To Suiu —

The real

Political Broker —

With warmest

regards,

Judy

political
brokers

political brokers

MONEY, ORGANIZATIONS, POWER AND PEOPLE

by the Editors and Reporters of
NATIONAL JOURNAL

edited by JUDITH G. SMITH

LIVERIGHT ✍ NEW YORK

A Liveright/National Journal Book

Copyright © 1972 by National Journal.

All rights reserved. No part of this book may be reproduced in any form without permission in writing from the publisher.   1.987654321

ISBN: 0-87140-552-0 (cloth); 0-87140-067-7 (paper)

Library of Congress Catalog Card Number 79-18337

Manufactured in the United States of America

CONTENTS

(v)

LIST OF TABLES

(viii)

FOREWORD

Have you ever heard of William Watson or Alexander Barkan, Charles McManus or Robert Humphrey, Russell Hemenway or John Calkins? The average American has not. But political Washington knows them well: these are some of the men who run the day-to-day operations of the political interest groups that gather and spend millions of dollars to elect men to the U.S. Congress. Their success or failure, in achieving their frequently conflicting goals, can ultimately make the difference in what legislation passes in Congress, what course the American government will take.

This book is an intimate look at the American elective process today, not the ideal world of democratic theory, but the nitty-gritty, operational, practical way that money and expertise flow. It is packed with facts and figures aplenty, but constantly the themes of *National Journal*, whose reporters and editors prepared this volume, reappear: How, when, where is influence exerted within official Washington? Which are the salient forces? How are they organized? How do they operate? What is their actual impact on the course of policy that guides a nation?

Since its birth in 1969, the weekly *National Journal*, depending on the resources of one of Washington's largest reporting staffs, has been answering those questions, with lucidity and in depth, about the executive and legislative branches of the federal government, and the world of lobbyists and special interest groups. Current governmental policy disputes are examined in the light of those criteria, and so is the elective process. The decision about which are the "good guys" and which the "bad," of partisan merit and ideologies, is prudently

left to others. But the tools are provided so that the interested ob-
server—or participant in the process himself—can make his decisions
based on clear fact.

To set the stage, each chapter in this volume identifies the ideologic
and historic roots of the organization and recalls some of its triumphs
and disasters (and every group has had some of both). Then there is
an examination of each group's ties to other organizations and the
formal party structure, followed by a review of major personnel and
a look at its *modus operandi* today.

One glances back in time to see the progress of organized labor's
political activity, from the days when F.D.R. made his controversial
statement to "Clear it with Sidney" to the modern AFL-CIO Committee on Political Education's sophisticated, multi-million dollar election year effort replete with field staffs and complex computer data
banks on union member registration. There is the story of the Americans for Democratic Action, founded to assert a clarion call for
economic liberalism, foundering on the rocks of dissent in the 1968
McCarthy campaign, estranged from the New Left but still growing
in support. To understand why the liberal Democrats have done so
well in modern-day campaigns for the U.S. Senate, one must look at
the National Committee for an Effective Congress, an organization
born out of the liberals' discouragement with the postwar Republican
80th Congress. Over time, the NCEC has become a formidable instrument for funneling "Eastern establishment," liberal money to chosen
candidates (almost all Democrats). And then there is the Democratic
National Committee itself, reduced to impotence in the Johnson
years, now struggling to return to professionalism and real power
under the leadership of Lawrence O'Brien. The story of Common
Cause, not a direct participator in campaigns but the first broad-
scale "people's lobby" of U.S. history, suggests new channels of
pressure on the system to reform itself from within (as with campaign finance legislation and the constitutional amendment lowering
the voting age to 18, both issues Common Cause has worked hard on).

The reader will learn here how the battles of the Reconstruction
era, directly after the Civil War, gave birth to the National Republican Congressional Committee, now the most elaborately organized
of all groups trying to influence congressional elections. There is the
story of how businessmen's frustrations about what they saw as
labor's domination of Congress led to formation of the Business-
Industry Political Action Committee—a direct imitation of labor's
COPE. On the right wing, there is the Americans for Constitutional

Action, founded in 1958 by retired Admiral Ben Moreell as a counter-thrust to ADA, backed financially by several well-known Americans of strongly conservative views. Now the ACA competes for funds and backing with other groups of like persuasion, including the American Conservative Union, Liberty Lobby and United Republicans of America. On the opposite extreme of the Republican spectrum, one finds the Ripon Society, which was formed a decade ago by young Harvard and M.I.T. students who hoped to turn their party to more liberal avenues. Their success on that score has been mixed at best, but they have seen several of their members obtain important White House positions in the Nixon Administration.

And then there is the story of the physicians of the American Medical Association, faced with an era of increasing hostility to their free enterprise concept of medical services, who formed an immensely powerful, well-financed political action group, not for the crass purpose of buying votes or support as pressure groups did in earlier years, but just to get "the right to a dialogue" with Congress.

To document actual operations of the political interest groups, this book takes the 1970 mid-term election year as a test tube. Here one finds the full documentation: each group's battle plan for the year, how it got its money, the candidates it helped finance, insights into the kinds of candidates and operations favored. And then there are the results: full, official, for every Senate and House contest, as well as all gubernatorial elections of 1970.

Knowing 1970, it is then possible to look forward realistically to 1972, when the election of a President will be added to the congressional election picture. The chapters of this book discuss how the interest groups are likely to readapt their techniques and objectives for 1972. An important section of the story on the Democratic National Committee, for instance, reviews the unprecedented reform movement within that party, shows its possibilities, reviews its severe limitations in actual application to state parties (a story first broken by *National Journal* in June 1971), and sets the stage for the Presidential nomination battle of 1972.

For the student of politics, for the political activist, for those who will be voting for the first time in 1972, here is a unique roadmap to the world of political strategy, an overview of the men and women and organizations behind the political sloganeering, and the guidelines that will permit them to enter the arena of political participation at a high level of knowledge and sophistication.

Neal R. Peirce

PREFACE

Nine of the ten case studies contained in this book were published in *National Journal* as part of its coverage of the 1970 political campaigns. They have all been updated to reflect the outcome of the mid-term elections and any staff or structural changes within the organizations. The profile of Common Cause is the first report in *National Journal's* 1972 campaign series. It, like two of the other studies, was authored by Andrew J. Glass, who has reported politics for nine years and served as an aide to three U.S. Senators. Jonathan Cottin, who along with Andy Glass plans *National Journal's* campaign coverage, is responsible for the COPE and BIPAC studies. Charles Culhane, a contributor to the COPE study, is *National Journal's* labor expert. John L. Moore, an associate editor of *National Journal* and the author of the ADA profile, has been a journalist for 21 years. Neal Gregory, after five years of reporting, has joined the business side of *National Journal* and Judith Robinson is on the staff of a U.S. Senator.

I am grateful for the help of these reporters, and the editor of *National Journal*, John F. Burby, the research support of Monica Benderly, and in particular for the invaluable assistance of Kay D. Ingle, who bore the brunt of the updating task.

Judith G. Smith
November 1, 1971

political
brokers

1

Americans for Democratic Action

JOHN L. MOORE

Americans for Democratic Action, cleaved by the Vietnam issue three years ago, has yet to recover its political power of yester-year. Its problems were suggested in remarks to *National Journal* by a former aide to ex-Sen. Joseph S. Clark, D-Pa. (1957-69), a member of ADA's national board. "ADA used to be a home for labor leaders, professors and ladies who felt uncomfortable and were not welcome in machine politics," said the former aide, who asked not to be identified. "Now it's not a home for labor or for kids either. It's neither the new left nor the old left. The kids probably laugh at it. Nobody takes it seriously."

ADA does face an identity problem, but the association is taken seriously in some quarters. Too radical for labor unions and not radical enough for militant students, ADA is now aim-ing its appeal to the settled-down young and middle-aged adults who are against the war and who want more attention paid to the cities, minority group problems and other issues at home.

Leon Shull, ADA's national director, reports increases since 1968 in both members and money. "Some people hoped we would die," says Shull. "But we didn't die. We grew." The growth has not restored ADA to the same forceful role it played in American politics for 20 years as a labor-intellectual coalition pressing for a broad range of common social goals.

1

But ADA is still alive. New blood has been infused into its hierarchy in its effort to carve a niche in a changing political world. And, without letting up its pressure to end U.S. participation in the war, ADA is continuing its traditional activities, which include lobbying with skill and effectiveness.

As one of its "new blood" efforts, ADA in May 1971 elected activist Allard K. Lowenstein, 42, as national chairman. Lowenstein, an ADA member who in 1967-68 began the "dump Johnson" movement against the renomination of the President, replaced Joseph D. Duffey, who had served as national chairman since 1969 and is currently an ADA vice chairman. Lowenstein, a former Democratic Representative from New York (1969-71), received an A.B. degree from the University of North Carolina in 1949 and a law degree from Yale University in 1954. He served in the U.S. army as an enlisted man from 1954 to 1956 and was subsequently on the teaching staffs of Stanford University, North Carolina State University, City College of New York and Yale. He was special assistant to former Sen. Frank Porter Graham, D-N.C. (1949-50), in 1949 and served as foreign policy assistant to Sen. Hubert H. Humphrey, D-Minn., in 1959. He is the author of *Brutal Mandate*, published in 1962.

Following his election as national chairman, Lowenstein told the ADA convention that the organization's job is "to end war, right wrongs and heal wounds." Regarding the 1972 Presidential elections, Lowenstein told the delegates there is "an unprecedented amount of activity on the national political level precisely because there is an unprecedented amount of dissatisfaction with the national Administration, and because the lesson of 1967-68 is that an incumbent President in a democratic system is highly vulnerable to such dissatisfaction." Lowenstein credited ADA with having played "an important role in developing and focusing that public feeling." ADA Vice Chairman Joseph L. Rauh Jr. describes Lowenstein as "the ideal chairman for ADA at this moment in history." "Al is really in my book the greatest symbol of young liberalism in America today," Rauh said, adding that ADA's new chairman

represents "the things that are important—including movement and working within the system."

ADA was split wide open on February 10, 1968, when its national board, by a vote of 65-47, endorsed then-Sen. Eugene
J. McCarthy, D-Minn. (1959-71), for the Democratic Presidential
nomination. One ADA officer—Vice Chairman Leon H. Keyser-
ling, a former member of the Council of Economic Advisers
(1946-53)—and four board members, along with an undeter-
mined number of members, resigned in protest.

Organized labor, which had given ADA most of its strength,
pulled out almost en masse. Three influential union presidents
quit the board—I. W. Abel of the United Steelworkers of
America, Louis Stulberg of the International Ladies Garment
Workers Union, and Joseph A. Beirne of the Communications
Workers of America. Among ADA members to quit was
Evelyn Dubrow, a lobbyist for the International Ladies Garment Workers Union who was an original member of ADA
and its first director of organization (1947-49). "It was one
of the saddest days of my life," she recalls.

The steelworkers cut off their $10,000 annual contribution to
ADA and the communications workers stopped their $3,000 an-
nual contribution. The late Walter P. Reuther, president of
United Auto Workers, withdrew his union's annual $12,000
contribution, but he remained an ADA vice chairman until his
death. His brother, Victor G. Reuther, a UAW official, is still
on the board. David Dubinsky, retired president of the International Ladies Garment Workers Union, issued a statement
sharply criticizing the McCarthy endorsement, but he did not
quit the board. Other labor leaders still serving on the board
are David Selden, president of the American Federation of
Teachers; Jacob Clayman, administrative director of the AFL-
CIO Industrial Union Department; and Patrick E. Gorman, international secretary-treasurer of the Amalgamated Meat Cutters and Butcher Workmen of North America.

Although ADA switched its support to then-Vice President Hubert H. Humphrey after he received the Democratic nomination, the departed labor leaders did not return to ADA. For all practical purposes, labor is no longer integral to ADA. "What they did in 1968 was idiotic politics," says Albert J. Zack, public relations director of the AFL-CIO. "Since then, they go their way and we go ours."

Also quitting the board in protest was John P. Roche, then a special consultant on the staff of President Johnson. Roche, who had been ADA's national chairman (1962-65), said as he resigned that ADA was "off on a trip to political Disneyland." Asked by *National Journal* if he still feels the same, Roche replied: "The ADA took the trip to Disneyland and while it was there the people of the United States put Richard Nixon in the White House." Roche, now a professor of politics at Brandeis University and a syndicated newspaper columnist, said "it hurt to have to break with friends of 20 years standing. But I still cannot accept the notion that a Hanoi victory is inevitable or desirable." He stressed that he was not intending to imply that ADA is deliberately trying to aid the enemy. But he said, "my judgment is that the position espoused by ADA could be disastrous."

Among board members who opposed the McCarthy endorsement but remained on the board is Vice Chairman Robert R. Nathan, a Washington economist and an ADA founder and benefactor. Nathan told *National Journal* the Vietnam conflict has, in effect, made ADA a one-issue organization. "It can't let go of Vietnam, but holding on makes it difficult to attract non-peace groups for ADA's other worthwhile causes," he said. The former ADA national chairman (1957-59) says he agrees that "we ought to get the hell out of Vietnam," but believes the refusal of some ADA members to support Humphrey "makes no sense at all." "It's pure punishment," says Nathan. "It shows no understanding of what Humphrey has done in the past as a liberal leader who has been out front in issue after issue. It's a carry-over of the one-issue problem; a refusal to be realistic. So now they've got Nixon."

While ADA cannot be credited with or blamed for the events

that split the Democratic Party in 1968, some of its members had key parts in the drama. One of them, Allard Lowenstein, ADA's current national chairman, led the movement that brought Sen. McCarthy into the picture as a peace candidate against the renomination of President Johnson. When Lowenstein began touring college campuses in 1967 to make antiwar and "dump Johnson" speeches, his assistant was Curtis Gans, who had been a member of the ADA national office staff since 1964.

ADA was the first major political organization to endorse McCarthy. Until then his campaign had been regarded largely as a student movement. ADA's endorsement gave the campaign a wider credibility and improved accessibility to financial support. Blair Clark, who managed McCarthy's campaign, told *National Journal:* "It would have been embarrassing if ADA had not supported McCarthy. But it did, and the endorsement was helpful." ADA leaders John Kenneth Galbraith, Joseph Rauh and others actively assisted the McCarthy campaign; they continued to do so after President Johnson decided not to run and Humphrey entered the race.

The Vietnam war, as such, is not a big issue in ADA. Few, if any, members are hawks. The conflicts in 1968, and since, have been chiefly over ways in which the issue manifests itself—particularly in the treatment of Humphrey, a founder of ADA when he was mayor of Minneapolis. Humphrey was rebuked by the ADA board October 11, 1969. The board released a statement, adopted by voice vote with some opposition, which said ADA was "shocked and saddened by the recent statement by former Vice President Hubert H. Humphrey supporting President Nixon's Vietnam policies. We condemn his stand."

The Minnesota chapter of ADA on August 14, 1970, endorsed Earl D. Craig Jr., an instructor in black studies at the University of Minnesota, in his unsuccessful campaign against Humphrey for the Democratic-Farmer-Labor nomination for the Senate seat being vacated by McCarthy. National Director Shull, who concedes having little success in attempts to heal the association's breach, had flown to Minneapolis the day before and tried to persuade the state unit to endorse Humphrey. ADA chapters have autonomy in making state and local endorsements. Shull said later that Minnesota members felt Craig was closer to their position that U.S. troops should be withdrawn immediately, even though he agreed with Humphrey that a withdrawal could not be accomplished overnight.

Following ADA's endorsement of Craig, a former member of Humphrey's Vice Presidential staff, who asked not to be quoted by name, said Humphrey "can't be pleased that his old ADA friends didn't endorse him, but it will probably gain him votes in November not to have the ADA's approval. In view of the burgeoning hard-hat sentiment, an ADA endorsement is probably a mark of being too liberal." (Humphrey, who served as a Senator from Minnesota from 1949 to 1964, when he resigned to become Vice President, was reelected to the Senate in 1970.) Besides helping found ADA, Humphrey served as national chairman in 1949-50. But after the McCarthy endorsement in 1968, he recalled that he had resigned as an ADA vice chairman upon campaigning for Vice President in 1964 and had not paid dues for several years. Shull says ADA and Humphrey are not enemies, "but he doesn't see it as his organization any longer."

ADA Vice Chairman Rauh says he had hoped the Minnesota chapter would endorse Humphrey "because it (Craig's endorsement) looks like vindictiveness and we're in politics for ideas and idealism, not to be vindictive." Rauh claims ADA would not have survived "if we hadn't backed the peace candidates and followed the road we did" in 1968. He noted that as early as April 2, 1965, he and other association leaders met with President Johnson to recommend against escalation of the war. ADA's opposition to the war, he says, brought it "tremendous popular strength" and although it cost the support of "the political muscle people (labor leaders), we never did have their support on things like that."

Duffey, then ADA national chairman and unsuccessful Democratic candidate in 1970 for the U.S. Senate from Connecticut, told *National Journal* that ADA "is in a transition period, forging new coalitions in terms beyond the New Deal."

Duffey, 39, a self-described "left-footed Irish protestant clergyman" and son of a coal miner, was selected by national convention delegates to assume the national chairmanship in 1969 from Harvard economist Galbraith, 62, who had held the position since 1967. At the time of Duffey's election, Galbraith, a founder of ADA, cracked that the change was made "not to bridge the generation gap but to jump it."

Duffey, now a professor at Yale Divinity School, does not believe Republicans have a monopoly on the so-called "silent majority." "This country will be torn apart if we cannot address the alienated subaffluent on social issues, in terms other than fear," he told *National Journal* the day after he won the Democratic primary nomination for the Senate seat held by Sen. Thomas J. Dodd, D-Conn. (1959-71). "We have to take them as seriously as we do the students and the blacks. I have applied that in my present campaign, and so far it's working."

Duffey spelled out his views on the silent majority in a speech July 26, 1969, to a New Democratic Coalition conference in Denver. He said "the group which constitutes our greatest political challenge . . . is the group that Mr. Nixon has already singled out to be a part of the coalition that he will seek to build. I am referring to what sometimes is called the 'average citizen,' the man who works hard to support his family on $10,000 a year or less. . . . These people have legitimate reason to protest what is going on in American society, and yet they have been neglected by liberal movements and by both political parties. For in a sense, liberalism has become an activity of the affluent for whom the concerns of these people, like the concerns of the very poor, emerge primarily in abstract terms and categories. . . . There are, I believe, in the discontent of the poor, the young and this third group some common concerns which can be brought together."

ADA was founded in 1947 as what it called an "organization of progressives, dedicated to the achievement of freedom and economic security for all people everywhere, through education

and democratic political action." Its founders were New
Deal adherents who feared that under President Truman the
programs and social philosophy of President Franklin D.
Roosevelt would wither and die. Mrs. Eleanor Roosevelt was
an active supporter and became ADA's honorary chairman
(1947-62). Among the founders and early supporters who had
held positions in the Roosevelt Administration were chairmen
Leon Henderson, former administrator of the Office of Price
Administration (1941-42), and Francis Biddle, former U.S.
Attorney General (1941-45).

ADA was an outgrowth of Union for Democratic Action
(UDA), a small New Dealist organization that wanted to ex-
pand into a major force between the pro-Communist left and
the rising post-World War II reaction. UDA had barred Communists since it was formed in 1941. At UDA's call, about 400
persons met January 3, 1947, at the Willard Hotel in Washington, D.C., to begin organizing the new group. James I. Loeb,
who had held a similar post with UDA, became ADA executive
director, and remained in the job until 1951. Wilson W. Wyatt, former Democratic Mayor of Louisville, Ky., (1941-45) and
administrator of the National Housing Agency in 1946, became
ADA's first national chairman (1947-48).

The statement of principles adopted by the conference
called for expansion of New Deal programs, extension of
civil liberties, support for the United Nations, and rejection of
"any association with Communists or sympathizers to communism in the United States as completely as we reject any association with fascists or their sympathizers." A rival Progressive Citizens for America (PCA), dominated by former
Vice President Henry A. Wallace (1941-45), was formed about
the same time. Without rejecting communism, PCA pressed
for "liberal unity" under its umbrella. PCA developed into
Wallace's Progressive Party, which petered out after his third
party suffered a decisive defeat in the 1948 Presidential
elections.

Embarrassing to ADA in later years was its effort in 1948
to deny Truman the Democratic nomination. ADA wanted
Dwight D. Eisenhower as the nominee, but Eisenhower made

it clear he would refuse the nomination if it were offered. Truman, after his election, turned out to be more to ADA's liking than it had expected, and President Eisenhower later ran an Administration that was decidedly unacceptable by ADA standards.

Several ADA members and ex-members were appointed to prominent positions in the Kennedy Administration. Appointments went to ADA founders Galbraith as Ambassador to India (1961-63), Arthur M. Schlesinger Jr. as a Presidential assistant (1961-63), and Chester Bowles as under secretary of state (1961-62). James Loeb, ADA's first director, was named Ambassador to Peru (1963-65). However, Mr. Kennedy showed no particular affinity for ADA as an organization, and ADA frequently criticized his policies.

The state, regional or local chapter is the basic unit of ADA's organizational structure. ADA claims an estimated 75,000 memberships in chapters in 18 states and the District of Columbia and an at-large membership category, covering states where there are no chapters and other countries. Spokesmen for the organization say there are no 1971 figures available showing membership breakdown. In 1970, ADA listed a total of 50,325 members. The greatest increase in membership since 1970, according to ADA officials, has been in the at-large category. Shull noted, however, that 750 of the increase was represented by a new Hawaii chapter; ADA also records Campus ADA (CADA) members in its general membership figures. Some of the organization's memberships represent husband and wife, but ADA does not know how many of its single memberships represent two people.

The organization claims to have posted steady gains in members as ADA became more identified with the antiwar effort. Shull said ADA had a net gain of 4,700 memberships in 1968 over the previous year, with 6,400 new memberships received and 1,700 dropped for non-payment of dues. Twelve of the large chapters have one or more full-time employees. They are Massachusetts, New York, New Jersey, Southeastern Pennsylvania, Western Pennsylvania, Baltimore, Ohio, Michigan, Illinois, Northern California, Southern California, and Metropolitan Washington, D.C.

ADA members pay $10 a year for a single membership or $15 for a double. Except for a small per capita assessment, this money remains with the chapters. Most of ADA's income comes from contributions. About 500,000 to 800,000 appeals for funds are mailed each year, mostly to ADA members.

Shull said ADA's income, which had been under $260,000 the two previous years, leaped to $345,000 in 1968 after the McCarthy endorsement. In 1969, ADA's income was $356,000 and expenditures were $351,000, he said. The comparable figures for 1970 were $317,000 and $341,000. Shull predicted ADA's 1971 income would be about the same as 1970. "We have suffered far less than other similar organizations . . . this year (1971) we seem to be holding our end up and may even receive a little more than last year (because of increased memberships)," Shull added.

"We don't have financial angels," Shull said. "To us, $1,000 is a big contribution." One reason is that contributions to ADA are not tax-exempt, as they would be to a charitable organization. If ADA were to seek tax-exempt status to attract larger contributions, it would have to forfeit its function as a political organization. Shull said ADA was not hurt financially by the drop in the stock market in early 1970, "because we don't get money from people who are apt to be big investors."

ADA's 32 officers include an ex-Senator and five House Members, all Democrats. (See Table 1.1.) The officers and a 146-member national board comprise the governing body of ADA. Most board members are chapter delegates, although some at-large members are elected at the annual convention. The board meets about five times a year. Members include Rep. Shirley Chisholm, D-N.Y.; Bayard Rustin, director of the A. Philip Randolph Institute; Rep. Robert F. Drinan, D-Mass.; Mrs. LaDonna Harris, wife of Sen. Fred R. Harris, D-Okla.; and Jane O'Grady, legislative representative of the Amalgamated Clothing Workers of America, AFL-CIO, and formerly on the staff of the Center for Community Change.

The executive committee, which meets monthly, is the governing body between meetings of the national board. The committee consists of all ADA officers plus chapter representatives from Baltimore, Philadelphia, Washington, New York and Boston. Since committee meetings are held week nights in Washington, other, more distant chapters are not expected to send representatives, Shull said. In 1969, ADA elected David Cohen, then 32, one of its former legislative representatives, as executive committee chairman. Cohen is currently director of field organization for Common Cause. Dolores L. Mitchell, immediate past secretary of national ADA, replaced Cohen as executive committee chairman in May 1971, when Cohen was named a vice chairman.

Guidelines for ADA policy are adopted at an annual three-day convention, usually held in Washington. National officers and some at-large board members are elected then. The 1970 convention began May 1, the day after President Nixon announced the Cambodia incursion. The delegates promptly adopted a resolution denouncing the move as "an illegal act of war." In all, the convention adopted 100 policy statements on a broad range of domestic and foreign issues. The 1971 convention adopted resolutions and policy statements on a variety of topics: urban development, income tax reform, drug law reform, decentralization of schools, the draft, qualifications for Presidential candidates and Pakistan and the Middle East.

There is nothing elaborate about ADA's national headquarters, which occupies about half of the seventh (top) floor of an old red-brick building at 1424 Sixteenth St. NW, in Washington's former "embassy row" area. Walls of the outer office are plastered with posters reflecting ADA views in such terms as "No More Vietnams," "Stop ABM" and "King Kong Died from Smog."

A staff that Shull describes as "small, young and badly paid" handles ADA's full-time activities. Assisted by six clerical employees, the professional staff of eight includes the director and two lobbyists:

- Shull, 56, has been national director since 1964. Before that, he was executive director of ADA's Southeastern

Pennsylvania chapter for 13 years. He owned Logan Furniture Company in Philadelphia from 1936 to 1941, and was active in the city's community affairs. He was director of the Jewish Labor Committee there from 1946 to 1950.

- Edward B. Lippert, 31, legislative representative, joined the ADA staff in 1967. He received an A.B. degree from New York University in 1961, a law degree from Brooklyn Law School in 1964 and an M.A. in international relations from American University in 1969. He was briefly an assistant corporation counsel for the District of Columbia in 1967 and was employed by the Internal Revenue Service in 1966-67.

- Lynn K. Pearle, 28, legislative representative, received an A.B. degree from Smith College in 1965 and a law degree from Boston College Law School in 1968. She was an associate at the New York City law firm of Breed, Abbott & Morgan for one year (1968-69). Mrs. Pearle joined the ADA staff in March 1971, replacing Verlin L. Nelson, who served as an ADA lobbyist from 1967 to 1970.

- Stina Santiestevan, 50, editor of the monthly *ADA World*, received an A.B. degree from Occidental College in 1942. The wife of a former United Auto Workers editor, Mrs. Santiestevan was active in civic affairs in Los Angeles, Detroit and Washington, D.C., before joining the ADA staff five years ago.

- Gertrude L. Riger, 54, became ADA development director in September 1969. She was chairman of ADA's Cleveland chapter for five years (1959-64). Mrs. Riger received the annual Helen Rotch award for outstanding ADA service at the organization's 1967 convention.

- Olga Tabaka, 55, has been on the staff since ADA's founding in 1947, as public relations department secretary for the first year and office manager since then.

- Amy F. Hamburger, 24, chapter relations coordinator, joined ADA as an intern in September 1969 and was promoted to the professional staff in January 1970. She has an A.B. degree from American University and taught English in Turkey.

- Sarah Trott, 23, ADA's first public relations director, joined the staff in March 1971. A native of Cincinnati, Ohio, Miss Trott received an A.B. degree from Hollins College in 1969. She came to Washington in September 1970 as an assistant press secretary to Sen. William B. Saxbe, R-Ohio, and remained in that position until she joined ADA. Mrs. Santiestevan handled ADA's public relations, in addition to her other duties, before Miss Trott joined the organization.

Missions of the staff include lobbying and rating the "liberal quotient" of House and Senate Members. The staff also publishes a monthly tabloid, *ADA World*. Other publications include a yearly statement of policy and periodic "backgrounders" on timely issues.

Looking to the 1972 elections, ADA in summer 1971 organized a nationwide youth voter registration program. It also set up a committee to oversee and assist in legal tests of state delegate selection and national convention procedures in both the Democratic and Republican Parties. ADA's 1972 Convention Task Force is chaired by Duffey and Kenneth A. Bode, director of the Washington-based Center for Political Reform and an ADA board member. Rauh serves as its chief legal counsel. (Rauh also is legal counsel to Bode's Center for Political Reform, organized in early 1971 to push for implementation of the Democratic National Committee's reform commission guidelines for the selection of delegates to the 1972 convention.) The task force was organized in part to ensure that all party members, including those of racial minorities, are given the opportunity to participate in the delegate selection process. It will provide legal assistance in the preparation of law suits against states and state parties whose laws and rules bar citizen participation in the Presidential nominating process and in the preparation of credentials challenges to the national conventions based on racial discrimination and closed delegate selection procedures.

In announcing the task force June 19, 1971, National Chairman Lowenstein stressed ADA's commitment to work for implementation of the party reform measures adopted by both national parties. In 1968, Lowenstein said, "there was more grassroots participation in the Presidential nominating process than ever before in the history of our country. As a result, our party procedures were put to a severe test—which they did not pass. In too many states, the official party structures remained closed and unresponsive to increased rank-and-file participation. . . ."

The voter registration program is "intended to defeat Nixon by a massive voter registration of young people across the nation," ADA says. National Director Shull described the project as "the most important and urgent program to be undertaken by ADA" in 1971. (Ratification of the 26th Amendment to the Constitution has expanded the electorate by 11.4 million people between the ages of 18 and 21. Another 13.7 million people between 21 and 25 will be eligible in 1972 to participate in their first Presidential election, bringing the potential new young vote to 25.1 million.)

Directed by Lowenstein and financed by a nationwide fund-raising campaign, the program includes student conferences in selected target states, registration rallies and ADA chapter registration drives in high schools and colleges. In late June 1971, ADA reported the program was underway in 15 states and that over 70,000 young people had attended rallies in Providence, R.I., Indianapolis, Ind., Minneapolis, Minn., and Long Island, N.Y.

When he accepted the ADA chairmanship, Lowenstein asserted: "No political activity in 1971 will have a more beneficial impact on the 1972 elections than registration of the great bulk of the newly eligible voters. Consequently, I hope to devote a good deal of my time, as well as the time and resources of ADA, to accomplishing this goal." During summer 1971, Lowenstein presided over ADA's student vote registration drive. He traveled to college campuses, encouraging student leaders to organize voter registration drives built around opposition to Mr. Nixon and the Administration. One of his allies in the drive was Rep. Paul N. McCloskey Jr., R-Calif., who is opposing Mr. Nixon for the Republican nomination for President.

As a self-styled "multi-issue, public interest pressure group," ADA lobbies on a wide array of legislation. ADA's two registered lobbyists are Lippert and Mrs. Pearle. They often are assisted by Joseph Rauh, who is not required to register as an ADA lobbyist because he is not paid for his work.

Rauh, 60, of Washington is often called "Mr. ADA" because of his close association with the organization he helped form in 1947. He was its national chairman in 1955-57 and remains a vice chairman. A tall and pleasant man with a ready smile, Rauh nevertheless relishes a good fight over political or social issues. Over the years he has been at the forefront of many of them, involving Democratic party politics, civil rights and liberties, labor and the peace movement. At the same time he keeps up a busy law practice, with several unions among his clients. He is Washington counsel of the United Auto Workers. He also represents the United Shoe Workers of America and Miners for Democracy, the dissident United Mine Workers group whose leader, Joseph A. Yablonski, was found shot to death January 5, 1970.

Born in Cincinnati, Rauh graduated *magna cum laude* from Harvard in 1932 and from Harvard Law School in 1935. He was law clerk to Supreme Court Justices Benjamin N. Cardozo and Felix Frankfurter from 1935 to 1939. He was a lawyer for several government agencies until World War II, when he served as an Army officer. At the Democratic National Convention in 1960, Rauh led a successful fight for adoption of a strong civil rights platform. As general counsel of the Leadership Conference on Civil Rights, another volunteer post, he was a leading lobbyist for the Civil Rights Act of 1964 (78 Stat 241) and the Voting Rights Act of 1965 (79 Stat 437). In 1971, Rauh was a leader in the fight against Senate confirmation of Supreme Court nominee William H. Rehnquist.

Another volunteer worker, David Cohen, is highly regarded for his efforts on behalf of ADA. Cohen was a registered lobbyist for ADA from 1963 to 1967. Verlin Nelson, then an ADA legislative representative, said of Cohen: "David was my mentor my first three years here, and he was a good one. He is one of the best social issue lobbyists in Washington. He is the best in parliamentary and strategy situations. You won't get any argument on that."

Cohen, who served on Humphrey's campaign task forces on consumer credit and housing in 1968, no longer does any lobbying for ADA but is still involved in policy making. Dark-haired, ruggedly built and intense, Cohen is regarded by his colleagues as an indefatigable and thorough worker. Cohen was a member of the student division of ADA at Temple University, where he received an A.B. degree in 1957. He worked for the Upholsterer's International Union in Philadelphia, and was active in the Southeastern Pennsylvania chapter of ADA. Cohen joined ADA's Washington staff as a legislative representative in 1963 and remained until 1967, when he became a staff member of the AFL-CIO Industrial Union Department. Before joining Common Cause, he was legislative representative of the Committee for Community Affairs, lobbying arm of the Center for Community Change.

During the 91st Congress (1969-70), ADA lobbyists were involved in the successful efforts to block the Supreme Court nominations of Clement F. Haynsworth Jr., of the 4th Circuit Court of Appeals, and G. Harrold Carswell, then of the 5th Circuit Court of Appeals; to obtain passage of voting rights for 18-year-olds (84 Stat 314); and to gain approval of the Philadelphia Plan (83 Stat 447) requiring more minority workers on federal construction projects. ADA opposed the no-knock, preventive detention and extended wire-tap provisions of the so-called D.C. crime bill (84 Stat 473).

Along with other peace groups, ADA in 1970 made little headway in efforts to curb deployment of the Safeguard anti-ballistic missile (ABM), limit military aid to Cambodia or end the Vietnam war through legislative means. ADA supported the Cooper-Church amendment to the Foreign Military Sales Act Amendments (84 Stat 2053), which would have prohibited use of U.S. ground combat troops or military advisors in Cambodia. It also lobbied for Senate amendments to the Military Procurement Authorization Bill (84 Stat 905). The ADA-supported amendments would have prevented expansion of the ABM system and fixed a deadline for withdrawal of U.S. troops from Vietnam.

Current domestic issues ADA has given priority and support to include the Administration's family assistance proposals, draft repeal, public service jobs by the government as last-resort guaranteed employment and direct election of Presidents. In its 1971-72 legislative program, ADA also is focusing on such issues as efficient mass transit, low- and middle-income housing growth, improved health care, consumer protection and campaign-spending reform.

Not having a huge constituency, political war chest or any of the other requisites of an arm-twisting lobby, ADA relies heavily on persuasion and alliances to make its influence felt. While serving as ADA's legislative representative, Nelson said the organization had "to work in coalitions" because it did not have "enough clout" by itself. He said he worked "almost 100 per cent of the time" with the United Auto Workers and the activist Democratic Study Group (DSG) in the House. Both Nelson and Cohen said working through coalitions is largely a lobbyist-to-lobbyist operation. "We have to lobby other lobbyists," Cohen said. "We have to recognize that clout in the conventional sense is important." ADA is affiliated with the Leadership Conference on Civil Rights, an organization of 125 Negro, labor, religious, and civic organizations. Rauh is the Leadership Conference's general counsel. Lippert is on the governing board of the Coalition on National Priorities and Military Policy, of which ADA is one of 38 affiliates. ADA also is a member of the Ad Hoc Committee on the Defense Budget.

Because it lobbies across the board on a variety of issues, ADA sometimes joins forces with its foes on the right and opposes its friends on the left. For example, as a civil libertarian group, ADA supported Sen. Sam J. Ervin Jr., D-N.C., (who has a cumulative ADA rating of 16) in fighting the "no knock" search and seizure provisions of the D.C. crime bill. Ervin, chairman of the Senate Judiciary Committee's Subcommittee on Constitutional Rights, felt that the controversial provisions would be unconstitutional. ADA agreed. On the Philadelphia Plan issue, Rauh and ADA were on the winning side against the AFL-CIO, their frequent ally.

ADA lobbyists stress information gathering and dissemination in their work, along with personal contact with Senators, House Members and committee staffs. Lippert said ADA distributed from 800 to 5,000 copies of each separate ADA "backgrounder" on Cambodia and other Indochina issues. The issues prepared in 1970 went to House and Senate Members, the press and other opinion molders or policy makers.

On Capitol Hill, ADA's regular and reserve lobbyists are given high marks for their competence, even by those who frequently disagree with ADA views. But the extent of their impact on legislation, or whether ADA has declined in influence on the Hill, is largely a matter of opinion. Rauh, for example, contends that "I can't remember a time when ADA has been doing a better job" and that "there never would have been a fight against Carswell if it hadn't been for ADA. Not only were we the first to say so, but it was weeks before we could persuade anybody that this guy could be beaten."

Sen. Birch Bayh, D-Ind., gives a somewhat different picture. He agrees that Rauh's testimony attacking Carswell's civil rights record helped convince him that the nominee had to be opposed. But Bayh said ADA's potential assistance was not a significant factor in his decision to join Sen. Edward W. Brooke, R-Mass., in leading the fight against Carswell after he (Bayh) had spearheaded the successful campaign against Haynsworth. Bayh said ADA's help was enlisted against Carswell "when the battle began and we started looking around for allies." In that role, he said, ADA lobbyists were "very helpful." Lawrence M. Baskir, chief counsel and staff director of the Ervin subcommittee, told National Journal that ADA's lobbyists were effective, even though the D. C. crime bill was passed. "They were very good at what they did, because some groups in the Senate are responsive to the ADA," Baskir said.

Americans for Constitutional Action (ACA), founded in 1958 to counterbalance ADA's influence, still looks upon ADA as formidable opposition. Charles A. McManus, ACA president, said he considers ADA "very effective, very influential." He said ADA, as a lobbying organization, focuses on "working through the system, rather than making a lot of noise." ACA, on the other hand, tries to influence public and congressional opinion through publicity and other means without actual lobbying. Kenneth Meiklejohn, an AFL-CIO legislative representative, said ADA "has some pretty effective lobbyists." But while they sometimes work together on the same bills, he said, "there is no real relationship except through the Leadership Conference on Civil Rights."

ADA derives considerable propaganda value from its annual ratings of Members of Congress on a "liberal quotient" from zero to 100. The ratings are based on votes on issues selected by the executive committee from recommendations by the staff. The 1970 ratings were based on 32 votes in the Senate and 25 in the House. For example, a Senator could have increased his "liberal quotient" by opposing the D.C. crime bill and the Carswell nomination, or lowered his rating by supporting a freer Presidential hand in Cambodia, or restrictions on school desegregation. (See Table 1.2.)

A Member with a high ADA rating will usually rate low with ACA. Curiosities crop up occasionally. Rep. John R. Rarick, D-La., who backed George C. Wallace for President in 1968, received an ADA rating of 20 in 1969 because of three votes that, for different reasons, paralleled ADA views. This made Rarick one of the more "liberal" Southerners by ADA standards, but only temporarily: His 1970 score was four. Rarick rated a 95 in 1969 from ACA. ADA's Rauh says both ADA and ACA appear to have their rating systems "down pat." "Our ability to be the inverse of each other in ratings with such consistency shows that there is a quotient that pretty accurately distinguishes liberals from conservatives," Rauh said.

Rauh and Shull say there is no rigging of ratings by selecting issues to help individuals or groups have higher scores. They noted that after ADA had endorsed McCarthy in 1968, association leaders were dismayed to see that the Senator came out with a low 21 on the basis of issues selected for rating that year. Rauh said the executive committee rejected any thought of choosing different votes to improve McCarthy's rating, which was low mainly because he had missed several key votes. (McCarthy's 1970 ADA rating was 72.)

National ADA makes no financial contributions to candidates and its endorsements are confined to Presidential candidates. Decisions whether to endorse other candidates are made at the chapter level. In areas where an ADA endorsement is considered a liability, a chapter may withhold an endorsement to help the candidate it wants to win. At the chapter level, committees may be formed to raise funds for candidates or help their campaigns in other ways. The national ADA sometimes helps by supplying lists of persons to ask for money or sending out letters directly, usually in the candidate's name or that of a recognized ADA leader, such as Galbraith or Schlesinger.

Shull said he and other ADA leaders have views on whom should be endorsed in virtually every congressional race, but that "our advice isn't always needed." For example, he said, there was no need for ADA to tell the California chapter that Democratic Rep. John V. Tunney (ADA rating 50), should be supported in his successful campaign for the Senate against Republican Sen. George Murphy (ADA rating zero) in 1970.

Occasionally chapter endorsement actions will kick up a storm. Early in 1970, the Pittsburgh ADA unit endorsed Byrd R. Brown, a black attorney and local ADA leader, in his unsuccessful Democratic primary race against Rep. William S. Moorhead, who had a cumulative ADA rating of 92. Former Sen. Joseph Clark denounced the action and drew an irate reply from Molly Yard Garrett, the chapter chairman and long-time Clark supporter.

Three years ago in Massachusetts, the state ADA incensed U. S. Rep. Torbert H. Macdonald, D, who has a consistently high ADA rating, by asking him to be interviewed if he was interested in an ADA endorsement. "After 14 years in Congress that seemed kind of silly to me," Macdonald said. "All they had to do was look up my record. I wouldn't humiliate myself by submitting to an interview under those circumstances." Gordon A. Martin Jr., then first vice chairman of the Massachusetts chapter and now chapter chairman, conceded to National Journal that the unit had failed in that instance "to make adequate distinction between an incumbent with a long voting record and a challenger without a voting record to appraise." He said the request to Macdonald was made in a form letter that went to all candidates. The ADA made no endorsement in the 1968 contest, which Macdonald won handily. In 1970, Macdonald received ADA's endorsement in his successful reelection bid.

While many students sided with ADA in the McCarthy campaign for President and many were active in Duffey's 1970 Senate campaign, they have not been attracted to the ADA banner in any significant numbers. The student branch of ADA, called Campus ADA or CADA, had in 1970 about 600 members in chapters at Minneapolis, Norfolk, Va., New York, Ohio State University and Georgetown University. ADA currently is revising its membership structure to include student members in the state and local chapters.

Joseph J. Minarik, 22, chairman of CADA in 1970, told National Journal the student branch is being abolished by ADA in a general consolidation effort. ADA also is making the change, he said, in response to the voting eligibility of 18-year-olds. Minarik, a graduate of Georgetown University and director of research for the Youth Citizenship Fund in Washington, D.C., assisted ADA's lobbyists in draft reform and other issues of special interest to youth while serving as CADA chairman. Minarik concedes that students today "tend to go to more radical organizations." But he said that during the Cambodia protests in May 1970, several student groups sought ADA

advice on effective political action and that ADA responded
with seminars for them. He says this suggests "there may
be a change; activism within the system may become more
popular."

Different views on ADA are expressed by Sam Brown, who
organized Students for McCarthy in 1968 and the October 15,
1969, moratorium demonstrations on campuses, and Gregory
F. Stone, 21, chief of research for Continuing Presence in
Washington. Stone, who joined ADA after the moratorium,
told National Journal he believes ADA has "some of the top
expertise on our side." Stone also said he "would not diverge
from the vast majority of their viewpoints." Brown wrote in
the August 1970 issue of The Washington Monthly that coordinators of the moratorium demonstrations felt that to succeed,
"we had to avoid following the ADA path (drifting to the right
ideologically without gaining new support) and alienating the
left at the same time."

In a special "Statement of Principles—1970," the 23rd ADA
convention repudiated "those who engage in, counsel or con-
done violence even when their objectives appear to be similar
to our own." ADA found "striking similarities between those
on the left who counsel or engage in violent acts and those on
the right—both in and out of government—who counsel or engage in repressive acts. Each seeks to dehumanize its opposition by the use of epithets—'pigs' and 'bums' and the like.
Each seeks to intimidate and to tear down such institutions as
universities, the media and the courts. . . ." The statement re-
affirmed ADA's "commitment to work through constitutional
processes to achieve our goals and our confidence that in doing so we will be successful." It concluded: "We will continue
to join with young people who have brought new vigor and
ideas to the liberal movement and we are confident that they
are ready to cooperate with us in achieving common goals. . . ."

In the May-June 1970 issue of ADA World, Shull urged student groups to "eschew and deny the use of violence or ob-
scenity in the course of the campaign" and to "stay in the political system, win or lose. . . ." He wrote that "today it is the
use of violence, primarily on the left, that has given the con-

servatives their greatest weapon. It would almost seem as if Gov. Ronald Reagan depends for his reelection upon violence on the campuses of California. . . ."

Vice Chairman Cohen says that while students are sought and welcomed by ADA, the organization's "target population" is somewhat older: "People in their middle or late 20s or early 30s, who are beginning to make a mark in their careers." A younger element has been more conspicuous in recent ADA conventions, as signified by the elections of Lowenstein, Cohen and Duffey to top ADA posts. Cohen believes these elections symbolize "recognition within the leadership that ADA has to include people who came to political maturity in the 1960s and those who will be coming to maturity in the 1970s." At the same time, he says, there is no reason for ADA's veteran leaders to fade away. "I don't consider Joe Rauh, for instance, an old-timer," Cohen said. "Joe is still full of zest and makes a valuable contribution."

ADA stresses that it is Americans for Democratic Action "with a small 'd'." There are no Republicans among the association's leadership. ADA has endorsed only Democratic Presidential candidates, and the overwhelming number of chapter-endorsed candidates have been Democrats. But Rauh says ADA "has demonstrated its independence from the Democratic Party in many ways, including hundreds of press releases attacking the party."

In his 1962 book, *Americans for Democratic Action: Its Role in National Politics*, Clifton Brock states: "Looked at from the outside, ADA's over-all relationship with the Democratic Party resembles a French farce, with ADA coyly jumping in and out on the left side of the big Democratic bed and peering jealously at the Southerners and big-city bosses resting on the right. From inside ADA, however, this relationship has been a frustrating courtship of a party—attractive and repellent at the same time—which ADA suspects might resort to marriage, then leave it at home while consorting with other mistresses." The quote, while somewhat outdated, still pretty well describes the relationship between ADA and the national Democratic Party.

The frustrating relationship was not tranquilized by the suggestion put forth by Galbraith in his 1970 book, *Who Needs the Democrats*. In it, Galbraith suggested that Democrats vote with Republicans in January 1971, to allow Republicans to organize the House of Representatives and break the Southern Democrats' hold on committee chairmanships. "Nothing is lost by exchanging conservative or reactionary Democrats for conservative or reactionary Republicans," Galbraith wrote. "Once lost, the traditional southern power will never again be restored. . . ."

The suggestion was rejected July 23, 1970, by Lawrence F. O'Brien, Democratic national chairman, who told a group of congressional interns that Democratic control of the House "is vital to continuing Democratic social programs." A staff member of the Democratic National Committee, who would not speak for attribution, said the committee "doesn't pay much attention to ADA. Its social motivation is just great, but its conception of how to get things done is totally unrealistic and unattuned to the way politics works in this country." Another Democratic National Committee staffer, who also requested anonymity, said, "Many years ago ADA was a vital force in the liberal community. Now it seems old, stodgy and set in its ways. When you get beyond Rauh, Galbraith and Schlesinger, who have they got?"

While some Republicans (Sen. Jacob K. Javits of New York, Sen. Clifford P. Case of New Jersey, Rep. Paul N. McCloskey Jr. of California) have been endorsed by ADA, the party leadership tends to dismiss the association as an entity of the Democratic Party. "It's the arm of another political organization," says Leslie C. Arends, R-Ill., House assistant minority leader. ADA is "not nearly as effective as it used to be," says Arends, whose cumulative ADA rating is 14. Gordon Wade, then communications director at the Republican National Committee, cited the Minnesota chapter's endorsement of Earl Craig and Galbraith's prescription for renewing the Democratic Party, and said, "that is extremism, and in my opinion extremism does not win elections." Wade said ADA is likely to grow weaker "as the country at large becomes more conservative."

Writing in the September 1971 issue of *ADA World*, Joseph Rauh discussed the role of "liberals" in the 1972 elections and criticized the Democratic Party leadership for "seeking to move the party to the center of the political spectrum" in its efforts to defeat President Nixon. Rauh proposed that "the way to block this Democratic trend to the center is by working for the most liberal announced or unannounced candidates for the Democratic nomination and by not relinquishing the threat of a fourth party ticket. . . ." The ADA vice chairman concluded: "Liberalism is the only way to a Democratic victory in 1972, but victory for a middle-of-the-road candidate, were it possible, would be fraught with very real dangers . . . . One more failure of governmental liberalism would bring dismay and despair to many who already have begun to question the system."

Considering its all-but-lost coalition with labor, and the slim chance of this bond being renewed while Vietnam is an issue, ADA's future appears to hinge upon its success in furthering the "middle-class involvement" it began under Duffey's leadership. But other groups also perceive a rich vein of political energy in the restive masses, and the competitors' ability to tap that source could affect ADA's effort to broaden its own constituency. One of these groups is Common Cause, which was launched in September 1970 by John W. Gardner, then chairman of the National Urban Coalition (1968-70) and former HEW Secretary (1965-68). In agenda, scope and approach, Common Cause closely resembles what ADA is trying to be. Common Cause aims to be a nonpartisan, mass-membership "citizens' lobby," pressing for a speedy end to the war, congressional reform and enactment of social programs.

ADA leaders are optimistic that the organization can remain viable for a long time to come. Even their former ally, John Roche, is confident the split over the war issue can be mended. He said: "I refuse to get into polemics with them on this disagreement, because I feel that ultimately we can get together on our common objectives." Cohen believes that "the ability to work at politics in the broadest sense will sustain ADA." Duffey, who had to fend off complaints during his Connecticut campaign that ADA is growing old and stale, is convinced that "ADA is still lively.... It's got a lot of life to it yet." But to Robert Nathan, from his perspective as a founder of ADA, "the acid test is still ahead." "When Vietnam is out of the way," he asks, "can ADA bend enough to return to the multi-issue stance it always had?"

Table 1.1   ADA Officers

Officers of Americans for Democratic Action are:

Allard K. Lowenstein, 42, national chairman. U.S. Representative, D-N.Y. (1969-71).

Eugene M. Lang, 52, treasurer. Businessman, president of Research and Facilities Corporation, New York, N.Y., and ADA assistant treasurer in 1969 and 1970.

Marvin Rich, 40, assistant treasurer. President of Scholarship, Education and Defense Fund for Racial Equality Inc., New York, N.Y.

Dolores L. Mitchell, 42, executive committee chairman. Former state chairman of Massachusetts ADA chapter and national secretary of ADA in 1970.

Barney Frank, 31, secretary. Administrative assistant to Rep. Michael J. Harrington, D-Mass., and executive assistant to Democratic Boston Mayor Kevin H. White in 1968-71.

Leon Shull, 56, national director. Former executive director of ADA's Southeastern Pennsylvania chapter.

ADA's 26 vice chairmen are:

Meyer Berger, 59. Businessman, president of M. Berger Company, Pittsburgh, Pa., and national treasurer of ADA in 1968-70.

Ramsey Clark, 44. Member New York law firm of Paul, Weiss, Goldberg, Rifkind, Wharton & Garrison, Attorney General (1967-69) and former ADA national board member.

David Cohen, 34. Director of field organization for Common Cause, Washington, D.C., former lobbyist for ADA (1963-67) and the Committee for Community Affairs (1968-71), and chairman of ADA's executive committee in 1970.

John Conyers Jr., 42. U.S. Representative, D-Mich., and former ADA national board member.

David Dubinsky, 79. President emeritus, International Ladies Garment Workers Union.

Joseph D. Duffey, 39. Professor, Yale Divinity School and national chairman of ADA in 1969 and 1970.

Bob Eckhardt, 58. U.S. Representative, D-Tex.

Marian Wright Edelman, 32. Attorney, Director of the Washington Research Project, Washington, D.C., and former ADA national board member.

Don Edwards, 55. U.S. Representative, D-Calif.

Walter E. Fauntroy, 38. Delegate to the U.S. House of Representatives from the District of Columbia.

Donald M. Fraser, 47. U.S. Representative, D-Minn.

Douglas A. Fraser, 55. Vice president of United Auto Workers.

John Kenneth Galbraith, 62. Economist, author and educator, Harvard University, and Ambassador to India (1961-63).

Maynard H. Jackson, 33. Vice-mayor of Atlanta, Ga., and former ADA national board member.

James I. Loeb, 63. Ambassador to Peru (1963-65), an ADA founder and former ADA national board member.

Abner J. Mikva, 45. U.S. Representative, D-Ill.

Hans J. Morgenthau, 67. Political scientist, director of the Center for Study of American Foreign and Military Policy, University of Chicago.

Wayne L. Morse, 70. U.S. Senator from Oregon (R, 1945-52; Ind., 1952-55; D, 1955-69), currently practicing law and arbitrating labor disputes.

Robert R. Nathan, 62. Economist, president Robert R. Nathan Associates Inc., Washington, D.C., and an ADA founder.

Albert A. Pena Jr. Commissioner of Bexar County, Tex., officer of Southwest Council of La Raza and former ADA national board member.

Joseph L. Rauh Jr., 60. Washington, D.C., counsel for United Auto Workers, counsel for Miners for Democracy and United Shoe Workers of America, and an ADA founder.

Marvin Rosenberg, 65. Businessman, chariman of Cameo Curtains Inc., New York, N.Y.

Arthur M. Schlesinger Jr., 53. Historian, City University of New York, an ADA founder and White House staff assistant (1961-63).

Nancy C. Swadesh, 49. Activist in California Democratic politics.

Jerry Wurf, 52. President of State, County and Municipal Employees Union.

Andrew J. Young Jr., 39. Former director of the Southern Christian Leadership Conference and a close associate of the late Martin Luther King Jr.

Table 1.2   ADA Rates Members of Congress, 1970 Session and Cumulatively

---

Using votes on selected legislative issues, Americans for Democratic Action rates the "liberal quotient" of each Senator and House Member for each session of Congress. ADA stresses in a preface that the ratings are offered as a guide in judging the performance of Members of Congress on certain important issues and are "no measure of a legislator's creative ability or the diligence with which he performs his work in committee. . . ."

Senate Ratings

For the second session of the 91st Congress (1970), ADA rated Senators on the basis of 32 selected issues. The 1970 ratings are compared below with the cumulative ratings of each Senator. Except where noted, Senators listed were serving in the first session of the 92nd Congress, as of November 1, 1971.

Democrats	Cumulative	1970		Cumulative	1970
Allen, Ala.	13	16	Bayh, Ind.	76	72
Anderson, N.M.	58	31	Bible, Nev.	36	9

Democrats (cont'd)	Cumu-lative	1970		Cumu-lative	1970
Burdick, N.D.	82	84	Tydings, Md. **(4)**	82	63
Byrd, Va.	7	22	Williams, N.J.	88	94
Byrd, W. Va.	41	31	Yarborough, Tex. **(3)**	67	66
Cannon, Nev.	44	19	Young, Ohio **(9)**	84	78
Church, Idaho	79	75			
Cranston, Calif.	81	91	**Republicans**		
Dodd, Conn. **(4,10)**	67	16	Aiken, Vt.	52	34
Eagleton, Mo.	92	91	Allott, Colo.	20	3
Eastland, Miss.	16	3	Baker, Tenn.	16	13
Ellender, La.	28	16	Bellmon, Okla.	18	19
Ervin, N.C.	16	13	Bennett, Utah	9	0
Fulbright, Ark.	52	66	Boggs, Del.	24	31
Gore, Tenn. **(4)**	65	53	Brooke, Mass.	84	88
Gravel, Alaska	72	72	Case, N.J.	81	88
Harris, Okla.	72	94	Cook, Ky.	45	41
Hart, Mich	94	97	Cooper, Ky.	53	47
Hartke, Ind.	71	66	Cotton, N.H.	13	0
Holland, Fla. **(9)**	23	16	Curtis, Neb.	3	0
Hollings, S.C.	17	22	Dole, Kan.	6	13
Hughes, Iowa	93	97	Dominck, Colo.	13	13
Inouye, Hawaii	72	72	Fannin, Ariz.	3	8
Jackson, Wash.	78	56	Fong, Hawaii	42	38
Jordan, N.C.	13	22	Goldwater, Ariz.	11	3
Kennedy, Mass.	89	84	Goodell, N.Y. **(4)**	90	97
Long, La.	37	13	Griffin, Mich.	31	28
Magnuson, Wash.	80	72	Gurney, Fla.	2	6
Mansfield, Mont.	75	75	Hansen, Wyo.	4	3
McCarthy, Minn. **(9)**	80	72	Hatfield, Ore.	24	84
McClellen, Ark.	14	0	Hruska, Neb.	5	0
McGee, Wyo.	71	47	Javits, N.Y.	84	75
McGovern, S.D.	84	84	Jordan, Idaho	8	9
McIntyre, N.H.	70	50	Mathias, Md.	78	78
Metcalf, Mont.	83	72	Miller, Iowa	13	13
Mondale, Minn.	93	97	Mundt, S.D.	10	0
Montoya, N.M.	63	63	Murphy, Calif. **(4)**	5	3
Moss, Utah	82	69	Packwood, Ore.	53	50
Muskie, Maine	86	91	Pearson, Kan.	19	28
Nelson, Wis.	94	97	Percy, Ill.	61	56
Pastore, R.I.	82	78	Prouty, Vt. **(10)**	36	34
Pell, R.I.	90	84	Saxbe, Ohio	54	47
Proximire, Wis.	83	78	Schweiker, Pa.	76	75
Randolph, W.Va.	72	59	Scott, Pa.	48	31
Ribicoff, Conn.	90	94	Smith, Ill. **(4)**	23	18
Russell, Ga. **(10)**	19	3	Smith, Maine	43	22
Sparkman, Ala.	52	13	Stevens, Alaska	26	25
Spong, Va.	38	41	Thurmond, S.C.	1	0
Stennis, Miss.	13	9	Tower, Tex.	1	3
Symington, Mo.	76	69	Williams, Del. **(9)**	11	16
Talmadge, Ga.	9	3	Young, N.D.	15	3

House Ratings

ADA used 25 votes to rate House Members for the second session of the 91st Congress (1970). Cumulative rating is based on ADA-selected votes since 1947. Listed below are 1970 and cumulative ADA ratings for House Members. (House Speaker John W. McCormack did not participate in House votes.) Except where noted. Members listed were serving in the first session of the 92nd Congress, as of November 1, 1971.

Democrats	Cumu-lative	1970		Cumu-lative	1970
Abbitt, Va. 4	10	0	Chisholm, N.Y. 12	90	80
Abernethy, Miss. 1	15	0	Clark, Pa. 25	74	32
Adams, Wash. 7	87	88	Clay, Mo. 1	92	84
Addabbo, N.Y. 7	84	80	Cohelan, Calif. 7 **(1)**	97	100
Albert, Okla. 3	69	48	Collins, Ill. 6 **(11)**	67	67
Alexander, Ark. 1	17	20	Colmer, Miss. 5	13	0
Anderson, Calif. 17	86	84	Conyers, Mich. 1	98	92
Anderson, Tenn. 6	54	40	Corman, Calif. 22	89	88
Andrews, Ala. 3	23	8	Culver, Iowa 2	83	96
Annunzio, Ill. 7	77	60	Daddario, Conn. 1 **(7)**	86	76
Ashley, Ohio 9	93	100	Daniel, Va. 5	4	0
Aspinall, Colo. 4	74	28	Daniels, N.J. 14	88	72
Baring, Nev. AL	40	12	Davis, Ga. 7	28	4
Barrett, Pa. 1	89	80	Dawson, Ill. 1 **(9)**	80	33
Bennett, Fla. 3	37	24	de la Garza, Tex. 15	32	28
Bevill, Ala. 7	11	20	Delaney, N.Y. 9	82	40
Biaggi, N.Y. 24	66	52	Dent, Pa. 21	78	60
Bingham, N.Y. 23	100	100	Diggs, Mich. 13	87	80
Blanton, Tenn. 7	19	24	Dingell, Mich. 16	89	68
Blatnik, Minn. 8	86	76	Donohue, Mass. 4	78	72
Boggs, La. 2	67	48	Dorn, S.C. 3	15	16
Boland, Mass. 2	89	76	Dowdy, Tex. 2	7	4
Bolling, Mo. 5	90	52	Downing, Va. 1	17	8
Brademas, Ind. 3	90	92	Dulski, N.Y. 41	78	80
Brasco, N.Y. 11	86	84	Eckhardt, Tex. 8	93	92
Brinkley, Ga. 3	5	4	Edmondson, Okla. 2	62	28
Brooks, Tex. 9	64	36	Edwards, Calif. 9	98	88
Brown, Calif. 29 **(3)**	88	88	Edwards, La. 7	21	12
Burke, Mass. 11	83	64	Eilberg, Pa. 4	78	84
Burleson, Tex. 17	20	0	Evans, Colo. 3	76	84
Burlison, Mo. 10	41	48	Evins, Tenn. 4	53	20
Burton, Calif. 5	97	96	Fallon, Md. 4 **(1)**	61	36
Byrne, Pa. 3	91	84	Farbstein, N.Y. 19 **(1)**	99	88
Cabell, Tex. 5	13	12	Fascell, Fla. 12	66	56
Caffery, La. 3	8	8	Feighan, Ohio 20 **(1)**	83	56
Carey, N.Y. 15	81	84	Fisher, Tex. 21	7	8
Carney, Ohio 5 **(11)**	50	50	Flood, Pa. 11	77	36
Casey, Tex. 22	18	16	Flowers, Ala. 5	11	8
Celler, N.Y. 10	92	80	Flynt, Ga. 6	14	4
Chappell, Fla. 4	8	8	Foley, Wash. 5	75	88

Democrats (cont'd)	Cumu- lative	1970		Cumu- lative	1970
Ford, William, Mich. 15	94	92	Kazen, Tex. 23	48	28
Fountain, N.C. 2	23	4	Kee, W. Va. 5	53	28
Fraser, Minn. 5	97	96	Kluczynski, Ill. 5	83	40
Friedel, Md. 7 (1)	88	80	Koch, N.Y. 17	100	100
Fulton, Tenn. 5	63	44	Kyros, Maine 1	71	72
Fuqua, Fla. 2	12	16	Landrum, Ga. 9	24	8
Galifianakis, N.C. 4	24	40	Leggett, Calif. 4	90	84
Gallagher, N.J. 13	88	80	Lennon, N.C. 7	7	8
Garmatz, Md. 3	82	52	Long, Md. 2	73	64
Gaydos, Pa. 20	66	72	Long, La. 8	6	8
Gettys, S.C. 5	7	8	Lowenstein, N.Y. 5 (2)	100	100
Giaimo, Conn. 3	76	56	Macdonald, Mass. 7	82	80
Gibbons, Fla. 6	61	60	Madden, Ind. 1	92	72
Gilbert, N.Y. 22 (1)	97	88	Mahon, Tex. 19	36	8
Gonzalez, Tex. 20	87	64	Mann, S. C. 4	2	4
Gray, Ill. 21	67	40	Marsh, Va. 7 (9)	1	0
Green, Ore. 3	83	40	Matsunaga, Hawaii 1	89	88
Green, Pa. 5	96	100	McCarthy, N.Y. 39 (3)	81	80
Griffin, Miss. 3	5	8	McCormack, Mass. 9 (9)	91	—
Griffiths, Mich, 17	77	64	McFall, Calif. 15	86	52
Hagan, Ga. 1	20	12	McMillan, S.C. 6	18	4
Haley, Fla. 7	8	8	Meeds, Wash. 2	81	84
Hamilton, Ind. 9	58	80	Melcher, Mont. 2	73	68
Hanley, N.Y. 34	72	72	Mikva, Ill. 2	100	100
Hanna, Calif. 34	74	72	Miller, Calif. 8	84	56
Hansen, Wash. 3	80	68	Mills, Ark. 2	42	12
Harrington, Mass. 6	94	88	Minish, N.J. 11	84	84
Hathaway, Maine 2	89	88	Mink, Hawaii 2	97	96
Hawkins, Calif. 21	94	84	Mollohan, W. Va. 1	42	36
Hays, Ohio 18	73	32	Monagan, Conn. 5	76	68
Hebert, La. 1	30	4	Montgomery, Miss. 4	2	0
Hechler, W. Va. 4	86	88	Moorhead, Pa. 14	91	80
Helstoski, N.J. 9	96	96	Morgan, Pa. 26	85	56
Henderson, N.C. 3	18	8	Moss, Calif. 3	92	72
Hicks, Wash. 6	77	68	Murphy, N.Y. 16	71	56
Holifield, Calif, 19	90	60	Murphy, Ill. 3 (9)	86	52
Howard, N.J. 3	82	76	Natcher, Ky. 2	59	28
Hull, Mo. 6	30	8	Nedzi, Mich. 14	90	92
Hungate, Mo. 9	54	60	Nichols, Ala. 4	6	8
Ichord, Mo. 8	31	12	Nix, Pa. 2	90	88
Jacobs, Ind. 11	84	84	Obey, Wis. 7	88	84
Jarman, Okla. 5	27	0	O'Hara, Mich. 12	91	92
Johnson, Calif. 2	82	56	Olsen, Mont, 1 (2)	80	84
Jones, Tenn. 8	29	24	O'Neal, Ga. 2 (9)	4	4
Jones, Ala. 8	62	24	O'Neill, Mass. 8	85	76
Jones, N.C. 1	8	12	Ottinger, N.Y. 25 (4)	90	84
Karth, Minn. 4	89	88	Passman, La. 5	22	0
Kastenmeier, Wis. 2	97	92	Patman, Tex. 1	56	24

Democrats (cont'd)	Cumulative	1970
Patten, N.J. 15	84	80
Pepper, Fla. 11	78	56
Perkins, Ky. 7	77	40
Philbin, Mass. 3 **(1,2)**	76	56
Pickle, Tex. 10	37	16
Pike, N.Y. 1	67	84
Poage, Tex. 11	34	8
Podell, N.Y. 13	93	92
Powell, N.Y. 18 **(1)**	76	60
Preyer, N.C. 6	34	40
Price, Ill. 24	92	56
Pryor, Ark. 4	36	48
Pucinski, Ill. 11	78	48
Purcell, Tex. 13	29	12
Randall, Mo. 4	60	32
Rarick, La. 6	6	4
Rees, Calif. 26	91	88
Reuss, Wis. 5	97	88
Rivers, S.C. 1 **(10)**	17	4
Roberts, Tex. 4	26	12
Rodino, N.J. 10	93	84
Roe, N.J. 8	78	80
Rogers, Colo. 1 **(1)**	77	64
Rogers, Fla. 9	21	24
Rooney, Pa. 15	74	72
Rooney, N.Y. 14	88	60
Rosenthal, N.Y. 8	98	96
Rostenkowski, Ill. 8	80	52
Roybal, Calif. 30	96	100
Ryan, N.Y. 20	97	96
St. Germain, R.I. 1	85	72
Satterfield, Va. 3	2	4
Scheuer, N.Y. 21	97	96
Shipley, Ill. 23	62	64
Sikes, Fla. 1	28	12
Sisk, Calif. 16	83	44
Slack, W. Va. 3	64	24
Smith, Iowa 5	77	48
Staggers, W. Va. 2	77	52
Steed, Okla. 4	47	24
Stephens, Ga. 10	28	8
Stokes, Ohio 21	98	96
Stratton, N.Y. 35	64	48
Stubblefield, Ky. 1	51	20
Stuckey, Ga. 8	8	8
Sullivan, Mo. 3	89	68
Symington, Mo. 2	73	72
Taylor, N.C. 11	21	20

	Cumulative	1970
Teague, Tex. 6	26	8
Thompson, N.J. 4	94	92
Tiernan, R.I. 2	81	80
Tunney, Calif. 38 **(5)**	73	60
Udall, Ariz. 2	82	76
Ullman, Ore. 2	77	52
Van Deerlin, Calif. 37	83	84
Vanik, Ohio 22	90	96
Vigorito, Pa. 24	65	72
Waggonner, La. 4	5	4
Waldie, Calif. 14	89	96
Watts, Ky. 6 **(10)**	50	20
White, Tex. 16	24	32
Whitten, Miss. 2	18	4
Wilson, Calif. 31	73	68
Wolff, N.Y. 3	78	84
Wright, Tex. 12	54	32
Yates, Ill. 9	97	96
Yatron, Pa. 6	64	68
Young, Tex. 14	47	24
Zablocki, Wis. 4	84	44

Republicans

	Cumulative	1970
Adair, Ind. 4 **(2)**	8	4
Anderson, Ill. 16	11	28
Andrews, N.D. 1	14	24
Arends, Ill. 17	14	20
Ashbrook, Ohio 17	2	4
Ayres, Ohio 14 **(2)**	33	20
Beall, Md. 6 **(5)**	20	20
Belcher, Okla. 1	5	8
Bell, Calif. 28	24	28
Berry, S.D. 2 **(9)**	8	6
Betts, Ohio 8	5	12
Biester, Pa. 8	47	76
Blackburn, Ga. 4	0	0
Bow, Ohio 16	8	12
Bray, Ind. 6	19	0
Brock, Tenn. 3 **(5)**	5	4
Broomfield, Mich. 18	36	32
Brotzman, Colo. 2	12	24
Brown, Ohio 7	12	24
Brown, Mich. 3	33	24
Broyhill, N.C. 10	2	8
Broyhill, Va. 10	14	4
Buchanan, Ala. 6	2	4
Burke, Fla. 10	6	8

Republicans (cont'd)	Cumulative	1970		Cumulative	1970
Burton, Utah 1 **(4)**	6	16	Halpern, N.Y. 6	81	76
Bush, Tex. 7 **(4)**	7	12	Hammerschmidt, Ark. 3	4	16
Button, N.Y. 29 **(2)**	66	64	Hansen, Idaho 2	20	32
Byrnes, Wis. 8	18	20	Harsha, Ohio 6	7	8
Camp Okla. 6	6	12	Harvey, Mich. 8	16	20
Carter, Ky. 5	13	16	Hastings, N.Y. 38	12	16
Cederberg, Mich. 10	9	16	Heckler, Mass. 10	61	72
Chamberlain, Mich. 6	19	12	Hogan, Md. 5	22	24
Clancy, Ohio 2	4	0	Horton, N.Y. 36	63	76
Clausen, Calif. 1	5	16	Hosmer, Calif. 32	23	24
Clawson, Calif. 23	5	8	Hunt, N.J. 1	7	8
Cleveland, N.H. 2	23	44	Hutchinson, Mich. 4	5	12
Collier, Ill. 10	8	16	Johnson, Pa. 23	2	4
Collins, Tex. 3	0	0	Jonas, N.C. 9	4	0
Conable, N.Y. 37	16	28	Keith, Mass. 12	23	40
Conte, Mass. 1	60	72	King, N.Y. 30	3	4
Corbett, Pa. 18 **(10)**	52	20	Kleppe, N.D. 2 **(4)**	10	16
Coughlin, Pa. 13	56	64	Kuykendall, Tenn. 9	5	12
Cowger, Ky. 3 **(2)**	25	28	Kyl, Iowa 4	12	28
Cramer, Fla. 8 **(4)**	12	0	Landgrebe, Ind. 2	6	12
Crane, Ill. 13	4	8	Langen, Minn. 7 **(2)**	7	12
Cunningham, Neb. 2 **(1)**	13	12	Latta, Ohio 5	6	8
Davis, Wis. 9	10	20	Lloyd, Utah 2	10	16
Dellenback, Ore. 4	36	32	Lujan, N.M. 1	25	36
Denney, Neb. 1 **(9)**	5	8	Lukens, Ohio 24 **(6)**	6	8
Dennis, Ind. 10	6	12	MacGregor, Minn. 3 **(4)**	22	24
Derwinski, Ill. 4	11	20	Mailliard, Calif. 6	43	32
Devine, Ohio 12	5	4	Martin, Neb. 3	2	8
Dickinson, Ala. 2	1	8	Mathias, Calif. 18	7	20
Duncan, Tenn. 2	5	12	May, Wash. 4 **(2)**	10	16
Dwyer, N.J. 12	57	52	Mayne, Iowa 6	11	24
Edwards, Ala. 1	2	4	McClory, Ill. 12	16	24
Erlenborn, Ill. 14	10	24	McCloskey, Calif. 11	55	64
Esch, Mich. 2	48	52	McClure, Idaho 1	8	12
Eshleman, Pa. 16	7	12	McCulloch, Ohio 4	9	28
Findley, Ill. 20	14	28	McDade, Pa. 10	49	56
Fish, N.Y. 28	41	48	McDonald, Mich. 19	30	24
Ford, Mich. 5	25	12	McEwen, N.Y. 31	5	12
Foreman, N.M. 2 **(2)**	3	4	McKneally, N.Y. 27 **(2)**	18	16
Forsythe, N.J. 6 **(11)**	33	33	Meskill, Conn. 6 **(8)**	20	28
Frelinghuysen, N.J. 5	39	40	Michel, Ill. 18	12	20
Frey, Fla. 5	2	4	Miller, Ohio 10	14	40
Fulton, Pa. 27 **(10)**	62	56	Minshall, Ohio 23	14	12
Goldwater, Calif. 27	0	0	Mize, Kan. 2 **(2)**	8	16
Goodling, Pa. 19	3	8	Mizell, N.C. 5	0	0
Gross, Iowa 3	14	20	Morse, Mass. 5	59	56
Grover, N.Y. 2	16	12	Morton, Md. 1 **(9)**	11	16
Gubser, Calif. 10	23	20	Mosher, Ohio 13	41	88
	73	80	Myers, Ind. 7	5	12
Hall, Mo. 7	2	8	Nelsen, Minn. 2	11	16

Republicans *(cont'd)*	Cumu-lative	1970		Cumu-lative	1970
O'Konski, Wis. 10	44	40	Snyder, Ky. 4	7	8
Pelly, Wash. 1	33	24	Springer, Ill. 22	23	16
Pettis, Calif. 33	12	28	Stafford, Vt. AL **(12)**	39	60
Pirnie, N.Y. 32	24	24	Stanton, Ohio 11	22	52
Poff, Va. 6	7	8	Steele, Conn. 2 **(11)**	17	17
Pollock, Alaska AL **(6)**	17	16	Steiger, Ariz. 3	6	12
Price, Tex. 18	1	4	Steiger, Wis. 6	22	24
Quie, Minn. 1	22	40	Taft, Ohio 1 **(5)**	20	20
Quillen, Tenn. 1	3	4	Talcott, Calif. 12	7	24
Railsback Ill. 19	34	48	Teague, Calif. 13	18	8
Reid, Ill. 15 **(9)**	5	20	Thompson, Ga. 5	2	0
Reid, N.Y. 26	78	84	Thomson, Wis. 3	5	24
Reifel, S.D. 1 **(9)**	10	12	Vander Jagt, Mich. 9	30	48
Rhodes, Ariz. 1	16	24	Wampler, Va. 9	15	16
Riegle, Mich. 7	58	80	Ware, Pa. 9 **(11)**	0	0
Robison, N.Y. 33	28	64	Watson, S.C. 2 **(7)**	3	4
Roth, Del. Al **(5)**	11	20	Weicker, Conn. 4 **(5)**	40	40
Rouqebush, Ind. 5 **(4)**	3	0	Whalen, Ohio 3	70	88
Rousselot, Calif. 24	29	29	Whalley, Pa. 12	11	8
Ruppe, Mich. 11	39	56	Whitehurst, Va. 2	12	16
Ruth, N.C. 8	0	0	Widnall, N.J. 7	40	40
Sandman, N.J. 2	14	16	Wiggins, Calif. 25	6	16
Saylor, Pa. 22	37	40	Williams, Pa. 7	7	12
Schadeberg, Wis. 1 **(2)**	5	8	Wilson, Calif. 36	17	20
Scherle, Iowa 7	4	8	Winn, Kan. 3	3	4
Schneebeli, Pa. 17	12	28	Wold, Wyo. AL **(4)**	10	12
Schwengel, Iowa 1	41	40	Wyatt, Ore. 1	14	40
Scott, Va. 8	3	4	Wydler, N.Y. 4	34	56
Sebelius, Kan. 1	4	8	Wylie, Ohio 15	12	24
Shriver, Kan. 4	5	12	Wyman, N.H. 1	6	8
Skubitz, Kan. 5	4	4	Zion, Ind. 8	10	12
Smith, Calif. 20	5	12	Zwach, Minn. 6	23	44
Smith , N.Y. 40	16	20			

(1) Defeated in House primary, 1970.
(2) Defeated November 3, 1970, in House election.
(3) Defeated in Senate primary, 1970.
(4) Defeated November 3, 1970, in Senate election.
(5) Elected to Senate November 3, 1970.
(6) Defeated in gubernatorial primary, 1970.
(7) Defeated November 3, 1970, in gubernatorial election.
(8) Elected Governor, November 3, 1970.
(9) resigned or retired
(10) deceased
(11) Sworn in November 16, 1970, to fill vacancy.
(12) Appointed September 16, 1971, by Gov. Deane C. Davis, R, as interim replacement for the late Winston L. Prouty, R, pending a special primary and general election.

Source: ADA, *National Journal*

2

Americans for Constitutional Action

ANDREW J. GLASS

An economic slump has upset efforts by Americans for Constitutional Action to move Congress to the political right. ACA—which has spent $1,543,150 to send "constitutional conservatives" to Washington and keep them there—is suffering from the worst financial setback of its 13-year lifespan as a political pressure group. "Contributions are 65 per cent of what we would like them to be at this time of year," ACA President Charles A. McManus told *National Journal* in July 1971. Receipts for January to May 1971 were $43,694, he said, while disbursements amounted to $43,767.

McManus blames the business downturn—and, in particular, a sharp 1970-71 drop in the stock market—for the organization's plight. As a consequence, McManus says ACA presently "is not in a position to make any firm commitments for financial assistance" in the 1972 election campaigns. The organization is raising money on behalf of Senate candidates up for reelection in 1972 through receptions and other special fundraising efforts, which, McManus hopes, "will relieve ACA of the responsibility of major financial contributions" from its own treasury in 1972. (He said more than $30,000 had been raised by the first week of August 1971 for Sen. Strom Thurmond, R-S.C., and the figure was expected to reach $40,000.) ACA found itself in the same financial situation in early 1970. In previous campaign years, ACA by mid-May had already

targeted swing congressional districts and had put experts on
its own payroll who, in turn, went to work for key candidates.

Despite the problems, McManus remains determined to
make ACA "the paramount voice of responsible conservatism
in the nation." The group—formed in 1958 as a direct counter-
force to Americans for Democratic Action (ADA)—feels "the
long-range picture is not a bleak one." An April 1970 ACA
report cites the emergence of Vice President Spiro T. Agnew
"from relative obscurity to the position of a national spokesman . . . for popular concern over the abuses of liberalism and
social 'permissiveness.' " The report makes clear ACA is prepared to ride the Agnew tide.

Six inscribed photographs from "our friends on the Hill," as
McManus calls them, line the walls of the ACA president's
office. These Republican Senators serve as an informal advisory board to ACA. Chief among them is Karl E. Mundt, S.D.,
now recuperating from a stroke he suffered in November 1967.
The others are Robert Dole, Kan., Barry Goldwater, Ariz.,
Edward J. Gurney, Fla., John G. Tower, Tex., and Thurmond.

Despite ACA's "nonpartisan" status, McManus is an avowed
Republican with close ties to such key members of the Nixon
Administration as William E. Timmons, assistant to the Presi-
dent for congressional relations. ACA has yet to support a
Northern Democrat in a campaign and has endorsed only two
Western Democrats—Reps. Walter S. Baring of Nevada and
John Jarman of Oklahoma. Baring has an ACA cumulative
rating of 66 and Jarman has a rating of 65, against a theoretically "perfect" score of 100. In a promotion brochure,
Mundt describes ACA as "a thoroughly respectable, depend-
able, patriotic, democratic and effective political action
organization which dares fight openly for what it believes
to be right. . . . "

ACA is formally governed by a 25-member board of trustees, to whom McManus, as chief administrative officer and
acting chief executive officer, is responsible. The trustees

include eight former members of Congress, a retired Supreme Court Justice, a locomotive engineer, and two current members of the John Birch Society. (See Table 2.1.) Since September 1970, ACA has operated from a four-room suite at 955 L'Enfant Plaza in the District of Columbia, paying approximately $465 a month rent for its new quarters. Until 1968, ACA's power center in Washington was an apartment at 1301 Massachusetts Ave. NW, maintained by Admiral Ben Moreell, ACA founder and long-time chairman. "Until his health gave out, the Admiral *was* ACA," a congressional friend of the group told *National Journal.*

Moreell, 79, founded ACA in 1958 as a third career, after retiring from the military and from industry. The Navy promoted Moreell to full admiral in 1946 — a rare distinction for a non-Annapolis officer. During World War II, Moreell set up and ran the Seabees. In the wave of nationwide oil and soft coal strikes that followed the war, President Truman named Moreell to run these industries for the government. Leaving Washington, Moreell began a new career as president and chairman of Jones and Laughlin Steel Corporation (1947-58). President Eisenhower called him back to serve as chairman of the water resources and electric power task force of the second Hoover Commission (1953-55).

Moreell is big, square-jawed and broad-shouldered, carrying his solid poundage on a six-foot frame. Until a recent illness, he traveled widely as a spokesman for "constitutional conservatism." He currently is writing his memoirs at the Navy's Civil Engineers Corps officers school, Port Hueneme, Calif., where a museum and library are dedicated to him. While Moreell views freedom chiefly in economic terms, he can sound like a civil libertarian in defending extremists. "I'm very wary," he says, "of telling people what they should think or what they should say."

Now Charles McManus runs ACA, with calls and letters to Moreell in Port Hueneme on vital policy matters. McManus, 43, is both efficient and pleasant-mannered, and is drawn only against his will into ideological controversies. "I try to steer clear of polemical issues so far as I can," McManus confesses.

As ACA's executive director between 1961 and 1969, he kept out of the limelight and ran the shop. After work, he likes to mingle with reporters ("my favorite people") at the National Press Club or, perhaps, hurry home to Bowie, Md., for a round of twilight golf. Unlike others in ACA's hierarchy, McManus is not a joiner. His lone outside affiliation is the Knights of Columbus. In Bowie, McManus refrains from engaging in local GOP politics. "Seven children and the ACA," he says, "provide enough politics."

McManus is a native of Wilkes-Barre, Pa., a Navy veteran and a graduate of Wyoming Seminary Dean's School of business, Kingston, Pa. He attended night school at Temple University in Philadelphia for seven years and King's College in Wilkes-Barre for three years, majoring in business administration at both schools. While attending Temple's night school, McManus was employed in the eastern regional office of U.S. Steel Corporation. In that seven year period (1952-59), he was given increasingly larger lobbying duties for the company at the state level. Associates in the steel industry recommended McManus for the ACA staff job which he took in 1959.

The ACA staff consists of an office manager, two secretaries, a research aide and one volunteer. Rather than maintaining a large staff, ACA prefers to hire consultants. They perform such services as public relations, speech writing, campaign work and preparation of ACA's widely publicized index, which seeks to measure the extent to which a Member of Congress is a "constitutional conservative." ACA also utilizes college students, working on a volunteer basis, for research projects. McManus points with pride to his small staff which, he says, "contrasts most favorably with other political action groups on the right." In a review of 1969 activities, McManus notes "the proliferation of new political groups—many of them self-identified as 'conservative'—whose conflicting appeals for funds have put increasing demands on established contributors to the conservative cause." McManus told *National Journal:* "With funds now so tight, I become deeply disturbed when I see money being wasted for plush quarters, big staffs and extravagant methods of fund raising."

In contrast to political action groups which use professional fund-raisers, ACA makes its own solicitations—with the aid of two leased magnetic-tape automatic typewriters. McManus reported: "We never use 'fear letters' or scare techniques—like other people do. We don't tell people the organization is about to fold unless they send us a check right away. And we never buy brokers' lists." McManus said Sens. Mundt, Thurmond and Carl T. Curtis, R-Neb., have written letters on their Senate stationery seeking financial support for ACA.

As a political action group subject to the Federal Corrupt Practices Act (2 USC 241), ACA files its receipts and disbursements with the Clerk of the House of Representatives. Individuals who donate $100 or more are named. House records reveal that ACA has a loyal group of frequent contributors, although these gifts are not tax-deductible.

The organization's financial backers include some well-known Americans. Among them are the following—all of whom, according to records on file with the House clerk, have contributed at least $100 (some of them several thousand dollars), and most of whom have been regular contributors to ACA over the years: Lemuel R. Boulware, retired executive vice president (for labor relations), General Electric Company (New York, N.Y., and Del Ray Beach, Fla.); Avery Brundage, president, International Olympic Committee (Chicago, Ill.); James S. Copley, publisher, *The San Diego Union* and other newspapers in the Copley chain (La Jolla, Calif.); Roy H. Cullen, industrialist and oil executive (Houston, Tex.); Gaylord Donnelley, chairman, R. R. Donnelley & Sons Company (Libertyville, Ill.); Walter B. Knott, owner, Knott's Berry Farm (Buena Park, Calif.); Eli Lilly, chairman, Eli Lilly & Company (Indianapolis, Ind.); Jeremiah Milbank Jr., chairman, Republican Finance Committee (Greenwich, Conn.); A. C. Nielsen, chairman, A. C. Nielsen Company (Winnetka, Ill.); Peter O'Donnell, chairman, Texas Republican Party (Dallas, Tex.); J. Howard Pew, chairman, Sun Oil Company (Philadelphia, Pa.); Henry Salvatori, oil geologist, former finance chairman, California Republican State Central Committee (Los Angeles, Calif.); Maurice H. Stans, Secretary of Commerce (Washington,

D.C.) contributed $100 in 1964; Dewitt Wallace, publisher, *Reader's Digest* (Mount Kisco, N.Y.); and Albert C. Wedemeyer, author and retired military officer, former chief of staff to Generalissimo Chiang Kai-Shek (Boyds, Md.).

As of June 30, 1971, ACA's net worth was $48,343.45. (Of that amount, approximately $13,300 is the value of furnishings and equipment at ACA headquarters; the remainder is in cash or savings and checking accounts.) In the first seven months of 1971, the organization's receipts totaled $55,570.83. ACA said its May report to the Clerk of the House of Representatives showed $43,694.19 in receipts and $43,767.39 in expenditures. McManus told *National Journal* in early August, "I admit we're in financial straights, but we're not hard up." Receipts for 1970 totaled $138,475 — considerably less than in 1968, ACA's peak year, when $202,800 was received, and only $2,915 more than the $135,560 ACA raised in 1969. ACA spent a total of $188,875 in 1970, including $82,150 in campaign assistance. At the end of the year, ACA had only $3,810 in carryover money, compared to a $54,210 balance carried forward in 1969.

ACA has only five chapters now, although the program had a peak of 38 in 1964. There are statewide ACA chapters in Alabama, Texas and Georgia, a regional chapter in eastern Massachusetts and a chapter in Jefferson County, Ky. Chapters are encouraged to rate state legislators for their "conservatism" in the same way the parent group rates Congress. But application forms for new charters urge chapter sponsors "not (to) permit their efforts to be diverted from the attainment of (basic) objectives by becoming involved in other issues which are not relevant to the fundamental purposes (of ACA)." New chapters are provided with three comprehensive nuts-and-bolts political organization manuals. They are entitled: "Your Decision" (introduction by Tower), "Your Challenge" (introduction by Goldwater), and "Your Victory" (introduction by Thurmond). McManus says ACA is not attempting to organize new chapters at the present time. "We don't have the money or staff required for organizing (new chapters)," he explained. "I don't want to do it until I can do it right."

Despite recent reversals, which McManus attributes mainly to lack of money, no thought is being given to a merger with like-minded political groups or to a common fund-raising program. "I can only see ACA losing stature that way," McManus said. "We once discussed something like that in Goldwater's apartment (when the Senator was a moving force behind the now defunct Free Society Association). But nothing ever came of it."

Fund-raising problems have heightened the competition between ACA and a number of like-minded organizations which draw their funds from the same sources. The other Washington-based political pressure groups seeking to exert a rightward pull on Congress include:

• American Conservative Union, which traces its roots to the successful campaign to secure the 1964 Republican Presidential nomination for Sen. Barry Goldwater and the unsuccessful campaign to elect him. A 1970 fund-raising letter by Rep. John M. Ashbrook, R-Ohio, then ACU chairman, notes ACU's primary mission of countering "liberal propaganda" by making sure "conservative views receive the attention they deserve in Congress." In 1970, ACU denounced President Nixon's welfare plan and the Ford Foundation's alleged "illegal involvement in political activities." ACU claims a membership of 60,000, which receives its monthly newsletter, *Republican Battle Line*. ACU reported 1969 receipts of $234,850 and spending of $231,707, about the same as 1968. 1970 receipts totaled $319,758; expenditures were $355,716. M. Stanton Evans, editor of the *Indianapolis News*, was named ACU chairman in February 1971. Ashbrook remains an ACU national board member. In July 1971, ACU joined with other conservative groups in "suspending" support of President Nixon, in part for his decision to visit Peking.

• Liberty Lobby, which was shaken in 1969 when columnist Jack Anderson accused the group's organizer, Willis A. Carto, of anti-Semitic activities. A number of staff members subsequently left to form a competing group, American Lobby. In April 1970, Liberty Lobby's policy chairman, Curtis B. Dall, denounced Sen. J. W. Fulbright, D-Ark., for refusing to let the group testify before the Senate Foreign Relations Committee, which Fulbright chairs. Dall claims 24,500 "board of policy members" and 250,000 subscribers to the group's "legislative report," *Liberty Letter*. Liberty Lobby, founded in 1955 by "conservatives and anti-Communists" to promote individual liberty and patriotism, reported 1969 receipts of $83,790 and expenses of $79,927, about the same as 1968.

- United Republicans of America, which has no official ties to the Republican Party. It was necessary for the GOP's former finance director, C. Langhorne Washburn, to make this clear in a news release after a late 1967 fund-raising appeal by URA. The appeal included a nationwide Presidential preference questionnaire. Responses to the URA poll over the next six months showed Richard Nixon leading with 44 per cent and Ronald Reagan runner-up with 28. URA indicated its preference for Reagan, reporting in its monthly newsletter, *The Campaigner*, that Reagan was coming up rapidly in popularity and that late returns in the URA straw poll showed him running even with Nixon as the nominating convention neared. URA's chairman, Wainwright Dawson Jr., former executive director of Young Americans for Freedom, runs his own public relations firm, Dawson Associates, which URA retains. House records show URA plows back about half its contributions into promotional mailings. URA, founded in 1965 with the goal of "no-nonsense conservative" control of the Republican Party, reported 1969 receipts of $10,812 and expenses of $12,673, but 1968 receipts of $475,453 and spending of $496,360. In 1970, URA reported receipts of $83,172 and expenditures totaling $81,711.

In discussing the scope of ACA's operations, McManus observed: "We don't lobby. We don't make a lot of noise. We really don't have very much political clout." However, *Danger on the Right*, published in 1964, describes ACA as "an effective political action group which already exerts a certain impact on the U.S. Congress and whose influence may well be growing." (The book's authors are Benjamin R. Epstein and Arnold Forster, national director and general counsel, respectively, of the Anti-Defamation League (ADL) of B'nai B'rith, organized to protect minorities against attack.)

One reason for ACA's continued effectiveness is the ACA index, which rates Members of Congress on specific roll calls chosen by ACA. "Lets face it," said a Senator whose ACA rating is in the low 80s, "it's the only game in town. You have to pay attention. I look at it like the (television) Nielsen ratings." Senators who score well in the eyes of ACA usually do badly on similar ratings prepared by Americans for Democratic Action (ADA) and the Committee on Political Education (COPE) of AFL-CIO. The reverse is also true. While ACA prepares several subsidiary indexes, the score most often cited is its "cumulative consistency rating" of incumbent Members of Congress in both Houses. This includes all votes tallied by ACA in prior Congresses, beginning in 1955 for the Senate and 1957 for the House. A total of 315 Senate votes and 253 House votes have been analyzed.

In the first session of the 91st Congress (1969), a Senator could have boosted his ACA rating by voting against ratification of the Nuclear Nonproliferation Treaty (Exec H), and against federal development of a safe automobile (83 Stat 454); and by voting for imposing a $20,000 limit on individual farm subsidy payments (83 Stat 244). Conversely, a Senator's overall ACA rating would have fallen had he supported lifting the ceiling on the national debt (83 Stat 7), opposed deployment of the ABM (antiballistic missile system) (83 Stat 204), or favored the Philadelphia Plan for employing more minority workers in federal construction projects (83 Stat 447)—a system ACA terms "forced hiring." In the second session of the 91st Congress (1970), a Senator could have raised his ACA rating by voting against legislation to lower the voting age to 18 (84 Stat 314) and against amendments to the Military Procurement Authorization Bill (84 Stat 905) that would have fixed a deadline for withdrawal of U.S. troops from Indochina. A Senator's rating would have been lowered had he favored amendments increasing funds for higher education (84 Stat 800) and for the food stamp program (84 Stat 1480).

ACA tabulated 16 key issues in the Senate and 17 comparable ones in the House in 1969. On these issues, a Senate majority agreed with ACA five times and disagreed 11 times. In the House, ACA got its way on six votes. In 1970, ACA based its ratings on 24 issues in the Senate and 19 in the House. The Senate agreed with ACA on 10 of the chosen issues and the House was in agreement on nine of the issues. (See Table 2.3.) A *National Journal* study revealed President Nixon would have scored 50 — in the exact center of the ACA scale — based upon ACA's judgment of the rightness or wrongness of positions taken by the White House on ACA's Senate test votes in 1969. By contrast, the GOP leader in the Senate, Hugh Scott, Pa., scored 25; the deupty leader, Ropert P. Griffin, Mich., scored 38. House GOP leader Gerald R. Ford, Mich., scored 53, while the No. 2 Republican in the House, Leslie C. Arends, Ill., ended 1969 with a 71.

In an April 1970 statement, ACA deplored "a general lowering of ACA ratings among traditionally conservative Members" and observed: "Changes in . . . national administration(s) switched many conservative legislators from the position of outsiders attacking federal government policies and bureaucracy to that of defenders of the new Administration, and, however unwittingly, of the governmental status quo. . . . "

ACA ratings have at times proved useful to incumbents seeking to overcome primary challenges from members of the John Birch Society. For example, in a 1966 South Dakota GOP primary, Richard Murphy, an avowed Bircher, assailed Sen. Karl Mundt. While conceding that Mundt was a "conservative," Murphy attacked Mundt's votes on civil rights and federal aid to education. Mundt's cumulative ACA rating of 80 helped him swamp Murphy at the polls, 4-to-1. Sen. Wallace F. Bennett, R-Utah, whose ACA score is 86, underwent a similar experience in defeating his 1968 primary challenger, Mark Anderson, also a John Birch Society member.

In 1961, ACA began a program of "distinguished service awards" to Members of Congress with cumulative ratings of 65 or better. (The awards are given only in off-election years.) In that year, 136 (of 535) Representatives and Senators qualified. Since then, the number of qualifiers has risen slightly: 153 in 1963; 154 in 1965; 149 in 1967; 184 in 1969 and 177 in 1971. Each ACA award winner receives a "personalized" news release from the group praising his record — that is, if he wants one. "Some people seek open support; some do not," McManus noted. In an average year, some eight legislators decline to accept ACA plaques, despite achieving scores held satisfactory by ACA. In 1963, the seven Representatives who declined included two who have since been elected to the Senate: Griffin and Richard S. Schweiker, R-Pa. Those declining in 1969, according to ACA records, were Reps. Charles E. Chamberlain, R-Mich.; James C. Cleveland, R-N.H.; Barber B. Conable Jr., R-N.Y.; John Kyl, R-Iowa; James H. Quillen, R-Tenn.; and Burt L. Talcott, R-Calif.

Sometimes, awards have been coupled with an evening reception for recipients. Past contributors to ACA are invited to attend, for $25. "The girls (on Capitol Hill staffs) volunteer as hostesses and we all have a great time," McManus recalled. At the last such reception, held in 1967, all members of the GOP leadership in Congress attended, except Thomas H. Kuchel, Calif. (1953-69), then minority whip in the Senate.

In its 1969 report, ACA cites "an improved image of conservative office holders" which, it says, results from "the opening of new channels of communication with Washington news media." McManus, a member of the National Press Club (ACA pays his dues), in late April 1970 gave a party for political reporters and editors at the conclusion of a Press Club-sponsored "Congressional Night." Also at McManus's party were Presidential Assistant Timmons and several of ACA's House "friends" who were planning to run for statewide office in the 1970 general elections.

McManus also helps sponsor a dinner group known as the "Off-the-Record Club," to which 28 leading members of the Washington press corps belong. Its only non-press members who are not in government are McManus and Paul A. Theis, public relations director of the National Republican Congressional (Campaign) Committee. (There are two non-press members in government: Timmons and Lewis M. Helm, deputy assistant secretary of Interior for mineral resources. Timmons, Helm and McManus were the original founders of the club.) McManus reported ACA pays the check for the guest of the evening, who is usually "one of our friends on the Hill." Recent "Off-the-Record" guests have included former Sen. George Murphy, R-Calif. (1965-71), and Sen. Tower; Harry S. Dent, special counsel to the President; Lee R. Nunn, former staff director of the National Republican Senatorial Committee and currently director of the fund-raising division for the Committee for the Reelection of the President; and Sen. Dole, chairman of the Republican National Committee. ACA also serves as an informal speakers' bureau for ACA chapters and similar-minded groups. As McManus explained: "I'll call a Senator or Congressman and say, 'This is on your way home. Can you do it?' Some of the guys pick up a couple hundred bucks or so that way."

For the record, McManus reports that "we have no reason to have a relationship with the Nixon Administration, since we are not involved in lobbying nor do we get into Presidential races." On the other hand, ACA's president readily acknowledges the group's informal links to the Nixon team. "I have a lot of friends in government right now," McManus told *National Journal*. "Candidates come to me with local problems and I'm able to steer them to the right guy. Politically, it's a great situation. I tell him who to see. I help him out. It's the buddy system, you know."

In late April 1970, McManus telephoned Lyn Nofziger, then a deputy assistant to the President for congressional relations and a former communications secretary to California Gov. Ronald Reagan, R. "I have a candidate in the 3rd District of North Carolina (Republican Herbert H. Howell)," McManus told him. "Got any good speeches he can use?" Nofziger, who is now deputy national chairman for communications at the Republican National Committee, inquired into the candidate's political background and that of his opponent, Democratic Representative David N. Henderson who,McManus told Nofziger, "was once too liberal but he's running more our way now." Nofziger promised to see what he could do. (Howell, who was endorsed by ACA in 1968 and again in 1970, lost the election to Henderson, receiving 39.9 per cent of the votes cast.)

The assistance does not run one way. In 1970, McManus said, "we got wind of a group calling itself 'Friends of Agnew' without his permission. They wanted to use his name as a fund-raising gimmick for themselves. We told the White House. The White House got on it right away and stopped it cold."

In each congressional election year, ACA hires experienced campaign workers and publicity men and sends them into swing districts to aid primary and general election candidates pledged to further ACA objectives. "I prefer that the candidate find the person we hire . . . ," McManus said. "We never demand that he put our person on the campaign team. It's bad psychology and bad business." An ACA-paid staffer may serve as a press secretary, a research assistant or even a panel-truck driver hired to nail posters on rural highway telephone poles. Sometimes, ACA help comes in the form of an initial survey to determine if a potential candidate can be elected in the district. "Only in an emergency do we convey actual cash," McManus said. "It's not that we don't trust them, It's just that we think we can get more for our dollar that way."

ACA rarely gives less than $500 in services to a candidate and has never contributed more than $4,000 worth of help to one individual in a campaign. ACA gave direct financial assistance (in either cash or services) to approximately 50 candidates in 1964, 68 in 1966, 109 in 1968 and 56 in the 1970 elections. In 1968, 69 of the 109 candidates helped by ACA won (63.3 per cent); in 1970, 36 of the 56 candidates were winners (64.3 per cent). As a matter of policy, ACA keeps secret the names of candidates who get helpers. But the helpers' names are filed under law with the House clerk as ACA expenses. It is sometimes possible to identify who got how much aid and of what kind.

ACA also has expanded a new service which it calls "programmed financial support." It reports: "By working closely, in confidence, with key friends and financial supporters, our national office has channeled additional financial support to specifically earmarked conservative candidates." For the 1968 elections, $115,805 was raised in this way. In 1970, 49 candidates received $82,375 through the special assistance program. As part of its over-all campaign assistance program, ACA in 1970 also helped organize 11 fund-raising receptions for congressional candidates. According to ACA, the receptions raised between $10,000 and $25,000 for each candidate.

In 1969 special elections to Congress, ACA assisted Rep. Philip M. Crane, R-Ill., elected to the seat vacated when Donald Rumsfeld was named director of the Office of Economic Opportunity; Rep. Barry M. Goldwater Jr., R-Calif., elected to the seat Edward Reinecke gave up to become Lieutenant Governor of California; and W. S. Mather, an unsuccessful candidate for the seat vacated by Rep. Jim Battin, R-Mont., for a federal judgeship. "Two out of three isn't bad," McManus reflected. McManus said ACA's 1970 elections plan was "to put more of our effort into Senate races, particularly in the Deep South and Far West, than has been our practice." In 1970, ACA endorsed 15 Senate candidates. Six of the 15 were winners. All but 23 of the 157 House candidates endorsed by the organization were elected. (See Table 2.2.)

ACA maintains detailed dossiers on incumbents it would like to see defeated by "constitutional conservatives." These files—covering, in the main, Northern Democrats—contain data from the *Congressional Record* as well as press clippings. "Occasionally, we'll put together a hurry-up job against a liberal Republican," McManus said. In June 1967, a former ACA research aide, David M. Percy, prepared a fact-oriented 27-page memo to McManus on the National Committee for an Effective Congress (NCEC), a nonpartisan group which often supports candidates that ACA opposes. "We made sure (the ACA report) got into the hands of the right people," McManus said.

In March 1970, ACA broke its customary no-lobbying rule to enter into the unsuccessful effort to confirm G. Harrold Carswell, then of the 5th Circuit Court of Appeals, to the Supreme Court. ACA noted in a press release that 19 Senators who opposed Carswell had approved prior nominees who, the ACA said, "lacked judicial experience," such as former Chief Justice Earl Warren (1953-69). Regarding its role in the Carswell fight, McManus said: "It was not an attempt to lobby; it was an attempt to educate." McManus stressed ACA's policy not to get involved in specific political issues when asked about a July 1971 meeting of several like-minded organizations that resulted in a statement suspending support of the Nixon Administration. The July 26 statement criticized President Nixon for not following certain goals in domestic and foreign policy, citing in part his "overtures" to China and the "deteriorated" American military position. It was signed by representatives of the American Conservative Union, *National Review, Human Events*, Young Americans for Freedom, the New York State Conservative Party, the Conservative Book Club and the Southern States Industrial Council. McManus told *National Journal* that although ACA officials were not invited to attend the meeting, "because of our policy not to get involved in specific issues, we would not have attended had we been asked." He added that neither he nor Admiral Moreell intend to make any statement regarding the meeting.

ACA was formed in June 1958 as a counter-thrust to ADA. The announcement of its creation, which Sen. Mundt placed in the *Congressional Record* August 4, 1958, said the new group "could force back together the conservative coalition which for over 20 years successfully stopped the greatest excesses toward statism in this country but which (was then being) . . .

torn apart and destroyed" by the desertion of Southern Democrats on the issue of federal power development and by Northern Republicans on the issue of civil rights.

At the time, Mundt recalled that he had joined the late Sen. Owen Brewster, R-Maine (1941-52), in spawning the ideological parent of ACA, known as the National Committee for Political Realignment. This coalition group was created in September 1951 as a result of a Mundt-Brewster meeting in Washington, which also included as participants former Sen. Albert W. Hawkes, R-N.J. (1943-49), who had also served as president of the U.S. Chamber of Commerce, and the late Edward A. O'Neal of Selma, Ala., president of the American Farm Bureau Federation (1931-47). Brewster traveled widely for ACA in its early years, seeking support, while Hawkes became an ACA contributor.

McManus noted ACA was a direct financial offshoot of yet another now-defunct group, The Campaign for the 48 States, "although their purposes were quite different." That organization was set up in 1955 to lobby for the adoption of constitutional amendments that would limit income taxes, curb the voting power of urban areas and clamp a ceiling on federal spending. The chairman of The Campaign for the 48 States was Robert B. Snowden, then a resident of Memphis. Snowden became ACA's first finance chairman and has since been a major contributor. In a 1962 John Birch Society brochure, Snowden was listed as an endorser of the society.

ACA's first offices were in Memphis. As The Campaign for the 48 States folded, some $25,000 that remained in its treasury was used to open a bank account for ACA. The new group opened a Washington office in May 1959 and closed its Memphis operation six months later. ACA's original charter was drawn up and signed by Admiral Moreell; the late Charles Edison, then chairman of McGraw-Edison Company, a former Governor of New Jersey, D (1941-44), and son of inventor Thomas A. Edison; the late Dr. Walter B. Martin of Norfolk, Va., a past president of the American Medical Association (1954-55); the late T. Jefferson Coolidge, then chairman of United Fruit Company, and Loyd Wright, who is still an ACA trustee. (Wright unsuccessfully opposed then-Sen. Thomas Kuchel in the 1962 California GOP senatorial primary. Wright's campaign manager at the time was Murray M. Chotiner, a former special counsel to President Nixon who is now associated with the Washington, D.C., law firm of Reeves & Hamilton. Kuchel was beaten in a 1968 primary by ACA trustee Max Rafferty, who then lost the general election to Sen. Alan Cranston, D. ACA supplied "research" for an anti-Kuchel campaign ad paid for by Patrick J. Frawley Jr., another ACA trustee.)

McManus, who joined the staff in August 1959, recalls the early years as being quite stormy for the fledgling ACA. Its first executive director, Kenneth W. Ingwalson, who had been on the staff of the Farm Bureau, resigned in December 1960, and McManus took over. A complete shift in the professional staff followed shortly. "With my predecessor, everything was hush, hush—secret," McManus said. "I don't operate that way. I see no point in that when our records must be disclosed under the law anyway."

Ingwalson went on to become an assistant publisher of *Human Events*. (He is now publisher of Crestwood Books Inc., Arlington, Va.) For a short while ACA and the weekly publication shared offices on Capitol Hill. "Our relationship with *Human Events* was cordial—a little too cordial in some respects," McManus said. Initial publication rights to the ACA index were granted to *Human Events*, which sold the compilation for $15 a copy and paid ACA for its research efforts. "This *Human Events* promotion put us on the map in conservative circles," McManus said. "And it was also quite profitable for them." McManus broke the arrangement upon succeeding Ingwalson. One reason for the change, McManus said, was that in the opinion of ACA's lawyers, the arrangement jeopardized ACA's nonprofit tax status. Another was that it "made it look like ACA was merely a rating agency for *Human Events*." (Under McManus, ACA annually prints approximately 12,000 copies of the index and about 100,000 copies of an index summary, making it freely available to the new media.)

ACA's hierarchy remained relatively stable until 1969, when events brought what McManus calls "a major reorganization." This forced ACA to forego its biennial reception that year for ACA-backed Members of Congress. On July 31, 1969, Charles Edison, who had served as ACA's treasurer since its inception, died at age 78. Edison, who had also served as President Roosevelt's Secretary of the Navy (1939-40), had become increasingly disenchanted with New Deal politics. In 1956, he became co-chairman of the National Committee for T. Coleman Andrews and Thomas H. Werdel, third-party candidates for President and Vice President in 1956. (Later, Andrews, a former commissioner of internal revenue (1953-55), joined the national council of the John Birch Society.)

At the time of Edison's death, ACA's president and chief executive officer was Thomas A. Lane, a retired major general who had served as a plans and operations officer for the late Gen. Douglas MacArthur in World War II. Lane had served during the Eisenhower Administration as engineer commissioner of the District of Columbia (1954-57). "It was the death of Charles Edison that made the Admiral think of a successor," Lane recalled for *National Journal*. "We met at Edison's funeral in New York, talked it over and reached our decision at that time."

The decision, announced October 31, 1969, was that Lane would resign from ACA, that Moreell would retire and assume the title of chairman emeritus and that McManus would become its president and acting chief executive officer. "Lane has a (newspaper) column that was syndicated beginning in 1969," Moreell told *National Journal*. "His ability to devote time and effort to ACA was gradually diminishing. He felt we ought to make a clean break," Moreell added. Lane's column, "Public Affairs," published three times a week, appears in the *St. Louis Globe-Democrat* and 16 other newspapers. In addition, Lane was completing work on a book, *America on Trial: The Loss of Vietnam*, published in 1971. "In trying to sell the syndicated column, ACA was a distinct handicap," Lane said. "Editors didn't like me to have that kind of label. And the Admiral was getting up in years. Either I had to take over or somebody else did."

In early 1970, Moreell commented on the changes in ACA's leadership: "I'll be 78 in September. My health is failing. I just couldn't take the burden of this organization any longer. McManus is just at the right age to grasp responsibility by the nape of the neck." Moreell said there were "no policy differences" in the realignment. But Rep. Edward J. Derwinski, R-Ill., one of ACA's friends in Congress who was consulted at the time, told *National Journal:* "General Lane had a tendency to be politically naive. He allowed his name to be used by some people . . . and he let his emotions detract from the hard-nosed decisions that had to be made." McManus called Lane "a great guy." But he also acknowledged that Lane had accepted speaking engagements from "ultra-right groups." Lane's successor added: "The Admiral was convinced by friends on the Hill that we should use great discretion in associating with other groups. These groups were taking on the (Nixon) Administration and other Republicans. We simply couldn't have that."

"Mundt and Derwinski, among others, persuaded the Admiral that Charlie McManus could handle the job," a Capitol Hill source who declined to be identified told *National Journal.* "He (Moreell) was convinced that Lane's associations could embarrass ACA by permitting its enemies to tie them up with extremists," the source reported. ACA is now actively searching for a new chairman. "We need a nationally-known figure who is a man of stature and who is discreet in lending his name," Moreell said.

Over the years, ACA has been assailed by some Northern Democrats in Congress as well as by the Anti-Defamation League as a front for political extremists and bigots. ACA spokesmen categorically deny such charges. In their 1964 study of ACA and related groups, *Danger on the Right,* authors Epstein and Forster concluded: "If the extreme conservatives are not card-carrying Birchers, they often make common cause with them, and the similarities between their views are often more compelling than the differences."

Whenever ACA is attacked as an extremist group, McManus issues a standard press release. "Fortunately," he said, "I haven't had to use this in some time." The ACA's release quotes Sen. Hubert H. Humphrey, D-Minn., as having said in 1964 on CBS' "Face the Nation" that ACA represents "a legitimate conservative point of view," and " . . . I don't criticize the organization, for they have a function to perform." The release notes that ACA "is not related to nor affiliated with any other group." And, in an indirect reference to the Birch Society, the release quotes the late Edgar N. Eisenhower, an ACA trustee, as saying: "Certainly I would not be associated with an organization related to any group which has challenged the patriotism of my brothers, Ike and Milton." (In his 1958 book, *The Politician*, Robert H. W. Welch, founder of the John Birch Society, charged President Eisenhower — the "politician" of the title — with being a "dedicated, conscious agent of the Communist conspiracy." *The Politician* also charges that "Milton Eisenhower is an outright Communist.")

Asked about ACA's views on the Birch Society, McManus said: "Rightly or wrongly, the John Birch Society is not held in high esteem. They are counter-productive politically, from what I can determine. These controversial associations tend to embarrass (ACA-backed) candidates. There are many good people in the John Birch Society and many misguided people. But the only (ACA) board member I know of that is an active member of the society is Thomas Parker." (Parker is a member of the Birch Society's 26-member policy council.)

Another ACA trustee, Frank de Ganahl, contacted by *National Journal* in Carefree, Ariz., said that he, too, belonged to the Birch Society. In addition, Bonner Fellers, former ACA vice chairman and trustee (1960-70), was listed in a 1962 Birch brochure as an endorser. (Fellers, a retired brigadier general, served on the staff of Gen. MacArthur in World War II, as did former ACA President Thomas Lane.) Asked whether Fellers' past associations disturbed him, McManus said: "Having known Bonner personally, the answer is 'no'. But I can say the relation that has been established (with the Birch Society) has not been particularly helpful in terms of the political realities."

Twelve persons are listed on the masthead of the July-August 1971 issue of *American Opinion*, the official publication of the Birch Society, as members of the magazine's "editorial advisory committee." Five of the 12 have contributed $100 or more to ACA, according to records filed with the Clerk of the House. The five are: F. Gano Chance, a Centralia, Mo., businessman; Robert B. Dresser, a Providence, R.I., lawyer; N. Floyd McGowin, a Chapman, Ala., industrialist; William J. Grede, a Milwaukee industrialist; and Robert W. Stoddard, board chairman of The Worcester Telegram & Gazette Company and Wyman-Gordon Company, Worcester, Mass. Both Grede and Stoddard also are listed as members of the Birch Society's executive committee. Derwinski was unperturbed by these associations when queried about them. "You can't reject somebody's money as long as you don't let them dictate policy," he said. McManus responded: "We don't look up the biographical background of people who send us money. But, I must say, when it comes to this sort of thing, I'm very naive."

On April 30, 1966, a now-defunct group know as The 1976 Committee was organized in a Chicago meeting and announced by its chairman, William Grede, the next week. Grede told The *Milwaukee Journal* May 3, 1966, that "about half" of the 30 founding members of The 1976 Committee were also Birchers. ACA's Moreell became one of the four vice chairmen of the committee. The remaining three were Clarence Manion, former dean of Notre Dame Law School, originator of the "Manion Forum" broadcasts and, currently, an editorial adviser to *American Opinion*; W. B. McMillan, a former member of the Birch Society's national council and now an editorial adviser; and Loyd Wright.

Setting 1976 as a "target date" to halt a "wholesale nightmare of insanity and subversion," the committee took as its interim goal "to create massive support for Ezra Taft Benson"—Agriculture Secretary in the Eisenhower Cabinet (1953-61)—for President in 1968 and Strom Thurmond for Vice President. Moreell described The 1976 Committee to *National Journal* as "an abortive activity that never got off the ground." He noted that "the organization of a new political party is a stupendous venture." Regarding this interlock, McManus said:

"I felt the Admiral's name was too valuable to be given to an organization over which he has no control. The Admiral disagreed. After all, it's his life. . . . We can't do too much about former relationships. But any future officer of ACA will understand that he has certain responsibilities. I've personally declined any number of invitations to join groups. We must be very selective in lending our names. . . . "

Wesley McCune, editor of a Washington-based private weekly newsletter, *Group Research Report*, that monitors activities of what it calls extremist groups on the right, told *National Journal:* "Wittingly or unwittingly, ACA still provides a conduit of respectability for real Birchers. The situation is more serious than in 1963 because they know more about it and it hasn't changed." McCune, who has written several detailed reports on ACA, was referring to a colloquy in the House on May 20, 1963, just before that year's ACA awards ceremony. Then-Rep. Ronald Brooks Cameron, D-Calif. (1963-67), took the floor to urge his colleagues to boycott the ACA function. "It was a real crisis for us," McManus recalls. Cameron, speaking from research supplied largely by McCune, charged ACA was "attempting to clothe itself and the John Birch Society with an aura of respectability to which it is not entitled."

Rising to defend ACA were GOP Reps. Bruce Alger, Tex. (1955-65), now an ACA trustee; Frank T. Bow, Ohio; Thomas B. Curtis, Mo. (1951-69); Ed Foreman, N. Mex., then representing a Texas district (1963-65; 1969-71); Charles M. Teague, Calif.; and the late James B. Utt, Calif. (1953-70). They were joined by several Southern Democrats, including James A. Haley, Fla., and Albert W. Watson, S.C. (D, 1963-65; R, 1965-71). McManus is still smarting over the 1963 broadside against ACA in the House, although he is personally friendly with McCune, whom he calls "a real pro" and whom he consults from time to time.

For an April 1970 report, McManus prepared an eight-paragraph section dealing with extremist groups which was later deleted at the insistence of Moreell and other ACA trustees. The previously unpublicized section said in part:

"Another important service ACA has recently developed is a specialized and confidential information service to conservative Members of Congress. This consists of basic research and background information on organizations, many of which are self-designated patriotic, conservative lobbying and/or political action groups. In the last few years there has been a proliferation of such groups. In some cases, political opportunists and purely letterhead organizations solicit funds through the mails, using appeals on issues such as the drug problem, busing of school children, sex education, communism, taxation, treaties with Russia, gun legislation, law and order, etc. Some unscrupulous promoters have raised sizeable amounts of money in this way, without accounting to anyone for the distribution and dispersal of these funds. . . . "

In explaining why he vetoed this ACA statement, Moreell told *National Journal:* "We shouldn't attempt to establish our own stature by tearing down somebody else. We shouldn't engage in condemnation of other organizations, on the right or on the left. Why go out and pick a fight when there's so much useful work to be done?" Despite their sharp disagreements over the ACA policy toward dealing with extremist groups, McManus and Moreell remain close. Said McManus of the Admiral: "He's quite a guy. He's so down to earth. Just a marvelous person."

ACA's stature in coming years is closely tied to its current search for a new chairman. To a large extent, its future ability to win strong financial support—in competition with other political groups drawing from the same money pool—rests upon the outcome of this executive talent hunt. "We are looking for a known and responsible conservative who has achieved the social and economic status he desires and is not going to use ACA to further his own personal aims," McManus said. A list of names, submitted by the group's friends in Congress, is still being narrowed. "I'm putting out a few feelers myself to make sure we don't get a supercontroversial conservative," Derwinski reported. So far, McManus said, four candidates, all businessmen, have declined the ACA chairmanship due to "other commitments." Several new candidates are now under consideration.

If and when fresh funds become available and a new chairman is found, ACA is eager to engage in such new political techniques as:

- a computerized electronic processing center which would pool information for ACA-backed candidates on such data as opponents' public policy views, voter registration, direct mail solicitations, analysis of electoral patterns and congressional district profiles.
- a politically oriented Telex teleprinter system designed to help ACA-supported incumbents keep in better touch with home offices and campaign headquarters while at the same time feeding news releases on federal grants directly to local news media.
- a year-round speech service offering legislators with high ACA ratings "a weekly documented draft on a major conservative issue that could also be blue-penciled for local angles."

Finally, McManus would like to institute a formal advisory board to be composed of Members of Congress. Such a group, the ACA's president noted, would undoubtedly help funnel more support to the organization. It would provide yet another way "we can help tilt the scales in favor of constitutional conservatism across the nation."

Table 2.1 ACA Trustees

Following is a list of the 25 trustees of Americans for Constitutional Action.

*Ben Moreell, chairman emeritus. Admiral (ret.) U.S. Navy; founder of ACA. Port Hueneme, Calif. (See page 37.)

*Charles A. McManus, president of ACA since 1969. Bowie, Md. (See page 37.)

*Edward G. Orbann, treasurer. Aide to the late Charles Edison. Totowa, N.J.

Bruce Alger. Real estate developer; Member of Congress, R-Tex. (1955-65). Now resides in Boca Raton, Fla.

E. Robert Anderson. Captain (ret.) U.S. Navy; former editorial policy director, Copley Newspapers. San Diego, Calif.

Ralph F. Beermann. Farmer and alfalfa dealer; Member of Congress, R-Neb. (1961-65). Dakota City, Neb.

Anthony Bouscaren. Professor, Le Moyne College. Syracuse, N.Y.

Walter Brennan. Movie and television actor. Moorpark, Calif.

Clarence B. Carson. Chairman of Social Studies Department, Okaloosa Walton Junior College. Ft. Walton Beach, Fla.

James C. Davis. Lawyer; Member of Congress, D-Ga. (1949-63). Atlanta, Ga.

Patrick J. Frawley Jr. Chairman and president, Eversharp Inc., Schick Safety Razor Company; executive, Technicolor Inc., Culver City, Calif.

Frank de Ganahl. Industrialist; member, John Birch Society. Carefree, Ariz.

Charles B. Hoeven. Lawyer; Member of Congress, R-Iowa (1943-61). Alton, Iowa.

T. Robert Ingram. Rector, St. Thomas Episcopal Church. Houston, Tex.

William Loeb. Publisher, *The Manchester (N.H.) Union Leader.* Reno, Nev.

Thomas Parker. Physician; president, Association of American Physicians and Surgeons (1964); member, John Birch Society policy council. Greenville, S.C.

John R. Pillion. Lawyer, civil engineer, industrialist; Member of Congress, R-N.Y. (1955-65). Lake View, N.Y.

James E. Price. Locomotive engineer. Birmingham, Ala.

Max Rafferty. Dean, School of Education, Troy State University, Troy, Ala.

Katherine St. George. Member of Congress, R-N.Y. (1947-65). Tuxedo Park, N.Y.

Gordon H. Scherer. Lawyer; Member of Congress, R-Ohio (1953-63). Cincinnati, Ohio.

***William M. Tuck.** Lawyer; Member of Congress, D-Va. (1953-69); Former Virginia Governor, (1946-50). South Boston, Va.

John Wayne. Actor and movie producer. Hollywood, Calif.

Charles E. Whittaker. Lawyer; Associate Justice, U.S. Supreme Court (1957-62). Kansas City, Mo.

Loyd Wright. Lawyer; president, American Bar Association (1940-41). Los Angeles, Calif.

---

*executive committee

Source: ACA, *National Journal*

Table 2.2   ACA Endorsements, 1970

Americans for Constitutional Action in 1970 publicly endorsed 157 House candidates—129 Republicans, 27 Democrats and one Conservative—and 15 Senate candidates—13 Republicans, one Democrat and one Independent. All but 23 of the House candidates endorsed won. Six of the Senate endorsees were winners. The candidates ACA endorsed in 1970 are listed below. (ACA says an endorsement is not made public if the candidate believes the endorsement a "political liability.") Winners are in bold type.

Senate

W. E. Brock, R-Tenn.
Laurence J. Burton, R-Utah
George Bush, R-Tex.
Harry F. Byrd Jr., Ind-Va.*
Anderson Carter, R-N.M.
William C. Cramer, R-Fla.
Paul J. Fannin, R-Ariz.*
Roman L. Hruska, R-Neb.*
Thomas S. Kleppe, R-N.D.
George Murphy, R-Calif.*
Richard L. Roudebush, R-Ind.
Ralph T. Smith, R-Ill.*
John Stennis, D-Miss.*
Robert Taft Jr., R-Ohio
John Wold, R-Wyo.

House

Watkins M. Abbitt, D-Va.*
Thomas G. Abernethy, D-Miss.*
E. Ross Adair, R-Ind.*
John B. Anderson, R-Ill.*
George W. Andrews, D-Ala.*
W.A. Archer, R-Tex.
Leslie C. Arends, R-Ill.*
John M. Ashbrook, R-Ohio*
William H. Ayres, R-Ohio*
LaMar Baker, R-Tenn.
Walter S. Baring, D-Nev.*
Page Belcher, R-Okla.*
Tom Bevill, D-Ala.*
Benjamin B. Blackburn, R-Ga.*
Frank T. Bow, R-Ohio*
Fred D. Brady, R-S.D.
William G. Bray, R-Ind.*
Jack Brinkley, D-Ga.*
Clarence J. Brown, R-Ohio*
James T. Broyhill, R-N.C.*
Joel T. Broyhill, R-Va.*
John Buchanan, R-Ala.*
J. Herbert Burke, R-Fla.*
Danny L. Burton, R-Ind.
John W. Byrnes, R-Wis.*
John N. Happy Camp, R-Okla.*
Robert A. Carter, R-Fla.
Tim Lee Carter, R-Ky.*
Bill Chappell Jr., D-Fla.*
Donald D. Clancy, R-Ohio*

Don H. Clausen, R-Calif.*
Del Clawson, R-Calif.*
Richard Cockey, R-Hawaii
Harold R. Collier, R-Ill.*
James M. Collins, R-Tex.*
William M. Colmer, D-Miss.*
Bob Cooper, R-Ga.
Philip M. Crane, R-Ill.*
W. C. Daniel, D-Va.*
Glenn R. Davis, R-Wis.*
David W. Dennis, R-Ind.*
Edward J. Derwinski, R-Ill.*
Samuel L. Devine, R-Ohio*
William L. Dickinson, R-Ala.*
Ken Doll, R-W.Va.
W. J. Bryan Dorn, D-S.C.*
John Dowdy, D-Tex.*
Pierre S. du Pont IV, R-Del.
Jack Edwards, R-Ala.*
Edwin D. Eshleman, R-Pa.*
Paul Findley, R-Ill.*
O C. Fisher, D-Tex.*
Walter Flowers, D-Ala.*
John J. Flynn, Con.-N.Y.
Gerald R. Ford, R-Mich.*
Ed Foreman, R-N.M.*
L. H. Fountain, D-N.C.*
Louis Frey Jr., R-Fla.*
Barry M. Goldwater Jr., R-Calif.*
George A. Goodling, R-Pa.*
Charles H. Griffin, D-Miss.*
H. R. Gross, R-Iowa*
James R. Grover Jr., R-N.Y.*
Charles S. Gubser, R-Calif.*
Dexter H. Gunderson, R-S.D.
James A. Haley, D-Fla.*
Durward G. Hall, R-Mo.*
John Paul Hammerschmidt, R-Ark.*
William H. Harsha, R-Ohio*
James Harvey, R-Mich.*
R. (Jack) Hawke, R-N.C.
Craig Hosmer, R-Calif.*
Herbert H. Howell, R-N.C.
John E. Hunt, R-N.J.*
John Jarman, D-Okla.*
Albert W. Johnson, R-Pa.*
Charles Raper Jonas, R-N.C.*

House *(cont'd)*

Walter B. Jones, D-N.C.*
William J. Keating, R-Ohio
Carleton J. King, R-N.Y.*
Dan Kuykendall, R-Tenn.*
Earl F. Landgrebe, R-Ind.*
Delbert L. Latta, R-Ohio*
Alton Lennon, D-N.C.*
Norman F. Lent, R-N.Y.
Sherman P. Lloyd, R-Utah*
James R. Mann, D-S.C.*
Dave Martin, R-Neb.*
Robert B. (Bob) Mathias, R-Calif.*
Catherine May, R-Wash.*
Wiley Mayne, R-Iowa*
Robert McClory, R-Ill.*
James A. McClure, R-Idaho*
William M. McCulloch, R-Ohio*
Robert C. McEwen, R-N.Y.*
John L. McMillan, D-S.C.*
Robert H. Michel, R-Ill.*
Clarence E. Miller, R-Ohio*
William E. Minshall, R-Ohio*
John C. (Jack) Mitchell Jr., R-Colo.
Chester L. Mize, R-Kan.*
Wilmer Mizell, R-N.C.*
G. V. Montgomery, D-Miss.*
Rogers C. B. Morton, R-Md.* #
John T. Myers, R-Ind.*
Ancher Nelsen, R-Minn.*
Bill Nichols, D-Ala.*
Otto E. Passman, D-La.*
Thomas M. Pelly, R-Wash.*
Jerry L. Pettis, R-Calif.*
B. Leonard Phillips, R-S.C.
Richard H. Poff, R-Va.*
Walter E. Powell, R-Ohio
Robert Price, R-Tex.*
Charlotte T. Reid, R-Ill.*†
John J. Rhodes, R-Ariz.*
Richard Richards, R-Utah

Harry Roberts, R-Wyo.
J. Kenneth Robinson, R-Va.
Paul G. Rogers, D-Fla.*
John H. Rousselot, R-Calif.*
Earl B. Ruth, R-N.C.*
David E. Satterfield III, D-Va.*
John P. Saylor, R-Pa.*
William J. Scherle, R-Iowa*
John G. Schmitz, R-Calif.*
Herman T. Schneebeli, R-Pa.*
William Lloyd Scott, R-Va.*
Keith G. Sebelius, R-Kan.*
Garner E. Shriver, R-Kan.*
Joe Skubitz, R-Kan.*
H. Allen Smith, R-Calif.*
Henry P. Smith III, R-N.Y.*
Malcolm E. Smith Jr., R-N.Y.
M. G. Snyder, R-Ky.*
Floyd Spence, R-S.C.
Sam Steiger, R-Ariz.*
William J. (Bill) Teague, R-Calif.
Fletcher Thompson, R-Ga.*
Vernon W. Thomson, R-Wis.*
Sam Van Dyken, R-Calif.
Guy Vander Jagt, R-Mich.*
Victor V. Veysey, R-Calif.
William C. Wampler, R-Va.*
J. Irving Whalley, R-Pa.*
Jamie L. Whitten, D-Miss.*
Charles E. Wiggins, R-Calif.*
Jay G. Wilkinson, R-Okla.
Lawrence G. Williams, R-Pa.*
Bob Wilson, R-Calif.*
Wendell Wyatt, R-Ore.*
John W. Wydler, R-N.Y.*
Chalmers P. Wylie, R-Ohio*
Louis C. Wyman, R-N.H.*
C. W. Young, R-Fla.
Roger H. Zion, R-Ind.*
John M. Zwach, R-Minn.*

*   incumbent
\#   Resigned January 29, 1971, to become Interior Secretary.
†   Resigned October 7, 1971, to become a commissioner on the Federal Communications Commission.

Source: ACA

Table 2.3　ACA Rates Members of Congress, 1970 Session and Cumulatively

Following each session of Congress, Americans for Constitutional Action rates each Senator and House Member on the basis of his votes on selected legislative issues. The organization selects issues which it believes most accurately reflect ACA criteria: "For safeguarding the God-given rights of the individual and promoting sound economic growth by strengthening constitutional government; against 'group morality,' a socialized economy and centralization of government power."

Senate Ratings

During the second session of the 91st Congress (1970), 24 Senate votes were selected for the ACA index. The cumulative index prepared by ACA rates each incumbent's voting record on 315 selected issues since 1955. Listed below are cumulative and 1970 ratings for each Senator. (Sen. Karl E. Mundt, R-S.D.,did not participate in 1970 votes.) Except where noted, Senators listed were serving in the first session of the 92nd Congress, as of November 1, 1971.

Democrats	Cumu- lative	1970		Cumu- lative	1970
Allen, Ala.	87	83	Magnuson, Wash.	12	21
Anderson, N.M.	22	29	Mansfield, Mont.	11	29
Bayh, Ind.	11	11	McCarthy, Minn. **(9)**	2	0
Bible, Nev.	40	59	McClellan, Ark.	71	83
Burdick, N.D.	18	22	McGee, Wyo.	6	32
Byrd, Va.	82	87	McGovern, S.D.	9	5
Byrd, W.Va.	32	50	McIntyre, N.H.	22	39
Cannon, Nev.	33	50	Metcalf, Mont.	5	0
Church, Idaho	16	11	Mondale, Minn.	2	5
Cranston, Calif.	0	0	Montoya, N.M.	11	20
Dodd, Conn. **(4, 10)**	22	71	Moss, Utah	8	6
Eagleton, Mo.	3	4	Muskie, Maine	6	10
Eastland, Miss.	73	80	Nelson, Wis.	8	6
Ellender, La.	56	78	Pastore, R.I.	11	14
Ervin, N.C.	64	78	Pell, R.I.	5	5
Fulbright, Ark.	24	22	Proxmire, Wis.	25	25
Gore, Tenn. **(4)**	21	25	Randolph, W.Va.	13	26
Gravel, Alaska	0	0	Ribicoff, Conn.	11	0
Harris, Okla.	10	0	Russell, Ga. **(10)**	73	82
Hart, Mich.	2	9	Sparkman, Ala.	29	80
Hartke, Ind.	17	21	Spong, Va.	52	57
Holland, Fla. **(9)**	65	83	Stennis, Miss.	70	80
Hollings, S.C.	58	55	Symington, Mo.	17	6
Hughes, Iowa	9	10	Talmadge, Ga.	63	86
Inouye, Hawaii	1	0	Tydings, Md. **(4)**	6	12
Jackson, Wash.	9	24	Williams, N.J.	5	5
Jordan, N.C.	61	74	Yarborough, Tex. **(3)**	7	0
Kennedy, Mass.	3	5	Young, Ohio **(9)**	14	0
Long, La.	34	67			

Republicans	Cumu-lative	1970		Cumu-lative	1970
Aiken, Vt.	40	43	Hruska, Neb.	93	87
Allott, Colo.	77	91	Javits, N.Y.	17	0
Baker, Tenn.	69	89	Jordan, Idaho	85	82
Bellmon, Okla.	81	85	Mathias, Md.	12	15
Bennett, Utah	86	90	Miller, Iowa	78	86
Boggs, Del.	54	57	Mundt, S.D.	79	—
Brooke, Mass.	23	9	Murphy, Calif. (4)	81	81
Case, N.J.	21	4	Packwood, Ore.	43	50
Cook, Ky.	53	67	Pearson, Kan.	64	56
Cooper, Ky.	36	43	Percy, Ill.	30	31
Cotton, N.H.	85	85	Prouty, Vt. (10)	52	50
Curtis, Neb.	94	95	Saxbe, Ohio	38	47
Dole, Kan.	71	76	Schweiker, Pa.	25	29
Dominick, Colo.	79	76	Scott, Pa.	42	60
Fannin, Ariz.	88	90	Smith, Ill. (4)	68	72
Fong, Hawaii	43	39	Smith, Maine	46	76
Goldwater, Ariz.	97	92	Stevens, Alaska	18	19
Goodell, N.Y. (4)	7	5	Thurmond, S.C.	94	96
Griffin, Mich.	54	74	Tower, Tex.	95	94
Gurney, Fla.	88	85	Williams, Del. (9)	92	92
Hansen, Wyo.	87	87	Young, N.D.	66	75
Hatfield, Ore.	36	17			

House Ratings

ACA used 19 votes to rate House Members for the second session of the 91st Congress (1970). The cumulative index is based on 253 ACA-selected votes since 1957. Listed below are cumulative and 1970 ratings for Members of the House. (Five House seats were vacant; House Speaker John W. McCormack did not participate in House votes.) Except where noted, Members listed were serving in the first session of the 92nd Congress, as of November 1, 1971.

Democrats	Cumu-lative	1970		Cumu-lative	1970
Abbitt, Va. 4	87	76	Barrett, Pa. 1	5	6
Abernethy, Miss. 1	83	89	Bennett, Fla. 3	57	68
Adams, Wash. 7	11	6	Bevill, Ala. 7	68	56
Addabbo, N.Y. 7	13	12	Biaggi, N.Y. 24	38	37
Albert, Okla. 3	4	16	Bingham, N.Y. 23	5	16
Alexander, Ark. 1	39	50	Blanton, Tenn. 7	47	53
Anderson, Calif. 17	15	12	Blatnik, Minn. 8	4	7
Anderson, Tenn. 6	20	47	Boggs, La. 2	8	16
Andrews, Ala. 3	74	78	Boland, Mass. 2	8	12
Annunzio, Ill. 7	2	6	Bolling, Mo. 5	2	6
Ashley, Ohio 9	7	11	Brademas, Ind. 3	6	22
Aspinall, Colo. 4	12	25	Brasco, N.Y. 11	4	6
Baring, Nev. AL	66	64	Brinkley, Ga. 3	76	74

Democrats *(cont'd)*	Cumu-lative	1970		Cumu-lative	1970
Brooks, Tex. 9	10	29	Flowers, Ala. 5	75	75
Brown, Calif. 29 **(3)**	9	17	Flynt, Ga. 6	64	88
Burke, Mass. 11	7	11	Foley, Wash. 5	16	22
Burleson, Tex. 17	74	72	Ford, William, Mich. 15	4	6
Burlison, Mo. 10	47	53	Fountain, N.C. 2	68	79
Burton, Calif. 5	3	6	Fraser, Minn. 5	3	12
Byrne, Pa. 3	6	6	Friedel, Md. 7 **(1)**	5	6
Cabell, Tex. 5	56	38	Fulton, Tenn. 5	12	21
Caffery, La. 3	89	91	Fuqua, Fla. 2	64	63
Carey, N.Y. 15	8	18	Galifianakis, N.C. 4	52	37
Casey, Tex. 22	63	56	Gallagher, N.J. 13	4	7
Celler, N.Y. 10	4	0	Garmatz, Md. 3	9	11
Chappell, Fla. 4	88	83	Gaydos, Pa. 20	32	21
Chisholm, N.Y. 12	27	25	Gettys, S.C. 5	57	62
Clark, Pa. 25	17	31	Giaimo, Conn. 3	13	19
Clay, Mo. 1	11	7	Gibbons, Fla. 6	19	39
Cohelan, Calif. 7 **(1)**	5	6	Gilbert, N.Y. 22 **(1)**	5	13
Colmer, Miss. 5	84	89	Gonzalez, Tex. 20	5	11
Conyers, Mich. 1	11	21	Gray, Ill. 21	10	18
Corman, Calif. 22	1	7	Green, Ore. 3	15	41
Culver, Iowa 2	8	0	Green, Pa. 5	5	6
Daddario, Conn. 1 **(7)**	7	8	Griffin, Miss. 3	84	83
Daniel, Va. 5	86	79	Griffiths, Mich. 17	7	0
Daniels, N.J. 14	7	20	Hagan, Ga. 1	62	76
Davis, Ga. 7	43	60	Haley, Fla. 7	92	83
Dawson, Ill. 1 **(9)**	1	0	Hamilton, Ind. 9	18	13
de la Garza, Tex. 15	29	40	Hanley, N.Y. 34	9	17
Delaney, N.Y. 9	16	47	Hanna, Calif. 34	9	35
Dent, Pa. 21	12	22	Hansen, Wash. 3	4	0
Diggs, Mich. 13	5	6	Harrington, Mass. 6	19	18
Dingell, Mich. 16	7	12	Hathaway, Maine 2	2	0
Donohue, Mass. 4	10	17	Hawkins, Calif. 21	2	0
Dorn, S.C. 3	74	56	Hays, Ohio 18	17	17
Dowdy, Tex. 2	84	72	Hebert, La. 1	55	64
Downing, Va. 1	63	61	Hechler, W.Va. 4	13	37
Dulski, N.Y. 41	15	22	Helstoski, N.J. 9	6	6
Eckhardt, Tex. 8	2	0	Henderson, N.C. 3	65	72
Edmondson, Okla. 2	10	37	Hicks, Wash. 6	12	24
Edwards, Calif. 9	5	12	Holifield, Calif. 19	5	0
Edwards, La. 7	48	60	Howard, N.J. 3	6	11
Eilberg, Pa. 4	6	11	Hull, Mo. 6	61	71
Evans, Colo. 3	13	21	Hungate, Mo. 9	29	32
Evins, Tenn. 4	24	42	Ichord, Mo. 8	59	63
Fallon, Md. 4 **(1)**	18	14	Jacobs, Ind. 11	10	32
Farbstein, N.Y. 19 **(1)**	6	23	Jarman, Okla. 5	65	75
Fascell, Fla. 12	12	17	Johnson, Calif. 2	6	6
Feighan, Ohio 20 **(1)**	15	19	Jones, Tenn. 8	50	60
Fisher, Tex. 21	79	76	Jones, Ala. 8	17	26
Flood, Pa. 11	8	29	Jones, N.C. 1	78	79

Democrats (cont'd)	Cumu-lative	1970		Cumu-lative	1970
Karth, Minn. 4	7	12	Patman, Tex. 1	15	40
Kastenmeier, Wis. 2	9	11	Patten, N.J. 15	7	16
Kazen, Tex. 23	14	39	Pepper, Fla. 11	3	13
Kee, W.Va. 5	12	32	Perkins, Ky. 7	10	21
Kluczynski, Ill. 5	4	13	Philbin, Mass. 3 (1, 2)	10	16
Koch, N.Y. 17	17	17	Pickle, Tex. 10	34	47
Kyros, Maine 1	11	26	Pike, N.Y. 1	28	37
Landrum, Ga. 9	42	82	Poage, Tex. 11	47	56
Leggett, Calif. 4	6	17	Podell, N.Y. 13	5	14
Lennon, N.C. 7	77	71	Powell, N.Y. 18 (1)	10	11
Long, Md. 2	16	56	Preyer, N.C. 6	31	37
Long, La. 8	84	75	Price, Ill. 24	4	17
Lowenstein, N.Y. 5 (2)	21	22	Pryor, Ark. 4	30	27
Macdonald, Mass. 7	14	16	Pucinski, Ill. 11	13	26
Madden, Ind. 1	6	18	Purcell, Tex. 13	38	61
Mahon, Tex. 19	44	58	Randall, Mo. 4	38	53
Mann, S.C. 4	69	75	Rarick, La. 6	91	75
Marsh, Va. 7 (9)	87	84	Rees, Calif. 26	3	0
Matsunaga, Hawaii 1	0	0	Reuss, Wis. 5	4	17
McCarthy, N.Y. 39 (3)	10	0	Rivers, S.C. 1 (10)	52	46
McCormack, Mass. 9 (9)	–	–	Roberts, Tex. 4	54	61
McFall, Calif. 15	4	12	Rodino, N.J. 10	8	16
McMillan, S.C. 6	67	67	Roe, N.J. 8	28	28
Meeds, Wash. 2	5	0	Rogers, Colo. 1 (1)	8	19
Melcher, Mont. 2	32	35	Rogers, Fla. 9	68	68
Mikva, Ill. 2	17	22	Rooney, Pa. 15	9	21
Miller, Calif. 8	3	11	Rooney, N.Y. 14	5	6
Mills, Ark. 2	38	59	Rosenthal, N.Y. 8	6	17
Minish, N.J. 11	6	21	Rostenkowski, Ill. 8	3	14
Mink, Hawaii 2	4	5	Roybal, Calif. 30	4	6
Mollohan, W.Va. 1	21	18	Ryan, N.Y. 20	5	13
Monagan, Conn. 5	17	31	St. Germain, R.I. 1	9	17
Montgomery, Miss. 4	85	87	Satterfield, Va. 3	88	79
Moorhead, Pa. 14	6	6	Scheuer, N.Y. 21	8	13
Morgan, Pa. 26	8	18	Shipley, Ill. 23	26	44
Moss, Calif. 3	3	7	Sikes, Fla. 1	52	59
Murphy, N.Y. 16	5	13	Sisk, Calif. 16	4	7
Murphy, Ill. 3 (9)	5	16	Slack, W.Va. 3	18	39
Natcher, Ky. 2	29	42	Smith, Iowa 5	12	13
Nedzi, Mich. 14	7	13	Staggers, W.Va. 2	13	26
Nichols, Ala. 4	76	73	Steed, Okla. 4	28	42
Nix, Pa. 2	5	17	Stephens, Ga. 10	41	63
Obey, Wis. 7	27	33	Stokes, Ohio 21	22	18
O'Hara, Mich. 12	4	17	Stratton, N.Y. 35	24	21
Olsen, Mont. 1 (2)	9	21	Stubblefield, Ky. 1	27	44
O'Neal, Ga. 2 (9)	81	86	Stuckey, Ga. 8	68	56
O'Neill, Mass. 8	5	6	Sullivan, Mo. 3	6	22
Ottinger, N.Y. 25 (4)	21	7	Symington, Mo. 2	16	24
Passman, La. 5	70	71	Taylor, N.C. 11	64	63

Democrats (cont'd)	Cumu-lative	1970		Cumu-lative	1970
Teague, Tex. 6	56	42	Bush, Tex. 7 **(4)**	75	58
Thompson, N.J. 4	5	0	Button, N.Y. 29 **(2)**	28	21
Tiernan, R.I. 2	9	13	Byrnes, Wis. 8	85	72
Tunney, Calif. 38 **(5)**	8	0	Camp, Okla. 6	81	88
Udall, Ariz. 2	5	0	Carter, Ky. 5	67	72
Ullman, Ore. 2	12	41	Cederberg, Mich. 10	85	65
Van Deerlin, Calif. 37	6	13	Chamberlain, Mich. 6	80	78
Vanik, Ohio 22	13	25	Clancy, Ohio 2	95	88
Vigorito, Pa. 24	18	21	Clausen, Calif. 1	78	72
Waggonner, La. 4	83	78	Clawson, Calif. 23	93	89
Waldie, Calif. 14	9	19	Cleveland, N.H. 2	75	84
Watts, Ky. 6 **(10)**	34	56	Collier, Ill. 10	93	89
White, Tex. 16	43	47	Collins, Tex. 3	91	84
Whitten, Miss. 2	74	71	Conable, N.Y. 37	71	79
Wilson, Charles, Calif. 31	5	13	Conte, Mass. 1	42	28
Wolff, N.Y. 3	24	27	Corbett, Pa. 18 **(10)**	47	47
Wright, Tex. 12	20	35	Coughlin, Pa. 13	56	65
Yates, Ill. 9	9	17	Cowger, Ky. 3 **(2)**	68	60
Yatron, Pa. 6	28	26	Cramer, Fla. 8 **(4)**	88	75
Young, Tex. 14	16	38	Crane, Ill. 13	100	100
Zablocki, Wis. 4	10	26	Cunningham, Neb. 2 **(1)**	79	75
Republicans			Davis, Wis. 9	87	79
			Dellenback, Ore. 4	56	47
Adair, Ind. 4 **(2)**	89	86	Denney, Neb. 1 **(9)**	90	81
Anderson, Ill. 16	80	67	Dennis, Ind. 10	83	84
Andrews, N.D. 1	59	36	Derwinski, Ill. 4	92	89
Arends, Ill. 17	84	68	Devine, Ohio 12	96	94
Ashbrook, Ohio 17	98	93	Dickinson, Ala. 2	93	94
Ayres, Ohio 14 **(2)**	66	31	Duncan, Tenn. 2	89	74
Beall, Md. 6 **(5)**	56	63	Dwyer, N.J. 12	50	53
Belcher, Okla. 1	88	79	Edwards, Ala. 1	95	83
Bell, Calif. 28	61	62	Erlenborn, Ill. 14	80	69
Berry, S.D. 2 **(9)**	87	69	Esch, Mich. 2	43	38
Betts, Ohio 8	95	89	Eshlemann, Pa. 16	85	94
Biester, Pa. 8	47	32	Findley, Ill. 20	85	54
Blackburn, Ga. 4	92	87	Fish, N.Y. 28	50	68
Bow, Ohio 16	88	60	Ford, Gerald, Mich. 5	78	68
Bray, Ind. 6	86	86	Foreman, N.M. 2 **(2)**	92	83
Brock, Tenn. 3 **(5)**	88	80	Frelinghuysen, N.H. 5	53	53
Broomfield, Mich. 18	64	50	Frey, Fla. 5	91	88
Brotzman, Colo. 2	73	67	Fulton, Pa. 27 **(10)**	44	28
Brown, Ohio 7	80	56	Goldwater, Calif. 27	89	88
Brown, Mich. 3	67	71	Goodling, Pa. 19	92	100
Broyhill, N.C. 10	90	87	Gross, Iowa 3	96	89
Broyhill, Va. 10	85	71	Grover, N.Y. 2	72	75
Buchanan, Ala. 6	94	79	Gubser, Calif. 10	71	50
Burke, Fla. 10	96	93	Gude, Md. 8	29	33
Burton, Utah 1 **(4)**	80	59	Hall, Mo. 7	98	89

Republicans *(cont'd)*	Cumu- lative	1970		Cumu- lative	1970
Halpern, N.Y. 6	25	22	Myers, Ind. 7	90	83
Hammerschmidt, Ark. 3	80	84	Nelsen, Minn. 2	82	72
Hansen, Idaho 2	41	47	O'Konski, Wis. 10	54	44
Harsha, Ohio 6	85	84	Pelly, Wash. 1	72	50
Harvey, Mich. 8	70	78	Pettis, Calif. 33	75	59
Hastings, N.Y. 38	59	60	Pirnie, N.Y. 32	64	47
Heckler, Mass. 10	42	38	Poff, Va.	95	83
Hogan, Md. 5	56	47	Pollock, Alaska AL **(6)**	67	50
Horton, N.Y. 36	40	25	Price, Tex. 18	91	86
Hosmer, Calif. 32	75	76	Quie, Minn. 1	71	53
Hunt, N.J. 1	89	89	Quillen, Tenn. 1	92	94
Hutchinson, Mich. 4	93	100	Railsback, Ill. 19	58	53
Johnson, Pa. 23	83	89	Reid, Ill. 15 **(9)**	93	67
Jonas, N.C. 9	90	95	Reid, N.Y. 26	23	12
Keith, Mass. 12	63	56	Reifel, S.D. 1 **(9)**	68	63
King, N.Y. 30	89	80	Rhodes, Ariz. 1	82	72
Kleppe, N.D. 2 **(4)**	79	71	Riegle, Mich. 7	46	35
Kuykendall, Tenn. 9	79	60	Robison, N.Y. 33	70	56
Kyl, Iowa 4	87	82	Roth, Del. Al **(5)**	81	79
Landgrebe, Ind. 2	94	100	Roudebush, Ind. 4 **(4)**	93	73
Langen, Minn. 7 **(2)**	86	79	Rousselot, Calif. 24	100	100
Latta, Ohio 5	87	71	Ruppe, Mich. 11	43	53
Lloyd, Utah 2	75	60	Ruth, N.C. 8	86	89
Lujan, N.M. 1	73	69	Sandman, N.J. 2	64	63
Lukens, Ohio 24 **(6)**	87	82	Saylor, Pa. 22	65	73
MacGregor, Minn. 3 **(4)**	68	44	Schadeberg, Wis. 1 **(2)**	93	89
Mailliard, Calif. 6	53	47	Scherle, Iowa 7	95	88
Martin, Neb. 3	92	89	Schneebeli, Pa. 17	77	73
Mathias, Calif. 18	68	61	Schwengel, Iowa 1	64	61
May, Wash. 4 **(2)**	73	67	Scott, Va. 8	94	89
Mayne, Iowa 6	72	78	Sebelius, Kan. 1	84	82
McClory, Ill. 12	74	58	Shriver, Kan. 4	79	67
McCloskey, Calif. 11	41	59	Skubitz, Kan. 5	84	67
McClure, Idaho 1	89	83	Smith, Calif. 20	96	89
McCulloch, Ohio 4	80	53	Smith, N.Y. 40	67	78
McDade, Pa. 10	41	39	Snyder, Ky. 4	90	76
McDonald, Mich. 19	67	63	Springer, Ill. 22	74	63
McEwen, N.Y. 31	81	65	Stafford, Vt. AL **(11)**	49	28
McKneally, N.Y. 27 **(2)**	41	44	Stanton, Ohio 11	64	41
Meskill, Conn. 6 **(8)**	70	55	Steiger, Ariz. 3	91	94
Michel, Ill. 18	87	82	Steiger, Wis. 6	65	58
Miller, Ohio 10	83	68	Taft, Ohio 1 **(5)**	65	61
Minshall, Ohio 23	85	71	Talcott, Calif. 12	79	74
Mize, Kan. 2 **(2)**	73	72	Teague, Calif. 13	79	62
Mizell, N.C. 5	82	94	Thompson, Ga. 5	82	89
Morse, Mass. 5	36	33	Thomson, Wis. 3	87	89
Morton, Md. 1 **(9)**	71	69	Vander Jagt, Mich. 9	69	69
Mosher, Ohio 13	58	42	Wampler, Va. 9	84	84

Republicans (cont'd)	Cumu-lative	1970		Cumu-lative	1970
Watson, S.C. 2 **(7)**	88	75	Winn, Kan. 3	81	72
Weicker, Conn. 4 **(5)**	41	41	Wold, Wyo. AL **(4)**	76	83
Whalen, Ohio 3	28	26	Wyatt, Ore. 1	67	69
Whalley, Pa. 12	78	95	Wydler, N.Y. 4	67	58
Whitehurst, Va. 2	58	50	Wylie, Ohio 15	88	89
Widnall, N.J. 7	57	47	Wyman, N.H. 1	81	84
Wiggins, Calif. 25	81	71	Zion, Ind. 8	88	89
Williams, Pa. 7	93	100	Zwach, Minn. 6	68	56
Wilson, Bob, Calif. 36	81	67			

(1) Defeated in House primary, 1970.
(2) Defeated November 3, 1970, in House election.
(3) Defeated in Senate primary, 1970.
(4) Defeated November 3, 1970, in Senate election.
(5) Elected to Senate November 3, 1970.
(6) Defeated in gubernatorial primary, 1970.
(7) Defeated November 3, 1970, in gubernatorial election.
(8) Elected Governor, November 3, 1970.
(9) resigned or retired
(10) deceased
(11) Appointed September 16, 1971, by Gov. Deane C. Davis, R, as interim replacement for the late Winston L. Prouty, R, pending a special primary and general election.

Source: ACA, *National Journal*

3

American Medical Political Action Committee

JUDITH ROBINSON

Ten years ago, the American Medical Association is frank to say, the medical profession had difficulty getting Members of Congress to listen to its views. That is not the case today, the AMA believes. The association thinks it has brought about the change through extensive use of the most powerful of political commodities: money. The money has been raised and distributed by the AMA's political arm, the American Medical Political Action Committee (AMPAC) and by its counterparts at state and local levels. AMPAC reports that since 1962 it has spent $3.09 million in support of candidates for congressional office; it estimates that the state and local groups have contributed four times that much.

AMPAC was formed in 1961 to provide the AMA with a legal vehicle for direct contributions to political candidates. The Federal Corrupt Practices Act (2 USC 241) forbids political contributions by tax-exempt organizations such as the AMA. Like the AFL-CIO's Committee on Political Education (COPE) and industry's Business-Industry Political Action Committee (BIPAC), AMPAC solicits individual contributions to support political candidates. The group was formed expressly for the purpose of giving organized medicine some influence in Congress and in state legislatures. Influence was needed, in the AMA's view, to fight against government domination of health insurance programs. "We recognized that Members of Congress were being asked to listen to the AMA side without having had any political support from the AMA," a former AMPAC official told *National Journal*. Walter C. Bornemeier, president of the AMA in 1970, expressed it this way: "Before AMPAC was formed 10 years ago, we couldn't even get an audience with Congressmen or legislators. Now, we are heard and respected. AMPAC has helped us buy that right to a dialogue."

AMPAC does not lobby; that function is performed by the AMA's Washington office. AMPAC has two objectives. The first is to provide political education for physicians and their wives, to encourage them to participate actively in politics. The second is to provide direct assistance to candidates for political office, by mobilizing volunteers and financial contributions. AMPAC sponsors surveys to determine how close congressional races are, and gathers intelligence, such as incumbents' voting records, on the contests from a variety of sources. Its support for candidates is bipartisan, and it sometimes gives money to candidates who have views it does not share. It has contributed, for example, to some Members of Congress who voted in 1965 for medicare, which the AMA bitterly opposed. Such contributions help buy the right to a dialogue, AMPAC thinks.

But for the most part, AMPAC helps candidates the AMA considers friendly to its own objective: minimizing government control over the medical profession. AMPAC's banner reads: "Back Medicine's Right to Remain Free." Physicians' participation in candidate support, an AMPAC pamphlet says, "will help put men and women into office who will safeguard the future our children will inherit; and who will work to preserve the world's finest system of medical care."

AMPAC and its state and local counterparts rank very high among political organizations in terms of the money they disburse to political candidates—perhaps second only to COPE. By its own account, AMPAC and its affiliates participated in some 335 congressional races in 1968, and many other state and local contests. In 1970, AMPAC and the state PACs were involved in approximately 350 congressional races and the state PAC's participated in some 750 state legislative campaigns, an AMA official reported. AMPAC estimates that the medical political movement spent $3.5 million to $4 million supporting candidates in 1968 and about $3.5 million in 1970. An AMPAC publication quotes an unidentified Member of Congress as saying: "If it hadn't been for AMPAC, a good many Members of Congress would not be here today."

AMPAC is a nonprofit, unincorporated body whose establishment was authorized by the AMA's House of Delegates in 1961 and whose initial funding ($50,000) was provided by the AMA. The organization's activities are supervised by a 10-man board of directors, appointed annually by the AMA's board of trustees. The board of directors consists of nine physicians and one member of the women's auxiliary to the AMA. It is bipartisan. Members serve no more than 10 years, officers no more than two one-year terms. Many members have been reappointed: three retired at the end of 1970 after the maximum 10 years service. The present board, with five new members, has had the greatest turnover in membership of any board since AMPAC was founded. (See Table 3.1.)

Current chairman is Hoyt D. Gardner, a Louisville, Ky., surgeon and a Republican. Gardner has been on the board since 1965 and served as its secretary-treasurer in 1967-68. He replaced George J. Lawrence Jr. of Flushing, N.Y., a Democrat and the first Northeasterner to ever serve on the board, who retired in 1970 after 10 years service.

Selection of members of the AMPAC board is based mainly on personal acquaintance by the AMA trustees with a candidate's political activity at the local level; other factors, such as geographical location and party affiliation, are also considered. "The trustees consider perhaps a dozen candidates in any one year," says AMPAC Executive Director William L. Watson. "A lot of people would love to sit on the AMPAC board."

The full-time AMPAC professional staff consists of Watson, Mrs. Lee Ann Elliott, assistant director, and four secretaries at AMPAC's Chicago headquarters, five blocks away from AMA headquarters. Watson, 47, succeeded Joe D. Miller in 1969 when Miller became director of the AMA's new public affairs division. Before assuming his current position, Watson served as assistant director of the Pennsylvania Medical Society (1958-65), an AMPAC field representative in Pennsylvania and AMPAC program coordinator in Chicago.

AMPAC provides leadership for many state and local physicians' political action committees (PACs). In a number of ways, the state and local PACs are more influential than their parent organization: chiefly, they provide the bulk of financial support and volunteer help for candidates. Beneficiaries—candidates for congressional or local office—are selected at the local level and then backed by "candidate support committees." As membership in the PAC movement expands, more time and money have been channeled to state legislative and gubernatorial candidates. State PACs, organized in all 50 states and the District of Columbia, are structured along the lines of AMPAC, with directors selected by state medical societies. Local PACs generally are set up to coincide with congressional districts, are informally structured and are less permanent than their state counterparts.

The doctors' political action movement has kept dues low to encourage members to give the bulk of their support to candidates. AMPAC dues are in three categories: active membership—$10 to $49 annually; sustaining membership—$50 to $5,000 a year (the maximum allowed under federal law); student, intern and resident membership—$5 to $10. Non-physicians may belong to AMPAC in another category of membership—called "friends of medicine." Their dues are the same. Members in this category comprise about three per cent of total AMPAC membership, Watson says, and include dentists, veterinarians, pharmaceutical company personnel and medical society personnel. Wives of physicians comprise approximately 12 per cent of AMPAC's total membership, leaving AMPAC with an estimated 85 per cent actual physician membership.

The AMA has 223,139 members, but how many of them belong to AMPAC is a well-guarded secret; AMPAC also will not reveal its total membership. State PACs are in charge of membership recruiting, and in most cases dues to both the national and local organizations are paid through the state PAC.

James H. Sammons, former AMPAC chairman (1969-70) and now an AMA trustee, told the AMA House of Delegates June 21, 1970, that 1970 would be "another record-breaking year for AMPAC membership." He said 12 states had broken their membership records and other states were expected to do so before the end of the year. Congressional and party leaders, Sammons said, acknowledge the PAC movement "as a vital political force." He added: "Perhaps the millions of dollars we've put into countless political campaigns have served as attention getters." But Sammons said, "The political action movement is not where it could be." He urged doctors to get involved actively in candidate support in addition to writing checks to the PAC. "We're not in a popularity contest," Sammons concluded. "We are trying to be effective."

In his address to the June 1971 AMA House of Delegates, AMPAC Chairman Gardner said "nearly one out of three AMA members is also an AMPAC member." (An AMA official, not speaking for attribution, said Gardner was referring to the 169,480 AMA dues-paying members as of May 1971, not the 223,139 total membership claimed by the AMA. This estimate would put AMPAC's membership at approximately 56,500.) Gardner told the delegates AMPAC's membership has doubled three times in the organization's 10-year history and is "15 per cent higher" than in 1970. "Thirty-one state PACs are now further ahead in membership than they were at a comparable time last year," he said. "Eight have already broken their all-time membership record set in the past years." AMPAC and its state affiliates, Gardner said, began in 1971 to organize the medical movement for the 1972 elections, evaluating candidates and mustering financial resources.

PAC membership is highest in the South and Midwest, where Executive Director Watson said about one-third of the state medical society members are dues-paying PAC members.

Indiana and Illinois consistently have led in the number of AMPAC members. Membership is growing fastest, he said, in the far West, where up to one-fourth of the state society members belong to the PACs. Watson estimates that 7,000 of California's 24,000 state society members are PAC members. Membership is moderate in the mid-Atlantic states, and weakest in the Northeast.

Some doctors find the PAC movement's methods of recruiting members offensive. In the main what they object to is the common practice of including in the mailing containing the local medical society's annual bill a solicitation for membership in AMPAC or the state PAC. Some 41 states have such joint billing in some form, according to Watson. The methods include: space for voluntary PAC contributions at the bottom of the state society bill; a letter accompanying the statement; a separate, enclosed bill; or the use of the medical society mailing list. A number of doctors have unwittingly sent in AMPAC dues without realizing they were not part of their state society dues, only to discover their error on receipt of AMPAC membership credentials. Some have asked for refunds: AMPAC records for January 1969 to June 1970 show 24 instances of such refunds; 16 requests for refunds were made between January and mid-July 1971.

Several physicians in the District of Columbia Medical Society (DOCPAC) fought such joint billing practices. Henry D. Ecker, 1967 medical society president, questioned in the society's August 1967 journal whether such joint billing was allowable under the society's constitution. The society is constituted solely for the purpose of promoting "the science and art of medicine, sanitation and the common interests of its members and the public," Ecker wrote. "The areas of interest of (DOCPAC and the society) are not antagonistic. By the same token, they are oriented in significantly different channels. It is my conviction that these purposes should remain separate and distinct. They should not be merged — by direct collaboration or by inference. My point is that (joint billing) would imply an obligation on the part of a member to join DOCPAC, and further would indicate direct sponsorship of DOCPAC by the medical society." Despite his efforts to prevent it, joint billing was approved when Ecker left office in 1968. DOCPAC also solicits membership in space given free by the medical society's monthly journal. A DOCPAC official said in 1970 that membership had "not gone up as much as we thought it would" when joint billing went into effect.

In a major reorganization of the AMA and AMPAC in 1969, a new AMA division of public affairs was created and two AMPAC officials were placed in top positions. AMPAC Executive Director Miller, now assistant executive vice president of the AMA, was named public affairs director in Chicago and AMPAC Assistant Director Harry R. Hinton became manager of the Washington public affairs office. Hinton now carries the dual title of deputy director of the AMA's public affairs division and director of the AMA's Washington office.

Another part of the reorganization merged the AMA and AMPAC field staffs under jurisdiction of the new AMA public affairs division. Seven of AMPAC's former eight field men became members of the AMA's 12-man force of field representatives. The dual use of field men was seen by some physicians as an effort to consolidate AMPAC power. They feared the close alignment of AMPAC to the AMA might threaten the AMA's tax-exempt status. Delegates from six New England states fought the move at the 1969 AMA convention by introducing a resolution demanding that the new division of public affairs be divested of its AMPAC responsibilities (supervising the field men). "This amalgamation," the resolution stated, "is likely to be detrimental to the AMA and AMPAC by undermining confidence in their sincerity." The amalgamation was approved, however.

Former AMPAC Chairman Sammons, in an open letter to members in October 1969, said: "Some press reports would have us believe that AMPAC has taken over the AMA. This charge is as ridiculous as charges that the reorganization deemphasized AMPAC activities. Despite what some have charged, AMPAC continues to remain aloof from issue-oriented situations. But if our activities throughout the years have permitted the AMA more influence in the public sector, then for heaven's sake, lets not be embarrassed by it." Watson said the reorganization was accomplished for reasons of efficiency and economy. "We probably saved $200,000 in overhead," he said. "We went from 20 (eight AMPAC and 12 AMA) to 12 field men. Services were being duplicated by field men for both bodies. Working through the same men gives AMPAC a better rapport with the AMA on educational activity."

A major function of AMPAC and its field representatives is what they call "political education." In simple terms, this means getting doctors actively involved in politics. AMPAC officials admit that persuading doctors to be political activists is a major problem. At least a dozen physicians interviewed by *National Journal* said that they resist mixing politics and professional practice for ethical reasons. They do not object to getting involved privately in politics.

AMPAC urges doctors to talk politics to their patients in the course of normal business, and also to friends and fellow members of the profession. AMPAC acknowledges that physicians are too busy to ring doorbells or man telephones, but it encourages them to lend support to individual candidates by recruiting volunteers, soliciting funds or becoming "opinion-makers" in the community. A film shown over closed-circuit television at the Chicago convention in June 1970, demonstrated how doctors can form candidate support committees. "Patients trust our judgment when they ask us to take care of their health. I think they'll buy our opinions on congressional candidates," said a doctor in the film.

Meeting resistance to political activity, Sammons said, requires education within the profession. "We need to educate doctors to all the obligations of citizenship, one of which is political activity. As doctors become better informed, they become more active. The educational activity is a very important part of AMPAC. We're not going to be as successful as I'd like us to be until every doctor in America is politically active." (He noted that five physicians were signers of the Declaration of Independence. There are four doctors in the House at present and none in the Senate. The four House Members are Durward G. Hall, R-Mo., Tim Lee Carter, R-Ky., Thomas E. Morgan, D-Pa., and William R. Roy, D-Kan.)

"AMPAC's activities," Sammons added, "are a reflection of the growing consciousness of the profession as a whole, the seriousness with which doctors and their wives accept their political responsibility." Edward M. Donelan, former AMA New England field representative and current executive director of the American Dental PAC, said: "With the growth of medical legislation there has been a comparable growth in physician political activity. They can no longer afford not to get involved."

To help overcome resistance to political activity, AMPAC distributes numerous educational training aids, including films, books, pamphlets and a four-session, do-it-yourself training course on how to win elections—all of which teach traditional political arts: techniques of effective personal contact, how to get out the vote. One AMPAC booklet says the doctor, "if he applies his talents as an opinion-maker, can win votes for his candidate without appreciably altering his daily routine. It boils down to expressing his own political opinion frequently and to as many people as possible." AMPAC films include one urging doctors' wives to make telephone calls in support of candidates, called "DIAL—Do It at Leisure," and another directed to the physicians, called "How the Opinion-Maker Makes Opinion in Politics." AMPAC answers local affiliates' requests for information about a candidate the local is thinking of supporting or opposing. AMPAC gets its intelligence—voting records and the like—from the AMA's public affairs and legislative liaison operations. (It also conducts surveys to decide which candidates most need and warrant support.)

As part of its educational program, AMPAC conducts national workshops every year in Washington, D.C., for state PAC representatives. About 500 persons attend. Speakers since 1963 have included Leonard W. Hall, former GOP national chairman; Rep. Gerald R. Ford, R-Mich., House minority leader; Sen. Edmund S. Muskie, D-Maine; Rep. Robert H. Michel, R-Ill.;

Susan Walker, vice chairman of Great Britain's Conservative Party Organization (1964-68); former Sen. George Murphy, R-Calif. (1965-71); then-Rep. Melvin R. Laird, R-Wis. (1953-69); and Sen. Daniel K. Inouye, D-Hawaii. In 1970, major speakers included Senate Minority Leader Hugh Scott, R-Pa., Senate Majority Leader Mike Mansfield, D-Mont., and Sen. Edward J. Gurney, R-Fla.

The field men bear primary responsibility for political education activities. They conduct workshops for physicians, letter campaigns and arrange for political speakers, in a general effort to inspire PAC membership and activity. The strategy is to attract physicians who are respected among their local colleagues and who will encourage other doctors to get involved in politics. Richard G. Layton, former West Coast field representative and now director of field services in the AMA's communications division, said: "We need the catalysts, a few stars, doctors who will talk to other doctors and have their respect." He also says: "We start by motivating people to get involved. But we never talk in terms of a candidate."

Since the reorganization, field representatives have had to tread a fine line between what they legally can do for the AMA and for AMPAC. AMPAC officials are careful to point out that the field men are used only for nonpartisan political education and intelligence — never in campaigns while on the AMA payroll. If they are involved in direct political activity, they are pulled off the AMA payroll and paid out of AMPAC's campaign funds. Watson said: "If there is any question in our minds as to whether there should or should not be an expenditure from the political account, we use the political account so that we comply with both the spirit and the letter of the law." He said the field men rarely have been used in direct political activity since the amalgamation. Donelan, then an AMA field representative, told National Journal: "We like to think of ourselves as pros in political education and organization."

There is one incident in AMPAC's political history, a source of considerable embarrassment to the group at the time, which AMPAC officials still are reluctant to discuss. In 1963, AMPAC circulated a phonograph record entitled "AMPAC Brings You the Voice of COPE." The voice on the record made threatening and coercive statements intended to promote labor contributions to COPE. AMPAC described the speaker as Paul Normile, of Pittsburgh, an official in the United Steelworkers of America.

In a flyer accompanying the disc, AMPAC said that it obtained the recording from a COPE member—"A man who opposes, as many members of the labor movement do, the high-pressure methods which COPE resorts to in its effort to dominate government at every level within the United States." Normile denied that his voice was on the record. He sued the AMA for libel, invasion of privacy and $400,000 in damages. The suit was settled out of court in 1966; according to the steelworkers' newspaper, *Steel Labor*, Normile was paid $25,000. The AMA publicly regretted the "error."

With this public disclosure, AMPAC hastily withdrew the record from circulation in 1963. COPE, which called it "the strange case of AMPAC's Slipped Disc," claimed 2,600 of some 5,200 records made had been circulated. According to court records, the recording was obtained through a series of cloak-and-dagger events in which the Pennsylvania PAC executive director was contacted by two persons identified only as "Irv" and "Cousin." The Pennsylvania PAC official purchased for $20 a tape that "Cousin" told him would be "very interesting to medicine" in its fight against medicare (which COPE was supporting). AMA and AMPAC officials in Chicago made efforts to authenticate the recording by contacting several nonunion persons. Some association officials were convinced of its authenticity, some were not. A number of AMPAC officials now express the opinion, privately, that labor itself foisted the hoax to embarrass AMPAC. In any case, AMPAC officials now admit they made a mistake. "We clearly were led up the garden path and we fell for it," said an AMA official who was with AMPAC at the time.

AMPAC officials do not divulge the exact amount of money that has gone for candidate support from state and local PACs. Public disclosure of PAC support is inconclusive, since AMPAC money is given to state PACs, which in turn apply it to candidates the movement is backing. All states do not have disclosure laws, and many laws are not strict enough to require complete PAC disclosures.

AMPAC has spent $3,093,000 in support of candidates since 1962, according to the AMA. AMPAC expenditures, filed with the Clerk of the House of Representatives under the Corrupt Practices Act, show that it spent $681,965 in the 1968 campaign year. The comparable figure for 1970 was $693,413, according to an AMA official. (See Table 3.2.) However, AMPAC officials say that for every dollar spent by AMPAC, an estimated $4 is raised at the state and local levels, which would mean that some $2.7 million went to candidates in 1968 and 1970 over and above AMPAC's contributions. AMPAC officials like to cite a case where the ratio was considerably higher: They say AMPAC donated $5,000 to former Sen. Thruston B. Morton, R-Ky. (1956-68), during his 1962 senatorial reelection campaign and the state and local PACs raised $80,000 more. Morton is a former chairman of the Republican National Committee (1959-61), and was a member of the Senate Finance Committee that handled the medicare legislation.

AMPAC is "second only to labor in support of political candidates," according to an AMA official. (COPE reports spending more than $1 million in 1968 and about $1 million in 1970 at the national level, as compared to AMPAC's $681,965 and $693,413.) John T. Calkins, executive director of the National Republican Congressional (Campaign) Committee, notes that although AMPAC may have fewer members than COPE, it has "an affluent constituency, which may make up for its smaller size."

The political action movement actually has two sources of financial support. The money it can give to candidates—called "hard dollars"—comes from individual contributions. But it also gets so-called "corporate support" or "soft dollars" from the AMA, which can be used to defray organizational expenses —administration and political education—but not to support candidates. AMA corporate support to AMPAC has increased from the $50,000 in 1961 to a high of $1,137,000 in 1968. Corporate support has decreased since the merger of the AMA and AMPAC field staffs. AMPAC received $686,800 in 1969 and

$711,133 in 1970. Despite the overall decrease in corporate aid since 1968, support for AMPAC remains one of the AMA's "top priorities," an AMA spokesman said.

The largest single recipient of AMPAC money is the Physicians Committee for Good Government in the District of Columbia. AMPAC contributions amounted to $16,500 in 1968, $26,500 in 1969, $40,800 in 1970 and $27,500 by June 1, 1971. Federal disclosure records say the money is used either for "honorarium" or for "political action" purposes. The committee is a bank account, which allows the AMA to purchase tickets for congressional fund-raising events held in Washington. Thus, AMPAC hard dollars are funneled into candidates' coffers and the AMA is credited with supporting them. The District of Columbia has no disclosure law, and so it is impossible to determine where all the money goes. However, a good part of it is paid out to general partisan functions rather than to individual candidates. In 1970, for example, the physicians committee funneled at least $5,000 to a Republican congressional fundraising dinner March 11 and an equal amount to a Democratic congressional fund raiser on May 27. (AMPAC also disclosed contributions of $5,000 to each of the dinners. By June 1971, AMPAC had reported donations of $5,000 each to the Kickoff '72 Republican Dinner, the Democratic National Dinner Committee and the Democratic Congressional Dinner Committee.)

AMPAC is secretive about whom it supports, leaving public disclosure up to the candidate except where public records indicate PAC support. As a general rule, PAC money goes to candidates for House seats, particularly those in tight races. Some Senate candidates receive support, especially those with low campaign budgets. State PAC money is going increasingly to state legislative candidates and even to primary candidates. AMPAC Board Member Joe T. Nelson of Texas said the Texas PAC had "helped elect a state supreme court judge and helped Bentsen beat Senator Yarborough in the May 2 (1970) primary." (Former U.S. Rep. Lloyd M. Bentsen Jr. (1948-55) beat Sen. Ralph Yarborough (1957-71) for the Democratic Senate nomination with about 53 per cent of the vote and went on to win in the general elections.)

The choice of whom to support is made first at the local level. A small group of doctors will meet with a candidate and his campaign manager to discuss the candidate's views and campaign needs. The doctors then form a candidate support committee and set goals for fund raising and other political assistance. The local committee may go to the state PAC for additional funds for their candidate. If the state PAC feels a congressional candidate is worthy of even more financial support, it will ask AMPAC for funds. A three-member congressional review committee, members of the AMPAC board of directors who are unknown to AMPAC members, actually decides what candidates to back. The full AMPAC board, however, is aware of, and agrees in principle to, the three-man committee's decisions. The full board does not vote on the candidates AMPAC supports.

Sammons said the review committee screens some 200 or more requests from states annually, depending upon whether or not it is an election year. "We encourage state PACs to select their requests carefully," he said. The committee bases its decisions "not on polls alone, but on political intelligence gleaned from a number of sources—both parties, state PACs, our field staff," Sammons said. Asked if AMPAC ever feels it has been betrayed by a candidate it supported, he replied: "No—but disappointed." As to the type of candidates AMPAC supports, Sammons says: "We're bipartisan. We're not going to be boxed into conservative or liberal categories."

A former AMPAC official—not speaking for attribution—said the organization has supported Members of Congress who voted for medicare, simply to "buy their attention and the right to ask them to listen to us, perhaps compromise with us." In 1968, AMPAC gave money to three incumbents who voted for medicare: Reps. Brock Adams, D-Wash. ($250); Thomas E. Morgan, D-Pa. ($500); and Fred B. Rooney, D-Pa. ($500). "This movement would have been doomed had it been reactionary," the official added.

Former AMA President Bornemeier said: "We don't consider

ourselves conservative. We simply want the right to a dialogue." Sammons said, however, that AMPAC's philosophy
does not differ from that of the AMA: "AMPAC supports men
and women for and in office whose approach to the policy of
the nation's physicians is consistent with AMA policies." He
said AMPAC has never had any objections from the AMA
about candidates it has supported.

Quentin Young, a Chicago internist who is an AMA member,
believes that AMPAC supports "reactionaries." Young is national chairman of the Medical Committee on Human Rights,
which has led vocal criticism of the AMA at the AMA's last
three conventions. The medical committee has some 10,000
members, many of whom shun the AMA. Young told *National
Journal*: "AMPAC is extremely wealthy, its influence is perni-
cious, it provides the underpinnings of many reactionary candidates. It is the most important source of reactionary, war-
mongering support on both sides of the House."

Spokesmen for the National Republican Congressional
(Campaign) Committee, the National Republican Senatorial
Committee, the Democratic Senatorial Committee and the
Democratic Congressional (Campaign) Committee noted they
have received equal amounts of money from AMPAC through
the years, generally $5,000 to each of the four groups. AMPAC
also is in touch with each party committee, particularly for
political intelligence. The Republican and Democratic congressional campaign committees both reported that AMPAC
tends to support candidates who espouse the AMA point of
view, which they characterized as conservative. A spokesman
for the GOP House committee said there are sometimes "conflicts over Democrats we want to defeat and ones AMPAC
supports, especially in the South." The Democratic House
committee said AMPAC support generally goes to Southern
Democrats.

After the 1968 elections, *Political Stethoscope*, which is published about every four months by AMPAC, claimed: "The

medical profession has more friends on both sides of the aisle than ever before." According to Sammons, some 80 per cent of AMPAC-backed candidates were winners in 1968. Sammons said that AMPAC or the state PACs participated in about 335 congressional races. AMPAC participated in 162 House and 23 Senate races, he said, and state PACs participated in an additional 150 congressional campaigns. Following the elections, former AMPAC Chairman Frank C. Coleman told the AMA House of Delegates: "The 90th Congress is composed of enough Republicans and Democrats of moderate to conservative bent to constitute a majority. This is the first political victory of such magnitude that we ourselves helped to bring about."

An AMA official reported that in 1970 AMPAC and its state affiliates participated in approximately 350 congressional races. AMPAC was involved in 214 races—185 in the House and 29 in the Senate—and state PACs participated in about 135 congressional races in addition to some 750 state legislative campaigns, he said. According to the AMA spokesman, 75.2 per cent of the candidates supported by AMPAC were elected.

Rep. Durward Hall, a surgeon, told *National Journal,* "There's no question about AMPAC being a strong political organization." It has influenced many elections in both the House and Senate, he said, and has given the AMA more influence on Capitol Hill. Hall decried the fact that few doctors seek elective office. "Doctors are prone to reserve their energy for their profession. They are liable to wrap themselves in the cloak of aiding humanity and ignore their political responsibility. Who are better trained to serve in government than doctors, who have been among the people?"

The medical political movement has given away millions of dollars since 1965, when the AMA lost in its bitter fight against medicare. Some indication of the impact of AMPAC's contributions on the AMA's influence in Congress was provided in the 1969 controversy over the choice of Dr. John H. Knowles for a top Health, Education and Welfare (HEW) post. The AMA frowned upon that nomination, and it was never sent to Congress. Rep. Bob Wilson, R-Calif., chairman of the House GOP campaign committee, was among influential Members of Congress who openly opposed Knowles. He told *National Journal* the AMA "had a feeling that perhaps Knowles had an unfriendly attitude toward medicine. And I sympathized with them." AMPAC's campaign support for Members of Congress gave the AMA a right to express its views about Knowles, he feels.

A real test of AMPAC's impact will come on the issue of national health insurance which will provide the biggest challenge to the AMA since medicare. The AMA opposes proposals in Congress for mandatory health insurance programs, and has offered its own legislation (HR 4901) to establish an alternative voluntary plan it calls "medicredit." The AMA says its legislation is designed to solve only "the most immediate and most obvious problem relating to the health care crisis" — financing. Although AMA officials expect no action by Congress on health legislation until after the 1972 elections, they actively are seeking support for the medicredit proposal.

Table 3.1   AMPAC Directors

Since 1961, the American Medical Political Action Committee's 10-man board of directors has had a total of 27 members. Fourteen of these members have been Democrats and 13 have been Republicans. Democratic representation has been dominated by the South, while Republican board members have come largely from the Midwest.

Current Directors

Mrs. John M. Chenault, Decatur, Ala. Board member since 1970. Past president, AMA Women's Auxiliary. Democrat.

William H. Cooper, Washington, D.C. Named to board in 1971. Former chairman of DOCPAC. Member of teaching staff of The George Washington School of Medicine. Obstetrician, gynecologist. Republican.

Hoyt D. Gardner, Louisville, Ky. Board member since 1965; secretary-treasurer, 1967-68; elected board chairman in 1971. Former chairman of KEMPAC. Surgeon. Active in Republican state central committee.

Blair J. Henningsgaard, Astoria, Ore.

Board member since 1963; chairman, 1967-68; secretary-treasurer, 1970. AMA delegate; former chairman, AMPAC congressional review and research committees. Internist. Republican.

W. J. (Jack) Lewis, Dayton, Ohio. Named to board in 1971. Former vice chairman of the Ohio PAC. General practitioner. Republican.

Joe T. Nelson, Weatherford, Tex. Board member since 1970. AMA delegate; former chairman of TEXPAC. Former member of the Committee for Government of the People, headed by the late Sen. Everett McKinley Dirksen, R-Ill., and formed in 1966 to support Dirksen's constitutional

amendment to nullify Supreme Court's one-man, one-vote ruling. General practitioner. Democrat.
Philip G. Thomsen, Dolton, Ill. Named to board in 1971. Former chairman of the Illinois PAC; former president and trustee of the Illinois State Medical Society. Surgeon. Republican.
Malcolm C. Todd, Long Beach, Calif. Board member since 1962. Former chairman of CALPAC; personal physician to then-Vice President Nixon, 1952-60. Surgeon. Republican.
William B. West, Huntingdon, Pa. Named to board in 1971. Chairman of PAMPAC; former president of the Pennsylvania Medical Society; AMA delegate. Obstetrician, gynecologist. Republican.
Otis D. Wolfe, Marshalltown, Iowa. Named to board in 1971. Immediate past chairman Iowa PAC; former president of the Iowa Medical Society. Ophthalmologist. Republican.

Former Officers

Following is a list of former AMPAC directors who have served as officers:
Frank C. Coleman, Tampa, Fla. Board member, 1961-71; chairman, 1965-66. AMA delegate; chairman, AMA Council on Legislative Activities. Pathologist. Democrat.
Milton V. Davis, Dallas, Tex. Board member, 1961-62; first secretary-treasurer, 1961-62. State chairman, Doctors for (Sen.) John Tower Committee, 1961; state chairman, Doctors for Nixon-Lodge, 1960; delegate to White House Conference on Aging, 1961. Surgeon. Republican.
Mrs. Frank Gastineau, Indianapolis, Ind. Board member, 1963-69; secretary-treasurer, 1969. Past president, AMA Women's Auxiliary. Republican. (Died February 1970.)
Gunnar Gundersen, LaCrosse, Wis. Board member, 1961-65; first chairman, 1961-62. Former member of Committee on Electoral College Reform of the American Good Government Society, whose members have included FCC Chairman Dean Burch, former campaign manager for Sen. Barry Goldwater in the 1962 Presidential election, and Sen. Karl Mundt, R-S.D. Surgeon. Republican.
John R. Kernodle, Burlington, N.C. Board member 1964-68; secretary-treasurer, 1965-66. AMA trustee. Obstetrician, gynecologist. Democrat.
George J. Lawrence Jr., Flushing, N.Y. Board member, 1961-71; secretary-treasurer, 1963-65; chairman, 1970-71. AMA delegate; former chairman of New York's EMPAC; member, Independent Physicians Committee for James B. Donovan, 1962. Obstetrician, gynecologist. Democrat.
James H. Sammons, Baytown, Tex. Board member, 1964-70; chairman, 1969-70. AMA trustee. General practitioner. Democrat.
Donald E. Wood, Indianapolis, Ind. Board member, 1961-71; chairman, 1963-64. AMA delegate; former chairman, AMA Legislative Activities Council. Internist. Republican.

Table 3.2   AMPAC Contributions to State Affiliates, 1970

The American Medical Political Action Committee does not disclose how much it gives to candidates, or even which candidates it supports. It makes its contributions to state PACs or to national political groups, which in turn funnel the money to candidates. These block AMPAC contributions are reported to the Clerk of the House of Representatives, as required by federal law.

State and local PACs do not voluntarily disclose where they put their own and AMPAC money. Although 45 states have some form of disclosure law, only a few require complete campaign contribution disclosures by candidate or donor. Even in those states with relatively strict disclosure laws, it is often difficult to identify PAC contributions since state and local medical groups go by a variety of names.

According to the Citizens' Research Foundation, records filed in the office of the Clerk of the House indicate AMPAC gave a total of $636,500 to its state affiliates or to political groups in 1970. (An AMA spokesman said AMPAC reported additional expenditures of $56,913 in 1970 for political action.) The amounts the organization declared in its reports to the clerk's office, as compiled by CRF, follow:

State	Amount	State	Amount
Alabama	$ 6,500	Nebraska	$15,000
Alaska	10,000	Nevada	7,500
Arizona	13,500	New Jersey	14,950
Arkansas	4,000	New Mexico	13,100
California	43,000 *	New York	30,000
Colorado	7,500	North Carolina	5,000
Connecticut	16,500		2,000 #
Delaware	5,000	North Dakota	9,500
Florida	14,200	Ohio	26,000
Georgia	16,000	Oklahoma	8,000
Hawaii	5,000	Oregon	2,000
Idaho	5,000	Pennsylvania	18,000
Illinois	20,500	South Carolina	6,500
Indiana	32,500	South Dakota	10,000
Iowa	17,000	Tennessee	18,000
Kansas	5,000	Texas	24,000
Kentucky	8,000	Utah	16,900
Louisiana	8,000	Vermont	5,000
Maine	2,500	Virginia	22,500
Maryland	14,300	Washington	3,500
Michigan	11,500	West Virginia	2,500
Minnesota	22,500	Wisconsin	29,250 †
Mississippi	2,500		
Missouri	6,500	District of Columbia	40,800 ‡
Montana	7,000	Virgin Islands	2,500

* Includes $500 contribution to chairman, 22nd congressional district (Los Angeles).
# Political Education and Action Committee (North Carolina).
† Professional Association for Civic Education (Wisconsin).
‡ Physicians Committee for Good Government (District of Columbia).

Source: Citizens' Research Foundation

4

Committee on Political Education

JONATHAN COTTIN and CHARLES CULHANE

While others turn increasingly to use of mass media for attracting voters, the Committee on Political Education (COPE) sticks with the old-fashioned essentials. COPE uses newfangled methods, some involving the computer, only to strengthen its traditional mission: making direct contact with citizens, through a well-financed and smoothly functioning organization, and persuading them to register and vote for friends of organized labor.

COPE is the political action arm of the AFL-CIO. It boasts an impressive record on the hustings. In 1970, its nuts-and-bolts registration and get-out-the-vote efforts helped elect 203 House Members and 19 of the 35 Senators chosen by America's voters. (See Table 4.2.) In the 1968 elections, COPE supported the victorious campaigns of 15 Senate candidates and 185 House candidates. Now in its 17th year, COPE has spawned many imitators. But none claims anything like the money, manpower and electoral clout of COPE. The organization can be a powerful ally to the politicians it supports and an ominous threat to those it has singled out for defeat.

An all-out Republican effort to wrest control of the Senate from the Democrats raised a critical challenge for COPE in 1970. Among the Senators picked as prime targets of the GOP were three of labor's best friends: Ralph Yarborough of Texas (1957-71), Albert Gore of Tennessee (1953-71), and Harrison A.

Williams Jr. of New Jersey. COPE lost the first round when former Rep. Lloyd M. Bentsen Jr., D-Tex. (1948-55), who was elected to the Senate in the 1970 general elections, defeated Yarborough in a May 2 Democratic primary. Yarborough was chairman of the Labor and Public Welfare Committee, which handles minimum wage and other legislation of crucial interest to union members. COPE worked hard to save Gore and Williams, who—said a COPE spokesman—were facing "the toughest campaigns of their careers" in 1970. (Gore was defeated in the general elections by Republican W. E. Brock. Williams, who has served in the Senate since 1959, was reelected with 54 per cent of the votes cast.)

COPE tried to avoid what its director, Alexander E. Barkan, called "phony issues"—law and order, gun control, school prayer—and stick with economic issues in 1970—unemployment, underemployment and inflation. COPE leaders noted with dismay that Bentsen made violence an issue in his campaign against Yarborough, presenting film clips of the disorders surrounding the 1968 Democratic National Convention. COPE was concerned about union members' reactions to issues such as Gore's votes against Supreme Court nominees Clement F. Haynsworth Jr., of the 4th Circuit Court of Appeals, and G. Harrold Carswell, then of the 5th Circuit Court of Appeals; and the support of federal gun control laws by another COPE-backed Senator, Joseph D. Tydings, D-Md. (Tydings was defeated in the November elections, after having served one term in the Senate.)

The pragmatic technicians at COPE attempted in 1970 to steer clear of emotional disputes that strained old Democratic alliances, and to concentrate on helping candidates favorable to labor's economic causes. Their goal, says Barkan, is to "win elections, not arguments." Barkan added: "I look on myself as a political pragmatist. I want to win. I'm not interested in winning arguments and losing elections. Groups have to be willing to make compromises. Even if we're hawks, that doesn't stop us from working for Gore and Pete Williams. You can't find anywhere a man more dovish than Gore. There are a hell of a lot more six-pack Democrats than there are campus Camelots." Asked about Republicans, Barkan said, "My bitch is that they don't give us more (Sen.) Clifford (P.) Cases (R-N.J.).''

Organized labor's sustained and systematic political effort on the ward and precinct level started to take definite shape in the 1940s. In 1943, national leaders of the Congress of Industrial Organizations (CIO), fearing a strong wave of public opposition to a fourth term for President Roosevelt, formed the Political Action Committee and appointed the late Sidney Hillman, an energetic leader of the Amalgamated Clothing Workers of America, as chairman.

The late Philip Murray, then president of the CIO, spelled out the purpose of the committee in a report to a CIO convention on November 15, 1943. The committee, he said, was aimed at "mobilizing five million members of the CIO and enlisting the active support" of other labor groups for effective political action. Hillman, working out of a headquarters in New York City, directed leaders of local CIO unions to canvass their members, urging them to register and vote. "On a door-to-door basis we are registering voters, persuading them that unless the 1944 vote is a mandate for full production, 1932 will seem like a picnic," Hillman said.

In 1944, Mr. Roosevelt was considering James F. Byrnes, director of the Office of War Mobilization (1943-45), a former Senator from South Carolina (1931-41) and a former Associate Justice of the Supreme Court (1941-42), as a possible Vice Presidential candidate. Hillman considered Byrnes unfriendly to labor and strongly opposed his candidacy. The New York Times reported that just before the 1944 Democratic National Convention, Mr. Roosevelt instructed one of his aides to get approval from Hillman on the final choice of a running mate. "Clear it with Sidney," the Times quoted the President. Mr. Roosevelt finally chose Sen. Harry S. Truman, D-Mo. (1935-45.)

Whether the story is apocryphal remains unclear, but Republican party strategists seized the phrase, using it to picture

Mr. Roosevelt as the CIO's captive candidate. Placards saying "Clear Everything With Sidney" soon sprouted up across the country. Some political writers credited Mr. Roosevelt's comfortable margin of victory in 1944 to the power of the CIO's drive in his behalf. The President wired Hillman soon after the election: "I cannot delay longer telling you how deeply I appreciate the splendid job you did from start to finish." Hillman died in 1946. Soon after, the headquarters of the PAC moved to Washington.

In 1947, the American Federation of Labor (AFL), alarmed by passage of the Taft-Hartley Act, voted to establish Labor's League for Political Education as a nationwide political action group. George Meany, now president of the AFL-CIO, then secretary-treasurer of the AFL, told the delegates at an AFL convention in December 1947, where the federation's leaders laid the groundwork for the formation of the league: "We have got to make our people politically conscious; develop them politically in their own interest, not for the purpose of attempting to run the country but for the purpose of protecting ourselves."

In March 1948, the league opened headquarters in Washington in a mansion built in 1836 across Lafayette Park from the White House. The building now houses the rectory of St. John's Episcopal Church. The league started raising money from union members and organizing state and local leagues. It distributed leaflets urging the members of AFL local unions to involve themselves in political activity. The CIO endorsed President Truman for election in 1948 but the AFL made no endorsement. Spokesmen for the AFL-CIO say that while AFL leaders worked for Mr. Truman's reelection it was the national policy of the AFL not to make a formal endorsement. In 1952, both the AFL and the CIO endorsed the late Adlai E. Stevenson for President.

In December 1955, when the AFL and the CIO voted to merge into a single national federation, they formed the AFL-CIO Committee on Political Education as a fusion of Labor's League for Political Education and the Political Action Committee. Veterans of the labor movement recall that several years before the merger, the two political action groups had started working together in loose, informal alliances on the national, state and local levels. Jack Kroll, director of the Political Action Committee and a former leader of the Amalgamated Clothing Workers of America, and James L. McDevitt, a one-time plasterer and the director of the League for Political Education, acted as co-directors of COPE from 1955 until Kroll retired in 1957 and McDevitt was named director. McDevitt died in 1963.

COPE's national staff, operating in a plainly furnished suite on the sixth floor of the AFL-CIO building in Washington, has increased only slightly since it started in 1955. But the operation has grown steadily in financial power and political sophistication, and now employs computerized voter identification lists and professional polls.

Barkan, 62, national director of COPE since 1963, sets the pace for his staff of seven professionals, their 16 assistants and the 18 field representatives. "We used to have off-years around here," said Mrs. Mary Zon, COPE research director. "But after Al became director, we've been on a dead run ever since." A broad-shouldered man who stands just under six feet, Barkan is warm and friendly when he wants to be. But labor and political sources say he is a tough, shrewd bargainer when it comes to brokering money and political power. The one-time organizer for the Textile Workers Union of America maintains close communication with top leaders of AFL-CIO and makes most of the major decisions on COPE's day-to-day operations. He also monitors many of the minute details of his staff's work. "Al is the last of the red-hot revivalists," says one associate in describing Barkan's zeal on the platform. He frequently speaks at large gatherings of unionists, exhorting them to give time, money and effort to elect labor's political friends.

Barkan, a Democrat, served as COPE's deputy director from 1957 to 1963 and assistant director from 1955 to 1957. A native of Bayonne, N.J., he graduated from the University of Chicago with a bachelor of philosophy degree in 1933. He joined the Textile Workers Organizing Committee, the forerunner of the Textile Workers Union of America, as an organizer in 1937 in New Jersey. He served four years in the U.S. Navy during World War II. Barkan was veterans director of the Congress of Industrial Organizations' community services committee in New York from 1945 to 1946 when he became executive secretary of the New Jersey state CIO council in Newark, N.J. He was political action director of the Textile Workers Union of America from 1948 to 1955. "If anybody is being paid for a labor of love, it's me," Barkan says. "I enjoy what I'm doing. In 17 years, I've had about a week's vacation. My wife forces me to have long weekends at Rehoboth (Del.). In the mornings, I run for the *Times* and the Washington papers. I'm always itchy to get back to work."

Barkan's seven-member professional staff working in COPE's national office guides the organization's intricate political machinery in the 50 states:

- Joseph M. Rourke, 66, deputy director since 1963. He was secretary-treasurer of the Connecticut State Labor Council, AFL-CIO, from 1946 to 1963. He served as a Democrat in the Connecticut state Senate from 1939 to 1943 and in the Connecticut House of Representatives from 1959 to 1963.
- John Perkins, 38, assistant director. He assumed his present post in January 1971, after having served as COPE's field representative for Illinois and Indiana for three years. Perkins, who is responsible for voter registration at COPE, has been a member of the Carpenters Union since 1952, and was business representative for the Carpenters local in Elkhart, Ind., from 1955 to 1966. He also served as a vice president of the Indiana State Building and Construction Trades Council.
- Mary Zon, 49, director of research. She worked on the staff of the CIO's Political Action Committee before joining COPE in 1955 after the AFL-CIO merger. She succeeded her husband, Henry Zon, as COPE's research director when he left the organization in 1959 to enter the public relations business.

- Margaret T. Cronin, 49, assistant director of research. Miss Cronin joined COPE's national staff in 1955. She worked in the accounting department of the AFL's Labor's League for Political Education from 1948 to 1955.
- Walter Bartkin, 50, comptroller. He is responsible for accounting all the money COPE receives and spends. He worked in the accounting department of the CIO's Political Action Committee from 1946 until 1955 when he joined COPE.
- Bernard (Ben) Albert, 44, publications director since 1962. He was a legislative aide to former Sen. Stephen M. Young, D-Ohio (1959-71), from 1959 to 1962. Previously, he had worked as a reporter and editor for newspapers in Colorado, New York, Maine, West Virginia and Iowa.
- Walter R. Markham, 49, director of automatic data processing since 1968. He was director of computer operations for the Pennsylvania Democratic State Committee before he joined COPE. He learned computer operations while working for the Underwood Corporation and Sperry Rand Corporation for 20 years as a computer sales representative.

One key function of the national office is supervision of local voter registration drives. LaRoy H. Purdy, on loan to COPE from the Communications Workers of America where he was responsible for legislative activities, headed COPE's registration program until Perkins assumed the position in early 1971. (Purdy is now retired and lives in Florida.) The state COPE organizations submit budget estimates to the national office for their proposed registration efforts. If they expect assistance, they must justify their spending requests. Typical expenses of a voter registration drive include headquarters rent, office supplies, salaries for clerical and telephone canvassing personnel.

One assist to COPE's registration program is its computerized voter identification program. The computer system is now operating in California, Maryland, Pennsylvania, Ohio, Texas, Oklahoma, Colorado, Michigan, Connecticut and the District of Columbia. It is designed to speed the process of registering unionists and getting them to vote. In areas of operation, COPE obtains from national and international

unions names of members in each state, gathers from state and
local COPEs data on the registration status of these members
and feeds the material into the computers. The machines compile the information and produce three-by-five cards listing all
pertinent data about every union member, including his registration status. The material is made available to local COPEs,
which use it to identify areas where a registration drive could
prove most productive. The electronic brains of the system—
which has five million names stored on magnetic tape—are a
Univac III and a Univac 9300 owned by the International Association of Machinists and located in the union's offices about a
mile from COPE headquarters in Washington. COPE pays the
union the cost of the time required of the computers to process
the registration data.

Albert, COPE's publication director, characterized COPE's
vast store of political intelligence as "the best political research files in the city." Mrs. Zon, the research director, heads
a staff of four which works in a large room lined with steel
filing cabinets and shelves piled high with bound volumes of
the Congressional Record. The staff members clip items from
newspapers, national magazines and the Record. The research
workers maintain individual files on all 535 Members of Congress, the 50 governors, congressional candidates and the political campaigns in each state.

"Normally, the people we oppose are the ones we keep
extensive files on," said Margaret Cronin, assistant research
director. "It's not worth our time and energy to keep extensive
files on liberals." She pointed to a file bulging with information about Rep. Joel T. Broyhill, R-Va., whom COPE considers
hostile to labor. A nearby folder on then-Rep. George E. Brown
Jr., D-Calif. (1963-71), a friend of labor, was almost empty. If
COPE-endorsed candidates seek information about their foes,
the researchers are happy to oblige. Often, members of COPE's
field staff advise candidates of the files and make arrangements for getting material to them.

The staff also collects facts and figures on registration laws
and voting patterns in all states and virtually all cities. The
files include details on the number of people registered and

voting in each state and congressional district. When possible, the information is broken down by political party. Primary and general election results and primary election dates are also on file. Researchers are in frequent touch with all 50 secretaries of state to keep the data up to date. Election statistics on all cities with populations above 15,000 are compiled by the research staff. It sends questionnaires to city clerks to gather facts about offices up for election, registration deadlines, final filing dates, primary and general election dates. COPE researchers often receive requests for routine information from such diverse groups as the Republican National Committee, the League of Women Voters and the British Broadcasting Corporation.

COPE makes extensive use of professional polls to gather fresh political intelligence. The organization sometimes commissions statewide polls where candidates with COPE backing are in tight contests. Where possible, it seeks to have the candidate share some of the poll costs. COPE seeks to measure public support for its candidates and to identify issues important to voters. COPE is experimenting in some areas with its own telephone polling techniques. "We think it can be twice as fast and cost us half as much," Barkan said. The phone polls will eventually replace the more costly house-to-house surveys if successful, he said. Albert says COPE will probably use the phone polls to supplement house-to-house surveys in 1972.

Barkan said COPE uses the data results to determine whether further grass-roots action is necessary. "We have a benchmark. If a COPE-endorsed candidate doesn't draw 60 per cent support in union households, we think he's in trouble. Then we can take steps to bolster him," he said. Barkan says polls are useful tools if "you recognize their limitations." Since conditions change so quickly, poll results are frequently out of date within a week, he said.

COPE inundates unionists with leaflets, pamphlets, posters and handbills. Some contain factual information on candidates and issues. Most make strong emotional appeals aimed at motivating the readers to vote for COPE's candidates. The only regular publication of the national office is *Memo From COPE,* issued biweekly to 70,000 subscribers paying $1 a year each. It gives information on candidates, issues and campaigns.

Albert said some of the material he publishes is "educational, quote, propagandistic, unquote, and some of it gets kind of shrill sometimes." A mid-1970 issue of the newsletter hammered at the economic downturn and showed photos from the depression-era 1930s depicting shantytowns, a street corner apple vendor and long lines of jobless persons. "History Can Repeat," the caption warned. "Don't let it! Vote for COPE's candidates." Some of the leaflets COPE distributed in 1970, urging people to register, were emblazoned with questions in bold red or blue headlines: "Do You Really Like High Prices? Do You Really Like High Interest Rates? Do You Like A Pay Check Every Week?" Similar leaflets are distributed in each election year.

One publication the national office disseminates contains a maximum of hard, factual information and a minimum of emotion. It is called *How to Win: A Handbook for Political Education.* Some politicians say the manual, put out in the late 1940s by the CIO Political Action Committee and revised since then, is the most compact and learned set of instructions available on the nuts and bolts of organizing a successful political campaign. Sen. Barry Goldwater, R-Ariz., who strongly differs with COPE's philosophy, says the manual is an effective campaign guide. The booklet provides detailed instructions on how to recruit campaign workers, collect money, generate publicity, register voters and get them to the polls. "If you have 20 active people in a precinct of 1,000, you're well on the way to controlling the primary machinery that nominates candidates," says *How To Win.* "And if you're in a position to nominate, especially in a traditionally majority party, you're well on the way to elect." One chapter explains, point-by-point, how to analyze election results. "The time to begin political organization for an election is on the day after the last election. Your comprehensive analysis of the results of the last election is bound to be a blueprint for the next one."

Near the end of each Congress, COPE compiles and publishes a score sheet on House and Senate Members, designed to show how faithfully they voted the union line. Barkan and Andrew J. Biemiller, director of the AFL-CIO's department of legislation, selected the issues on which the 91st Congress (1969-70) was rated. They included roll calls on overriding President Nixon's veto of the hospital construction spending bill, rejection of Clement Haynsworth and Harrold Carswell for membership on the Supreme Court, and a number of poverty war and social welfare spending measures. (See Table 4.3.)

COPE's Washington operation is bolstered by an aggressive program in the field. Barkan concedes that without the 18 field representatives who work the union hustings, much of what is developed in Washington would go unimplemented at the state and local levels, where the votes are. The grass-roots effort is the responsibility of 12 area directors, four minorities field representatives and two regional supervisors of the women's activities department. "We're kind of proud of our organization," Barkan commented. "We've got organizations in 50 damn states and it goes right down from the states to the cities. . . . We're at it the year 'round. We've got full-time people in every state of the union."

As the legmen of COPE, the area directors must tread softly in their regions. For while they are on the Washington payroll, and therefore primarily responsible to Barkan, they must have the confidence of state and local COPE leaders as well as the political action men in the internationals. Explains publications director Albert: "Area directors do not work for the state but can't work without them. They have to work with the state leadership and want to." The 12 regional representatives perform a variety of functions, but their primary assignments are to serve as the eyes and ears of national COPE and motivate state and local labor leaders to develop effective political action programs.

Although the national office gleans information from polls

and politicians, its most trustworthy barometers are the area directors, who file biweekly field reports directly to Barkan. These surveys detail the activities of the area directors, sum up the political situation, discuss voter registration programs and the progress of COPE "dollar drives" in each state. Typical of the work arriving each fortnight on Barkan's desk is a 1970 pre-election report from Walter F. Gray, the area director for the Far West (Alaska, Hawaii, Idaho, Oregon, Washington). In outlining the Washington state situation on July 15, Gray wrote: "There appears to be a good opportunity to knock off (Rep.) Catherine May (R) in the 4th District, if we do our homework in the Mexican-American community and on the Yakima Indian Reservation." (Rep. May was defeated in the 1970 elections.)

From the South, area director Daniel A. Powell reported June 12, 1970, to Barkan on the Florida Republican Senate primary situation between then-Rep. William C. Cramer (1955-71) and Carswell, who was rejected April 8, 1970, by the Senate for the Supreme Court. Powell said: "Had the primary been in May, as it formerly was, Carswell would have probably won the nomination, but by September (8), most of the sympathy he gained from his rejection for the Supreme Court will have evaporated, leaving him just another ambitious judge, no better qualified for the Senate than he was for the court. Since (Gov. Claude) Kirk (R) has opposition in the gubernatorial primary, the help he could give Carswell will be limited." Powell went on: "While Nixon pledged his support to Cramer prior to Carswell's entry into the primary, the President will probably keep his commitment, because of his dislike of Kirk, who has been a constant source of embarrassment to the Nixon Administration." (Carswell lost in the primary. Both Kirk and Cramer were defeated in the November general elections.)

In the same memo, Powell previewed the August 1970 Democratic Senate primary in Tennessee, where Sen. Gore picked up 51.3 per cent of the vote while his closest rival, Hudley Crockett, accumulated 44.9 per cent. Powell told Barkan: "Whether Crockett can give Gore a close race will depend primarily upon whether Crockett can get adequate campaign financing—$400,000 to $500,000. Without sufficient financing, Crockett's vote will range between 30 per cent and 35 per cent, but with enough money to do necessary media saturation Crockett might get 45 per cent or more of the vote. Should Crockett get no more than 35 per cent to 39 per cent of the vote, Gore will go into the general election stronger than he would have been without primary opposition. But if Crockett runs between 45 per cent and 49 per cent of the vote, then Gore will be hurt and weakened for the general election."

Powell, a veteran of 26 years with COPE whose region includes Alabama, Arkansas, Florida, Louisiana, Mississippi and Tennessee, told *National Journal* he has "probably been in more campaigns than anyone in America." The job requires a pragmatic diplomat with a keen sense of political organization, he says. "One of the difficulties is to get cooperation from state and city COPEs without making them feel that you're taking over. You have to be a real diplomat. If you don't succeed, it can be a real mess." Powell said there are campaigns without seasoned directors and he takes over: "In some cases, behind the scenes, I'm the campaign director."

Regarded by the Washington office as one of the best area directors, Powell says the job often entails considerable negotiation with the national office on behalf of state or local COPEs to pry money loose for programs or candidates. If a COPE organization has developed a voter registration drive for an area where union membership is clearly under-registered, Powell will often get in touch with Barkan and ask for money to get it off the ground. Powell also tries to seek potential candidates for office and encourage them to run. He advises some state COPE officials in the selection of candidates for support. In cases where two candidates seeking COPE endorsements for the same office appear to be about equal in ability, Powell will suggest the leaders consider which office-seeker has a better chance and find out what other interests support the man.

Powell says area directors have a say in how much money from national COPE is spent on a candidate. He gives national

COPE his impressions of an endorsed candidate's chances and an assessment of the political background leading to the endorsement. If friendship between the local labor leaders and the candidate was more persuasive than the organization's assessment of his actual chances for victory, and the area director figures the man has "no chance," there is a strong likelihood of little more than a "token contribution" from national COPE, says Powell.

Ten area directors, in addition to Gray and Powell, cover the remaining 39 states: Henry Murray (Connecticut, Maine, Massachusetts, New Hampshire, Rhode Island, Vermont); Frank McGrath (Delaware, Maryland, Pennsylvania, West Virginia); Clement D. Dowler (Georgia, Kentucky, North Carolina, South Carolina, Virginia); Peter Pesoli (Illinois, Indiana); LaMar Gulbransen (Arizona, California, Colorado, Nevada, Utah); Sherman A. Miles (Kansas, Missouri, New Mexico, Oklahoma, Texas); Jack E. McCoy (Montana, Nebraska, North Dakota, South Dakota, Wyoming); Charles L. McMahon (New York, New Jersey); Raymond S. Alvarez (Michigan, Ohio); and Richard E. Fallow (Iowa, Minnesota, Wisconsin).

Noting the growing numbers of racial minorities involved in the union movement, COPE has moved to involve them in politics. Currently, its principal efforts are aimed at Negroes and Mexican-Americans. Three of the four minorities representatives work in black communities, chiefly encouraging registration programs and tamping down what one field man calls "black militancy and white rage."

W. C. Young, who is based in Paducah, Ky., and is regarded in national headquarters as one of the most effective minorities field workers, sees his major task as "bringing the presence of the labor movement within the black community." To achieve this, he attempts to identify black wards and precincts, and develop voter registration and education drives. "We need black input into the voter registration plans" for citywide efforts by local COPEs, says Young. In the voter education thrust, he said, COPE's minorities representatives seek to cool animosities against whites. The two other field representatives working in black communities are Fannie Neal of Montgomery, Ala., and Earl W. Davis of Richmond, Va., national field coordinator for Negroes.

In the West, COPE's lone representative among the Mexican-Americans, Severiano Quinones (Chano) Merino, said many of his fellow Mexican-Americans are not even aware that they have a right to vote in the United States. Merino, who lives in Hurley, N.M., said "a lot of my people could care less about politics." His major job, he said, is to educate Mexican-Americans about the direct relationship between the kind of office-holder they elect and their own lives. Merino tries to identify each leader in Mexican-American communities or friendly labor unions throughout the West which will help him organize voter registration and education drives among his people.

The national office maintains two women on its staff to recruit women in the labor movement for political action work in state and local COPE organizations: Ruth Colombo, women's activities director for 27 states east of the Mississippi, and Margaret Thornburg, who is responsible for 23 states west of the Mississippi.

Mrs. Colombo says she spends about 95 per cent of her time in the field during an election year. Women volunteers, she said, do much of the drudgery of COPE's campaigns: compiling card files, conducting telephone canvasses, mailing voter information and recruiting other women workers. Mrs. Colombo, who lives in Washington, D.C., sends newsletters on women's activities to groups in her area, helps distribute the voting records of Members of Congress and tries to generate direct mail campaigns to union families briefing them on labor issues on Capitol Hill. Women also help test the political waters for candidates COPE supports. Several weeks before an election, she said, the volunteers call union families, asking the members if they are willing to talk to five of their friends in behalf of a candidate COPE backs. "We don't really expect them to do this but it is a way of testing the support a candidate has in a given campaign," she explained. "If a candidate has 65 to 70 per cent support among union people he can feel fairly confident about the outcome of the election."

The money that supports COPE's far-flung national operations is drawn from a complex web of relationships woven across the 50 states. The group's treasury is tightly interlaced with the general finances of the parent AFL-CIO, dealings with national and international unions and voluntary contributions from a substantial number of the estimated 13.5 million union members. COPE's national officials refuse to discuss the specific amounts of money received and expended. However, they provided some sketchy details on the group's complicated financial structure.

The national staff oversees the spending of four separate funds: the political fund, registration fund, education fund and administrative fund. The political fund is amassed through voluntary contributions from union members. A section (18 USC 610) of the Corrupt Practices Act forbids labor organizations from using dues collections to support candidates for federal offices. But it does not rule out voluntary contributions from individual members for political campaigns. COPE donates money from this fund to candidates it endorses for the Presidency, the House and Senate.

COPE's campaign spending fund depends on the amount collected through its dollar drives conducted by local unions. COPE keeps records of donations so as to have proof the cash gifts are voluntary. The organization uses 10-ticket receipt books for this purpose. Resembling church raffle booklets, millions of them are distributed to national and international unions, relay points for circulation to the rank and file. Collections are made by shop stewards and union members. The donor is given a COPE membership receipt. The ticket stub, with the giver's name, is forwarded to COPE for filing.

COPE sets a quota for national and international unions, asking each to collect at least $12.50 annually for each 100 members. Some unions exceed the quota; some meet it; others contribute less than the quota; some give nothing. The big industrial unions traditionally give COPE its strongest support. Among the organization's most cooperative fund-raisers are the United Steelworkers of America and the United Rubber Workers of America. Many of the building trades unions provide little or no backing. They often prefer to set up their own political movements independent of COPE.

A COPE spokesman estimated that union members, through the annual dollar drives, gave about $600,000 for political campaigns in 1966, more than $1 million in 1968 and about $1 million in 1970. The spokesman predicted that 1972 contributions will run "about the same" as 1970. Usually, the spokesman said, the national office gives about $10,000 to each COPE-supported Senate candidate and $2,500 to each House candidate with COPE backing. The national office generally channels these gifts to the state COPE organizations which then turn the money over to the candidates' finance committees. (See Table 4.1.)

The national staff devotes much of its time to guiding state, county and city drives to register union members and their families to vote and helping finance costs of these efforts. "It's the guts of the work," said Joseph Rourke, COPE's deputy director. The national office gives $2 for every $1 raised by local COPEs for registration. The national office obtains most of its registration drive money from the general treasury of the AFL-CIO and the rest in "dribs and drabs from the nationals and internationals," said COPE's comptroller Bartkin. Rourke estimates that in an election year COPE's registration fund swells to $750,000.

The national office receives money for its education fund through the AFL-CIO general treasury as well as the union affiliates. Unions give to the fund voluntarily. COPE uses the money to finance the distribution and printing of posters, leaflets and handbills. The fund also pays for publication of voting records of House and Senate incumbents compiled by AFL-CIO on bread-and-butter issues. "First you've got to register the voters, then you've got to educate them," explains

Bartkin. Rourke estimates the organization's education fund at $500,000 in an election year. The national office operates at a cost of about $1 million annually. This covers salaries, travel, printing and other expenses. Once again, the general treasury of the AFL-CIO, through union dues collections, is the source of the fund.

Campaign efforts in states, regions, counties and cities are geared primarily to elect candidates friendly to labor. Thus, COPE at all levels must decide who its friends are. To arrive at these decisions, it receives considerable help from the issue-oriented staff of AFL-CIO.

National COPE takes its marching orders on support of Presidential candidates from the national board of the AFL-CIO. Since the merger, only Democratic nominees have obtained the federation's endorsement. Each Presidential year, the AFL-CIO presents its platform proposals to both national party conventions. Invariably, the Democratic platform incorporates more of labor's proposals than does the Republican platform. Shortly after both conventions close, the national AFL-CIO board selects the Presidential candidate who will receive the money and manpower from the approximately 125 international unions represented on the board.

Responsibility for selection of candidates to receive COPE endorsement shifts to state AFL-CIO organizations for House and Senate races. Normally, after a screening and interviewing procedure for new candidates and scrutiny of incumbents' vote ratings compiled in Washington, state AFL-CIO memberships make their choice at conventions following the primaries. In some instances, state COPEs assist candidates in the primaries, particularly in the South.

Occasionally, there are deep divisions at state conventions over support of candidates. Most of the time, said publications director Albert, "There's very little difference between us and the state leadership." If a rift cannot be healed before a vote, endorsements are generally mild. When a division is evidenced, Barkan anticipates problems in galvanizing the labor movement of a state behind the candidate who picks up the COPE backing. "Unless an endorsement is overwhelming, endorsements don't mean much," he said.

An example of such a division occured in Vermont in the 1970 elections, where former Democratic Gov. Philip H. Hoff (1963-69) challenged the late Republican Sen. Winston L. Prouty (1959-71). Hoff was running with a strong pro-labor record, and Ralph E. Williams, president of the Vermont State Labor Council, AFL-CIO, said: "I don't know of a union in the state" which will back Prouty. However, Prouty said he expected some labor support; and Joseph Curran, president of the National Maritime Union of America, told *National Journal* the union leadership was torn between the two men. "I don't know what we're going to do yet, he declared. Hoff, who lost to Prouty in the November 1970 elections, eventually was endorsed by COPE.

COPE leaders in Washington are generally agreed that one of the most effective COPE programs has been developed by the 500,000-member Communications Workers of America. CWA is one of the few unions which meets its $12.50 per 100 members quota regularly. "It's the official program and policy of the union," says Glenn E. Watts, secretary-treasurer of CWA. "We use sales-type gimmicks to encourage participation and contributions—awards to locals, plaques, statues, and we present them to local presidents, then give them publicity." CWA also pushes its COPE dollar drives through its regular publications and special monthly letters. CWA's aggressive COPE program does not stop at money raising. The union of America's telephone operators, it has pressed into voluntary service as many as 20,000 operators during peak periods for telephone voter-registration campaigns.

COPE's power in the precincts is almost universally conceded. In the House and Senate, where COPE has helped forge victories for hundreds of the nation's lawmakers over the years, winners are frank in their admiration of the organization. So are some losers. Frank A. Kemp Jr., a Republican who lost to then-Rep. Byron G. Rogers, D-Colo. (1951-71), in 1968, credits COPE's endorsement of the Denver Democrat with a major role in his defeat. Kemp told *National Journal* in mid-1970: "COPE has a very strong influence in the state of Colorado and is a staunch supporter of Congressman Rogers. I don't see their support for him so much as far as money is concerned. So far he hasn't needed it. But they really do get out the vote for him. This has been a significant thing for him in five or six elections. There is a very active organizational effort to get out the vote. They drive cars during election day also, getting poor people and people who are house-bound out to vote." (In the 1970 Democratic primary in Colorado, COPE switched its support from Rogers to his opponent, Craig S. Barnes. Barnes lost in the general elections to Rep. James D. McKevitt, R.) "They've got manpower and wordpower," reports Sen. Thomas F. Eagleton, D-Mo., who received COPE's support in his successful 1968 general election bid. "They are especially effective through dissemination through their considerable channels of communication—almost every union in the state."

Barkan says most candidates, when given the choice, would rather have COPE's cash in hand than have the organization use its funds to get out the vote. "We ask a candidate: 'What would you rather have—$25,000 budgeted for working the union membership to vote for you or $5,000 in cash?' Almost everyone will take the $5,000. I never fail to be amazed at the short-sightedness of many candidates. I don't have a high regard for the pragmatic intelligence of most candidates."

Concern over COPE's effectiveness was translated into an amendment submitted to the Senate December 8, 1969, by Sen. Paul J. Fannin, R-Ariz., that would have taxed union dues and assessments used for political purposes, including voter registration. Fannin told the Senate his proposal was designed to be "protective of the (union) members' rights." Sen. Walter F. Mondale, D-Minn., termed the idea "harsh and unsound." It was rejected, 59-27. COPE opposed Fannin in 1964 and 1970 and backed Mondale in 1966.

If imitation is the most sincere form of flattery, COPE is

surrounded by flatterers—most of them on the opposite side of the philosophical fence. One of the most effective is the Business-Industry Political Action Committee (BIPAC), whose leaders readily concede they formed the group to counterbalance COPE's effectiveness. Robert L. Humphrey, BIPAC president, admits his group was modeled after COPE. Another group formed more recently to give businessmen more political muscle is the Bankers Political Action Committee (Bank-Pac), organized in spring 1970 in Chicago and headed by Lewis K. McKee, a Memphis, Tenn., banker. BankPac reported 1970 expenditures of $85,795, of which $67,050 went to House and Senate candidates friendly to the banking community.

COPE's leadership expresses little concern about political counterweights. Barkan says COPE "raised more money (in 1970) than we ever have in the past. . . . There's no party that can match us. Every election it gets better and better. Give us 10 or 15 years and we'll have the best political organization in the history of this country."

Table 4.1   COPE Donations to States, 1968 and 1970

The Committee on Political Education (AFL-CIO) usually channels its contributions to political campaigns through its state and local organizations in the 50 states. The records filed in the office of the Clerk of the House of Representatives indicate the organization gave a total of $742,320 in 1968 and $637,340 in 1970 to state and local political action groups. The amounts COPE declared in its reports to the clerk's office follow:

State	Year	Amount	State	Year	Amount
Alabama	1968	$12,000	Florida	1970	$14,500
Alaska	1970	12,500		1968	24,000
	1968	16,000	Georgia	1970	2,000
Arizona	1970	12,000		1968	6,000
	1968	9,250	Hawaii	1970	1,000
Arkansas	1968	6,000		1968	20,180
California	1970	40,500	Idaho	1970	3,500
	1968	45,390		1968	21,300
Colorado	1970	4,000	Illinois	1970	22,500
	1968	8,000		1968	25,000
Connecticut	1970	12,000	Indiana	1970	26,000
	1968	21,000		1968	32,500
Delaware	1970	16,000	Iowa	1970	15,600

State	Year	Amount	State	Year	Amount
Iowa (cont'd)	1968	$27,000	North Dakota	1970	$14,500
Kansas	1970	3,000		1968	6,300
	1968	15,000	Ohio	1970	28,000
Kentucky	1970	1,000		1968	70,700
	1968	13,000	Oklahoma	1970	6,500
Louisiana	1970	9,500		1968	9,000
	1968	13,000	Oregon	1968	6,000
Maine	1970	15,000	Pennsylvania	1970	22,500
	1968	12,800		1968	23,000
Maryland	1970	21,500	Rhode Island	1970	5,500
	1968	8,500		1968	5,000
Massachusetts	1970	6,500	South Carolina	1970	5,000
	1968	8,000		1968	9,000
Michigan	1970	19,500	South Dakota	1970	4,000
	1968	23,000	Tennessee	1970	28,250
Minnesota	1970	15,500		1968	7,500
	1968	14,000	Texas	1970	28,000
Mississippi	—	—		1968	41,000
Missouri	1970	18,650	Utah	1970	21,500
	1968	28,000		1968	6,000
Montana	1970	11,000	Vermont	1970	15,000
	1968	4,300	Virginia	1970	12,000
Nebraska	1970	11,000		1968	9,600
	1968	6,000	Washington	1970	15,750
Nevada	1970	11,000		1968	21,000
	1968	10,000	West Virginia	1970	12,500
New Hampshire	—	—		1968	9,000
New Jersey	1970	11,500	Wisconsin	1970	20,500
New Mexico	1970	12,500		1968	35,000
	1968	6,000	Wyoming	1970	18,500
New York	1970	20,000		1968	5,500
	1968	39,500	District of		
North Carolina	1970	2,000	Columbia	1970	8,090
	1968	4,000			

Source: Citizens' Research Foundation, *National Journal*

Table 4.2 COPE Endorsements, 1970

In the 1970 elections, the Committee on Political Education (AFL-CIO) endorsed 31 Senate candidates—all Democrats— and 336 House candidates— of which 315 are Democrats. Nineteen of the Senate candidates endorsed won and 203 of the House candidates endorsed were elected. A COPE endorsement does not always mean a cash investment in the candidate by the labor federation, an organization official said. But COPE declined to say who received money or how much those obtaining financial backing actually received. Following are the Senate and House candidates endorsed in 1970, with winners in bold type:

Senate

Quentin N. Burdick, D-N.D.*
Howard W. Cannon, D-Nev.*
Lawton Chiles, D-Fla.
Joseph D. Duffey, D-Conn.
Albert Gore, D-Tenn.*
Sam Grossman, D-Ariz.
Philip A. Hart, D-Mich.*
Vance Hartke, D-Ind.*
Philip H. Hoff, D-Vt.
Hubert H. Humphrey, D-Minn.
Henry M. Jackson, D-Wash.*
Wendell P. Kay, D-Alaska
Edward M. Kennedy, D-Mass.*
Mike Mansfield, D-Mont.*
Gale W. McGee, D-Wyo.*
Howard M. Metzenbaum, D-Ohio
Joseph M. Montoya, D-N.M.*
Frank B. Morrison, D-Neb.
Frank E. Moss, D-Utah*
Edmund S. Muskie, D-Maine*
Richard L. Ottinger, D-N.Y.
John O. Pastore, D-R.I.*
William Proxmire, D-Wis.*
George C. Rawlings Jr., D-Va.
William G. Sesler, D-Pa.
Adlai E. Stevenson III, D-Ill.
Stuart Symington, D-Mo.*
John V. Tunney, D-Calif.
Joseph D. Tydings, D-Md.*
Harrison A. Williams Jr., D-N.J.*
Jacob Zimmerman, D-Del.

House

James Abourezk, D-S.D.
Clifford R. Adams, D-Minn.
Brock Adams, D-Wash.*
Joseph P. Addabbo, D-N.Y.*
David S. Aland, D-Md.
Carl Albert, D-Okla.*
Glenn M. Anderson, D-Calif.*
Richard N. Anderson, D-N.Y.
William R. Anderson, D-Tenn.*
Frank Annunzio, D-Ill.*
Doug Arnett, D-Ohio
Thomas L. Ashley, D-Ohio*
Les Aspin, D-Wis.
Wayne N. Aspinall, D-Colo.*
Herman Badillo, D-N.Y.
Craig S. Barnes, D-Colo.

William A. Barrett, D-Pa.*
Joseph J. Bartolomeo, D-Ohio
Orren Beaty, D-Ariz.
Nicholas J. Begich, D-Alaska
Alphonzo Bell, R-Calif.*
Arthur L. Berger, D-Pa.
Bob Bergland, D-Minn.
David Bernstein, D-N.Y.
Mario Biaggi, D-N.Y.*
Jonathan B. Bingham, D-N.Y.*
Ray Blanton, D-Tenn.*
John A. Blatnik, D-Minn.*
Roger Blobaum, D-Iowa
H. Clifton Blue, D-N.C.
Hale Boggs, D-La.*
Edward P. Boland, D-Mass.*
Richard Bolling, D-Mo.*
Erwin L. Bornstein, D-N.Y.
John Brademas, D-Ind.*
Frank J. Brasco, D-N.Y.*
William J. (Bill) Brauner, D-Idaho
Joseph R. Breslin, D-Pa.
Jack Brooks, D-Tex.*
James E. Brooks, D-N.D.
Tate C. Buchanan, D-Va.
James A. Burke, D-Mass.*
Bill D. Burlison, D-Mo.*
George Bill Burrows, D-Neb.
Phillip Burton, D-Calif.*
James A. Byrne, D-Pa.*
Hugh L. Carey, D-N.Y.*
Charles J. Carney, D-Ohio
Emanuel Celler, D-N.Y.*
G. L. (Jerry) Chapman, D-Calif.
Fabian Chavez Jr., D-N.M.
Shirley Chisholm, D-N.Y.*
John A. Cihon, D-Mich.
Frank M. Clark, D-Pa.*
William Clay, D-Mo.*
George W. Collins, D-Ill.
John Conyers Jr., D-Mich.*
James C. Corman, D-Calif.*
Robert J. Cornell, D-Wis.
William R. Cotter, D-Conn.
Roger Cowan, D-Tenn.
Billie M. Cox, D-Ill.
Leslie W. Cravens, D-Calif.
James G. Cretekos, D-N.Y.
Edward Cuddy, D-N.Y.

House *(cont'd)*

John C. Culver, D-Iowa*
T. F. Gilroy Daly, D-Conn.
Eugene S. Daniell Jr., D-N.H.
John D. Daniello, D-Del.
Dominick V. Daniels, D-N.J.*
George E. Danielson, D-Calif.
Richard E. Davies, D-Mich.
James H. DeCoursey Jr., D-Kan.
James J. Delaney, D-N.Y.*
Ronald V. Dellums, D-Calif.
John H. Dent, D-Pa.*
John E. Devine Jr., D-Ill.
Charles C. Diggs Jr., D-Mich.*
John D. Dingell, D-Mich.*
Harold D. Donohue, D-Mass.*
John G. Dow, D-N.Y.
William Dretzin, D-N.Y.
Thaddeus J. Dulski, D-N.Y.*
Florence P. Dwyer, R-N.J.*
Bob Eckhardt, D-Tex.*
Ed Edmondson, D-Okla.*
Don Edwards, D-Calif.*
Edwin W. Edwards, D-La.*
Joshua Eilberg, D-Pa.*
Ronald C. Eisele, D-N.J.
Richard A. Enslen, D-Mich.
Frank E. Evans, D-Colo.*
Myrlie B. Evers, D-Calif.
Joe L. Evins, D-Tenn.*
Barry Farber, R-N.Y.
Dante B. Fascell, D-Fla.*
Joseph T. Fitzpatrick, D-Va.
Thomas P. Flaherty, D-N.Y.
Daniel J. Flood, D-Pa.*
Thomas S. Foley, D-Wash.*
William D. Ford, D-Mich.*
Donald M. Fraser, D-Minn.*
James G. Fulton, R-Pa.*†
Richard Fulton, D-Tenn.*
Lou Galetich, D-Iowa
Nick Galifianakis, D-N.C.*
Cornelius E. Gallagher, D-N.J.*
Edward A. Garmatz, D-Md.*
Joseph M. Gaydos, D-Pa.*
Richard G. Gebhardt, D-Colo.
Robert N. Giaimo, D-Conn.*
Sam Gibbons, D-Fla.*
Henry B. Gonzalez, D-Tex.*
James W. Goodrich, D-Ohio

Ella T. Grasso, D-Conn.
Kenneth J. Gray, D-Ill.*
John J. Greaney, D-N.Y.
Edith Green, D-Ore.*
Nino Green, D-Mich.
William J. Green, D-Pa.*
Martha W. Griffiths, D-Mich.*
Gilbert Gude, R-Md.*
Seymour Halpern, R-N.Y.*
Lee H. Hamilton, D-Ind.*
James M. Hanley, D-N.Y.*
Richard T. Hanna, D-Calif.*
Julia Butler Hansen, D-Wash.*
Cecil R. Harrington, D-Pa.
Michael J. Harrington, D-Mass.*
Fred L. Harris, D-Mich.
Gary K. Hart, D-Calif.
Royal Hart, D-Md.
William D. Hathaway, D-Maine*
Augustus F. Hawkins, D-Calif.*
Wayne L. Hays, D-Ohio*
Ken Hechler, D-W.Va.*
Margaret M. Heckler, R-Mass.*
Henry Helstoski, D-N.J.*
Floyd V. Hicks, D-Wash.*
John Hlavacek, D-Neb.
Chet Holifield, D-Calif.*
James C. Hood, D-Ohio
Frank Horton, R-N.Y.*
James J. Howard, D-N.J.*
J. David Huber, D-Ind.
David A. Hughes, D-Wash.
George R. Hughes Jr., R-Md.
William J. Hughes, D-N.J.
William L. Hungate, D-Mo.*
Richard H. Ichord, D-Mo.*
Andrew Jacobs Jr., D-Ind.*
Billy D. Jellison, D-Kan.
Harold T. Johnson, D-Calif.*
Ed Jones, D-Tenn.*
James R. Jones, D-Okla.
Robert E. Jones, D-Ala.*
James C. (Jim) Juhnke, D-Kan.
Joseph E. Karth, D-Minn.*
Victor J. Karycki Jr., D-Pa.
Robert W. Kastenmeier, D-Wis.*
Abraham Kazen Jr., D-Tex.*
William J. Keating, R-Ohio
James Kee, D-W.Va.*

House *(cont'd)*

N. (Toni) Kimmel, D-Calif.
John C. Kluczynski, D-Ill.*
Edward I. Koch, D-N.Y.*
William M. Kortum, D-Calif.
Peter N. Kyros, D-Maine*
Robert L. Leggett, D-Calif.*
Thomas B. Lenhart, D-Calif.
Arthur J. Lesemann, D-N.J.
Arthur A. Link, D-N.D.
Clarence D. Long, D-Md.*
Allard K. Lowenstein, D-N.Y.*
Torbert H. Macdonald, D-Mass.*
Ray J. Madden, D-Ind.*
Salvatore T. Mansi, D-N.J.
Spark M. Matsunaga, D-Hawaii*
Paul N. McCloskey Jr., R-Calif.*
David R. McCormack, D-Mich.
Mike McCormack, D-Wash.
Neal P. McCurn, D-N.Y.
Joseph M. McDade, R-Pa.*
Heyward McDonald, D-S.C.
John J. McFall, D-Calif.*
Manley L. McGee, D-Ohio
K. Gunn McKay, D-Utah
Jean McKee, D-Mich.
Stuart D. McLean, D-Calif.
John Mead, D-Tex.
Lloyd Meeds, D-Wash.*
John Melcher, D-Mont.*
Chester E. Merrow, D-N.H.
Ralph H. Metcalfe, D-Ill.
Edward Mezvinsky, D-Iowa
Abner J. Mikva, D-Ill.*
George P. Miller, D-Calif.*
Harold O. Miller, D-Va.
Milton S. Miller, D-Calif.
Robert C. Miller, D-Ill.
Russell R. Miller, D-Calif.
Joseph G. Minish, D-N.J.*
Patsy T. Mink, D-Hawaii*
Parren J. Mitchell, D-Md.
Robert H. Mollohan, D-W.Va.*
John S. Monagan, D-Conn.*
Terry Montgomery, D-Minn.
Fred H. Moore, D-Iowa
William S. Moorhead, D-Pa.*
Melvin W. Morgan, D-Ill.
Thomas E. Morgan, D-Pa.*
F. Bradford Morse, R-Mass.*

John E. Moss, D-Calif.*
Ronald M. Mottl, D-Ohio
John M. Murphy, D-N.Y.*
Morgan F. Murphy, D-Ill.
Virgil L. Musser, D-Ohio
A. H. (Bob) Nance, D-Utah
William H. Natcher, D-Ky.*
Lucien N. Nedzi, D-Mich.*
Robert N. C. Nix, D-Pa.*
David R. Obey, D-Wis.*
James G. O'Hara, D-Mich.*
Joseph F. O'Kicki, D-Pa.
Alvin E. O'Konski, R-Wis.*
Arnold Olsen, D-Mont.*
Thomas P. O'Neill Jr., D-Mass.*
Michael M. Osborn, D-Tenn.
Gerald J. Parent, D-Mich.
Wright Patman, D-Tex.*
Edward J. Patten, D-N.J.*
Edward W. Pattison, D-N.Y.
Thomas M. Pelly, D-Wash.*
Claude Pepper, D-Fla.*
Carl D. Perkins, D-Ky.*
John E. Pflum, D-Pa.
Philip J. Philbin, Ind.-Mass.*
John F. Pickett, D-Conn.
J. J. Pickle, D-Tex.*
Otis G. Pike, D-N.Y.*
Bertram L. Podell, D-N.Y.*
Donald Poe, D-Ark.
Gerald A. Pollock, D-Ariz.
Richardson Preyer, D-N.C.*
Melvin Price, D-Ill.*
Roman C. Pucinski, D-Ill.*
Ben Ragsdale, Ind.-Va.
William J. Randall, D-Mo.*
Charles B. Rangel, D-N.Y.
Thomas M. Rees, D-Calif.*
Ogden R. Reid, R-N.Y.*
Henry S. Reuss, D-Wis.*
George Rice, D-Minn.
Donald W. Riegle Jr., R-Mich.*#
O'Brien Riordan, D-Calif.
William D. Roach, D-Ind.
Peter W. Rodino Jr., D-N.J.*
Robert A. Roe, D-N.J.*
Charles Arthur Rogers, D-Mich.
Teno Roncalio, D-Wyo.
Fred B. Rooney, D-Pa.*

House (cont'd)

John J. Rooney, D-N.Y.*
Benjamin S. Rosenthal, D-N.Y.*
Dan Rostenkowski, D-Ill.*
J. Edward Roush, D-Ind.
William R. Roy, D-Kan.
Edward R. Roybal, D-Calif.*
Ralph Rudd, D-Ohio
James D. Ruppert, D-Ohio
William F. Ryan, D-N.Y.*
T. D. (Ted) Saar Jr., D-Kan.
Fernand J. St. Germain, D-R.I.*
Paul S. Sarbanes, D-Md.
James H. Scheuer, D-N.Y.*
August Scholle, D-Mich.
Donald Searcy, D-Neb.
John F. Seiberling Jr., D-Ohio
Philip R. Sharp, D-Ind.
Carl G. Sherer, D-Ohio
Harvey W. Sherman, D-N.Y.
David Bruce Shine, D-Tenn.
George E. Shipley, D-Ill.*
Ray Short, D-Wis.
Franklin Shumake, D-Ga.
Joseph Simmons, D-N.Y.
B. F. Sisk, D-Calif.*
John M. Slack, D-W.Va.*
Neal Smith, D-Iowa*
Philip A. Sprague, D-Ind.
Gerald N. Springer, D-Ohio
Harley O. Staggers, D-W.Va.*
J. William Stanton, R-Ohio*
James V. Stanton, D-Ohio
Darrel H. Stearns, D-Va.
Tom Steed, D-Okla.*
Raymond H. Stevens, D-Ohio
R. Michael Stillwagon, D-Mich.
Louis Stokes, D-Ohio*
Michael M. Stolzberg, D-Calif.

Terrence D. Straub, D-Ind.
Gerry E. Studds, D-Mass.
Leonor K. Sullivan, D-Mo.*
James W. Symington, D-Mo.*
Fred M. Tabak, D-Wis.
Lyle D. Taylor, D-Iowa
Roy A. Taylor, D-N.C.*
Frank Thompson Jr., D-N.J.*
Robert O. Tiernan, D-R.I.*
David A. Tunno, D-Calif.
Morris K. Udall, D-Ariz.*
Al Ullman, D-Ore.*
Lionel Van Deerlin, D-Calif.*
Charles A. Vanik, D-Ohio*
Joseph P. Vigorito, D-Pa.*
Jerome R. Waldie, D-Calif.*
Louis F. Waldmann, D-Pa.
Edward A. Warman, D-Ill.
James H. Weaver, D-Ore.
Charles W. Webster, D-Ky.
Charles W. Whalen Jr., R-Ohio*
Richard C. White, D-Tex.*
Roy R. White, D-Va.
J. Harvie Wilkinson III, R-Va.
Kathleen Z. Williams, D-Ind.
Murat Williams, D-Va.
Charles H. Wilson, D-Calif.*
Richard H. Winningham, D-Tenn.
Lester L. Wolff, D-N.Y.*
Chester M. Wright, D-Calif.
Jim Wright, D-Tex.*
Sidney R. Yates, D-Ill.*
Gus Yatron, D-Pa.*
Andrew Young, D-Ga.
John Young, D-Tex.*
Clement J. Zablocki, D-Wis.*
William P. Zurick, D-Pa.

---

*   incumbent
\#   Endorsed by Flint (Mich.) Central Labor Union COPE.
†   Died October 6, 1971.

Source: COPE

Table 4.3   COPE's Congressional Ratings, 1969-1970:
"Right" or "Wrong" on Labor Issues

The Committee on Political Education rates all Members of Congress on how they voted on issues the AFL-CIO regards as crucial to the labor movement. The political action group gives them an R for a vote labor considers "right" and W for votes that are "wrong" from labor's standpoint. COPE keeps cumulative scores on the Members from the time they are elected. These are the COPE ratings for the 91st Congress (1969-70). (Five House seats were vacant; House Speaker John W. McCormack did not participate in House votes.) Except where noted, Members listed were serving in the first session of the 92nd Congress, as of November 1, 1971.

SENATE RATINGS

Democrats	R	W		R	W
Allen, Ala.	2	9	McGovern, S.D.	65	3
Anderson, N.M.	68	16	McIntyre, N.H.	41	2
Bayh, Ind.	40	1	Metcalf, Mont.	85	3
Bible, Nev.	54	31	Mondale, Minn.	35	0
Burdick, N.D.	62	3	Montoya, N.M.	65	4
Byrd, Va.	4	25	Moss, Utah	56	4
Byrd, W.Va.	60	33	Muskie, Maine	60	2
Cannon, Nev.	48	15	Nelson, Wis.	44	0
Church, Idaho	64	8	Pastore, R.I.	87	4
Cranston, Calif.	12	0	Pell, R.I.	55	0
Dodd, Conn. **(4, 10)**	54	8	Proxmire, Wis.	73	6
Eagleton, Mo.	12	0	Randolph, W.Va.	56	10
Eastland, Miss.	16	79	Ribicoff, Conn.	50	1
Ellender, La.	30	69	Russell, Ga. **(10)**	23	69
Ervin, N.C.	23	66	Sparkman, Ala.	56	41
Fulbright, Ark.	44	46	Spong, Va.	8	17
Gore, Tenn. **(4)**	65	16	Stennis, Miss.	22	78
Gravel, Alaska	11	2	Symington, Mo.	84	4
Harris, Okla.	28	4	Talmadge, Ga.	18	61
Hart, Mich.	63	0	Tydings, Md. **(4)**	31	1
Hartke, Ind.	53	6	Williams, N.J.	70	1
Holland, Fla. **(9)**	18	85	Yarborough, Tex. **(3)**	72	7
Hollings, S.C.	8	16	Young, Ohio **(9)**	61	3
Hughes, Iowa	10	0			
Inouye, Hawaii	57	3	**Republicans**		
Jackson, Wash.	92	1	Aiken, Vt.	54	42
Jordan, N.C.	15	55	Allott, Colo.	20	68
Kennedy, Mass.	44	0	Baker, Tenn.	6	16
Long, La.	49	47	Bellmon, Okla.	3	10
Magnuson, Wash.	92	2	Bennett, Utah	3	90
Mansfield, Mont.	80	13	Boggs, Del.	27	31
McCarthy, Minn. **(9)**	82	1	Brooke, Mass.	21	1
McClellen, Ark.	19	76	Case, N.J.	72	17
McGee, Wyo.	53	7	Cook, Ky.	9	3

Senate Republicans (cont'd)	R	W		R	W
Cooper, Ky.	49	38	Baring, Nev. AL	42	41
Cotton, N.H.	12	77	Barrett, Pa. 1	99	0
Curtis, Neb.	2	88	Bennett, Fla. 3	43	58
Dole, Kan.	5	56	Bevill, Ala. 7	7	18
Dominick, Colo.	9	48	Biaggi, N.Y. 24	10	2
Fannin, Ariz.	1	34	Bingham, N.Y. 23	38	0
Fong, Hawaii	36	24	Blanton, Tenn. 7	9	16
Goldwater, Ariz.	1	63	Blatnik, Minn. 8	98	3
Goodell, N.Y. **(4)**	17	52	Boggs, La. 2	82	20
Griffin, Mich.	22	56	Boland, Mass. 2	90	5
Gurney, Fla.	2	47	Bolling, Mo. 5	95	1
Hansen, Wyo.	2	22	Brademas, Ind. 3	68	0
Hatfield, Ore.	20	4	Brasco, N.Y. 11	25	0
Hruska, Neb.	4	87	Brinkley, Ga. 3	4	20
Javits, N.Y.	85	12	Brooks, Tex. 9	78	16
Jordan, Idaho	7	40	Brown, Calif. 29 **(3)**	47	0
Mathias, Md.	39	20	Burke, Mass. 11	67	3
Miller, Iowa	7	48	Burleson, Tex. 17	22	74
Mundt, S.D.	10	84	Burlison, Mo. 10	7	5
Murphy, Calif. **(4)**	7	28	Burton, Calif. 5	40	0
Packwood, Ore.	9	4	Byrne, Pa. 3	94	0
Pearson, Kan.	12	35	Cabell, Tex. 5	9	28
Percy, Ill.	17	5	Caffery, La. 3	3	7
Prouty, Vt. **(10)**	41	45	Carey, N.Y. 15	56	1
Saxbe, Ohio	5	4	Casey, Tex. 22	23	46
Schweiker, Pa.	38	22	Celler, N.Y. 10	99	1
Scott, Pa.	57	36	Chappell, Fla. 4	3	9
Smith, Ill. **(4)**	2	9	Chisholm, N.Y. 12	12	0
Smith, Maine	52	50	Clark, Pa. 25	78	9
Stevens, Alaska	7	4	Clay, Mo. 1	12	0
Thurmond, S.C.	6	81	Cohelan, Calif. 7 **(1)**	69	0
Tower, Tex.	0	46	Colmer, Miss. 5	1	90
Williams, Del. **(9)**	8	94	Conyers, Mich. 1	36	1
Young, N.D.	23	72	Corman, Calif. 22	56	2
			Culver, Iowa 2	35	1
HOUSE RATINGS			Daddario, Conn. 1 **(7)**	62	5
			Daniel, Va. 5	2	10
Democrats			Daniels, N.J. 14	69	0
Abbitt, Va. 4	10	87	Davis, Ga. 7	24	33
Abernethy, Miss. 1	17	84	Dawson, Ill. 1 **(9)**	86	3
Adams, Wash. 7	38	0	de la Garza, Tex. 15	23	12
Addabbo, N.Y. 7	57	3	Delaney, N.Y. 9	94	6
Albert, Okla. 3	86	14	Dent, Pa. 21	67	3
Alexander, Ark. 1	4	6	Diggs, Mich. 13	81	1
Anderson, Calif. 17	12	0	Dingell, Mich. 16	79	2
Anderson, Tenn. 6	27	6	Donohue, Mass. 4	97	3
Andrews, Ala. 3	28	68	Dorn, S.C. 3	16	80
Annunzio, Ill. 7	36	2	Dowdy, Tex. 2	12	78
Ashley, Ohio 9	83	3	Downing, Va. 1	17	52
Aspinall, Colo. 4	81	18	Dulski, N.Y. 41	68	2

House Democrats *(cont'd)*	R	W		R	W
Eckhardt, Tex. 8	25	0	Hicks, Wash. 6	34	4
Edmondson, Okla. 2	78	16	Holifield, Calif. 19	99	3
Edwards, Calif. 9	46	0	Howard, N.J. 3	35	2
Edwards, La. 7	12	14	Hull, Mo. 6	37	49
Eilberg, Pa. 4	25	0	Hungate, Mo. 9	28	8
Evans, Colo. 3	35	2	Ichord, Mo. 8	32	24
Evins, Tenn. 4	58	35	Jacobs, Ind. 11	37	0
Fallon, Md. 4 **(1)**	76	23	Jarman, Okla. 5	27	65
Farbstein, N.Y. 19 **(1)**	81	0	Johnson, Calif. 2	67	1
Fascell, Fla. 12	66	21	Jones, Tenn. 8	5	7
Feighan, Ohio 20 **(1)**	93	7	Jones, Ala. 8	70	28
Fisher, Tex. 21	11	86	Jones, N.C. 1	6	21
Flood, Pa. 11	88	5	Karth, Minn. 4	69	0
Flowers, Ala. 5	3	8	Kastenmeier, Wis. 2	68	2
Flynt, Ga. 6	24	60	Kazen, Tex. 23	21	4
Foley, Wash. 5	33	5	Kee, W.Va. 5	34	3
Ford, William, Mich. 15	38	0	Kluczynski, Ill. 5	90	2
Fountain, N.C. 2	28	67	Koch, N.Y. 17	12	0
Fraser, Minn. 5	48	1	Kyros, Maine 1	25	0
Friedel, Md. 7 **(1)**	89	6	Landrum, Ga. 9	39	53
Fulton, Tenn. 5	44	4	Leggett, Calif. 4	48	1
Fuqua, Fla. 2	9	38	Lennon, N.C. 7	12	71
Galifianakis, N.C. 4	11	14	Long, Md. 2	40	6
Gallagher, N.J. 13	66	0	Long, La. 8	5	31
Garmatz, Md. 3	98	3	Lowenstein, N.Y. 5 **(2)**	12	0
Gaydos, Pa. 20	10	0	Macdonald, Mass. 7	78	8
Gettys, S.C. 5	6	31	Madden, Ind. 1	99	2
Giaimo, Conn. 3	62	6	Mahon, Tex. 19	35	65
Gibbons, Fla. 6	38	10	Mann, S.C. 4	1	10
Gilbert, N.Y. 22 **(1)**	65	0	Marsh, Va. 7 **(9)**	1	48
Gonzalez, Tex. 20	54	1	Matsunaga, Hawaii 1	47	1
Gray, Ill. 21	80	7	McCarthy, N.Y. 39 **(3)**	31	5
Green, Ore. 3	71	13	McCormack, Mass. 9 **(9)**		
Green, Pa. 5	40	0	McFall, Calif. 15	81	2
Griffin, Miss. 3	3	13	McMillan, S.C. 6	17	78
Griffiths, Mich. 17	80	4	Meeds, Wash. 2	36	1
Hagan, Ga. 1	17	41	Melcher, Mont. 2	9	3
Haley, Fla. 7	9	82	Mikva, Ill. 2	11	0
Hamilton, Ind. 9	29	8	Miller, Calif. 8	97	2
Hanley, N.Y. 34	37	1	Mills, Ark. 2	50	47
Hanna, Calif. 34	42	4	Minish, N.J. 11	48	0
Hansen, Wash. 3	56	1	Mink, Hawaii 2	38	0
Harrington, Mass. 6	9	0	Mollohan, W.Va. 1	19	0
Hathaway, Maine 2	38	0	Monagan, Conn. 5	61	8
Hawkins, Calif. 21	46	0	Montgomery, Miss. 4	2	21
Hays, Ohio 18	85	9	Moorhead, Pa. 14	66	3
Hebert, La. 1	32	66	Morgan, Pa. 26	97	3
Hechler, W.Va. 4	67	3	Moss, Calif. 3	90	2
Helstoski, N.J. 9	38	0	Murphy, N.Y. 16	46	2
Henderson, N.C. 3	16	44	Murphy, Ill. 3 **(9)**	69	1

House Democrats (cont'd)	R	W		R	W
Natcher, Ky. 2	65	26	Steed, Okla. 4	60	33
Nedzi, Mich. 14	52	1	Stephens, Ga. 10	25	34
Nichols, Ala. 4	5	20	Stokes, Ohio 21	12	0
Nix, Pa. 2	71	0	Stratton, N.Y. 35	56	9
Obey, Wis. 7	11	1	Stubblefield, Ky. 1	45	25
O'Hara, Mich. 12	67	3	Stuckey, Ga. 8	6	18
Olsen, Mont. 1 (2)	58	2	Sullivan, Mo. 3	92	1
O'Neal, Ga. 2 (9)	3	34	Symington, Mo. 2	11	1
O'Neill, Mass. 8	91	3	Taylor, N.C. 11	16	44
Ottinger, N.Y. 25 (4)	34	2	Teague, Tex. 6	26	67
Passman, La. 5	23	75	Thompson, N.J. 4	85	0
Patman, Tex. 1	69	25	Tiernan, R.I. 2	23	0
Patten, N.J. 15	49	0	Tunney, Calif. 38 (5)	32	2
Pepper, Fla. 11	46	2	Udall, Ariz. 2	49	7
Perkins, Ky. 7	92	8	Ullman, Ore. 2	71	10
Philbin, Mass. 3 (1, 2)	96	5	Van Deerlin, Calif. 37	45	3
Pickle, Tex. 10	26	16	Vanik, Ohio 22	84	3
Pike, N.Y. 1	44	15	Vigorito, Pa. 24	33	4
Poage, Tex. 11	42	56	Waggonner, La. 4	7	46
Podell, N.Y. 13	16	0	Waldie, Calif. 14	22	62
Powell, N.Y. 18 (1)	75	1	Watts, Ky. 6 (10)	55	40
Preyer, N.C. 6	6	6	White, Tex. 16	17	20
Price, Ill. 24	102	0	Whitten, Miss. 2	15	83
Pryor, Ark. 4	11	13	Wilson, Calif. 31	45	0
Pucinski, Ill. 11	66	4	Wolff, N.Y. 3	34	4
Purcell, Tex. 13	24	27	Wright, Tex. 12	58	27
Randall, Mo. 4	56	13	Yates, Ill. 9	85	5
Rarick, La. 6	3	20	Yatron, Pa. 6	11	1
Rees, Calif. 26	25	0	Young, Tex. 14	53	24
Reuss, Wis. 5	88	0	Zablocki, Wis. 4	101	0
Rivers, S.C. 1 (10)	22	74			
Roberts, Tex. 4	20	34	**Republicans**		
Rodino, N.J. 10	99	0	Adair, Ind. 4 (2)	9	85
Roe, N.J. 8	7	2	Anderson, Ill. 16	8	52
Rogers, Colo. 1 (1)	88	6	Andrews, N.D. 1	9	34
Rogers, Fla. 9	24	64	Arends, Ill. 17	8	93
Rooney, Pa. 15	43	2	Ashbrook, Ohio 17	4	55
Rooney, N.Y. 14	101	1	Ayres, Ohio 14 (2)	32	59
Rosenthal, N.Y. 8	53	0	Beall, Md. 6 (5)	5	7
Rostenkowski, Ill. 8	66	4	Belcher, Okla. 1	6	88
Roybal, Calif. 30	48	0	Bell, Calif. 28	15	40
Ryan, N.Y. 20	57	1	Berry, S.D. 2 (9)	4	91
St. Germain, R.I. 1	58	0	Betts, Ohio 8	6	90
Satterfield, Va. 3	3	35	Biester, Pa. 8	13	12
Scheuer, N.Y. 21	35	0	Blackburn, Ga. 4	3	21
Shipley, Ill. 23	57	10	Bow, Ohio 16	6	83
Sikes, Fla. 1	35	65	Bray, Ind. 6	19	75
Sisk, Calif. 16	80	3	Brock, Tenn. 3 (5)	1	45
Slack, W.Va. 3	61	9	Broomfield, Mich. 18	25	57
Smith, Iowa 5	63	4	Brotzman, Colo. 2	8	27
Staggers, W.Va. 2	94	6	Brown, Ohio 7	6	20

House Republicans (cont'd)	R	W		R	W
Brown, Mich. 3	11	13	Gubser, Calif. 10	18	74
Broyhill, N.C. 10	2	47	Gude, Md. 8	20	4
Broyhill, Va. 10	10	83	Hall, Mo. 7	1	57
Buchanan, Ala. 6	2	36	Halpern, N.Y. 6	59	9
Burke, Fla. 10	3	22	Hammerschmidt, Ark. 3	2	23
Burton, Utah 1 **(4)**	7	38	Hansen, Idaho 2	7	27
Bush, Tex. 7 **(4)**	1	21	Harsha, Ohio 6	7	52
Button, N.Y. 29 **(2)**	21	4	Harvey, Mich. 8	13	46
Byrnes, Wis. 8	9	93	Hastings, N.Y. 38	2	8
Camp, Okla. 6	1	23	Heckler, Mass. 10	16	7
Carter, Ky. 5	9	27	Hogan, Md. 5	3	9
Cederberg, Mich. 10	5	87	Horton, N.Y. 36	39	10
Chamberlain, Mich. 6	16	66	Hosmer, Calif. 32	19	74
Clancy, Ohio 2	4	54	Hunt, N.J. 1	5	20
Clausen, Calif. 1	5	41	Hutchinson, Mich. 4	0	48
Clawson, Calif. 23	7	38	Johnson, Pa. 23	2	42
Cleveland, N.H. 2	10	38	Jonas, N.C. 9	3	91
Collier, Ill. 10	7	76	Keith, Mass. 12	19	49
Collins, Tex. 3	1	11	King, N.Y. 30	3	55
Conable, N.Y. 37	5	32	Kleppe, N.D. 2 **(4)**	3	21
Conte, Mass. 1	37	33	Kuykendall, Tenn. 9	3	21
Corbett, Pa. 18 **(10)**	67	35	Kyl, Iowa 4	10	44
Coughlin, Pa. 13	5	7	Landgrebe, Ind. 2	1	11
Cowger, Ky. 3 **(2)**	11	12	Langen, Minn. 7 **(2)**	3	67
Cramer, Fla. 8 **(4)**	3	80	Latta, Ohio 5	10	59
Crane, Ill. 13	0	7	Lloyd, Utah 2	4	30
Cunningham, Neb. 2 **(1)**	20	59	Lujan, N.M. 1	3	7
Davis, Wis. 9	2	55	Lukens, Ohio 24 **(6)**	4	18
Dellenback, Ore. 4	10	15	MacGregor, Minn. 3 **(4)**	11	46
Denney, Neb. 1 **(9)**	0	24	Mailliard, Calif. 6	37	54
Dennis, Ind. 10	1	11	Martin, Neb. 3	4	55
Derwinski, Ill. 4	3	65	Mathias, Calif. 18	6	18
Devine, Ohio 12	5	64	May, Wash. 4 **(2)**	6	63
Dickinson, Ala. 2	0	38	Mayne, Iowa 6	1	23
Duncan, Tenn. 2	6	32	McClory, Ill. 12	11	37
Dwyer, N.J. 12	50	32	McCloskey, Calif. 11	8	8
Edwards, Ala. 1	0	37	McClure, Idaho 1	1	22
Erlenborn, Ill. 14	2	33	McCulloch, Ohio 4	14	85
Esch, Mich. 2	10	13	McDade, Pa. 10	33	16
Eshleman, Pa. 16	2	22	McDonald, Mich. 19	10	14
Findley, Ill. 20	6	53	McEwen, N.Y. 31	3	33
Fish, N.Y. 28	5	7	McKneally, N.Y. 27 **(2)**	5	7
Ford, Mich. 5	3	85	Meskill, Conn. 6 **(8)**	11	11
Foreman, N.M. 2 **(2)**	3	20	Michel, Ill. 18	16	67
Frelinghuysen, N.J. 5	27	68	Miller, Ohio 10	3	22
Frey, Fla. 5	0	10	Minshall, Ohio 23	10	76
Fulton, Pa. 27 **(10)**	69	31	Mize, Kan. 2 **(2)**	7	30
Goldwater, Calif. 27	1	11	Mizell, N.C. 5	1	11
Goodling, Pa. 19	1	44	Morse, Mass. 5	34	23
Gross, Iowa 3	15	86	Morton, Md. 1 **(9)**	8	39
Grover, N.Y. 2	10	37	Mosher, Ohio 13	21	38

House Republicans (cont'd)	R	W		R	W
Myers, Ind. 7	3	22	Skubitz, Kan. 5	5	44
Nelson, Minn. 2	5	62	Smith, Calif. 20	4	78
O'Konski, Wis. 10	68	22	Smith, N.Y. 40	6	31
Pelly, Wash. 1	31	60	Snyder, Ky. 4	7	28
Pettis, Calif. 33	9	16	Springer, Ill. 22	15	77
Pirnie, N.Y. 32	23	44	Stafford, Vt. AL (11)	25	35
Poff, Va. 6	5	90	Stanton, Ohio 11	10	27
Pollock, Alaska AL (6)	10	10	Steiger, Ariz. 3	0	25
Price, Tex. 18	0	25	Steiger, Wis. 6	8	17
Quie, Minn. 1	12	59	Taft, Ohio 1 (5)	9	25
Quillen, Tenn. 1	5	43	Talcott, Calif. 12	6	43
Railsback, Ill. 19	11	12	Teague, Calif. 13	8	76
Reid, Ill. 15 (9)	2	46	Thompson, Ga. 5	2	21
Reid, N.Y. 26	41	8	Thomson, Wis. 3	4	56
Reifel, S.D. 1 (9)	9	49	Vander Jagt, Mich. 9	8	16
Rhodes, Ariz. 1	7	86	Wampler, Va. 9	6	26
Riegle, Mich. 7	15	9	Watson, S.C. 2 (7)	2	43
Robison, N.Y. 33	16	56	Weicker, Conn. 4 (5)	7	4
Roth, Del. AL (5)	3	21	Whalen, Ohio 3	19	5
Roudebush, Ind. 5 (4)	5	52	Whalley, Pa. 12	8	46
Rousselot, Calif. 24	0	13	Whitehurst, Va. 2	5	7
Ruppe, Mich. 11	15	10	Widnall, N.J. 7	38	59
Ruth, N.C. 8	1	11	Wiggins, Calif. 25	2	21
Sandman, N.J. 2	7	16	Williams, Pa. 7	3	22
Saylor, Pa. 22	49	48	Wilson, Calif. 36	8	81
Schadeberg, Wis. 1 (2)	6	41	Winn, Kan. 3	3	22
Scherle, Iowa 7	4	19	Wold, Wyo. AL (4)	2	9
Schmitz, Calif. 35	0	2	Wyatt, Ore. 1	11	26
Schneebeli, Pa. 17	6	56	Wydler, N.Y. 4	19	29
Schwengel, Iowa 1	25	48	Wylie, Ohio 15	3	21
Scott, Va. 8	1	24	Wyman, N.H. 1	4	32
Sebelius, Kan. 1	1	11	Zion, Ind. 8	4	19
Shriver, Kan. 4	8	50	Zwach, Minn. 6	11	13

(1)   Defeated in House primary, 1970.
(2)   Defeated November 3, 1970, in House election.
(3)   Defeated in Senate primary, 1970.
(4)   Defeated November 3, 1970, in Senate election.
(5)   Elected to Senate November 3, 1970.
(6)   Defeated in gubernatorial primary, 1970.
(7)   Defeated November 3, 1970, in gubernatorial election.
(8)   Elected Governor, November 3, 1970.
(9)   resigned or retired
(10) deceased
(11) Appointed September 16, 1971, by Gov. Deane C. Davis, R, as interim replacement for the late Winston L. Prouty, R, pending a special primary and general election.

Source: COPE, National Journal

5

Business-Industry Political Action Committee

JONATHAN COTTIN

The Business-Industry Political Action Committee is dedicated to the principle that Congress governs best when controlled by lawmakers with a pro-business bias. Toward this end, BIPAC has invested more than $1 million in House and Senate campaigns since the organization was founded in 1963 by high officials in the National Association of Manufacturers.

The infusion of campaign cash from an organized, business-oriented conduit has largely benefited Republican incumbents facing tough opponents, although some Democrats, mostly in the South, have been BIPAC beneficiaries. Thus, many Republicans are enthusiastic about the organization. And even BIPAC's ideological adversary, the AFL-CIO's Committee on Political Education (COPE), acknowledges that in its eight years the organization has become an effective tool for the business community. BIPAC owes its existence to COPE, which has been giving money to labor-oriented candidates since 1955. "The idea was to find a counterpart to COPE," explains Robert L. Humphrey, BIPAC president. Humphrey, recalling the adversary many businessmen saw in COPE, said that in the early 1960s, "both Houses of Congress were dominated by labor."

At the National Association of Manufacturers (NAM), where Humphrey was director of public affairs, and at the U.S. Chamber of Commerce, many of the politically aware officers began to discuss a COPE alternative as early as 1958, recalled Jay Royen, manager of the NAM's Washington news bureau and former assistant to the executive vice president at NAM. Royen said the principal lobbyists within the two groups for a separate funding organization were Arthur H. Motley, former chamber president who now heads Parade Publications Inc., and Archie K. Davis, a former NAM board member, now chamber president (1971-72) and a member of BIPAC's board of directors. Motley said R. Downs Poindexter, a member of NAM's policy committees and current chairman of BIPAC, also pushed for a financial political participation unit.

Discussions about a joint NAM-chamber venture went on for some time. But chamber leaders decided against combining with NAM, apparently for several reasons. Former chamber President Motley and Arch N. Booth, current executive vice president of the organization, give different reasons for the chamber's veto of the merged effort. Motley said the chamber opposed participation because the idea was "directly competitive" with a program it was already conducting to encourage business executives to take part in local political contests.

Booth explains his group's refusal to team up with NAM this way: "It wasn't that we didn't want to go in with NAM. The lawyers on our board of directors were watching our tax-exempt status." Booth said chamber counsel advised against an affiliation in BIPAC to protect the organization's tax-exempt status. "I had the feeling the tax lawyers knew more than I did," said Booth. He added that the chamber is "a little more cautious" than NAM. But he noted that "many members of the chamber are quite active" in BIPAC. (A cross-check of chamber and NAM board members and officials with BIPAC's list of board members shows that 23 members of the BIPAC board are directors or high officials in the NAM. Only 2 chamber officials are on the BIPAC board.)

NAM officials decided to move ahead despite the chamber's rejection. Humphrey, who had been national director of public affairs at NAM since 1951, was asked to develop a blueprint for a campaign funding unit. An easygoing Texan who thrives on politics, Humphrey, then based in Washington, consulted with business and political leaders around the country, developed a plan of operation and presented a report to NAM's board. Official endorsement of the project followed quickly.

With a cash advance from NAM, the organization called Business-Industry Political Action Committee opened its doors August 4, 1963. First located at 14 East 49th St., in New York, the operation "started with some borrowed furniture in an anteroom," said Humphrey. In the beginning, former Rep. Laurie C. Battle, D-Ala. (1947-55), served as acting director while Humphrey returned briefly to his Washington assignment with NAM. Battle said the understanding was that he would only serve temporarily in the post. Now chief counsel to the House Rules Committee, Battle left BIPAC in October 1963 when Humphrey returned to New York to work full-time with the fledgling organization.

BIPAC's first chairman was Kenton R. Cravens of St. Louis, board chairman of Eagle Rubber Company and a director of the American Zinc Company. Cravens is now one of the organization's nine regional vice chairmen. In announcing BIPAC's creation, Cravens told a news conference August 4, 1963, that the group was "not affiliated with any political party." He stressed that it was "completely independent and not a part of any other organization." A brochure issued at the news conference and directed to "American management" described BIPAC as "the new force in politics." It set as its goal the protection of "the principle of individual freedom," and pledged to "represent the competitive, free enterprise viewpoint."

On August 8, four days after the announcement, BIPAC obtained formal backing of the NAM, whose staff and officers had been intimately involved with plans to build the funding unit. Werner P. Gullander, NAM president, told a service club luncheon in New York his organization supported BIPAC "not because we want business to dominate politics, but because we don't want the nation's politics and policies to be dominated by those who apparently do not understand the needs of our free economy." Gullander maintained that the business community had been slow to move on the political front. He said business should be "doing the things which are necessary if sound economics are to find expression in government actions." He blamed "over-regulation, over-investigation and over-control" by the federal government for impeding economic growth.

Financed initially with seed money from NAM, the BIPAC "staff" consisted of one secretary and the president. In 1966, BIPAC moved from its first headquarters to a larger suite of offices at 485 Madison Ave., in the heart of midtown Manhattan. As the organization matured and developed credibility in the business community, the need to remain in America's financial capital diminished. Thus, in September 1970, BIPAC shifted its headquarters to 1747 Pennsylvania Ave. NW, in Washington, less than a block from the White House.

Humphrey, who feels at home with the politicians in the nation's capital, says there are no plans to change the emphasis of the organization and declares that no lobbying will be done. New York, says Humphrey, "was a better place to start" because it is home to many of the nation's biggest companies. But BIPAC wanted to be nearer its beneficiaries. Humphrey observed that being in New York made BIPAC "look more like a fund-raising organization than a political organization." BIPAC combines elements of both, but Humphrey wanted greater emphasis placed on the political.

A small staff—never more than eight including Humphrey—operates the Washington office. The permanent staff consists of the president, an assistant treasurer, an editorial director, a director of political education, a research assistant, a part-time consultant and two full-time secretaries. During peak periods, when an influx of donations is heavy, or when the membership lists need updating, Humphrey will add temporary staff—normally college students—to handle the paper work.

Humphrey, 64, had a varied career in the promotional field before arriving at the campaign funding organization. He was sales promotion director of the *Dallas News* (1930-35); national advertising manager of the *Fort Worth Press* (1935-37); director of sports and entertainment at the 1937 Pan Am Exposition in

Dallas; sales promotion director of the *Houston Chronicle* (1937-39); vice president and general manager of Associated Publishers Inc. (1939-46) in Dallas; manager of sales personnel in the oil well supply division of U.S. Steel Corporation (1946-51); and national director of public affairs of the National Association of Manufacturers (1951-63).

The consultant, Edward I. Maher, 68, former vice president and editor of *Liberty* magazine (1942-47), was vice president for public relations at NAM (1956-64) during Humphrey's years as NAM's public affairs director. Maher, who is now retired and working with BIPAC part-time, formerly operated a public relations firm and is a trustee of the West Side Savings Bank in New York.

BIPAC produces two publications—*Politics*, issued bimonthly, and *BIPAC Newsletter*, sent to all contributors (they number more than 10,000, according to Humphrey). *Politics* is available by subscription at $10 a year. Its production and distribution are financed by donations from corporation officials, which are sufficient for BIPAC to send copies of the publication to every member of the House and Senate, said Humphrey. The eight-page publication is an intelligence report on the political enemy camp. It also airs BIPAC philosophy. *Politics*, in its March-April 1970 edition:

- said that COPE was preparing new pamphlets and films which suggest that "COPE believes inflation and recession will be major issues this year and hopes to saddle the Administration and congressional conservatives with the blame."
- declared that "hardly a week goes by but that some new national shortcoming isn't discovered, usually by liberal politicians looking for headlines. However, little is heard of the steady progress being made in most areas."
- warned that "union political activity is expected to reach an all-time high this year, with more money and manpower than ever before devoted to getting out every possible pro-liberal vote for organized labor's congressional friends."

The *Newsletter* is more directly concerned with BIPAC's interest in the philosophy of Congress. Its June 1970 issue listed for all Members of the House and Senate the "ideological ratings given them by national political organizations, together with a report on how they voted on close issues on which conservatives and liberals were divided." Used as barometers to gauge the thinking of incumbents were ratings of their work by Americans for Constitutional Action (ACA), "a conservative group"; Americans for Democratic Action (ADA), a "liberal group"; National Farmers Union, "a liberal agricultural group"; and COPE. (The descriptions are BIPAC's.) *Newsletter* also keeps close track of the candidates given BIPAC money, reporting how they fared in primary and general elections.

BIPAC's steady growth and increased visibility in the business community result largely from Humphrey's missionary zeal. He estimates that he is on the road two-thirds of the time, making speeches, meeting with businessmen and traveling. Well-known in the business community across the country, Humphrey often receives last-minute invitations to speak about BIPAC and has compressed his presentation into a brief talk designed to acquaint his listeners with the organization and encourage participation. Humphrey also ad-libs a run-down on "the political situation" during his talks. Humphrey considers an important part of the BIPAC operation to be his frequent personal, written and telephone contacts with businessmen and party leaders. They exchange information about races and the political climate in various regions of the country. Humphrey believes his intelligence network is one of the most accurate in the nation.

BIPAC policy, the basis for Humphrey's operation, is charted by a 59-man board of directors. (See Table 5.1.) Most of the directors are high-ranking executives in companies of varying size. Twenty-five of the board members are high officials of the top 1,000 companies listed in a 1970 compilation by *Fortune*. The other 34 come from smaller firms.

Humphrey says BIPAC has made no concerted effort to enroll upper-echelon executives from large firms as BIPAC directors. "We've only called on a few big companies," he said. The BIPAC president described recruitment of support from officials in large companies as a "slow process." Humphrey said the major companies were not snubbing BIPAC. "Business in particular accepts things rather slowly. They like to identify themselves with what they do," he explained. As "people of one company talk to people of other companies," more large firms will be represented on BIPAC's board, he predicted. Whatever the reason, only five of the firms on *Fortune* magazine's list of the 100 largest U.S. companies have representatives on BIPAC's policy-making board of directors. They are Gulf Oil Corporation, General Foods Corporation, Humble Oil and Refining Company (a subsidiary of Standard Oil of New Jersey), Phillips Petroleum Company and Republic Steel Corporation.

BIPAC directors, with a clear interest in politics, nevertheless steer away from involvement in the government, Humphrey said. To avoid "controversy," he said, none has served in any national Administration since BIPAC was organized. (One director, Robert B. Anderson, had served in the Eisenhower Cabinet as Treasury Secretary in 1957-61.)

The BIPAC board consists of nine regional vice chairmen, nine directors at large and 38 state directors, plus the chairman, president and secretary-treasurer. An executive committee, elected by the board, handles important policy decisions that arise between the annual meetings of the full board. A legal committee, which advises on law and tax matters, is also part of the board operation. The remaining committee is its most important: the Congressional Candidate Review Committee, which sifts reports on candidates and requests for assistance, and decides where the money will be dispatched. Its six members are elected at the board's annual meeting.

To protect its six-man candidate selection committee from money-hungry office-seekers, BIPAC keeps the membership's identity a secret. Humphrey will only say that the unit is composed of three Democrats and three Republicans. The candidate selection system is simple but offers ample checks and balances to protect the organization from rash judgments. Normally, a member of the board initiates the request for assistance to a candidate. In at least one case, a BIPAC official first sounded out a candidate on whether he would like to be considered for some BIPAC cash. Charles Fentress, former press assistant to Sen. Marlow W. Cook, R-Ky., said that in 1968 Cook's finance committee heard from the organization and expressed interest in an injection of BIPAC money. The response was affirmative. Cook received $3,500 from the group.

Once BIPAC receives oral or written requests for aid, the Washington office checks the candidate to determine his stand on economic issues, the degree of his support in the local business community and his potential for winning. Humphrey draws on his intelligence network to make these determinations. He reports his findings to the candidate review committee, which decides whom to support, and how much. The state director or regional vice chairman who made the initial request is then told of the decision. A check is forwarded to the BIPAC member who asked for the money, and he turns it over to the candidate or his campaign finance committee representative. The money is donated "on behalf of the businessmen of the state and nation, and to be used for the purposes for which it is requested," says a BIPAC memorandum. As insurance, the organization asks that "the candidate direct a brief letter to the BIPAC office . . . indicating that the contribution was received." BIPAC forbids its own representatives from announcing the cash awards. However, a policy statement makes it clear "this does not prevent the candidate himself indicating he has received BIPAC support if he feels this will help his campaign."

BIPAC uses its cash on races in which the victor in the previous contest picked up less than 55 per cent of the vote. Thus, the organization's money is rarely funneled into campaigns in which a candidate favored by BIPAC is the heavy favorite or underdog. "We only go where our money may tip the scales," says Humphrey. Also, he reported, if there exists an irreconcilable rift among local BIPAC advisers over who is to be supported, "we stay out of it."

BIPAC pumps its money solely into House and Senate races.

It has no plans to widen its funding program to include state government contests or Presidential races. Humphrey maintains that "the job to be done is in the House and the Senate." This is the reason BIPAC sees no need to do any lobbying on Capitol Hill. "If you get the right group down there, you don't have to lobby," says consultant Maher. As Humphrey tells businessmen: "BIPAC is not a lobbying organization or pressure group. It does not take stands on legislative issues. It does not exact any pledges in return for its support nor does it seek legislative favors from candidates after they are elected."

BIPAC's selection of candidates in 1968 and 1970 indicates a clear preference for Republicans over Democrats. In the 1968 Senate elections, BIPAC supported 12 Republicans who won but no Democrats. In the House, 70 Republicans were elected with BIPAC support; only eight of the Democrats elected were awarded money from the organization. On the losing side, only one Democrat obtained a BIPAC contribution in House contests, while 47 Republicans picked up BIPAC cash. In the Senate, no Democratic losers were supported in 1968, and eight defeated Republicans were beneficiaries. In addition, BIPAC money helped 13 of 23 endorsed House and Senate primary candidates to victory.

In the 1970 Senate elections, BIPAC contributed to the victorious campaigns of eight Republicans but no Democrats. Eight Republican beneficiaries were defeated. In the House, 61 of 97 Republicans supported were elected and all 10 of the Democratic candidates receiving BIPAC money won. In the primary elections, 10 House and Senate Democratic candidates, all winners, obtained BIPAC donations. (See Tables 5.2 and 5.3.)

Ideologically, most BIPAC recipients score considerably higher on the ACA cumulative rating than they do with COPE. ACA says its ratings are based on votes "for safeguarding the God-given rights of the individual and promoting sound economic growth by strengthening constitutional government against 'group morality,' a socialized economy and centralization of government power." An examination of 11 BIPAC-supported Senate winners in 1968 shows six with ACA averages higher than their COPE scores. Five scored better with COPE. On the House side, all eight Democrats supported by the organization had higher ACA ratings, while 59 of 68 Republicans did better with ACA.

The Consumer Federation of America (CFA), a group dedicated to consumer protection action, also rated the House Members. Based on their votes from 1967 through 1969 on 21 issues that "intimately involve consumers," the average CFA rating for all House Members was 66.8 per cent while the 78 BIPAC-endorsed Members averaged 49.9 per cent. (The numerical score is the percentage of the time a Member voted "right," according to CFA, out of the 21 selected votes. CFA lists only a Members "right" and "wrong" votes. The numerical scores were applied by *National Journal* for purposes of comparison. The same numerical formula is used by such organizations as ACA and COPE in developing their ratings.) (See Table 5.2.)

Interpreting his organization's support of some candidates with higher COPE ratings, consultant Maher said their opponents in many cases were more "radical" than the men supported by BIPAC. Thus, he said, Sen. Richard S. Schweiker, R-Pa., who had a 60 COPE score compared to a 19 from ACA, was preferable to the man he unseated in 1968, Sen. Joseph S. Clark, D (1957-69). Maher conceded some lawmakers who had BIPAC support in 1968 appeared to be moving away from the organization's principles. This caused some "shock" at BIPAC, he said. One surprise, he said, was Sen. Charles McC. Mathias Jr., R-Md., who defeated Sen. Daniel B. Brewster, D (1963-69).

BIPAC's track record since it began supporting candidates indicates substantial success. In the 1964 general elections, 10 of BIPAC's 12 Senate contestants and 61 of its 82 House choices were elected. In 1966, BIPAC candidates won 10 of 16 primary races, 10 of 12 Senate races and 71 of 94 House contests. In 1968, BIPAC candidates won 13 of 23 primaries, 12 of 20 Senate races and 78 of 126 House campaigns. In the 1970 elections, BIPAC gave money to 10 primary contestants, all of whom won; 10 of the 18 Senate candidates supported by BIPAC won and 71 of its 107 House candidates were elected. The victory rate went up from 60.9 per cent in 1968 to 67.4 per cent in

1970. The total number of victories decreased from 103 to 91, reflecting a decrease in the number of candidates receiving BIPAC support—from 169 in 1968 to 135 in 1970.

Although BIPAC pumps considerable cash into House and Senate campaigns, its donation record shows few heavy contributors. Humphrey estimated that the average individual contribution was $24.50 in 1969 and $24 in 1970. He predicted the average donation will be about the same in 1972. Only 142 individuals gave $100 or more to BIPAC throughout 1969, according to records on file with the Clerk of the House of Representatives. Of the 142, most were $100 each and only two were $1,000 gifts (from BIPAC Chairman Poindexter and Norman V. Kinsey of Shreveport, La.). In 1970, BIPAC received 109 contributions of $100 or more and six donations of $1,000. BIPAC encourages membership donations of $99 and less. Those who give less than $100 are not required by the Corrupt Practices Act to have their names listed with the House clerk. Most BIPAC subscribers prefer anonymity.

BIPAC has three annual membership classifications: sustaining member for $99, supporting member for $25, and regular member for $10. Membership dues—the funds used for political campaigns—are not tax deductible, BIPAC tells its subscribers. They go into a special bank account maintained for the organization's Political Action Division. However, BIPAC's other major division, Political Education, also has its own bank account and contributions to it are tax deductible, the organization's brochures say. The Political Education fund is used to finance the office operation—about $200,000 a year.

The businessman's group has established a divisional structure allowing it the flexibility to comply with federal regulations governing political action organizations. Tax-deductible gifts to the Political Education fund are not used to operate the office in the three-month period before every election. During that period, the entire BIPAC operation—salaries, rental and other overhead—is switched from the education division bank account to the political division fund. "We comply to the letter

of the law, not only the spirit," says Humphrey. Since the office staff will get involved in political campaigns before the
election, the transfer of funding responsibilities protects
BIPAC against charges of using tax-deductible contributions for
direct political action, BIPAC strategists believe. Humphrey
said he had no idea if other campaign funding groups follow a
similar practice, but he added: "I hope they are. I would encourage them to."

BIPAC's campaign spending has grown with the organization's increased visibility in the business community. Records
on file with the House clerk show it spent $203,283 in 1964,
$294,000 in 1966, $510,200 in 1968 and $461,000 in 1970 in direct
contributions to candidates. In election years, BIPAC spends
more than it earns, since donations are made for each campaign over a two-year cycle. In 1968, expenditures for candidate support and office operations prior to the election totalled $567,684.45; net receipts were only $360,303.96. However,
during 1967, the organization obtained $220,437 but spent only
$634, leaving more than enough over the two-year period to
finance its candidates in the 1968 elections. In the 1970 election year, BIPAC reported expenditures totaling $539,156.62;
net receipts were $302,553.54. Humphrey says it is difficult to
determine the number of BIPAC members because the total
fluctuates from year to year. He estimates there are more than
10,000. More members are recorded in election years than in
off years.

To avoid any possible clashes with the two major political
parties over money, BIPAC makes it clear it has no desire to dry
up cash sources for the national parties. With both parties under
pressure to help candidates with additional money, BIPAC tells
its subscribers: "A BIPAC membership is a supplement to, not
a substitute for, giving to the party and the individual candidate. BIPAC provides additional financial assistance to congressional candidates of both parties throughout the nation."

BIPAC's importance as a campaign funding tool increases as
the cost of running for office escalates. The Twentieth Century

Fund Task Force on Financing Congressional Campaigns reported in a 1970 study: "The cost of an effective campaign for Congress is rising rapidly. Today a competitive campaign for a House seat can cost each side more than $100,000, while a Senate contest can cost each campaigner a minimum of $250,000 even in a relatively small state." The task-force survey found that "with the exception of 'safe' districts, successful candidates for Congress must either be wealthy or have access to large sums of money. Challengers without such resources do run for Congress. Most lose."

Herbert E. Alexander, former chairman of President Kennedy's Commission on Campaign Costs and an authority on campaign financing, told a House Commerce subcommittee June 4, 1970, that "politics is not overpriced. It is underfinanced." Alexander, now director of Citizens' Research Foundation in Princeton, N.J., told the Subcommittee on Communications and Power that in all campaigns during 1968 about $300 million was spent. He said that this was 50 per cent more than the 1964 total and twice the cost of 1952.

The New York Times, in an editorial August 6, 1963, said formation of BIPAC "will undoubtedly be welcomed by many Members of Congress, faced as they are by the ever-rising costs of political campaigns." The newspaper continued: "If more Americans are stimulated to take an active interest in politics, then the new committee should be welcomed by everyone. Although the principles enunciated in the first announcement sound as though the committee probably would be more 'bipartisan' toward Republicans than Democrats—it will support candidates pledged to 'free, private and competitive enterprise,' it says—that also should be welcomed in a democratic society. Organized labor long has had its Committee on Political Education, which generally has supported Democrats against Republicans."

The Times' editorial sparked a letter to the newspaper the following August 19 from a labor official who termed "naive and mistaken" the view that before BIPAC's creation, business had nothing to match COPE. "Organized industry, big business, has always been in politics," wrote Louis Hollander, secretary-treasurer of the New York State AFL-CIO and chairman of

New York State COPE. Hollander also took issue with BIPAC's assertion of bipartisanship, arguing: "It can be no secret to *The New York Times* that there is a third party in this Congress — Dixiecrats of the South and Republicans of the North and of the West who make up the third party alliance in Congress — to block all liberal legislation for the good of the community as a whole. BIPAC will obviously support this alliance now existing in Congress."

At the Republican National Committee, BIPAC commanded considerable respect from former GOP Chairman Rogers C. B. Morton (1969-71), a House Member from Maryland who needed no help from BIPAC in his own campaign. Morton, who resigned from the House in 1971 to become Interior Secretary, said: "I believe BIPAC has an important place in the campaign processes. BIPAC provides individuals with a *more learned way of expressing* preference for party or candidate of their choice." (Italics are Morton's.) Lyn Nofziger, the RNC's deputy national chairman for communications, says the committee considers BIPAC "a welcome addition to the political scene, effective and doing a good job." Lawrence F. O'Brien, chairman of the Democratic National Committee, said he and his staff at the committee have had little communication with BIPAC. But O'Brien added: "If BIPAC helps make business-men more interested in the political process and more in-volved, then it serves a worthwhile purpose. We'd like the organization to have more contact with us."

At the national office of COPE, there is some admiration for the business committee. Ben Albert, publications director, said BIPAC is "obviously successful in raising money." In the Senate and House, many BIPAC beneficiaries profess to have little knowledge about the group. Sen. J. Glenn Beall Jr., R-Md., then a Member of the House (1969-71), said he knew nothing about the organization, had "never heard from them" since taking office, but thought he remembered his campaign com-mittee receiving a donation from the organization. BIPAC gave him $2,000 in 1968. (BIPAC also contributed $5,000 to Beall's 1970 Senate campaign.) Sen. Cook, who received $3,500 from BIPAC in 1968, said through a spokesman he knew nothing at all about the organization.

Rep. Lawrence J. Hogan, R-Md., was an exception. He said he knew about the committee. "I know they're business-oriented," he said. "Their job is to serve as a conduit from business and industry for contributions to people who are sympathetic to business and industry," said Hogan. He was given $2,000 in the 1968 elections and $2,500 in 1970. Sen. Wallace F. Bennett, R-Utah, a member of the Senate Ethics Committee, said he knew of BIPAC before coming to the Senate because he was a businessman. During his 1968 campaign, enriched with a $5,000 BIPAC donation, however, he said he "made it my business not to know what went on." Because of his political views, Bennett told *National Journal,* "I imagine I would be the candidate" to pick up money from the committee. Bennett said he was grateful for the BIPAC contribution. "Anybody who comes along with $10 — he's a friend," said the Utah Republican.

Although BIPAC went into the 1970 general elections with an expanded treasury, it suffered from low recognition on Capitol Hill and elsewhere among national politicians. However, BIPAC director Motley reported that some of the organization's 1970 beneficiaries used their BIPAC endorsements to stimulate local giving from businessmen who knew about the organization. If BIPAC candidates use the committee backing properly, Motley said, "it can produce more money." He said the committee candidates who make this extra fund-raising effort argue to local members of the commercial community that since BIPAC is the "voice of business," they should contribute to one of their own.

Despite Motley's optimism, BIPAC is still a long way from matching COPE's cash clout. COPE gave more than $1 million in 1968 for labor supported candidates and about $1 million in 1970, Albert said. Federal law prohibits political action groups from giving more than $3 million a year. COPE's Albert says he doubts if BIPAC will reach the limit in the foreseeable future because there is "so much competition for the dollar" among many groups.

Installed in Washington for one year, BIPAC President

Humphrey believes his organization has kept closer track of what its beneficiaries are doing and is beginning to win more political attention. "It's better to be here where the action is now that we are established," Humphrey said. "I think BIPAC's members feel we have a better grasp of what's going on and we're able to do a better job for our people."

Table 5.1 BIPAC Directors

The Business-Industry Political Action Committee's board of directors consists of three officers, nine regional vice chairmen, nine directors at large and 38 state directors:

R. Downs Poindexter, chairman. President, Superior Iron Works & Supply Company Inc., Shreveport, La.
Robert L. Humphrey, president.
Richard A. Young, secretary-treasurer. President, Bemis Company Inc., Minneapolis, Minn.

Regional vice chairmen

Kenton R. Cravens, chairman, Eagle Rubber Company, St. Louis, Mo.
Archie K. Davis, chairman, Wachovia Bank & Trust Company, Winston-Salem, N.C.
Joseph B. Lanterman, chairman, Amsted Industries Inc., Chicago, Ill.
Oral L. Luper, vice president and director, Humble Oil and Refining Company, Houston, Tex.
Harold S. Mohler, president, Hershey Foods Corporation, Hershey, Pa.
Glenn E. Nielson, chairman, Husky Oil Company, Cody, Wyo.
Kinsey M. Robinson, chairman, Washington Water Power Company, Spokane, Wash.
James W. Sikes, chairman, Florida Tile Industries Inc., Lakeland, Fla.
Robert F. Smith, senior vice president, Wells Fargo Bank, San Francisco, Calif.

Directors at large

Robert B. Anderson, attorney, New York, N.Y. Treasury Secretary (1957-61).

J. Robert Fluor, chairman, The Fluor Corporation Ltd., Los Angeles, Calif.
Paul W. Kayser, partner, Golightly & Company International Inc., New York, N.Y.
W. W. Keeler, chairman, Phillips Petroleum Company, Bartlesville, Okla.
H. C. Lumb, vice president, Republic Steel Corporation, Cleveland, Ohio.
Arthur H. Motley, president, Parade Publications Inc., New York, N.Y.
David W. Richmond, lawyer, partner, Miller & Chevalier, Washington, D.C.
Royce H. Savage, retired director, Gulf Oil Corporation, Pittsburgh, Pa.
H. A. True, partner, True Drilling Company, Casper, Wyo.

State directors

Olof V. Anderson, president and treasurer, Anson Inc., Providence, R.I.
John H. Batten, president, Twin Disc Inc., Racine, Wis.
Byron V. Boone, president, *Tulsa World*, Tulsa, Okla.
James M. Boyd, vice president, Southwest Forest Industries, Phoenix, Ariz.
Arthur P. Burris, chairman, Turbodyne Corporation, Minneapolis, Minn.
H. Z. Carter, president, Avondale Shipyards Inc., New Orleans, La.
James Cashman Jr., president

Cashman Enterprises, Las Vegas, Nev.
James A. Chapman Jr., president, Inman Mills, Inman, S.C.
Herbert M. Cleaves, senior vice president, General Foods Corporation, White Plains, N.Y.
Martin J. Condon III, president, Conwood Corporation, Memphis, Tenn.
William L. Davis, vice chairman, Emerson Electric Company, St. Louis, Mo.
E. M. deWindt, chairman, Eaton, Yale & Towne Inc., Cleveland, Ohio.
Frank D. Gorham, president, Pubco Petroleum Corporation, Albuquerque, N.M.
W. J. Holman Jr., director, Johnson & Johnson, New Brunswick, N.J.
Cass S. Hough, president, Daisy/Heddon Division, Victor Comptometer Corporation, Rogers, Ark.
J. R. L. Johnson Jr., vice president, Hercules Inc., Wilmington, Del.
Leon C. Jones, president, Food Division J. R. Simlot Company, Caldwell, Idaho.
Milton L. Kapp, chairman, Interstate Power Company, Dubuque, Iowa.
Jack P. Keith, president, First National Bank, West Point, Ga.
Kenneth C. Kellar, vice president and chief counsel, Homestake Mining Company, Lead, S.D.
Herman W. Lay, chairman, PepsiCo Inc., Dallas, Tex.
William C. Liedtke Jr., president and director, Pennzoil United Inc., Houston, Tex.
Earl T. Luff, president, Lincoln Steel Corporation, Lincoln, Neb.
W. P. McMullan Jr., president, Deposit, Guaranty National Bank, Jackson, Miss.
J. Clifford Miller Jr., president, Miller Manufacturing Company Inc., Richmond, Va.
Merle E. Minks, general counsel, Gulf Oil Corporation, Pittsburgh, Pa.
E. A. Morris, chairman, Blue Bell Inc., Greensboro, N.C.
C. Neil Norgren, president, C.A. Norgren Company, Littleton, Colo.
George W. O'Connor, president and director, Montana Power Company, Butte , Mont.
Bruce F. Olson, chairman, Sundstrand Corporation, Rockford, Ill.
Burt F. Raynes, chairman and chief executive officer, Rohr Corporation, Chula Vista, Calif.
E. A. Simonson, president, Fargo Foundry Steel & Manufacturing Company, Fargo, N.D.
Joseph T. Simpson, chairman, Harsco Corporation, Harrisburg, Pa.
Harold J. Steele, president, First Security Bank of Utah, Salt Lake City, Utah.
Oliver L. Stone, vice president and general counsel, Shell Oil Company, New York, N.Y.
J. P. Van Winkle Jr., president, Stitzel Weller Distillery, Louisville, Ky.
Anthony E. Wallace, president, Connecticut Light & Power Company, Hartford, Conn.
Robert C. Warren, president, Cascade Corporation, Portland, Ore.

Table 5.2   BIPAC's Beneficiaries, 1968

In 1968, the Business-Industry Political Action Committee contributed to the victorious campaigns of 12 Senate Republicans, 70 House Republicans and eight House Democrats. One of the Senators, Everett M. Dirksen of Illinois (1951-69), has since died. Two of the winning Republican House Members— Edwin Reinecke of California (1965-69) and James F. Battin of Montana (1961-69)—have resigned. Listed below are the remaining 87 winners. (In the general election, BIPAC also endorsed 56 losers, who are not listed.) Included in the summary are the BIPAC funds received by each winning candidate, with his ideological ratings by Americans for Constitutional Action (ACA), the AFL-CIO's Committee on Political Education (COPE) and, for House winners, the Consumer Federation of America (CFA).

ACA and COPE ratings are cumulative through the first session of the 91st Congress (1969). (More recent ratings are listed in Tables 2.3 and 4.3.) The CFA tabulated Members' "right" and "wrong" votes on consumer protection legislation from 1967-69. For comparison purposes, *National Journal* converted CFA's tabulation to a numerical score, using the same formula (percentage of "right" votes in a Member's total) used by ACA, COPE and others. Except where noted, Members listed were serving in the first session of the 92nd Congress as of November 1, 1971.

House Republicans	Donation	ACA	COPE	CFA
Adair, Ind. **(1)**	$2,000	89	13	47
Beall, Md. **(3)**	2,000	47	70	42
Blackburn, Ga.	2,000	88	20	35
Bow, Ohio	2,000	91	9	41
Brotzman, Colo.	5,000	75	30	57
Brown, Mich.	2,000	66	55	41
Broyhill, Va.	2,000	87	13	57
Buchanan, Ala.	500	75	20	42
Burke, Fla.	500	97	18	38
Camp, Okla.	2,500	73	10	42
Cowger, Ky. **(1)**	2,000	70	50	33
Dellenback, Ore.	2,500	58	48	44
Denney, Neb. **(7)**	2,500	92	5	50
Dennis, Ind.	500	81	10	42
Dickinson, Ala.	3,500	93	0	44
Esch, Mich.	2,500	44	50	70
Fish, N.Y.	2,500	29	80	85
Foreman, N.M. **(1)**	2,000	96	10	40
Frey, Fla.	3,000	94	20	42
Goodling, Pa.	2,000	91	5	45
Gross, Iowa	1,750	97	15	35
Hammerschmidt, Ark.	4,000	79	9	42
Hansen, Idaho	1,000	35	60	60
Heckler, Mass.	2,000	38	20	70
Hogan, Md.	2,000	65	30	66
Hunt, N.J.	3,500	89	22	50
King, N.Y.	500	90	4	36
Kleppe, N.D. **(2)**	4,000	82	22	52
Kuykendall, Tenn.	3,000	71	11	44
Kyl, Iowa	2,000	88	18	44
Landgrebe, Ind.	2,000	88	6	40
Lloyd, Utah	2,500	77	12	50
Lujan, N.M.	2,000	76	44	40
Mathias, Calif.	2,000	71	27	60

House Republicans *(cont'd)*	Donation	ACA	COPE	CFA
Mayne, Iowa	$1,000	70	14	57
McClure, Idaho	500	91	10	33
McDonald, Mich.	3,000	69	48	66
McKneally, N.Y. **(1)**	4,500	38	60	60
Meskill, Conn. **(6)**	2,000	73	48	61
Miller, Ohio	1,000	87	9	47
Minshall, Ohio	1,000	87	13	40
Myers, Ind.	750	91	13	42
Pettis, Calif.	2,000	79	30	62
Pollock, Alaska **(4)**	2,500	68	33	60
Railsback, Ill.	2,000	29	80	41
Riegle, Mich.	1,000	49	65	68
Roth, Del. **(3)**	2,500	82	18	57
Ruppe, Mich.	2,000	39	73	62
Sandman, N.J.	2,000	65	42	57
Schadeberg, Wis. **(1)**	2,500	82	40	52
Scherle, Iowa	1,000	97	9	26
Schwengel, Iowa	2,500	65	39	60
Scott, Va.	2,000	95	13	33
Sebelius, Kan.	1,000	86	11	50
Snyder, Ky.	2,000	93	21	40
Steiger, Ariz.	2,000	90	4	35
Taft, Ohio **(3)**	1,000	66	36	40
Thompson, Ga.	750	81	15	36
Wampler, Va.	2,000	83	23	55
Watson, S.C. **(5)**	1,000	89	4	50
Weicker, Conn. **(3)**	2,000	41	70	83
Whitehurst, Va.	2,000	67	30	80
Wiggins, Calif.	2,000	75	22	35
Wold, Wyo. **(2)**	3,000	69	22	50
Wylie, Ohio	2,000	73	40	50
Wyman, N.H.	2,000	80	12	66
Zion, Ind.	2,000	88	24	45
Zwach, Minn.	1,000	72	46	68

House Democrats

Daniel, Va.	1,500	94	20	42
Dorn, S.C.	2,000	76	16	60
Fisher, Tex.	1,500	79	11	50
Gettys, S.C.	750	57	14	68
Marsh, Va. **(7)**	2,500	87	6	38
Montgomery, Miss.	2,000	86	10	42
Rogers, Fla.	2,000	68	28	83
Satterfield, Va.	2,000	89	6	43

Senate

BIPAC-supported Senate winners, all Republicans, are listed with ACA and COPE ratings only. CFA did not rate all 100 Senators.

Senate *(cont'd)*	Donation	ACA	COPE
Bellmon, Okla.	$5,000	75	27
Bennett, Utah	5,000	85	3
Cook, Ky.	3,500	33	78
Cotton, N.H.	5,000	85	13
Dominick, Colo.	5,000	79	16
Goldwater, Ariz.	5,000	98	0
Gurney, Fla.	5,000	93	2
Mathias Jr., Md.	2,500	7	65
Packwood, Ore.	5,000	33	73
Saxbe, Ohio	3,000	27	63
Schweiker, Pa.	5,000	19	60

(1)   Defeated November 3, 1970, in House election.
(2)   Defeated November 3, 1970, in Senate election.
(3)   Elected to Senate November 3, 1970.
(4)   Defeated in gubernatorial primary, 1970.
(5)   Defeated November 3, 1970, in gubernatorial election.
(6)   Elected Governor, November 3, 1970.
(7)   resigned or retired

Source: **BIPAC,** *National Journal,* **Clerk of the House of Representatives**

Table 5.3   BIPAC's Beneficiaries, 1970

In the 1970 general elections, the Business-Industry Political Action Committee contributed to the campaigns of 18 Senate candidates and 107 House candidates. Ten of the Senate candidates supported won: eight Republicans, one Conservative and one Independent. (One of the Senators, Winston L. Prouty, R-Vt. (1959-71), has since died.) Seventy-one of the House candidates were elected: 61 Republicans and 10 Democrats. In the primary elections, BIPAC supported 10 Democrats—one Senate contestant and nine House candidates, all of whom went on to win in the general elections. Reports filed by BIPAC with the Clerk of the House of Representatives show the organization gave a total of $461,000 to Senate and House candidates in 1970. Listed below are the candidates supported and amounts contributed. Winners are in bold type.

Senate‡	Donation
J. Glenn Beall Jr., R-Md.	$5,000
Lloyd M. Bentsen Jr., D-Tex.#	5,000
W. E. Brock, R-Tenn.	5,000
James L. Buckley, Con.-N.Y.	5,000
Laurence J. Burton, R-Utah	5,000
Harry F. Byrd Jr., Ind.-Va.*	5,000
Anderson Carter, R-N.M.	5,000
Paul J. Fannin, R-Ariz.*	5,000
Nelson G. Gross, R-N.J.	5,000
Thomas S. Kleppe, R-N.D.	5,000

Senate *(cont'd)*	Donation
George Murphy, R-Calif.*	$5,000
Winston L. Prouty, R-Vt.*	5,000
William V. Roth Jr., R-Del.	5,000
Richard L. Roudebush, R-Ind.	5,000
Ralph T. Smith, R-Ill.*	5,000
Ted Stevens, R-Alaska*	5,000
Robert Taft Jr., R-Ohio	5,000
Lowell P. Weicker Jr., R-Conn.	5,000
John Wold, R-Wyo.	5,000

House Republicans

E. Ross Adair, Ind.*	3,500
William H. Ayres, Ohio*	2,000
LaMar Baker, Tenn.	4,000
Page Belcher, Okla.*	1,500
Benjamin B. Blackburn, Ga.*	2,000
Frank T. Bow, Ohio*	2,000
Fred D. Brady, S.D.	2,000
William S. Broomfield, Mich.*	2,500
Donald G. Brotzman, Colo.*	2,000
James T. Broyhill, N.C.*	2,500
Joel T. Broyhill, Va.*	2,500
J. Herbert Burke, Fla.*	4,000
Danny L. Burton, Ind.	1,500
Edward A. Costigan, N.J.	5,000
William O. Cowger, Ky.*	1,500
John Dellenback, Ore.*	1,000
David W. Dennis, Ind.*	3,000
Michael C. Donaldson, Calif.	3,500
Charles F. Dougherty, Pa.	1,000
Pierre S. du Pont IV, Del.	1,500
Marvin L. Esch, Mich.*	4,000
Adrian Fink, Ohio	3,000
Alfred E. Fontanella, N.J.	3,000
Ed Foreman, N.M.*	2,000
Edwin B. Forsythe, N.J.	2,000
William Frenzel, Minn.	5,000
George A. Goodling, Pa.*	3,000
H. R. Gross, Iowa*	1,000
Dexter H. Gunderson, S.D.	2,000
Orval Hansen, Idaho*	2,000
Tom Hayden, Calif.	1,000
Margaret M. Heckler, Mass.*	1,000
Elwood H. Hillis, Ind.	1,000
Henry L. Hoebel, N.J.	3,500
Lawrence J. Hogan, Md.*	2,500
John E. Hunt, N.J.*	1,000
Hastings Keith, Mass.*	2,000
Jack F. Kemp, N.Y.	2,750
Richard C. Kilbourn, Conn.	4,000

House Republicans (cont'd)	Donation
Carleton J. King, N.Y.*	$ 750
Dan Kuykendall, Tenn.*	500
John Kyl, Iowa*	3,500
Odin Langen, Minn.*	4,000
Norman F. Lent, N.Y.	4,000
Andre E. Le Tendre, Wis.	3,500
Sherman P. Lloyd, Utah*	1,500
Manuel Lujan Jr., N.M.*	3,500
Catherine May, Wash.*	2,000
Robert P. McCarney, N.D.	2,000
James A. McClure, Idaho*	1,500
John Y. McCollister, Neb.	3,500
Jack H. McDonald, Mich.*	1,000
Robert C. McEwen, N.Y.*	1,000
John McGlennon, Mass.	1,000
James D. McKevitt, Colo.	5,000
Stewart B. McKinney, Conn.	5,000
Tom McMann, Calif.	3,000
William E. Minshall, Ohio*	4,000
Wilmer Mizell, N.C.*	2,000
Frank H. Murkowski, Alaska	5,000
John F. O'Connor, N.Y.	2,000
Peter Parker, Md.	1,500
John E. Parks, Calif.	1,000
Thomas M. Pelly, Wash.*	2,000
Peter A. Peyser, N.Y.	4,000
Walter E. Powell, Ohio	1,000
Jack Rehberg, Mont.	2,000
Raymond J. Rice, N.Y.	4,000
Richard Richards, Utah	5,000
Harry Roberts, Wyo.	5,000
J. Kenneth Robinson, Va.	2,000
Earl B. Ruth, N.C.*	4,500
Charles W. Sandman Jr., N.J.*	1,000
Henry C. Schadeberg, Wis.*	5,000
Phyllis Schlafly, Ill.	2,000
Herman T. Schneebeli, Pa.*†	2,000
Fred Schwengel, Iowa*	1,000
William Lloyd Scott, Va.*	1,000
Keith G. Sebelius, Kan.*	2,000
Richard G. Shoup, Mont.	4,000
David D. Smith, N.Y.	2,000
Floyd Spence, S.C.	2,000
Robert H. Steele, Conn.	5,000
Sam Steiger, Ariz.*	2,500
William J. (Bill) Teague, Calif.	5,000
John H. Terry, N.Y.	2,000
Fletcher Thompson, Ga.*	5,000
Charles J. Thone, Neb.	5,000
Antonina P. Uccello, Conn.	4,000
Sam Van Dyken, Calif.	1,000

House Republicans *(cont'd)*	Donation
Victor V. Veysey, Calif.	$5,000
William C. Wampler, Va.*	2,000
Richard B. Wathen, Ind.	3,000
G. William Whitehurst, Va.*	2,000
Larry Winn Jr., Kan.*	2,500
Roger H. Zion, Ind.*	4,000
John M. Zwach, Minn.*	2,000

House Democrats	
Watkins M. Abbitt, Va.*	2,000
Walter S. Baring, Nev.*#	2,000
Earle Cabell, Tex.*#	2,000
Patrick T. Caffery, La.*#	3,000
Bob Casey, Tex.*#	2,000
Bill Chappell Jr., Fla.*	2,000
W. C. Daniel, Va.*	2,000
O. C. Fisher, Tex.*	3,000
Charles H. Griffin, Miss.*	1,500
James A. Haley, Fla.*	2,000
David N. Henderson, N.C.*	2,000
Alton Lennon, N.C.*#	2,000
Speedy O. Long, La.*#	2,000
Otto E. Passman, La.*#	1,000
John R. Rarick, La.*#	2,000
David E. Satterfield III, Va.*	3,500
Samuel S. Stratton, N.Y.*	2,000
Roy A. Taylor, N.C.*	1,500
Richard C. White, Tex.*#	1,000

---

* incumbent
\# Support provided in primary election only.
† Support provided in primary and general election.
‡ In addition to individual donations listed, BIPAC reported contributions of $5,000 each to the following 14 political committees whose benefactors could not be identified: Businessmen for Good Government, Virginia; Tennessee Businessmen's Committee; Connecticut Businessmen's Committee for Better Government; Ohio Businessmen for Progress; North Dakota Committee for Better Government; New Mexico Businessmen's Committee; Indiana Committee for Good Government; Businessmen's Committee of California; Good Government Committee, New Jersey; Utah Businessmen for Good Government; Wyoming Businessmen for Good Government; Maryland Businessmen for Good Government; Illinois Businessmen for Good Government; and BIPAC of New York.

Source: BIPAC, Citizens' Research Foundation

6

The National Committee for an Effective Congress

NEAL GREGORY

The National Committee for an Effective Congress calls itself "an independent political action group supported by a national constituency of eighty thousand concerned citizens." It might better be labeled "an effective committee for a national Congress" — effective, because the candidates it endorses and helps finance usually get elected; and national, because its aims are clearly directed toward foreign policy and other issues usually removed from the parochial interests of a congressional district. "It's not the best name," admits Russell D. Hemenway, the NCEC's national director. "But it has been the name for 23 years, so I guess we'll keep it."

Begun in the 1948 elections, the organization from the first has focused most of its interest and resources on the Senate, where foreign policy is affected most directly. In addition to endorsing candidates and contributing funds, the NCEC has worked behind the scenes in many nonelectoral activities. None of its staff or members is registered as a lobbyist, because it contends that most of its activities do not come within the legal definition of the term.

The NCEC was active in the battles which led to the 1954 censure of Sen. Joseph R. McCarthy, R-Wis. (1947-57); was a major factor in the formation of the bipartisan Fair Campaign Practices Committee; and was instrumental in the creation of the Democratic Study Group in the House of Representatives.

145

More recently, the NCEC has been a participant in the stepped-up fight against military spending, particularly through opposition to ABM, the antiballistic missile system. The organization now is concentrating its major efforts on campaign-spending reform, an issue it has been actively involved in since 1969.

"Whether we like to admit it or not," Sen. Barry Goldwater, R-Ariz., once told the National Republican Senatorial Committee, "the National Committee for an Effective Congress is a most effective tool to elect a so-called liberal Congress. I do not dispute their right to do so. I only warn the conservative element." All its opponents do not speak so kindly. In a 1954 speech on the House floor, the late Rep. Kit F. Clardy, R-Mich. (1953-55), called the NCEC a "band of leftists (who) are spending unlimited amounts to throttle every congressional voice raised in defense of the American system of free economy."

But the NCEC has built up quite a coterie of supporters in Congress during its two decades of existence. With more than $830,000 channeled to congressional candidates in 1970, the NCEC called that year "the most successful non-Presidential campaign in NCEC history." The NCEC, Hemenway told *National Journal,* was second only to the AFL-CIO's Committee on Political Education (COPE) in its contributions to "liberal" candidates. In the 1970 elections, the organization endorsed 22 Senate candidates, all Democrats; 13 of these were elected. In the House, 71 candidates received an NCEC endorsement: 63 Democrats, six Republicans, one Liberal and one Independent. Of these, 38 were winners. (See Table 6.3.) In the elections of 1968, the NCEC endorsed 13 Senate candidates: 11 Democrats and 2 Republicans. Nine of the 13 won. The NCEC endorsed 61 House candidates: 50 Democrats, 10 Republicans and one Independent. Of these, 43 were elected.

Hemenway says his organization gets involved only in marginal races. Three criteria are applied to candidates before the NCEC makes endorsements: Can he win the election? Is there a clear philosophical difference with his opponent? Will aid from the NCEC make any difference? Positive answers are generally required to all three questions. Decisions to endorse and proffer financial assistance rest in the hands of the 12-man executive board composed of Hemenway, the five officers and six members.

Harry M. Scoble, a political scientist at the University of California at Los Angeles, points out that formal organizational structure of the committee is designed to avoid the threat of cohesion that could lead to a takeover by Communists or other interest groups. The NCEC was not intended to be a mass-membership organization. In his 1967 book, *Ideology and Electoral Action*, Scoble quotes George E. Agree, Hemenway's predecessor as national director: "We are essentially a staff organization, not a constituent organization. Most members of our board are inactive, and even the others are not very active. We have no general membership, and our contributors—except insofar as they support our work financially and are informed of and support our determinations—do not participate in our activities or decision-making processes."

Hemenway says the operation today is basically the same. As a tax-paying political organization chartered in New York State, the NCEC is a self-perpetuating group. Its bylaws provide for no more than 50 members; however, no minimum number is set. Most of the 34 members currently listed on the NCEC letterhead are inactive, yet the group of prestigious names is undoubtedly a factor in attracting contributions.

Of the $832,619 the NCEC reported it raised for candidates for the 1970 campaign year, $489,100 was donated by more than 80,000 NCEC supporters in all 50 states and given as direct contributions from the committee to candidates. (Records filed with the Clerk of the House of Representatives show the NCEC donated $68,150 to candidates or political committees in 1969 for the 1970 campaigns.) Another $6,450 was donated to the NCEC by "one to three" persons for a series of 21 research papers on selected national and international issues distributed to all NCEC-endorsed candidates. In addition to the

$495,550 that passed through the NCEC's treasury, $337,069 in candidate support was generated by the organization through 25 parties and receptions and through individual contributions to specific candidates on the basis of advice and consultation of the NCEC. (See Tables 6.2 and 6.3.) During 1967-68, some 70,000 persons contributed a total of $702,795 for NCEC candidate support in the 1968 elections. The NCEC estimated that another million dollars in support for Senate and House candidates was generated through its efforts in 1968.

Maurice Rosenblatt, a Washington publicist who founded the NCEC and now serves as its unofficial adviser, calls the organization "the first liberal group without labor orientation" and "an unofficial political action group for the Eastern establishment." The membership list bears him out. It includes men whose family names connote wealth and philanthropy — George Biddle, Fairleigh Dickinson Jr., Thomas K. Finletter, Robert B. Gimbel, Orin Lehman, Stewart R. Mott. There are lawyers who counsel the rich and the corporate elite — Thibaut de Saint Phalle, Telford Taylor and Gerhard P. Van Arkel. And for balance, there are academic and literary figures such as Henry Steele Commager, James Michener, Hans J. Morgenthau, David B. Truman and Barbara Tuchman. (See Table 6.1.)

Rosenblatt recalls the beginnings of the organization as an outgrowth of the practice of Southern and Midwestern progressives making election-year pilgrimages to New York, seeking political contributions from the late Bernard M. Baruch. He envisioned the NCEC as a vehicle to gather financial aid from such Wall Street sources and pass it on to congressional candidates.

Concerned with isolationist views emerging in the postwar years, Rosenblatt and several friends saw Congress, and particularly the Senate, as an area being neglected in the 1948 election campaign. Rosenblatt had met many Congressmen and other influential Washington figures during his work as a public relations specialist for the American League for a Free Palestine (ALFP), a group interested in keeping U.S. publicity focused on the Middle East until the nation of Israel was established. Many of these acquaintances (among them such New

Deal and Fair Deal stalwarts as Elliott and Faye Emerson Roosevelt, the late Sen. Harley M. Kilgore, D-W.Va. (1941-56), former Interior Secretary Oscar L. Chapman (1949-53) and Eleanor Roosevelt) shared his fears of a conservative takeover of the Senate and supported his idea for a group to support progressive congressional candidates.

Joining Rosenblatt as NCEC founding members were Stewart McClure and Harry L. Selden, close friends and fellow publicists who had been associated with him at the ALFP; Marshall MacDuffie, a New York lawyer and expert on the Soviet Union; Marshall K. Skadden, also a lawyer in New York and NCEC legal adviser until his death in 1961; and Sidney H. Scheuer, an international textile broker and industrial consultant. Now 73, Scheuer has been chairman of the NCEC since 1956.

The initial group, meeting with Kilgore, picked out the following Senate candidates to support in 1948: an incumbent—the late James E. Murray of Montana (1934-61); two former Senators trying for a comeback—the late Matthew M. Neely of West Virginia (1923-29, 1931-41, 1949-58) and Guy M. Gillette of Iowa (1936-45, 1949-55); and three men making their first try—the late Estes Kefauver of Tennessee (1949-63), Paul H. Douglas of Illinois (1949-67) and Hubert H. Humphrey of Minnesota. The six men, all Democrats, were elected; and the NCEC was off to an auspicious start. Only $12,601 was raised for the candidates in 1948, a far cry from the financial support provided 22 years later. In 1949, the NCEC worked in the special election which sent the late Herbert H. Lehman, D (1949-57), to the Senate from New York. After a somewhat less active involvement in 1950 (only $9,000 was disbursed), the group began what Scoble calls its "negativist role," sparked by NCEC opposition to activities of Sen. Joseph McCarthy.

Congressional Report, a newsletter published several times each year, was started by the NCEC in 1952, and an early issue focused on McCarthy, seeking to portray him as an operating political force and to develop an understanding of the underlying causes and bases of his support. The NCEC attempted to bolster the morale of incumbent liberal Senators through analysis of McCarthy's electoral weaknesses. Eventually, the organization became a clearinghouse for information about the Wisconsin Senator and helped coordinate the Democratic and Republican efforts that led to the 1954 censure resolution.

Anticipating McCarthy's announced intent to pose himself as the central issue of the 1954 mid-term elections, the Fair Campaign Practices Committee was created. The NCEC claims to be "at least 50-per cent responsible" for this nonprofit group which attempts to raise the ethical level of election campaign tactics in federal and statewide races. The NCEC continued with an attack on 24 Senate Republicans whom it called "extremists . . . who oppose social legislation and bipartisan foreign policy." It encouraged opponents in both primaries and general elections.

Throughout the '50s, the NCEC continued to evolve its philosophy, supporting liberal causes — civil rights, pro-labor legislation, congressional reorganization. But foreign policy considerations remained paramount, as indicated by this 1958 statement in the NCEC's *Congressional Report:* "As a rule, foreign policy-oriented people tend to be the most interested and articulate, and are well represented in every leadership echelon. But their political influence in the determination of foreign policy is not at all comparable to the influence of workers in determining labor policy, or of farmers in determining agricultural policy. Their activities are just not organized for political impact. Unless they become so organized, it is unlikely that America will ever be able to pursue a coherent and consistent foreign policy free from domination by irrelevant domestic interests and pressures."

Although the NCEC clearly had a New Deal tone from its beginning, it began a heavy emphasis on electing Republicans who shared its views following the McCarthy censure. It went so far as to set up a special fund for Sen. Clifford P. Case of New Jersey, helping assure his election in 1954. Two years later it furnished staff assistance and set up a special "Citi-

151

zens for Cooper" account which received $42,523.91 for Sen. John Sherman Cooper, who resigned as Ambassador to India and was persuaded to make a late Senate campaign in Kentucky.

In 1958, a "Citizens for Scott" account provided $17,500 in special contributions for Senate Minority Leader Hugh Scott, then a Philadelphia House Member making his first try for the Senate. And in 1960, Case received almost $10,000 in a special fund-raising effort for a difficult primary. In the general elections that followed, $21,645 was raised by "Citizens for Cooper, Case and Boggs," a special fund paid for and operated by the NCEC on behalf of three GOP incumbents: Cooper, Case and Sen. J. Caleb Boggs of Delaware.

This continuing search for Republicans to support remains a major problem for the group, which has difficulty maintaining its self-styled bipartisan status. In the 1968 elections, NCEC involvement in two Republican Senate races proved particularly embarassing. The organization refused to support Rep. Thomas B. Curtis, R-Mo. (1951-69), even though it had backed him in four earlier races for the House. Support given GOP nominee Marlow W. Cook in Kentucky was publicly withdrawn in the closing days of the campaign. The two incidents demonstrate that once a candidate is backed by the NCEC, he has no guarantee of continued support.

Curtis, having represented a suburban St. Louis constituency in the House since 1951, had been floor leader for the Eisenhower trade bill, legislation in which the NCEC was actively interested. Faced with major opposition in 1958, he approached the NCEC through a Republican associate, seeking the group's endorsement. In the political lexicon of the day, Curtis was frequently referred to as an "enlightened conservative." As a ranking member of the tax-writing Ways and Means Committee, he had built a reputation as one of the most knowledgeable men in the House on economic matters. After lengthy debate over the feasibility and desirability of endorsing such a candidate, the NCEC gave him its blessing for 1958 and again in the next two elections. Curtis provided key Republican support in the 1961 fight over increasing the size of the Rules Committee and in civil rights legislation of the late 1950s and early 1960s. He co-authored a legislative reorganization bill and, in 1963, received the Congressional Distinguished Service Award from the American Political Science Association. With Goldwater heading the GOP ticket in 1964, Curtis did not want—and did not get—the NCEC's public endorsement; however, at least one large contribution was routed through the organization to the Curtis campaign that year. The NCEC endorsed Curtis for re-election in 1966.

When Missouri Republicans nominated Curtis as their Senate candidate in 1968, he expected NCEC endorsement. Members could not decide; National Director Hemenway visited Curtis personally to quiz him on his views (despite the group's 10-year familiarity with him). The NCEC finally endorsed his Democratic opponent, Lt. Gov. Thomas F. Eagleton, who won the election.

The deciding factor, added to his over-all conservative voting record, was Curtis' leadership role in the 1967 House refusal to seat then Harlem Rep. Adam C. Powell (1945-71). Peace groups also influenced the committee in favor of Eagleton. A former Curtis aide, who would not be quoted by name, said flatly that the refusal to endorse Curtis, a leader in efforts for congressional reform, proves the fallacy of the NCEC's claims to either bipartisanship or interest in an "effective" Congress. "They ought to change their name to . . . Liberal Congress or . . . Democratic Congress," he said. "They never make any effort to defeat the Southern Democratic chairmen. That would really help make an effective Congress."

In Kentucky in 1968, the Republican nominee for the seat being vacated by Sen. Thruston B. Morton, R (1957-69), was Marlow Cook. The NCEC had previously contributed $5,000 to Morton, who returned the money after deciding against a reelection bid. Accompanied by Sen. Cooper, long a favorite with the NCEC, Cook met with the committee and received its endorsement. When the Kentucky campaign got under way, the NCEC began receiving press reports and letters from Kentucky contributors attacking Cook's speeches on Vietnam and the issue of crime. For the first time in its 20-year history, the NCEC—following a survey of its executive board—withdrew an endorsement. Cook denounced the action, which became an issue in the closing days of his campaign.

"We felt they (the NCEC) were incredibly naive," said Mitch McConnell, then legislative assistant to Cook. "In the rhetoric of 1968, I suppose you would call him (Cook) a hawk on Vietnam. He questioned the bombing halt . . . and said some things about the Pueblo, going in and getting the men back— that sort of thing. But there was nothing about civil rights any liberal could disagree with. . . . Look at Sen. Cook's record. He's voted for defense cuts. He voted against ABM. They're (the NCEC) supposed to be a sophisticated group. They ought to know *The Courier Journal*—except for Sen. Cooper—always backs Democrats. They just overreacted to things said in the heat of the campaign." Elected by a margin of 35,000 votes, Cook ignored an NCEC telegram asking him to return its $5,000 contribution.

In 1970, none of the Republican Senate candidates received the NCEC's endorsement. (Scott, an NCEC favorite since 1952, was not endorsed by the group in his successful reelection bid. Hemenway told *National Journal* that the Senate minority leader did not ask for an endorsement and the organization did not consider the race marginal, a prime prerequisite for NCEC aid. "We thought Hugh Scott was going to win handily. The narrowness of the margin came as a surprise," explained Hemenway.) Asked about the NCEC's difficulty in maintaining its bipartisan credentials, Hemenway said the organization will have no problem finding Republican candidates to endorse in 1972. He named as examples Sens. Case of New Jersey, Edward W. Brooke of Massachusetts, Charles H. Percy of Illinois and Mark Hatfield of Oregon.

While keeping its emphasis on the Senate, the NCEC has cautiously taken a greater interest in House elections. Its first two choices—in 1952—were the late Gracie Pfost, D-Idaho (1953-63), and Hugh Scott of Pennsylvania. Both candidates won. In both cases, the NCEC had a double purpose. Mrs. Pfost was challenging John Wood, a leading Republican isolationist, and the NCEC had a long-term desire to encourage the Democratic Party in Idaho in hopes of later defeating the state's two GOP Senators, Herman Welker (1951-57) and Henry C.

Dworshak (1946-49, 1949-62), both now deceased. Scott, facing a tough reelection fight, had been in the House since 1941. He had served as Republican National Chairman (1948-49) under the late Thomas E. Dewey and he was prominent among Eisenhower boosters. Foreseeing a Republican majority in Congress in 1952, the NCEC hoped support of Scott would give them access to the new House leadership.

Since that first effort, NCEC interest in the House has grown considerably. By its own account, the NCEC in 1970 devoted more attention to House primary elections than at any time in its 22 years. The NCEC views the primaries as its best opportunity for challenging "entrenched" incumbents and says it will intensify its candidate-support efforts in these contests in 1972. In a December 1970 report outlining its program for the '72 primary elections, the NCEC said: "To try to retire the entrenched House reactionaries in the general election is an exercise in futility, for their districts are safe. If they have an Achilles' heel, it is the primaries, where they have rarely been challenged. Only such an effort, beamed at both parties' pre-primary activities where candidates are created, will revitalize the House as a modern, contemporary institution."

The organization encouraged the formation of the Democratic Study Group, a band of Representatives formed in 1959 to provide an activist role for House liberals frustrated by the coalition of Republicans and Southern Democrats that controlled legislation. The NCEC has solicited funds for the DSG and provided block grants to the organization for redistribution to DSG members facing rough reelection battles. In 1964, this grant totaled $80,000; in 1968, it was $30,000; in 1970, it was $22,500. In December 1969, the NCEC purchased a table ($1,000) at the DSG 10th Anniversary Dinner, proceeds of which went to pay for research activities.

Reflecting on the 1970 elections, NCEC Director Hemenway said: "We entered the '70 elections with a great deal of trepidation — the climate was such that we could lose heavily, we were unsure of what was happening in the House. But the

Republicans overstepped their bounds. They made every wrong political step they could; they badly assessed what was happening in America and the strategy failed. We had far fewer losses than we could have expected."

Of particular concern to the NCEC was the loss of two Democratic incumbents in the Senate—Albert Gore of Tennessee and Joseph D. Tydings of Maryland. (Gore, who had served in the Senate since 1953, was defeated by W. E. Brock, R; Tydings lost to J. Glenn Beall Jr., R, after one term in the Senate.) The NCEC was pleased, however, with primary defeats of "several senior Members of the House . . . who hadn't come into the 20th century or were so tied to special interests that they couldn't vote their conscience," Hemenway said. He cited as examples five Democrats: Philip J. Philbin of Massachusetts (1943-71), second-ranking Democrat on the Armed Services Committee, defeated in the primary and again as "sticker" candidate in the general elections; George H. Fallon of Maryland (1945-71), Public Works Committee chairman: Samuel N. Friedel of Maryland (1953-71), House Administration Committee chairman and the second-ranking Democrat on the Interstate and Foreign Commerce Committee; and Michael A. Feighan of Ohio (1943-71) and Byron G. Rogers of Colorado (1951-71), second- and fourth-ranking Democrats on the Judiciary Committee. "Heartened by that success in 1970," Hemenway said, "we are going after some of these similarly entrenched Members of the House in 1972."

The NCEC's plan for 1972 is a greatly expanded candidate-support program, with major emphasis on defeating incumbents in the primaries. In its 1970 year-end analysis of Congress, the organization discussed its strategy for the next election year: "Its (the NCEC's) role must be invisible in specific primaries, because it would be obviously self-defeating to hand a targeted incumbent the issue of outside 'interference.' This imposes a special burden of faith on the NCEC's 80,000 supporters, who will now be asked to contribute not to a specific candidate but to a campaign method, and not in the heat of a general election but in the early months when this program must be implemented. . . . If on a selected basis one were to replace no more than half a dozen senior Members of each party, it would ventilate the system and cause a psychological revolution in the House."

To determine its best chances of defeating incumbents, the NCEC has undertaken an extensive survey of the demographic characteristics and voting patterns of existing congressional districts and new districts that will be created in 14 states before the 1972 elections. The result, according to Hemenway, is a list of 30 districts where the NCEC believes it has a good opportunity to unseat incumbents in the primary elections, and a second list of 20 districts where the NCEC sees some chance of defeating the opposition. The NCEC is actively recruiting challengers for the primaries. These candidates will receive research and consultant services, "substantial" financial assistance and "every other resource at our command," Hemenway said. The NCEC director is optimistic that despite the committee's stepped-up primary activities, "the resources we are expected to provide will be there" when needed. "Our 80,000 supporters have been very generous in the past and many liberals have come to depend on our assistance."

Hemenway believes the economy and the Administration's economic program — "how it works and the way the country uses its resources" — will be major issues in the 1972 election year. "I think the President with his announcement of the China visit and withdrawal of troops has done a great deal to defuse this (Vietnam war) issue," he added. Commenting on the NCEC's expectations of the Republican effort in 1972, Hemenway said: "The Republicans handed us the issue in 1970. . . . Agnew set the tone on law and order . . . but the Administration was dead wrong. . . . I think they (the Administration) are capable of making unlimited mistakes again. On occasion, the President has shown that he is a very shrewd politician, but we're counting on them continuing to be as inept (in the 1972 campaigns)."

Campaign-spending reform has received more attention and active support from the NCEC over the past three years than any other issue—domestic or foreign. In fact, the NCEC is acknowledged to be the most effective pressure group working for campaign reform; it was a principal force behind the broadcast-spending bill (S 3637), vetoed by President Nixon in late 1970, and the campaign reform bill (S 382) passed by the Senate in August 1971. NCEC Chairman Scheuer told the Senate Rules Subcommittee on Privileges and Elections in May 1971 that the NCEC has been on record with Congress since 1957 in favor of campaign reform.

The NCEC became actively involved in the current campaign reform movement in 1969, when it drafted legislation to limit broadcast spending. The NCEC measure, introduced in 1969 but not acted on, was the basis for the broadcast-spending bill passed by Congress in 1970 and later vetoed by Mr. Nixon. Nicholas Zapple, staff counsel of the Senate Commerce Committee's subcommittee on communications, credited the NCEC with "supplying the concepts" that went into the vetoed bill. (Zapple works under Sen. John O. Pastore, D-R.I., chairman of the subcommittee and a co-sponsor of the 1971 bill.) Susan Bennett King, head of the NCEC's Washington office, said the broadcast bill would have died in committee "if at any time the NCEC had relaxed" its efforts. In his veto message October 12, 1970, Mr. Nixon complained that the bill to limit broadcast spending discriminated against broadcasters, since it did not limit nonbroadcast media, and that it failed to provide an effective accounting and reporting system. The Senate sustained the veto November 23 by a vote of 58-34—four votes short of the two-thirds majority needed to override.

The NCEC stepped up its role in the campaign reform movement after the Senate failed to override the President's veto. Senate architects of campaign-reform bills began consulting with Hemenway and Mrs. King in the wake of the veto, and the organization's role became more influential. Hemenway explained his group's long-range strategy during an interview with *National Journal* in May 1971:

"We kept newspapers out (of the 1970 bill) because TV was federally regulated. The President brought newspapers in. Now we're writing the new bill to satisfy him." Hemenway said the Nixon veto paved the way for serious reform. "He added to public sentiment with the veto, which was sheer stupidity. After the veto, we had a new climate." Hemenway also said the President's original mistake was that he never believed the bill to limit campaign broadcasts would pass in 1970. When it did, "they made the additional mistake of attacking it for what it didn't do. It didn't go far enough. It didn't plug all the loopholes."

Hemenway, who speaks with great enthusiasm about campaign reform, said the issues of spending limits and disclosure engage major disparate political elements in a classic national confrontation, because they affect all segments of American society. He told *National Journal:* "This is a cosmos. It is Democrats versus Republicans, public interest versus private interest, House versus Senate, Congress versus the executive, incumbents versus challengers, liberals versus conservatives, open government versus closed government, seniority versus freshmen."

Hemenway, who is regarded by Sen. Philip A. Hart, D-Mich., a member of the Commerce Committee, as "the hero" of campaign reform, said the proposal is "not anti-Nixon." "This is more anti-oil and -steel. This bill will take the power away. If a guy is rich, he has more votes than the guy who is poor." He said that since a wealthy man is now relatively free to donate large sums of money to many candidates for federal office, he has more influence in Congress than a man without means. It is for this reason that "the President doesn't want to sign this bill," said Hemenway. "It will kill them (the Administration)," he said. "We will use everything we can — press, public opinion, Presidential candidates — until we get a bill."

The campaign reform bill, passed by the Senate August 5, 1971, by an 88-2 vote, went beyond the limited broadcast-spending bill to include the print media and establish a more comprehensive financial accounting and reporting system. "We're on the road to public financing of political campaigns," Hemenway told *National Journal.* He said the NCEC hoped to have a bill on the President's desk by early November 1971. The new bill would limit a candidate's expenditures for radio, television, newspaper, periodical and billboard advertising to 10 cents per eligible voter in primary, general and special elections. A candidate could spend no more than six cents per voter – of the 10 cents allowable – for either broadcast or print services, and all media would be required to sell time to candidates at the lowest rate available to advertisers. The bill also would repeal the "equal-time" requirement for federal elections, establish an independent federal elections commission to oversee candidate and political committee reporting of finances and limit the contribution of a candidate or his family to his campaign.

The NCEC operates from two offices – with the principal one in New York and a smaller operation in Washington. National Director Hemenway supervises a staff of eight secretaries and researchers. He lives in New York and commutes to Capitol Hill two or three days each week. Why is the headquarters of a committee concerned with Congress located in New York? "That's where the money is," says Hemenway. New York is also headquarters for most of the national news media which the NCEC cultivates with information and its views about the activities of Congress and the White House.

Located on the sixth floor of a commercial office building at 10 East 39th St., the four-room suite of offices is the site of the committee's fund-raising activities. Response to direct-mail solicitation through a list of 100,000 names provides about half the NCEC receipts. The balance is raised through direct contact of would-be donors by Chairman Scheuer, Hemenway and active members of the committee.

Hemenway, 45, came out of the Democratic reform movement in Manhattan. In 1966, he resigned as director of the New York Committee for Democratic Voters, to take over direction of the NCEC. Born in Leominster, Mass. (near Worcester), he is a graduate of Dartmouth and studied in Paris before joining the U.S. Foreign Service. He was secretary of commerce under New York Gov. W. Averell Harriman (1955-59) and later was in the investment business. He succeeded George Agree who resigned in 1966 amid dissension within the committee. Agree had insisted that NCEC founder Rosenblatt, who represented several commercial clients in Washington, had a conflict of interest as a member of the NCEC. He contended that Congressmen did not know whether Rosenblatt was speaking for the committee or his clients. The membership backed Rosenblatt, and Agree joined the staff of philanthropist Stephen R. Currier, then an NCEC board member.

Concurrently with Hemenway's arrival, Rosenblatt resigned from the NCEC. He maintains contact with Scheuer and other members and contributes information on issues and candidate evaluation. Rosenblatt, 53, who was called by *Time* magazine "a Washington operator with a green thumb for controversy," terms himself an "unofficial adviser" to the NCEC. Although he has no authority to promise support or commit funds to campaigns, Rosenblatt is still firmly identified with the organization in the minds of many journalists, congressional staffers and Members of Congress.

The NCEC Washington office—formerly in Rosenblatt's Capitol Hill home—has been moved a block away, to the basement of a town house at 435½ New Jersey Ave. SE, two blocks from the House Office Buildings. In charge is Susan King, 30, who greets a steady stream of prospective candidates seeking NCEC support. A *cum laude* graduate of Duke University, she was a legislative and research assistant for the Administrative Office of the U.S. Courts and a legislative aide to the late Sen. Thomas J. Dodd, D-Conn. (1959-71), before joining the NCEC in December 1966.

Table 6.1 NCEC Membership

The 34 officers and members of the National Committee for an Effective Congress are:

*Sidney H. Scheuer, chairman. International textile broker and philanthropist, New York, N.Y.; former president Ethical Culture Society.

*Henry Steele Commager, vice chairman. Educator, author and historian of U.S. political and social development; professor of history, Amherst College, Mass.

*George R. Donahue, vice chairman. Labor relations consultant, New York, N.Y.; former president, Association of Catholic Trade Unionists.

*S. Jay Levy, secretary. Economist, publisher and analyst, Chappaqua, N.Y.

*Thibaut de Saint Phalle, treasurer. Lawyer, economist, counselor to Coudert Brothers, New York, N.Y.; investment banker, Stralem and Saint Phalle.

*Harry Ashmore. Director, Center for the Study of Democratic Institutions, Santa Barbara, Calif.; former editor, *Arkansas Gazette* (Little Rock).

George Backer. Author, publisher and businessman; former publisher, *New York Post.*

George Biddle. Artist and author, Croton-on-Hudson, N.Y.

Stimson Bullitt. Broadcaster and author; president, King Broadcasting, Seattle, Wash.

Robert B. Choate. Expert on hunger and malnutrition, Phoenix, Ariz.; an initiator and assistant on 1969 White House Conference on Food, Nutrition and Health.

Fairleigh Dickinson Jr. Philanthropist and industrialist; New Jersey Republican state Senator; chairman of the board, Fairleigh Dickinson University.

Thomas K. Finletter. Attorney, Secretary of the Air Force (1950-53), U.S. Ambassador to NATO (1961-65); partner, Coudert Brothers, New York, N.Y.

Paul Foley. Board chairman, McCann-Erickson Advertising Agency, Detroit, Mich.

Robert B. Gimbel. Department store executive, New York, N.Y.

Alan Green. Publisher and advertising executive, New York, N.Y.

Alvin H. Hansen. Author and educator, Cambridge, Mass.

Orin Lehman. Publisher and educator, New York, N.Y.; chairman of the board, New School of Social Research.

Isidore Lipschutz. Philanthropist, New York, N.Y.

Joseph P. McMurray. President, Queens College, City University of New York.

James Michener. Pulitzer Prize-winning author, Pipersville, Pa.

*Francis Pickens Miller. Soldier and churchman, Washington, D.C.

*Hans J. Morgenthau. Political philosopher and author, University of Chicago.

*Stewart R. Mott. Philanthropist, General Motors heir, New York, N.Y.

George E. Outland. Professor of government, San Francisco State College; Member of Congress, D-Calif. (1943-47).

Laughlin Phillips. Founder and editor, *Washingtonian* magazine; president of the Phillips Gallery, Washington, D.C.

George D. Pratt Jr. Farmer, conservationist and philanthropist, Connecticut.

Charles Rose. Investment banker, New York, N.Y.

Francis B. Sayre Jr. Clergyman. Dean of Washington Cathedral, Washington, D.C.

David E. Scoll. Attorney, New York, N.Y.

*Telford Taylor. Soldier, lawyer, writer and educator, New York, N.Y.; chief prosecutor, Nuremberg War Crimes Trials.

David B. Truman. Educator, political scientist; president, Mt. Holyoke College.

Barbara Tuchman. Historian and Pulitzer Prize-winning author, New York, N.Y.

*Gerhard P. Van Arkel. Attorney, Van Arkel and Kaiser, Washington, D.C.; general counsel, National Labor Relations Board (1946-47).

George Wald. Author, educator; Higgins Professor of biology, Harvard University; co-recipient 1967 Nobel Prize for medicine.

---

*   executive board

Table 6.2   NCEC Contributions, 1969

Disbursements made by the National Committee for an Effective Congress to congressional candidates during 1969, as filed with the Clerk of the House of Representatives, are listed below. Where not specified in the listing, the beneficiary is noted in parentheses.

Maryland Friends of Tydings	$ 5,000
(Sen. Joseph D. Tydings, D-Md.)	
Friends of Proxmire	5,000
(Sen. William Proxmire, D-Wis.)	
Golden Spike Committee	5,000
(Sen. Frank E. Moss, D-Utah)	
Re-elect Senator Moss Committee	5,000
Interregional Civic Association, Utah (Moss)	2,000
Hart for Senate Committee	5,000
(Sen. Philip A. Hart, D-Mich.)	
Hart for Senate Finance Committee	5,000
Citizens Committee for Senator Burdick	5,000
(Sen. Quentin N. Burdick, D-N.D.)	
Committee for Gore	5,000
(Sen. Albert Gore, D-Tenn.)	
Volunteers for Gore	5,000
Missourians for Symington	5,000
(Sen. Stuart Symington, D-Mo.)	
Texas Committee for Responsible Government	5,000
(Sen. Ralph Yarborough, D-Tex.)	
Committee for Responsible Government	5,000
(Yarborough)	
Harrington for Congress	2,000
(Rep. Michael J. Harrington, D-Mass.)	
Melcher for Congress Committee, Billings, Mont.	1,000
(Rep. John Melcher, D-Mont.)	
Seventh District Good Government Committee, Wausau, Wis.	1,000
(Rep. David R. Obey, D-Wis.)	
Democratic Study Group Dinner	1,000
Warman for Congress Committee, Skokie, Ill.	500
(Edward A. Warman, D, candidate special election, defeated.)	
Sam Gibbons Dinner Committee, Tampa, Fla.	200
(Rep. Sam Gibbons, D-Fla.)	
Adams for Congress Committee	200
(Rep. Brock Adams, D-Wash.)	
Citizens for Meeds Committee	250
(Rep. Lloyd Meeds, D-Wash.)	
Total	$68,150

Source: Clerk, U.S. House of Representatives, *National Journal*

Table 6.3   NCEC Contributions, 1970

In the 1970 elections, the National Committee for an Effective Congress endorsed 22 Senate candidates—all Democrats—and 71 House candidates— 63 Democrats, six Republicans, one Liberal and one Independent. (All but nine of the endorsees received NCEC money.) Thirteen of the Senate candidates endorsed won and 38 of the House endorsees were winners.

Citizens' Research Foundation reported that the NCEC filed with the Clerk of the House of Representatives contributions of $399,605 to Senate and House candidates in 1970, although the NCEC's records show that the organization reported a total of $489,100 in direct contributions. NCEC officials said the discrepancy resulted from failure to pick up all of the contributions made to candidates, particularly those made through political committees. The $399,605 figure represents only direct contributions made by the NCEC to individual candidates, since the organization is required to report only those contributions that pass through its treasury. The total does not include indirect contributions —funds raised through NCEC-sponsored parties and receptions for candidates and donations from individuals to designated candidates on the basis of advice and consultation of the NCEC.

Listed below are the candidates endorsed by the NCEC and the direct contributions received. (NCEC funds channeled to a candidate through a political committee are listed below the beneficiary's name.) Winners are in bold type.

Senate	Donations
Quentin N. Burdick, N.D.*	$ 6,500
Committee of North Dakotans	5,000
Joseph D. Duffey, Conn.	25,400
Albert Gore, Tenn.*	11,000
Tennesseans for Good Government	5,000
Sam Grossman, Ariz.	5,000
Philip A. Hart, Mich.*	15,000
Vance Hartke, Ind.*	10,000
Citizens for Good Government, Indiana	5,000
Philip H. Hoff, Vt.	28,000
Joe Josephson, Alaska #	15,000
Edward M. Kennedy, Mass.*	
Mike Mansfield, Mont.*	5,000
Howard M. Metzenbaum, Ohio	20,000
Joseph M. Montoya, N.M.*	15,000
Frank E. Moss, Utah*	10,000
Utahans for Good Government	5,000
Interregional Civic Association, Utah	5,000
Edmund S. Muskie, Maine*	5,000
William Proxmire, Wis.*	
George C. Rawlings Jr., Va.	2,500
Adlai E. Stevenson, III, Ill.	25,000
Stuart Symington, Mo.*	6,000
John V. Tunney, Calif.	33,000
Joseph D. Tydings, Md.*	
Harrison A. Williams Jr., N.J.*	25,000

Senate *(cont'd)* — **Donations**

Ralph Yarborough, Tex.*#	$ 200
Committee for Good Government, Texas	5,000
Committee for Effective Representation, Texas	5,000

House

James Abourezk, D-S.D.	2,000
Brock Adams, D-Wash.*	———
Doug Arnett, D-Ohio	2,000
Les Aspin, D-Wis.	2,000
Jesse H. Bankston, D-La.#	1,000
Craig S. Barnes, D-Colo.	3,000
Nicholas J. Begich, D-Alaska	2,000
Arthur L. Berger, D-Pa.	1,000
Bob Bergland, D-Minn.	4,000
Roger Blobaum, D-Iowa	5,000
John Brademas, D-Ind.*	1,000
William J. (Bill) Brauner, D-Idaho	1,000
Daniel E. Button, R-N.Y.*	2,000
Fabian Chavez Jr., D-N.M.	2,000
John C. Culver, D-Iowa*	1,000
James H. DeCoursey Jr., D-Kan.	2,000
Ronald V. Dellums, D-Calif.	1,000
John G. Dow, D-N.Y.	1,500
Robert F. Drinan, D-Mass.	2,000
Don Edwards, D-Calif.*	———
Peter E. Eikenberry, Lib.-N.Y.	2,000
Marvin L. Esch, R-Mich.*	1,000
Frank E. Evans, D-Colo.*	1,000
Myrlie B. Evers, D-Calif.	1,000
Joseph T. Fitzpatrick, D-Va.	1,000
Thomas S. Foley, D-Wash.*	———
Donald M. Fraser, D-Minn.*	1,000
Richard G. Gebhardt, D-Colo.	1,000
Sam Gibbons, D-Fla.*	———
James W. Goodrich, D-Ohio	2,000
Ella T. Grasso, D-Conn.	4,000
Michael J. Harrington, D-Mass.*	1,000
Royal Hart, D-Md.	2,000
Henry Helstoski, D-N.J.*	1,000
J. David Huber, D-Ind.	———
Andrew Jacobs Jr., D-Ind.*	1,000
Arthur J. Lesemann, D-N.J.	500
Allard K. Lowenstein, D-N.Y.*	2,000
Romano L. Mazzoli, D-Ky.	1,000
Paul N. McCloskey Jr., R-Calif.*	1,000
John Melcher, D-Mont.*	1,000
Parren J. Mitchell, D-Md.	1,000
Ronald M. Mottl, D-Ohio	2,000
David R. Obey, D-Wis.*	3,000

House (cont'd)	Donations
Ben Ragsdale, Ind.-Va.	$1,500
Charles B. Rangel, D-N.Y.	2,000
Otto Ravenholt, D-Nev.#	500
A. A. Rayner Jr., D-Ill.#	1,505
Ogden R. Reid, R-N.Y.*	1,000
Donald W. Riegle Jr., R-Mich.*	———
Teno Roncalio, D-Wyo.	
Wyoming Development Committee	1,000
Charles G. Rose, D-N.C.#	500
J. Edward Roush, D-Ind.	3,000
William R. Roy, D-Kan.	1,000
Paul S. Sarbanes, D-Md.	1,000
John F. Seiberling Jr., D-Ohio	3,000
Philip R. Sharp, D-Ind.	2,000
John H. Simmons, R-Mo.#	1,500
Philip A. Sprague, D-Ind.	2,000
Gerald N. Springer, D-Ohio	2,000
James V. Stanton, D-Ohio†	1,000
Claude Stephens, D-S.C.#	500
Gerry E. Studds, D-Mass.	3,500
James W. Symington, D-Mo.*	1,000
Frank Thompson Jr., D-N.J.*	1,000
Charles A. Vanik, D-Ohio*	1,000
Marden E. Wells, D-Idaho	1,000
Murat Williams, D-Va.	500
Clyde Wilson, D-Mo.#	1,000
Lester L. Wolff, D-N.Y.*	1,000
Andrew Young, D-Ga.	1,000

* incumbent
\# Defeated in primary election.
† Support provided in primary election only.

Source: NCEC, Citizens' Research Foundation

7

National Republican Congressional Committee

ANDREW J. GLASS

The National Republican Congressional (Campaign) Committee — self-directed and independently financed — will face in 1972 the added factor of a Presidential election in its effort to increase the GOP phalanx in the House beyond its present 176-Member strength. While a strong national ticket tends to aid both congressional incumbents and challengers, the national campaigns of 1972 will drain money away from congressional candidates and into the Presidential race, thus intensifying the committee's fund-raising problems.

"The big point in 1972 is that the President needs a Republican House and Senate," says Rep. Bob Wilson, R-Calif., the committee's veteran director. "If he (Mr. Nixon) sells this hard like Truman did in 1948 . . . it will be of great benefit to the Republicans running for the House." Whether or not 1972 emerges as a "sleeper year" for House Republicans will depend, Wilson said, on several factors — "if we can keep (George C.) Wallace out of the race, if the economy picks up, if Vietnam is over and if the President has a good landslide." Wilson also emphasized the importance of 1972 as a reapportionment year, which, he said, "could be most valuable" to the Republicans in picking up additional seats in the November elections. Although the congressional committee will experience more difficulty in raising funds for House candidates in 1972 than it would in a non-Presidential election year, Wilson said he is confident the committee can raise enough money to provide the financial assistance needed.

The House GOP campaign committee spent a record sum in 1970 in an effort to keep the 187 seats held by Republicans. One hundred and eighty Republican Members were elected, a loss of seven seats. But the committee was successful in helping to reverse an off-year trend: Since the turn of the century, the party controlling the White House has lost an average of 37 House seats in off-year elections. (Although the committee's 1970 contributions failed to reach the $4.3 million goal announced early in the year, the committee still operated under the largest budget of its 105-year history. Its annual payroll for 1970 totaled $439,700 and its paid staff reached a peak campaign level of 65 persons.) Assessing the GOP losses in the House, Wilson told *National Journal* the major problem was the number of Republican incumbents who gave up their seats for what turned out to be "hopeless" Senate races. "We had some shots (in the House) we lost," he said. "I don't blame the President for shooting for the Senate . . . but it may have been well to go for both," Wilson added.

Five years ago, when the Democrats controlled the White House, the Republicans gained 47 House seats. This drive was spurred by private citizen Richard M. Nixon, who toured the country on behalf of incumbents and challengers aboard a chartered jet. The congressional committee subsequently paid the full $120,000 bill for the Nixon tour. Some committee staff veterans, feeling that such campaigning benefited Mr. Nixon more than it helped the candidates, are still nettled by that, although none of them can afford to say so publicly.

Two years later, Mr. Nixon won the White House and problems arose again. "Originally, the Nixon White House had a disturbing tendency to regard us as part of the (Republican) National Committee," Wilson told *National Journal*. "But the national committee, I think it is widely understood, is and should be a creature of the President," Wilson added. "This doesn't mean we're disloyal," Wilson said. "Our *Newsletter* is practically a Nixon house organ. But we very definitely want to run our own operation." Wilson said that although the

White House often gets involved in Senate races, it does not take a great interest in House races. The President's top political advisers deny that there has ever been a rift between the White House and the congressional committee. In any event, both groups agree that current relationships are excellent.

The National Republican Congressional Committee was founded 105 years ago because of a power struggle between President Andrew Johnson and Republicans in Congress over how to deal with former Confederate states. Under the leadership of Rep. Thaddeus Stevens, Pa., and Sen. Charles Sumner, Mass., the Radical Republicans, as they were known then, organized the committee. Their purpose was to achieve undisputed dominance of Congress in the elections of 1866, a dominance that would enable them to nullify Johnson's vetoes for the next two years.

Having achieved their sought-for overwhelming majority, the Radical Republicans decided to preserve their instrument of success. They viewed the fledgling committee as a means of enabling them to act independently of both the White House and the Republican National Committee. Under Sen. Zachariah Chandler, one of the founders of the Republican Party, who took over as chairman in 1870, the congressional committee trained its efforts on the South, where Chandler sought to form newly emancipated blacks into a Republican voting mass. During Chandler's tenure, the committee launched a monthly publication, *The Republican,* which was the first regularly published organ of a political party in the United States and is the direct forerunner of the present committee *Newsletter.* In this period, the committee's paid staff rose to more than 100 persons.

In 1876, Sen. Simon Cameron, Pa., former Secretary of War in Lincoln's Cabinet, was chosen to head the committee. The Republicans gained 30 seats in the House and Rutherford B. Hayes entered the White House. At that time, the committee moved into offices in downtown Washington. Following Hayes' election, the committee fell into gradual eclipse, failing to designate a chairman for the next 10 years. The fallow period ended under Rep. Joseph W. Babcock, Wis., who directed a campaign in 1894 in which the Republicans gained 120 House seats. Under Babcock, the committee created a "literary department," precursor of the present public relations division, which circulated millions of GOP campaign pamphlets throughout the country. In preparation for the 1902 congressional campaign, the committee moved to New York, reflecting Babcock's conviction that New York was "an extremely convenient center for conducting a campaign." The committee's headquarters remained there until 1908, when they were shifted back to Washington, where they have been ever since.

The Taft-Roosevelt "Bull Moose" split of 1912 also tore apart the congressional committee. In that year, only 127 Republicans were elected to the House. In 1919, the committee was further weakened when Republican Senators (who had been elected by popular vote since 1913) formed their own campaign committee. The division continues to the present day. With the election of Franklin D. Roosevelt in 1932, the Republican Congressional Committee suffered another decline. Rep. Chester Bolton, Ohio, was elected its chairman in 1932, only to lose his own seat in the Roosevelt landslide of 1936. (Bolton later returned to Congress. Upon his death in 1940, the seat was filled by his wife, Frances, who held it until 1969.)

After the Republicans' 1936 setback, the committee began to rebuild its professional staff under a new chairman, the late Rep. Joseph W. Martin Jr., Mass. (1925-67). Martin shifted the burden of fund raising, a major problem in the Depression years, to the Republican National Committee. Under this consolidation, the national committee subsidized the operations of the congressional unit for the next 10 years. In 1948, however, the unsuccessful Presidential campaign of the late Thomas E. Dewey, Governor of New York in 1943-55, absorbed virtually all of the national committee's resources. The GOP lost 75 seats in the House.

Rep. Leonard W. Hall, N.Y. (1939-52), for the first time in

modern years established a permanent year-round professional staff. As in the post-Civil War period, the committee
once more began to enjoy an independent role. Hall had taken
over in 1947 from Rep. Charles A. Halleck, Ind. (1935-69), when
Halleck moved up to majority leader and Martin to speaker
in the GOP-run 80th Congress. In 1949, Hall shifted the committee's offices from the National Press Building in downtown
Washington to the since-demolished George Washington Inn
on Capitol Hill. Six years later, the committee moved across
the street to its present quarters in the Congressional Hotel.

After directing the 1952 House campaign, the last one which
produced a congressional majority for the Republicans, Hall
became Republican national chairman (1952-57). He was succeeded by the late Rep. Richard M. Simpson, Pa. (1937-60).
Simpson's death in early 1960 led to the election of Rep.
William E. Miller, N.Y. (1951-65), as chairman of the congressional committee. Miller, a scrappy GOP partisan, helped
produce a net gain of 21 GOP seats in the 1960 campaign, despite the election of a Democratic President, John F. Kennedy.
(In the 1964 Presidential elections, Miller ran as the Vice Presidential nominee on the Republican ticket with Sen. Barry Goldwater of Arizona.) Miller was succeeded in 1962 by Wilson,
who has held the House campaign post since.

As chairman, Wilson runs his own show, although he nurtures
good relations with his fellow Republicans of all political
leanings as carefully as he tends the prize flowers at his
Potomac, Md., home. In nearly a decade as chairman of the
campaign committee, Wilson, 55, has escaped serious criticism
from party factions in the House, although his voting record
falls sharply to the right of the Republican spectrum. (Wilson's
cumulative "liberal quotient" rating from the Americans for
Democratic Action (ADA) is a low 17 per cent.) Wilson's dedication to the political arts is illustrated by an incident that
occurred during the 1964 Presidential campaign. Goldwater,
the Republican Presidential nominee, boarded a special train

from Los Angeles to San Diego. This was Wilson's home territory—his 36th District is in San Diego—and Wilson urged Goldwater "to pour it on" at the various campaign stops. But Goldwater, affectionately absorbed with a young granddaughter who was put aboard the train, made only a few perfunctory appearances before the crowds. While Wilson was then and is now ideologically close to Goldwater, he was distressed by the Senator's campaign performance which, he told friends at the time, "lacked professionalism."

Wilson told *National Journal:* "I think this committee is the most professional political organization in Washington. I really do. These people are *trained.* Admittedly, some of them are new. But some others have been around a long while. We try to be innovative. My background before coming to Congress was in PR and in campaign management and I've tried to bring professionalism into that committee." Wilson is the sole advertising man in Congress. He began his advertising career in 1936 and now serves as vice president of Tolle Company, a San Diego-based advertising and public relations firm. Wilson is also an accomplished chef and the author of five cookbooks heavily spiced with campaign notes. He is a skin diver and an award-winning flower grower. He entered Congress in 1953 and has risen to the No. 4 GOP position on the House Armed Services Committee. (He is a lieutenant colonel in the Marine Corps Reserves.) In 1970, Wilson was reelected to the House with 71.5 per cent of the votes cast.

Wilson's congressional campaign committee role makes him a member of the House Republican leadership. Wilson has long dealt amiably with President Nixon, a fellow native Californian. He was national coordinator of the Nixon Vice Presidential campaign in 1956 and the Nixon national campaign schedule director in the 1960 Presidential campaign. He shows no inclination of seeking a higher berth in the House Republican leadership, as some of his predecessors in the campaign job have done. "I think the continuity is helpful," Wilson said, adding: "I'm not a legislator. I don't get up on the House floor and make speeches. This is my way of making a contribution to the legislative process."

In theory, Wilson is accountable to the full Republican Congressional Committee, which consists of one Member of Congress from each of the 39 states that has GOP representation, plus Wilson. Each Member casts as many votes as there are GOP Members in his state delegation. The full committee also elects regional vice chairmen while Wilson appoints an executive committee. This combined steering group meets, on the average, every six weeks. The full committee, however, meets only once or twice a year to ratify major policy moves taken under Wilson's direction by the smaller executive unit. (See Table 7.1.)

At the beginning of the second session of the 91st Congress (1970), Wilson reorganized the top-level staff of the campaign committee. In the reshuffle, Wilson removed I. Lee Potter, 62, a wealthy Northern Virginia businessman, as the committee's $30,000-a-year executive director and replaced him with John T. (Jack) Calkins, 46, a veteran executive assistant to Rep. Howard W. Robison, R-N.Y. He arranged for Potter to be named executive director of the Republican Congressional Boosters Club, which helps finance campaigns of GOP Senate and House candidates running against Democratic incumbents. Wilson's final reorganization move was to streamline the committee staff into four divisions operating under Calkins, creating a more clearly defined division of responsibility and authority than had existed under Potter. (See Chart 7.1.)

"There was White House pressure to remove him (Potter)," Wilson said in an interview. "I refused to do it. He wanted to resign for a year but I said no. Finally, when the Boosters thing came along, it was a good opportunity for him and we made the change." In the battle for the 1968 GOP Presidential nomination, Potter, Republican national committeeman from Virginia since 1964 and the congressional commitee's director since 1967, was not known as a "Nixon man." He did not oppose Mr. Nixon but, when other key Virginians were getting on the Nixon bandwagon, he sought unsuccessfully to keep the delegation uncommitted prior to the 1968 GOP National Convention in Miami. This pre-convention independence cost Potter potential friends at the Nixon White House in 1969. The

President also was displeased because Republicans had lost four of five 1969 by-elections in the House — two of them for seats the GOP had held for decades. Mr. Nixon and his key political advisers laid part of the blame for these failures at Potter's feet while Wilson staunchly defended Potter's performance.

"Bob Wilson first called me in mid-December (1969)," Calkins recalled. "Since I took this job, I've never been vetoed in a decision. I have wide latitude and day-to-day operational authority. The chairman and I talk at least once each day and we get together for an hour each Tuesday." Wilson is pleased with the change. He has told House colleagues that "I consider Jack one of the top professionals in this business." Calkins served for 17 years as an executive assistant to Rep. Robison before assuming the committee's top staff post in 1970. Calkins first came to Washington in 1949 as an aide to former Rep. John C. Davies, D-N.Y. (1949-51), leaving two years later to become an advertising man in his native Elmira, N.Y. He returned to the capital in 1953 as an aide to Rep. W. Sterling Cole, R-N.Y. (1935-57), serving until Cole left Congress to head the International Atomic Energy Agency in Vienna. In 1958, after obtaining a law degree, Calkins joined Robison, Cole's successor in the House, as chief of staff.

The congressional committee's four division chiefs report to Calkins:

● Curtis R. Fulton, 44, joined the committee in 1967 after retiring from the Air Force with 20 years of active duty. Fulton directs the committee's finance division. He is also director of the sustaining membership fund of the Republican National Finance Committee as well as treasurer of Capitol Hill Associates Inc., which is building the office complex that houses the Republican National Committee. Among associates, Fulton, who flew 100 combat missions in Korea, is known as "The Major." He holds a masters degree in business administration from the Air Force Institute of Technology.

● Edward A. Terrill, 52, was named director of the committee's campaign division in February 1970. Previously, he served nine years as its field representative for the Midwestern states. Terrill directed field operations for the Wisconsin Republican Party between 1957 and 1959. In the 1960 campaign, he was field director of the Republican National Committee's farm division. Between 1951 and 1963, Terrill operated a 300-acre dairy and hog farm in Wisconsin.

- Paul A. Theis, 47, director of the public relations division, joined the committee in 1957 after serving as executive assistant to former Rep. Oliver P. Bolton, R-Ohio (1953-57, 1963-65). Prior to that, Theis worked as a Washington correspondent for *Newsweek*, for Fairchild Publications and for the *Army Times*. Theis graduated from Notre Dame in 1948. During World War II, he was a bomber pilot in Europe.

- J. Lee Wade, 54, director of services, in 1950 helped reorganize the committee — which, for the previous 75 years, had always functioned with three or fewer staff members. Wade was picture editor and art director of the now-defunct *Washington Times-Herald* when he joined the committee. Previously, he worked as a Washington columnist and illustrator for the *Chicago Tribune*. In his 21 years on the committee, Wade has also served as public relations director and campaign director.

Since 1955, the congressional committee has occupied rooms at the Congressional Hotel, across from the Cannon House Office Building. Divisions have suites on different floors, increasing the committee's internal communication problems. The committee pays an annual rent to the hotel of about $35,000. "I think it's wrong to run a political operation on government property," Wilson said. "I know it's done. The Senate does it. The head guy for the Democrats' (campaign arm) is on the House payroll." He referred to Kenneth R. Harding, who serves both as an assistant sergeant at arms in the House and as executive director of the Democratic National Congressional Committee, and is paid for both jobs. "Paying your own way gives you greater independence with a Democrat-controlled Congress," Calkins observed. "But it also raises expenses." The Congressional Hotel is owned by the federal government. It is leased back by the General Services

Administration to the Knott hotel chain. The full committee, including the finance division and Potter's Boosters operation, will move in early 1972 into a new office complex on Capitol Hill known as the Dwight D. Eisenhower National Republican Center. The center also houses the Republican National Committee — and will eventually bring together all official GOP campaign functions in Washington.

The committee's independence from the Republican National Committee depends on a continuing ability to finance its own operations. In 1968, the committee's budget was $2.8 million. It began 1970 with an announced budget of $4.3 million. However, Calkins told *National Journal* in August 1970: "We're not going to raise it and we're not going to spend it. Realistically, I hope we can do the job for $3.2 million, some of which still has to be raised."

The final figure was $2.9 million, reflecting the widespread difficulty most political groups encountered in raising funds in 1970, much of which was due to a weaker economy and depressed stock prices. The committee started 1970 with a campaign kitty of more than $1 million, having raised about $1.7 million and spent only $672,000 in 1969. In the first eight months of 1970, its income and spending both came to about $1.8 million, leaving about $1.1 million to be spent in September and October.

About 25 cents of each dollar the committee raises goes toward raising additional dollars to finance its political work. "We have a sophisticated computer operation," Fulton, chief of the finance division, told *National Journal*. The committee's extensive list of actual and potential contributors is kept on magnetic tape. A computer is used to prepare mailing labels and write solicitations. Each donor receives a computerized receipt and those who contribute $100 or more receive a letter signed by Wilson.

The committee's median contribution is $17.50. Four-fifths of its budget is met with contributions of $100 or less. The largest single source of funds is the committee's weekly *News-letter*, which nets about $1.5 million a year through a $25 annual subscription price. Much of the remaining budget is raised through the committee's share of proceeds from an annual Senate-House Republican Dinner. The 1970 share came to about $620,000; the 1971 dinner produced about $500,000 for the committee. (Proceeds from the dinner go to the House GOP campaign committee, the National Republican Senatorial Committee and the Republican National Committee.)

Fulton said that about $1.3 million of the committee's funds was spent in 1969-70 in direct support of GOP incumbents in the House — 167 of whom were seeking reelection. Direct aid comes in two forms — drawing accounts and direct cash contributions. Each Member was provided an annual public relations drawing account of $3,000 that could be spent on such items as newsletters, speech reprints, constituent questionnaires and the use of the House recording studio. GOP freshmen and incumbents who won in 1968 with 55 per cent or less of the vote got an additional $2,000, giving them a total drawing account of $5,000. (In all, 32 Members qualified for the additional aid.)

An unrestricted campaign cash contribution of $4,000, known as "an organization and education" fund, was made available to each GOP House Member. The name of the fund was chosen to counter the Committee on Political Education (COPE) of the AFL-CIO which the congressional committee has traditionally viewed as its chief anti-Republican nemesis. Each marginal GOP Member and freshman got an additional $3,000 cash, giving them $7,000 apiece in addition to their annual public relations drawing account. These subsidies were somewhat more generous than those provided in 1968 when much of the party's fund-raising efforts were directed toward aiding the Nixon-Agnew ticket. In that year, the public relations account amounted to $2,000 (with an extra $1,000 for marginal and freshmen Members), while the campaign fund

came to $3,500 (with an extra $1,500 for marginals and freshmen.) In 1970, marginal Republicans and freshmen—key targets for Democratic challengers—received a total of $12,000
each in direct aid from the committee—a new record for financial support. The committee dispenses aid to incumbents
before July 1 if they have filed for reelection without opposition. The aid is deferred if an incumbent faces a primary hur-
dle. Except for Members with primary opposition, an entire
state delegation usually receives its campaign checks at the
same time.

The committee sets no political loyalty tests for its subsidies and support, a policy that increases its popularity
among GOP Members. "I have to fight this with lobbyists all
the time," Calkins told National Journal. (Lobbyists are among
the committee's large benefactors. In particular, the annual
Senate-House fund-raising dinners sponsored by both Republicans and Democrats are heavily subscribed by lobbyists
based in Washington.) "In the 1950s," Calkins said, "conservatives got most of the money. That's not the way we operate
now. We've got to spread the (political) base as much as possible. If they're willing to say they're Republicans, that's
enough." Wilson told National Journal: "Philosophy won't
enter into it—not while I'm around. I won't let it. We have
people sniping at the formula, trying to change it. But I won't
let them."

In addition to direct aid, the committee's public relations
division, under veteran director Paul Theis, provides a number of services for House incumbents. A cameraman equipped
with portable sound-on-film equipment is available to film
GOP Members at locations other than the recording studio.
Coaching in television techniques and counseling on the
effective use of the medium was provided in 1970 by actor
Lee Bowman two weeks a month; for the remaining two
weeks, Bowman was employed by the GOP Senate Campaign
Committee. Theis said Bowman, whose contract expired in
1971, will probably be employed again in the 1972 campaign
year. The committee has a news bureau that prepares and
distributes press releases which, as Wilson explains, a Mem-

ber "might consider too self-serving to put out from (his) own office" and a taping service that records radio press releases by freshmen and marginal GOP Members and sends the Members' recorded reports directly to radio stations in their districts. A public relations seminar for top Republican House staff members is held every two years. Candidates also receive editing assistance in the preparation of speeches—but no outright ghostwriting. A large file of speeches by Republicans is available, broken down by subject matter and the audience for which is is suited.

Services available for Republican incumbents from the committee's other divisions include: professional art work for newsletters, press releases and campaign letterheads; a photographic service that employs two full-time photographers who take and process pictures at Members' request (the photographers have facilities in the Rayburn House Office Building and are the only committee staffers that work from offices within the Congress); a running tabulation of incumbent voting records for both Republicans and Democrats (a complete voting analysis on each issue that came before the House is sent to every GOP Member after the session adjourns); and comprehensive briefings for new Members held at Airlie House, a Northern Virginia retreat, every two years at the start of a new Congress.

The committee has developed two programs for the 1972 Republican congressional campaigns. In cooperation with its Senate counterpart, the National Republican Senatorial Committee, the committee is sponsoring a program to instruct campaign managers in methods of running a successful campaign. The candidates, both incumbents and non-incumbents, must cover the costs required to send their campaign managers to the conferences, slated for fall of 1971 and spring of 1972. The congressional committee also is undertaking a program called "Young Voters for a Republican Congress," directed by William A. Russo, 21, a graduate of the University of North Carolina and a 1971 summer intern at the committee. Russo said the program is designed to "tell congressional candidates how to find and involve the 18- to 25-year-old voter in their campaigns." It will also "advise candidates on how to set up programs in their districts which are of concern to this age group," Russo explained. These programs "must be a continuing year-round thing," he said. "They (the candidates) have to prove to this age group that they are interested and involved (in the issues that concern young people), and not just at election time."

The congressional committee devotes an estimated 40 to 50 per cent of its total resources to helping GOP candidates who are seeking to oust Democratic House Members. Challengers receive no direct cash subsidies from funds raised by the committee. Such funds are raised through the seven-year-old Republican Congressional Boosters Club, which is directed by Lee Potter, and channeled through the committee to the candidates.

The Boosters' 1970 goal was $1.5 million. Potter told *National Journal* that the club fell short of this goal by "several thousand dollars." There are two classes of membership in the club: $3,000 and $1,000, although smaller donations are accepted. Two-thirds of the Boosters' income is spent on House races; the remaining third goes into Senate contests. Reports filed with the Clerk of the House of Representatives show the Boosters contributed a total of $1,297,227 to House and Senate challengers in 1970—$452,917 to 21 Senate candidates and $844,310 to 119 House candidates. (See Table 7.2.)

The Boosters have no overhead. All costs, including Potter's salary, are absorbed by the congressional committee and the GOP Senate Campaign Committee in the same two-to-one ratio as disbursements. "With the Boosters, we have more flexibility," Wilson observed. "We try to make a hard judgment where the money will do the most good. We must continually evaluate the chances of winning because the money is raised on that basis."

In 1970, much of the committee's resources, including the funds made available through the Boosters, were funneled into 82 key congressional districts, where—through research and intelligence—the committee staff determined Republican candidates had the best chance of defeating Democrats in November, or where a GOP seat was threatened because there was no incumbent seeking reelection. The committee's all-out effort focused on 56 "target" areas, 23 of which the Republicans won. Included in the target areas were 22 "open" GOP House districts and 11 out of 21 "open" Democratic districts— those without an incumbent seeking reelection. (Since, statistically, an incumbent has a 97 per cent chance of retaining his seat, the 22 open GOP seats were viewed as high-priority targets by the Democrats and, therefore, were of prime concern to the congressional committee. The Republican seats were not being defended by incumbents for varying reasons: 12 Members were running for the Senate, four were entering gubernatorial races, three were retiring, one Member was defeated in the primary elections and two seats were vacant.) GOP candidates successfully challenged the opposition in 19 of the 33 open districts pinpointed by the committee.

The 56 target districts got the top Boosters Club money the committee distributed to GOP challengers in 1970: $10,000. (A committee spokesman said the committee's policy is to distribute no more than $10,000 to any one challenger—donations in excess of this amount represent funds earmarked for a specific candidate by the contributor.) "We regard all of our contributions as seed money and as an expression of confidence at the national level," Executive Director Calkins said. "If a challenger who receives a check for $10,000 from us can't go out and raise 10 times that amount, then I regard our money as misspent," Calkins added. "But, usually, if they can flash a check from Washington, that can trigger substantial further support." In 1970, Calkins said, the strategy "at the top" was to concentrate on the Senate. He said the committee did not "quarrel" with the strategy, but viewed as an "unfortunate aspect" the large number of House seats being vacated by Congressmen running for the Senate. In a handful of House districts the committee was willing to pledge the $10,000 campaign-aid limit to attract a strong candidate to make the race. Usually however, the committee's checks reflected the tempo of the contest and were spread over several months.

In its selection of target areas for 1972, the congressional committee will examine the shift in congressional seats resulting from redistricting. Fourteen states are required to redistrict before the 1972 elections; nine of these states will lose one or more seats, and five will gain one or more seats. Terrill, chief of the campaign division, told *National Journal* the committee hopes to "gain six to seven of the new seats." California and Florida are two of the states the committee will be watching closely, he said. California will gain five seats, giving the state a total of 43 Representatives, and Florida will pick up three seats, bringing its total delegation to 15. The 1972 target areas were to be determined by the committee in October and November 1971, the customary time when the committee sets its financial goals for the election year.

Although it occasionally assists incumbents with severe problems, the committee's campaign division exists primarily to help GOP challengers who are trying to unseat House Democrats. "We run a very low-profile shop," Terrill said in an interview. "Generally speaking, we don't talk to the press." Terrill supervises the committee's extensive field program, a section for women's campaign activities directed by Mrs. Mary Ellen Miller as well as sections that compile voting statistics and perform political research. The committee's original plan for 1970 called for 18 field representatives. (The field men were redesignated as "regional directors" by Terrill to "increase their prestige.") Budget cuts, stemming from fundraising problems, curtailed the field program to seven men and one woman, Mrs. Miller. "Our men are never in Washington except for meetings," Terrill said, adding: "By the end of September, they zero in on three to five congressional districts in their areas where our sustained help could really make a difference. The field representatives act as coordinators. Often, they hand over our checks and set the conditions. They provide aid in any and every field where the candidate and his staff are deemed to be weak—organization, finance or public relations."

The congressional committee hires outside consultants on a regular basis to perform special services, such as poll-taking. The committee's field men are instructed not to recommend political management firms to candidates. "We give them a list of competent people and let them make their own contacts," Terrill said. Calkins explained that the field men "try to fit their political views to the district." "They also try to take an objective view and seek a totally professional image," he said. If a candidate should be defeated at the polls, the field man returns to the district after the election to conduct a political postmortem and to help spur planning for the next election, two years hence.

The committee sponsors a biennial pre-campaign conference for non-incumbent GOP candidates, their wives and their aides. In 1970, the three-day meeting, held in Washington in mid-June, attracted about 125 candidates and a total of 350 wives and staff assistants. All of the visitors paid their own travel and hotel expenses, plus a $60 registration fee. "This is the single most important thing the committee does," Calkins said, referring to the series of tightly packed briefings given to the candidates by veteran Republican lawmakers and such GOP political notables as Harry S. Dent, a special counsel to the President. Only one of the campaign school sessions, a closing address by Vice President Agnew, was open to the press. The GOP candidates also had a picture-taking session and reception at the White House given by the President and Mrs. Nixon on the evening of June 10. The congressional committee paid the $2,000 entertainment bill.

The committee's public relations division runs a publications section under L. David LeRoy, former congressional correspondent for *U.S. News and World Report* and 1967 president of the National Press Club, who joined the committee in 1970. LeRoy's chief publication is the eight-page multi-colored *Newsletter,* published every Thursday while Congress is in session and through November in election years.

The *Newsletter* compiles GOP activities in a crisply worded, large-type, well-illustrated format. Few issues pass without a swipe at the Democrats. The *Newsletter* is sent to about 55,000 paid subscribers. In addition, 50 copies are distributed to each GOP House office and copies are circulated to Washington reporters. Until recently, the *Newsletter* was the subject of considerable controversy within GOP circles. A Member from a Northeastern state who requested anonymity said: "We would throw our copies in the trash can. It had a blatant right-wing bias." LeRoy acknowledges this criticism but maintains that it is no longer valid. "We can't be in the business of rating Republicans," he said. Calkins, who is also aware of the "image" problem, said: "The *Newsletter* is now aimed at the broad range of Republicans in the United States."

The committee also publishes: *Daily News Digest*, a one-page fact sheet culled from wire-service reports that is distributed to GOP Members and to the Press; and *Newsletter Notes*, a weekly publication discussing a current issue in the news from the House Republican point of view that is designed to provide material for Members to use in newsletters to constituents. *Political Punch Lines*, a popular compendium of anti-Democratic quips and stories that LeRoy describes as "toastmaster stuff," was published during the 1970 campaigns and will probably be put out again in 1972. Other publications are *Speech of the Week*, delivered by a leading Republican, that is reprinted in full and sent to GOP Members and candidates; and *Daily Campaign Memo*, published in election years between September and November, that is sent to GOP candidates on a private wire leased by the committee. (One 1968 sample urged candidates to condemn former President Johnson for his pre-election decision to halt the bombing of North Vietnam but then cautioned: "Don't come out looking like you're for war and against peace in your comments.")

Despite its relative independence, the congressional committee still negotiates daily with other power centers in the Republican hierarchy. "As recently as two decades ago this committee was a two-room suite in the National Press Building; it was a 'white-envelope operation,' " Calkins recalled, referring to the years when it was primarily a conduit for campaign funds from other sources without fund raising or services of its own. "What made the difference was the decision in the late 1950s to take on our own fund-raising arm. Before that we were really at the mercy of the national committee and the White House."

The National Republican Finance Committee, a coordinating body, still approves the congressional committee's budget each year. The original 1970 budget, approved in December 1969, was cut to $4.3 million by mutual consent. "We feel a moral sense of obligation to make up their deficits either through loans, grants or services in kind," a member of the GOP Finance Committee who asked not to be identified told *National Journal*. "We get weekly reports on contributions and expenditures so we're able to keep pretty good tabs on that."

Regarding the congressional committee's dealings with the Republican National Committee, Calkins said that communication "at the top management level is steady but not day-to-day." One area of cooperation, he noted, is in the finance field, since the committee's budget is approved by the GOP Finance Committee. In addition, an effort is made to coordinate general policy, publications and research as well as to stagger fund-raising drives, Calkins said. "We're able to talk turkey with them. We try not to duplicate their work." Lyn Nofziger, deputy national chairman for communications at the RNC, described the relationship as "cordial and cooperative." But, he said, "we are not close because their job is to elect and re-elect Members of the House and our job is to build the national party and reelect the President."

While the President and his political staff were concentrating their attention in 1970 on Senate races, the House GOP campaign committee was not being neglected. "We have a very good liaison with the White House these days," Calkins told *National Journal* in September 1970. "We deal exclusively with their political arm, which is to say Dent, Chotiner and Lias. I talk to Murray Chotiner almost daily. It's a very good set-up." (Dent is a political adviser to President Nixon; Thomas L.

Lias, formerly a deputy assistant to the President who served as an aide to Dent, is currently a special assistant in the office of the U.S. Representative to the United Nations; Murray M. Chotiner, a former special counsel to the President, is now associated with the Washington, D.C., law firm of Reeves & Hamilton.) Herbert G. Klein, director of communications for the executive branch, said he was unaware of any past problems between the White House and the congressional committee. Calkins, he noted, regularly attended the White House meetings of the Administration's 1970 election task force. According to Rep. Wilson, the campaign committee has continued to maintain a good relationship with the White House. Currently, he said, the committee's dealings are with Dent and, to a lesser extent, with Charles W. Colson, a special counsel to the President, and Clark MacGregor, counsel to the President for congressional relations.

The committee's most crucial and most delicate relationships are those it maintains with individual Republicans in Congress and their staffs. In general, the relationship is an excellent one. "They deserve very high marks for their performance over the years. They do a truly superb job," Rep. Gerald R. Ford, R-Mich., the House minority leader, said. Some money-short incumbents have pressured Wilson and Calkins to release contributions earlier in the year. Yet the level of controversy has been dampened through a strict application of the fixed formula for disbursements—insuring all incumbents that, sooner or later, they will receive their fair share of committee funds. Among reform-minded Republicans in the House there is a widespread feeling that Calkins, in succeeding Potter, has striven to deal even-handedly with Members—whether or not they happen to be staunch supporters of the Nixon Administration's programs.

Wresting control of the Senate from the Democrats became a prime Republican goal when President Nixon entered the White House in 1968. But this effort fell short in 1970. (A net shift of eight seats into the GOP column would have brought about a Republican-run Senate in the 92nd Congress; the GOP gained only two seats.) In 1972, the Republican effort will focus on holding its own as President Nixon seeks reelection. Much of the political intelligence and financial muscle for this effort is funneled through a cramped two-room suite on the fourth floor of the Old Senate Office Building — home of the 52-year-old National Republican Senatorial Committee.

The coordinating group for this thrust, familiarly known as the Senate GOP Campaign Committee, has a more limited operation — in staff, budget and services performed — than its counterpart in the House. The committee is directed by Sen. Peter H. Dominick of Colorado, a member of the committee in 1965-66 who was renamed to the panel in 1969. When he took the chairmanship in January 1971, Dominick said, "My primary responsibility as chairman of this committee will be to get the 19 incumbent Republican Senators whose terms expire in 1972 reelected. In order to get a Republican majority in the Senate, we will have to work harder than ever, because there are only 14 incumbent Democrats up for reelection, and a good deal of the national attention will be focused on the Presidential election. I firmly believe that some of the Democratic Senators will be vulnerable in 1972."

Dominick began organizing the committee's 1972 election strategy shortly after he was elected chairman by the 45-member GOP Senate contingent. His first step was to divide the country into 12 regions and assign each member of the committee responsibility for determining in his region the vulnerability of Democratic and Republican seats up in 1972. Dominick's aim is to gather the basic political intelligence early and keep constant tabs on political developments in each region to determine where Republican candidates have the best chance of defeating Democrats.

Aside from Dominick, the Senate GOP Campaign Committee consists of 12 Senators, six of whom are freshmen: J. Glenn Beall Jr. of Maryland, W. E. Brock of Tennessee, James L. Buckley of New York, William V. Roth, Jr. of Delaware, Robert Taft Jr. of Ohio, Lowell P. Weicker Jr. of Connecticut,

William B. Saxbe of Ohio, Charles McC. Mathias Jr. of Maryland, Barry Goldwater of Arizona, Robert Dole of Kansas, Paul J. Fannin of Arizona and Hiram L. Fong of Hawaii. Senators are ineligible to serve on the campaign panel in the final two years of their Senate term. Consequently, Dominick, whose term of office expires in 1975, must step down as chairman in January 1973.

Dominick was preceded as chairman of the committee by Sen. John G. Tower of Texas, who had served in the post since 1969; by former Sen. George Murphy of California (1967-69), who was defeated in 1970 after serving one term in the Senate; by former Sen. Thruston B. Morton of Kentucky (1965-67), who declined to run for reelection in 1968 after having served 12 years in the Senate; and by Goldwater (1963-65), whose wide-ranging activities as Senate campaign chairman served as a springboard for his party's Presidential nomination in 1964.

Much of the actual money-raising is coordinated by the committee's director, Buehl Berentson, 46, former director of the Republican Governors' Association. Berentson took the committee's top administrative post in April 1971, replacing Lee R. Nunn, who had served as director since 1967. Nunn, a former director of the Republican National Finance Committee (January to May 1970) and currently director of the fund-raising division for the Committee for the Reelection of the President, remained in the background more than Berentson, believing that the chairman should be the sole spokesman for the committee. Berentson, a native of Washington state, received an A.B. degree from Pacific Lutheran University, Tacoma, Wash. Following service in the Navy in World War II, he set up a real estate and investment firm in the Anacortes, Wash., area. He came to Washington, D.C., in 1960, as an aide to former Rep. Jack Westland, R-Wash. (1953-65). After Westland's defeat in 1964, Berentson joined the Republican Congressional Campaign Committee as field representative for the 13 western states. He remained with the House committee until he was named director of the Republican Governors' Association in January 1969. Dominick and Berentson consult frequently and operate the committee with a skeleton staff. Berentson's principal aide is Mrs. Glee D. Gomien, former executive secretary to the late Sen. Everett McKinley Dirksen, R-Ill. (1951-69). The committee also employs a five-member clerical and secretarial staff.

During 1970, the committee raised and spent far more than it did during the 1968 campaign year. The committee reported receipts of $1,520,222.64 in 1970. About 90 per cent of the committee's total proceeds are raised through annual $1,000-a-plate all-star GOP dinners held in Washington. The manner in which the proceeds are divided is a matter of intense, if highly private, negotiations; no two dinners are handled in exactly the same way. The last such dinner, held in March 1971, netted approximately $1.5 million. The Senate committee's share of the proceeds was one-third, according to Berentson. In 1970, the committee, which paid the expenses of the dinner, received a total of $1,013,286.31.

Unlike its House counterpart, which makes direct contributions to incumbents only, the Senate GOP Campaign Committee provides direct cash subsidies to challengers and incumbents. Berentson told *National Journal* that while the committee obviously was set up by incumbents to support incumbents, it realizes an incumbent Senator often has the resources and political knowledge to win elections that challengers may not have. "They (incumbents) can take care of themselves given the material (money and people). You have to concentrate a little more effort where challengers are concerned," Berentson said. Reports filed with the Clerk of the House of Representatives, as required under the Corrupt Practices Act, show the campaign committee in 1969 and 1970 spent a total of $1,847,566.06, of which $546,836 was in direct contributions to 18 challengers and the nine Senate incumbents seeking reelection in 1970. (The Republican Congressional Boosters Club, which provides additional financial assistance to challengers through the committee, reported donations totaling $452,917 to 21 candidates in 1970. (See Tables 7.2 and 7.3.)

The committee's financial reports revealed that the amount provided incumbents may vary widely. In 1969 and 1970, the committee made payments totaling $72,948 to Sen. George Murphy, the most given to any of the nine incumbents. (However, Murphy's total was surpassed by Rep. George Bush, Texas GOP Senate candidate, who received payments totaling $76,099 from the committee, and an additional $55,500 from the Boosters Club.) Trailing the list of incumbents was Sen. Charles E. Goodell, R-N.Y., who received only $16,531 during the same period. (All three candidates were defeated in the November 1970 elections.) Goodell felt the reason he had received less was that funds were being "earmarked" through the committee to other candidates who had a firmer record of support for the President's positions. However, Nunn denied that any funds raised by the committee are earmarked for a particular incumbent or candidate.

At times, the campaign committee effectively masks its fiscal operations from public scrutiny by funneling funds to other committees whose ultimate benefactors cannot readily be identified. For example, in 1970, the Tower group gave $5,000 to the "Committee to Further Educational Opportunities," which was based in Washington, D.C., but which it did not otherwise identify. Two other groups involved in an unspecified manner in the Senate Republican political scene also received contributions: the "D.C. Committee for Effective Legislation" ($5,000) and the "Citizens for Good Government Committee" ($4,780).

"There's no formula over here on giving out funds as there is in the House," Tower told National Journal in 1970. "We'll help incumbents regardless of primary foes and we'll help challengers after they have surmounted all of their primary problems and if we think they have a chance of winning. All of it goes out on a purely cold basis of who stands the best chance at the polls. There are no political reprisals. You can't get into that. What we're aiming at is votes to organize the Senate. After we give it to them, we don't dictate how they should spend it, although we do make recommendations." Tower declined to discuss the policy process under which committee funds are divided and distributed. Other Senate sources said, however, that Tower and Nunn made the decisions after consulting with key White House staffers. Tower's secrecy led to protest from his Republican colleagues. Subsequently, further funds were distributed to Republicans who had received less money on the first go-round.

The committee maintains a continuing program of subsidies and services to Republican Senators to enhance their chances of reelection. The committee generally provides a minimum of $5,000 to each GOP incumbent in each of the last two years of his Senate term. Berentson said $5,000 was given to each incumbent in 1971, with the exception of Sen. John Sherman Cooper of Kentucky, who has said he will retire, and several others Berentson said "have left themselves in positions of indecision."

In addition, each GOP incumbent facing reelection receives for two years a committee air travel card which he may use for an unrestricted amount of personal travel between Washington and any point in his home state. (A Senate expense account, funded from the Treasury, covers 12 such round-trips a year, but the Senator must state that his trip was made on "official business.") The committee also subsidizes the use of the Senate Recording Studio by all Republican Senators, to a limit of $500 monthly for each Senator. The committee recording studio payments were $67,927.24 in 1970.

In the two months preceding the November 1970 elections, Tower organized "flying squads" of GOP Senators to tour key states as a group on behalf of promising GOP challengers. Such squads normally numbered from four to six Senators, although 12 GOP Senators campaigned in Illinois for Sen. Ralph T. Smith on September 14. (Smith, who had served in the Senate since 1969 as the interim replacement for the late Sen. Dirksen, was defeated in the general elections.) Within GOP councils, it was felt such "flying squads" provided the advantage of creating more publicity than a single Senator could generate. Furthermore, the "flying squads" by their composition, could appeal to a wider segment of the electorate. Tower and Nunn conferred regularly with the 1970 group of GOP challengers. Nunn also arranged a series of informal briefings by key Administration officials for the challengers. One such briefing featured Peter M. Flanigan, an assistant to the President, and Paul W. McCracken, chairman of the Council of Economic Advisers. McCracken and Flanigan discussed the political implications of the economic situation.

In preparation for the 1972 campaigns, the Senate committee is developing a campaign managers training program in cooperation with its House counterpart. It also is considering a "candidates conference" for spring 1972, which, Berentson explained, would "give the challengers the benefit of press coverage, tips from incumbents and discussion of basic Republican issues and positions with incumbents and members of the Administration." Dominick and Berentson began in summer 1971 canvassing states to determine the committee's '72 target areas. "We're going to look at the statistics . . . look at the vulnerability of incumbents (Democrats and Republicans) and determine the defense and offense target areas," Berentson said. Berentson believes the committee has "a shot at" several of the 14 Democratic Senate seats up in 1972: "There are not many big opportunities in the South . . . but in the mountain states we have a chance and there are one or two seats in the central states and even some in the New England area. . . ."

Table 7.1   National Republican Congressional Committee

The National Republican Congressional Committee consists of one Member from each of the 39 states having Republican representation in the House, plus the chairman. (Robert T. Stafford of Vermont, a member of the committee since his election to the House in 1960, was appointed September 16, 1971, by Gov. Deane C. Davis, R, to fill the Senate seat held by Winston L. Prouty, R, who died September 10. Stafford is an interim replacement, pending a special primary and general election; Vermont's lone House seat will be filled in a special election, probably in January 1972.)

Members of the committee are younger and newer to Congress than those of the comparable committee on the Democratic side. They average 53 years of age and nearly 10 years in Congress, compared with 56 and 16, respectively, for Members of the House Democratic Campaign Committee.

	Years in Congress	Age
Bob Wilson, Calif. (36) *	19	55
William S. Broomfield, Mich. (18) #	15	49
Donald G. Brotzman, Colo. (2) #	7	49
Silvio O. Conte, Mass. (1) #	13	50
Carleton J. King, N.Y. (30) #	11	67
William M. McCulloch, Ohio (4) #	25	70
John P. Saylor, Pa. (22) #	23	63
William L. Springer, Ill. (22) #	21	62
William B. Widnall, N.J. (7) #	22	65
Benjamin B. Blackburn, Ga. (4) †	5	44
J. Herbert Burke, Fla. (10) †	5	58
Del Clawson, Calif. (23) †	9	57
James M. Collins, Tex. (3) †	4	55
Glenn R. Davis, Wis. (9) †	17	57
John Dellenback, Ore. (4) †	5	53
Dan Kuykendall, Tenn. (9) †	5	47
Wilmer Mizell, N.C. (5) †	3	41
Thomas M. Pelly, Wash. (1) †	19	69
Sam Steiger, Ariz. (3) †	5	42
Charles J. Thone, Neb. (1) †	1	47
Mark N. Andrews, N.D. (1)	9	45
Page Belcher, Okla. (1)	21	72
Joel T. Broyhill, Va. (10)	19	52
John Buchanan, Ala. (6)	7	43
James C. Cleveland, N.H. (2)	9	51
Pierre S. du Pont IV, Del. (AL)	1	36
Durward G. Hall, Mo. (7)	11	61
John Paul Hammerschmidt, Ark. (3)	5	49
Orval Hansen, Idaho (2)	3	45
Lawrence J. Hogan, Md. (5)	3	43
Sherman P. Lloyd, Utah (2)	7	57
Manuel Lujan Jr., N.M. (1)	3	43
Stewart B. McKinney, Conn. (4)	1	40
Albert H. Quie, Minn. (1)	14	48
Fred Schwengel, Iowa (1)	15	64
Richard G. Shoup, Mont. (1)	1	48
Joe Skubitz, Kan. (5)	9	65
M. G. Snyder, Ky. (4)	7	43
Floyd Spence, S.C. (2)	1	43
Roger H. Zion, Ind. (8)	5	50

* chairman
# vice chairman
† executive committee

States not represented: Alaska, Hawaii, Louisiana, Maine, Mississippi, Nevada, Rhode Island, South Dakota, Vermont, West Virginia, Wyoming.

Table 7.2 Republican Congressional Boosters Club Contributions, 1970

In 1970, the Republican Congressional Boosters Club gave a total of $452,917 to 21 Republican Senate candidates. On the House side, 119 Republican candidates received contributions totaling $844,310. Five of the Senate candidates supported won and 25 of the House candidates were winners. The Boosters Club restricts its contributions to those GOP candidates who are seeking to oust Democratic Members. Funds are raised by the Boosters and channeled to the candidates through the National Republican Congressional (Campaign) Committee and its Senate counterpart, the National Republican Senatorial Committee. Listed below are the 1970 Boosters' contributions, as reported to the Clerk of the House of Representatives. (Boosters Club funds channeled to a candidate through a political committee are listed below the beneficiary's name.) Winners are in bold type.

Senate	Contribution
J. Glenn Beall Jr., Md.	$28,000
Neil S. Bishop, Maine	367
W. E. Brock, Tenn.	33,200
Laurence J. Burton, Utah	25,000
George Bush, Tex.	45,500
Senatorial Committee for Better Government, Texas	5,000
Tejanos Senatorial Committee, Texas	5,000
Anderson Carter, N.M	17,000
William C. Cramer, Fla.	24,100
Conservative Action Committee, Florida	5,000
Concerned Parents	5,000
John C. Danforth, Mo.	10,000
Raymond L. Garland, Va.	500
Nelson G. Gross, N.J.	12,000
Thomas S. Kleppe, N.D.	25,000
Concerned Citizens	5,000
Clark MacGregor, Minn.	18,700
John J. McLaughlin, R.I.	2,000
William J. Raggio, Nev.	30,000
Lenore Romney, Mich.	7,000
William V. Roth Jr., Del.	14,000
Delaware Senatorial Campaign Committee	5,000
Richard L. Roudebush, Ind.	36,450
Open Convention Committee, Indiana	5,000
Josiah A. Spaulding, Mass.	1,500
Robert Taft Jr., Ohio	32,600
Lowell P. Weicker Jr., Conn.	30,000
John Wold, Wyo.	25,000

House	
W. A. Archer, Tex.	11,300
Luke Atkinson, N.C.	10,000
LaMar Baker, Tenn.	10,250

House *(cont'd)*	**Contribution**
Clifton B. (Pete) Barham Jr., N.C.	$ 2,500
Edward B. Baskin, S.C.	3,500
Fred D. Brady, S.D.	10,000
Danny L. Burton, Ind.	7,100
Arthur W. Busch, Tex.	5,000
Gerald R. Ford Dinner Committee for Busch	2,500
Daniel E. Button, N.Y. *	1,000
Fred L. Casmir, Calif.	6,000
Richard K. Cockey, Hawaii	2,500
Bob Cooper, Ga.	5,000
Edward A. Costigan, N.J.	10,000
Frank Crowley, Tex.	6,000
Elmer Davies Jr., Tenn.	2,000
Margaret Dennison, Ohio	4,500
Ken Doll, W.Va.	5,000
Michael C. Donaldson, Calif.	10,000
Charles F. Dougherty, Pa.	5,000
William F. Dowd, N.J.	5,000
Elmore J. Duffy, Calif.	2,500
Robert J. Dunn, Conn.	2,500
Pierre S. du Pont IV, Del.	12,100
Dick Enroth, Minn.	3,100
Fred Evans, Ill.	2,500
R. Frank Everett, N.C.	8,500
Barry Farber, N.Y.	7,500
Adrian Fink, Ohio	6,000
Alfred E. Fontanella, N.J.	10,000
Edwin B. Forsythe, N.J.	10,000
William Frenzel, Minn.	10,700
Dick Fullerton, Ga.	2,500
Peter P. Garibaldi, N.J.	5,000
Richard Gill, Tex.	7,000
Bill Gossard, Colo.	3,350
Mark Guerra, Calif.	5,000
Dexter H. Gunderson, S.D.	10,000
R. (Jack) Hawke, N.C.	10,000
Tom Hayden, Calif.	10,000
John E. Healy, Calif.	10,000
James M. Helm, Va.	4,500
Morris Herring, Ariz.	6,500
Elwood H. Hillis, Ind.	5,000
Henry L. Hoebel, N.J.	10,000
Herbert H. Howell, N.C.	10,000
George R. Hughes Jr., Md.	10,000
John F. Jacobs, N.Y.	5,000
Griffith H. Jones, N.J.	2,500
Henry S. Kaplinski, Ill.	1,000
William J. Keating, Ohio	10,000
Jack F. Kemp, N.Y.	5,000
Committee for Republican Candidates	5,000

House *(cont'd)*

	Contribution
Richard C. Kilbourn, Conn.	$10,000
Michael Kitsock, Pa.	7,500
James B. Kuhn, Calif.	5,000
Ray Lee, Miss.	5,000
Norman F. Lent, N.Y.	11,000
Andre E. Le Tendre, Wis.	10,660
Brian Lewis, Wash.	2,500
Joe Z. Lovingood, Fla.	5,000
Robert P. McCarney, N.D.	10,000
John Y. McCollister, Neb.	10,000
John McGlennon, Mass.	10,250
James D. McKevitt, Colo.	10,000
Project '70, Colorado	250
Stewart B. McKinney, Conn.	10,000
Tom McMann, Calif.	10,250
Cole McMartin, Iowa	3,500
Mrs. Joe (Marian) McQuade, W.Va.	2,500
Wayne R. Merrick, Pa.	5,000
Howard A. Miller Jr., Mass.	1,500
Walter J. Miska, R.I.	1,000
Frank H. Murkowski, Alaska	10,450
Donald M. Newman, Ind.	7,500
John F. O'Connor, N.Y.	10,000
Peter Parker, Md.	5,000
John E. Parks, Calif.	7,500
James T. Patterson, Conn.	2,500
Gustine J. Pelagatti, Pa.	5,000
Peter A. Peyser, N.Y.	10,000
B. Leonard Phillips, S.C.	10,000
Howard Phillips, Mass.	5,000
Ross Z. Pierpont, Md.	6,500
Walter E. Powell, Ohio	10,000
Henry Pressler, Tex.	500
Thomas (Tom) Ragsdale, Ga.	2,500
Richard Marshall Reddecliff, W.Va.	5,500
Jack Rehberg, Mont.	10,000
Raymond J. Rice, N.Y.	8,500
Richard Richards, Utah	10,000
Harry Roberts, Wyo.	10,000
J. Kenneth Robinson, Va.	10,350
John H. Rousselot, Calif.#	7,750
Gary Rust, Mo.	10,000
Allen T. St. Clair, Va.	1,300
Phillip V. Sanchez, Calif.	10,000
Phyllis Schlafly, Ill.	10,000
John G. Schmitz, Calif.	7,750
Allen H. Shapiro, Ohio	4,500
Richard G. Shoup, Mont.	10,000
James W. Shue, N.J.	2,500

House *(cont'd)*	Contribution
David D. Smith, N.Y.	$ 7,500
Ronald T. Speers, Maine	2,500
Floyd Spence, S.C.	10,000
Hugh A. Sprague, Mo.	2,500
Peter J. Sprague, N.Y.	7,500
Committee for Better Government	3,000
Joe Staley, Tex.	10,000
Robert H. Steele, Conn.	9,000
William J. (Bill) Teague, Calif.	5,000
"11-70" Club	5,000
Lincoln Club	5,000
John H. Terry, N.Y.	10,250
Charles J. Thone, Neb.	10,000
Antonina P. Uccello, Conn.	10,000
Sam Van Dyken, Calif.	6,500
Victor V. Veysey, Calif.	10,300
John H. Ware III, Pa.	10,000
Richard B. Wathen, Ind.	2,500
Jay G. Wilkinson, Okla.	12,000
Republican Congressional Committee,D.C.	10,000
J. Harvie Wilkinson III, Va.	7,100
Leonard V. Wood, Fla.	5,000
C. W. Young, Fla.	10,000
Alex J. Zabrosky, Ill.	5,250

*   Not considered an incumbent by the Boosters Club due to redistricting.
\#   Contribution for June 1970 special election to fill vacancy created by the death of Rep. Glenard P. Lipscomb, R-Calif. Rousselot was reelected to the House November 3, 1970.

Source: Citizens' Research Foundation.

Table 7.3   National Republican Senatorial Committee Contributions, 1969-1970

In 1969-70, the National Republican Senatorial Committee contributed a total of $348,946 to the nine incumbents running for reelection in 1970. A total of $197,890 was contributed to 18 challengers in 1970. Listed below are the Senate GOP Campaign Committee's direct contributions to incumbents and challengers as reported to the Clerk of the House of Representatives.* Winners are in bold type.

Incumbents	Contribution
George Murphy, Calif.	$72,948 #
Ralph T. Smith, Ill.	56,654
Ted Stevens, Alaska	36,952
Paul J. Fannin, Ariz.	36,877

(Incumbents, cont'd)	Contribution
Hugh Scott, Pa.	$35,341 #
Winston L. Prouty, Vt.†	35,222
Hiram L. Fong, Hawaii	31,608
Roman L. Hruska, Neb.	26,813 #
Charles E. Goodell, N.Y.	16,531

Challengers

George Bush, Tex.	76,099
Lowell P. Weicker Jr., Conn.	13,810
Lenore Romney, Mich.	13,705
W. E. Brock, Tenn.	13,630
Clark MacGregor, Minn.	13,507
Laurence J. Burton, Utah	12,183
J. Glenn Beall Jr., Md.	11,560
William C. Cramer, Fla.	10,465
Robert Taft Jr., Ohio	8,270
John C. Danforth, Mo.	5,900
Richard L. Roudebush, Ind.	1,210
Open Convention Committee, Indiana	4,270
Anderson Carter, N.M.	3,465
William V. Roth Jr., Del.	2,610
John Wold, Wyo.	2,206
Nelson G. Gross, N.J.	2,050
William J. Raggio, Nev.	2,050
Thomas S. Kleppe, N.D.	850
John E. Erickson, Wis.	50

*   In addition to the direct contributions listed, the National Republican
Senatorial Committee reported in 1970 a total of $14,780 in contributions,
which could not be identified by candidate, to political committees: Citizens for Good Government ($4,780); D.C. Committee for Effective Legislation ($5,000); and Committee to Further Educational Opportunities, Washington, D.C. ($5,000).

\#   Includes funds contributed to the Republican State Committee for candidate's campaign.

†   Died September 10, 1971.

Source: Citizens' Research Foundation, *National Journal*

Chart 7.1

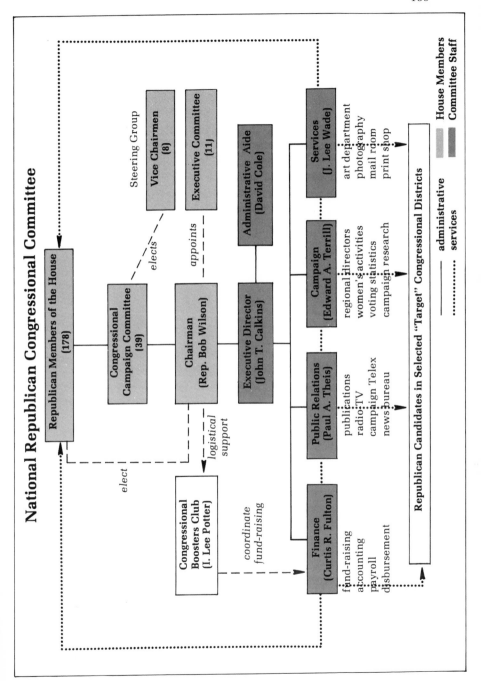

National Republican Congressional Committee

8

The Ripon Society

NEAL GREGORY

The Ripon Society has shown that a political organization can have an impact in Washington without a large membership, a lot of money or a prestigious roster of names on its letterhead. The young people behind the Republican research and policy group are moving to increase the organization's visibility within the party and are seeking a wider voice for its "progressive" political philosophy.

While winning the praise of some party leaders, the Ripon Society has aroused the ire of other prominent Republicans by its critical comments on the policies and practices of the Nixon Administration. Attorney General John N. Mitchell, on January 17, 1970, called Ripon members "little juvenile delinquents." Ironically, a few hours later, the White House dispatched a telegram to the society's seventh anniversary dinner, in President Nixon's name, praising the group for its thoughtful approach to contemporary public problems.

How the Ripon Society looks depends entirely on one's vantage point. One of its friends, Senate Minority Leader Hugh Scott, Pa., has called it a "strong and persuasive Republican voice, addressing the intelligence of the party and stimulating its conscience." The editorially hostile *Chicago Tribune*, has called it a "diehard rear guard of eastern liberal Republicanism." Press reports usually characterize it as "liberal" or "moderate" or "ultra-liberal"—labels which Ripon officials disdain. "We are primarily progressive Republicans," says Howard F. Gillette Jr., Ripon's national president. Gillette, who is an assistant professor of American studies at George Washington University, explains Ripon's philosophy this way: "We are trying to bring the kind of intellectual honesty and creativity to American politics that we ideally foster in the universities. This is the main thrust of what we are trying to do, whether it is in politics—supporting or endorsing candidates—or in creating position papers. I would say 90 per cent of the membership is committed to this intellectual honesty in politics."

Gillette and other Ripon officials, in defining the organization's long-range objectives, stress a commitment to strengthen the progressive wing of the GOP and to build an "open" Republican Party. These objectives can best be served, they believe, by working within the party structure. In response to New York Mayor John V. Lindsay's August 1971 announcement that he was leaving the Republican Party to become a Democrat, Gillette said, "We wish him well, but we intend to fight rather than switch. We urge all progressive Republicans to do likewise." Although Ripon has in the past looked to Lindsay as one of its leaders, he said, it disagrees that progressive Republicans cannot build and sustain a power base in the Republican Party. "We shall carry on the fight within the Republican Party because we believe it has demonstrated in many areas of the country and can demonstrate nationally its viability as the most effective vehicle for constructive change in our country. . . . Despite the urgings of reactionary Republicans and liberal Democrats, we are not about to leave our party and abandon our view that our nation cannot afford to have one irresponsible political party. . . ."

Without deemphasizing its research and policy role, the society recently has begun to focus more of its attention on direct political activity and fund-raising for progressive Republican candidates. By building a national network of Ripon people and organizing the membership to support the election of progressive GOP candidates, Ripon hopes to give more weight in party circles to its concept of an open-minded political strategy and progressive Republican leadership. At one time, Ripon attributed whatever influence it has in the party to its ability to attract the attention of the news media. But, Gillette said, We have moved from that early perception to a sense of political organization." Robert D. Behn, Ripon's executive director, said the society's "basic strength comes from the individual influence" of its members. "Some have been elected to public office; others hold appointed positions in government; and members of the society are becoming more active as political workers and advisors, both at the grass roots and national levels," he said.

The Ripon Society traces its beginnings to 17 Harvard University and MIT graduate students who sought to stimulate new ideas within the Republican Party. The students first met in December 1962 and discussed several names before settling on Ripon, after the town in Wisconsin that claims to be the birthplace of the Republican Party. The society, which in eight years has expanded to 14 chapters with members from the business, professional and academic communities, is modeled in part after the Bow Group, formed in 1951 by younger members of Britain's Conservative Party.

After a year of periodic meetings for discussion and debate, the Ripon Society first attracted national attention in January 1964 with publication of "A Call to Excellence in Leadership." This paper, an open letter urging the younger generation of Republicans to restore their party to its earlier role of leadership in such fields as civil rights, received widespread distribution and publicity. Lee W. Huebner, former Ripon president (1967-68) and now a White House staff assistant, recalls that the response "reinforced members' conviction that one could contribute to the American dialogue by saying the right thing at the right time."

In the early months of 1964, Ripon began to concentrate on

the coming Presidential election, emphasizing the party's civil rights heritage. Just before the Republican National Convention in San Francisco, members of the society met in Ripon and issued a "Declaration of Conscience," a statement warning against any attempt to compromise with the South. After the November election, Ripon issued a 124-page *Election '64* report, presenting it to a meeting of the Republican National Committee in Chicago in January 1965. The report attributed the party's massive defeat to the "conservative" slant of the campaign. Author Theodore H. White, in *The Making of the President 1964*, called the Ripon report "the best state-by-state analysis of the elections that I know . . . an indispensable document for any further study of the 1964 election." The American Conservative Union (ACU) dissented, maintaining the Ripon report "ignored the crucial role of Lyndon Johnson's campaign strategy, which precluded serious debate on philosophy and issues, and instead focused its venom on the Republican campaign." Dean Burch, then Republican national chairman and now chairman of the Federal Communications Commission, commented, "It's amazing to me that a group of eighty members can write a report and get so much attention." Sen. Barry Goldwater, R-Ariz., the defeated 1964 GOP Presidential candidate, was irked by the report. He told *The New York Times*: "The Ripon Society is a group no responsible Republican understands. . . . The Ripon Society is more secret than the John Birch Society."

The society in 1965 extended its operations to the West Coast, establishing a chapter in Los Angeles. It rented permanent office space in Cambridge, Mass., and began publishing the *Ripon Forum*, a monthly magazine featuring research papers on public policy and political analysis. By 1967, the society had hired Thomas E. Petri, a founding member who had recently returned from the Peace Corps, as a full-time executive director. Its budget—for rent, salaries, printing and mailing—approached $50,000. During this period, Ripon's research papers and *Forum* articles advocated such proposals as more diplomatic contact with China, replacement of the draft with a volunteer army, civil rights for the mentally ill and adoption of the negative income tax. Its first book, *From Disaster to Distinction*, was published in 1966. In a foreword, Sen. Scott called the book "not merely a challenge to Republicans, calling on them to rise above a narrow and outmoded rightist conservatism. It is a challenge to all Americans. . . ."

Most of the Ripon membership supported the Presidential candidacies of Gov. Nelson A. Rockefeller of New York and Gov. George W. Romney of Michigan before the 1968 Republican National Convention. After the convention, the society gave the Nixon-Agnew ticket its unenthusiastic support. (A poll of 500 *Ripon Forum* readers before the 1968 elections showed that four out of five of them had supported Rockefeller, and only a third had made up their minds to support Mr. Nixon in November. "Frankly, Nixon-Agnew was not our dream ticket," the *Forum* said in an editorial. But many Ripon members worked in the Presidential campaign, as well as in races for other Republican candidates. These included the successful Senate race of William B. Saxbe in Ohio, the election of Richard B. Ogilvie as Governor in Illinois, the unsuccessful Senate race of Rep. Thomas B. Curtis (1951-69) in Missouri and James E. Farmer's unsuccessful try for the House from New York's 12th district.)

With Mr. Nixon elected, Ripon members debated whether they should take positions with the new Administration and try to guide it their way or sit on the sidelines and criticize. John S. Saloma III, who served as Ripon president during the society's first four years and is now an associate professor of political science at MIT, warned in a February 17, 1969, article in *The Nation:* "If the Nixon Administration absorbs the best Ripon talent and the society becomes in effect an arm of the Administration, we've lost our most important function—independent thought and criticism. Anybody who goes to work for the Administration may try to use their Ripon contacts to get the society to tone down its criticism." Others disagreed. Josiah Lee Auspitz, then president of Ripon (1969-71), said,

"The question is whether we want to be effective, or exhibit our virtue." Clair W. Rodgers Jr., then executive director of Ripon (1969-70), recalled that one of the society's goals is to recruit and train talent for Republican political life.

As it turned out, a number of Ripon members accepted key positions in the Nixon Administration. Four members of the society currently are working in the White House. John R. Price Jr., former chairman of Ripon's national governing board (1968-69) and a former New York attorney, is a special assistant to the President and a staff member of the Domestic Council, specializing in urban-rural affairs. Ronald L. James, who joined the White House staff in 1971, is special assistant to Donald Rumsfeld, counselor to the President. Les Janka is staff assistant to Henry Kissinger, Presidential assistant for national security affairs. The fourth is Lee Huebner, who had succeeded Saloma as Ripon president. Huebner took leave from that post to work in the Nixon campaign in 1968, then resigned to become a staff assistant to the newly elected President. He works on the speechwriting staff of Presidential special assistant Raymond K. Price Jr.

Huebner feels that he and his Ripon associates have had "some effect" on the decision-making at the White House. In a *National Journal* interview, Huebner conceded that he frequently gets pointed questions from fellow Ripon members. "It's sort of like the salesman-to-cocktail-waitress question: 'What's a nice girl like you doing in a place like this?' " he related. "I just point to the family assistance plan, for instance," Huebner said. "This is a highly complex place. Publicity often focuses on the bad news, but there are lots of good things happening, too." Huebner cited such achievements as the work of the now-disbanded President's Advisory Council on Executive Organization (Ash Council), whose recommendations resulted in 1970 in the establishment of a Domestic Council in the White House and a restructuring of the Budget Bureau, which became the Office of Management and Budget. The advisory council had three Ripon members on its staff—Auspitz, Peter J. Wallison, Ripon finance chairman, and Thomas Petri, current president of the Sabre Foundation, which directs the

Ripon Society's Open Presidency Task Forces, a project designed to involve young people in the governmental process.

In addition to the White House staff, Ripon members are in policy-making or key advisory positions in several departments and agencies. Six members currently are with the Health, Education and Welfare Department (HEW): Stephen Kurzman, assistant secretary for legislation; Frank E. Samuel Jr., executive assistant to Kurzman; J. Stanley Pottinger, director of the Office for Civil Rights; Michael S. Lottman, director of Equal Educational Opportunity; Howard Cohen, deputy assistant secretary for legislation (welfare); and Paul Niebank, deputy assistant secretary for community development. Other Riponers serving in the Administration are: Woodward L. Kingman, president of the Government National Mortgage Association at Housing and Urban Development (HUD); William Matuszeski, staff member of the Council on Environmental Quality; Nelson Crowther, special assistant to the assistant secretary of Labor for wage and labor standards; and William J. Kilberg, associate solicitor for labor relations and civil rights at the Labor Department. Stephen Horn, former aide to Sen. Thomas H. Kuchel, Calif. (1953-69), and now president of California State College, Long Beach, serves in the part-time post of vice chairman of the U.S. Commission on Civil Rights.

President Nixon in May 1970 endorsed the Ripon Society's proposal for Open Presidency Task Forces, terming the proposal "an exciting experiment in giving government the benefit of the fresh ideas and careful scrutiny of responsible young people." The task force program grew out of a December 1969 meeting in which Ripon representatives discussed with the President the society's 1969 report on youth. The report, entitled "Bring Us Together," made 60 recommendations, ranging from tax credits for political contributions to defining the rights of draftees and creating an all-volunteer army. Attending the meeting with the President were Sen. Howard H. Baker Jr., R-Tenn., co-sponsor of the study, Presidential assistants Leonard Garment and Eugene S. Cowan, who has since resigned, and six Ripon members — Auspitz; Rodgers; Howard

L. Reiter, then editor of the *Ripon Forum* and current vice president of Ripon; Bruce K. Chapman, senior author of the report and a former editorial writer for the defunct *New York Herald Tribune*; and Franklin D. Raines and Robert W. Davidson, co-authors of the report and both Harvard undergraduates. (A book based on the study, entitled *Instead of Revolution*, was edited by Reiter and published by Hawthorn Books in 1971.)

Davidson, director of the Open Presidency Task Forces, said the object of the program is to "tap the energies of young people to examine important areas of public policy and government performance." Davidson says the approach is similar to investigations undertaken by consumer advocate Ralph Nader, with a major difference: "We have chosen to work with Administration and other authorities within the bureaucracies on our studies, rather than adopt the confrontation style which is in some respects a drawback to Nader's effectiveness. . . ." The program is administered by the Sabre Foundation of Fond du Lac, Wis., a non-profit, independent organization established in 1969. In addition to Petri, who serves as president of the foundation, the 10-member, bipartisan task force advisory board includes: Auspitz; Martin H. Peretz, assistant professor of social studies at Harvard and formerly an adviser to 1968 Presidential candidate Sen. Eugene J. McCarthy, D-Minn. (1959-71); William A. Rusher, publisher of the *National Review* and a board member of the American Conservative Union; Robert Shrum, speechwriter for Sen. Edmund S. Muskie, D-Maine; and Andrew M. Rouse, a member of the management consultant firm of Arthur D. Little Inc. and former executive director of the Ash Council (1969-71). By late 1971, the task forces had completed two reports—one on the Administration's proposal for an all-volunteer army and, the other, on expanded ownership.

Any doubts that Ripon could maintain its independence during a Republican Administration have been dispelled by the positions it has taken since 1968. The society has directed some well-publicized and frank criticism at several of Mr. Nixon's policies. Nevertheless, Gillette contends Ripon is supporting the Administration "70 per cent of the time." He also stresses that a number of proposals advanced by Ripon since its founding have been adopted in some form by the Nixon Administration.

Major issues on which Ripon has sided with the Administration include revenue sharing, the need to disperse the ghetto poor to white suburbs, welfare reform, an all-volunteer army, support for minority-owned enterprise and increased contact with mainland China. The proposals advanced by Ripon and the positions it adopts on public policy issues—published in the *Ripon Forum* as editorials or policy papers—are determined primarily by the society's six national officers, the co-editors of the *Forum* and the national political director.

Ripon first publicly advocated the concept of general revenue sharing in 1965 when it joined with the Republican Governors' Conference in issuing *Government for Tomorrow: A Proposal for the Unconditional Sharing of Federal Tax Revenues with State and Local Governments*. The 18-page report supported the plan of Walter W. Heller, a Democrat and a former chairman of the Council of Economic Advisers (1961-64) and an early advocate of the concept incorporated in the Administration's revenue sharing package for distributing a portion of federal income tax revenues to the states. While Ripon supports the concept of revenue sharing as an appropriate method of decentralizing power from the federal to the state and local levels, it opposes the Nixon plan under which local governments would share the revenue.

Ripon has given its unqualified support for Administration policies on the so-called "open communities" issue. A policy paper published in the October 1971 *Forum* credited Housing and Urban Development Secretary George W. Romney with having convinced the Administration to "institutionalize access of ghetto residents to the suburbs as an objective of the federal government." As a long-time advocate of welfare reform, Ripon has endorsed the Administration's family

assistance plan, maintaining that chances for passage are better under a Republican Administration which lacks "the free-
spending image of the Great Society." Ripon contends the
President in his welfare reform speeches has accepted a program it has advocated since its founding—a negative income
tax. The society in December 1969 defended Mr. Nixon's proposal for an all-volunteer army and attacked the opposition
of Sen. Edward M. Kennedy, D-Mass.

The January 1970 issue of the *Forum* featured a cover car-
toon of Attorney General Mitchell and went on to charge that
he has allowed "political strategy to shape law enforcement
strategy" in the Justice Department. "Too often last year was
the Justice Department cast in the role of delaying and even
reversing the great strides for equality by Southern blacks,"
Ripon said. "The Attorney General and the politicians who
serve as his chief assistants are motivated by a desire to 'sell'
the President to the white Southerner."

The Justice Department and President Nixon came under attack by Ripon during the 1970 Senate debate on the confirmation of G. Harrold Carswell, then of the 5th Circuit Court of
Appeals, for a seat on the Supreme Court. The society urged
Republican Senators to reject the nomination on the grounds
that Carswell "lacks even the minimal legal qualifications necessary for competent service." A Ripon position paper released
March 5, entitled "The Case Against Carswell," was placed in
the *Congressional Record* by Sen. Birch Bayh, D-Ind., who,
with Sen. Edward W. Brooke, R-Mass., led the successful fight
against Carswell. In an editorial March 30, the *Indianapolis
News* commented: "Bayh's use of Ripon material makes it rather clear that, so far as the White House is concerned, the enemy
is within the gates. It seems doubtful the President is going to be
able to deal successfully with liberal types like Bayh on Capitol Hill until he has ousted Bayh's 'Republican' soul brothers
from their positions of influence at 1600 Pennsylvania Avenue."

The President's opposition to the use of federal desegregation funds for busing of public school children also has drawn
criticism from Ripon. In the April 15, 1971 issue of the *Forum*,
the society charged that Mr. Nixon's position would not effect

desegregation but only place added financial burdens on local school districts. Characterizing the President's strategem as one of placating all sides, Ripon said the "President's histrionics also made it all but impossible for local officials in the South to ignore the racial issue."

In a *Forum* editorial August 15, 1971, following Mr. Nixon's announced plans to visit China, Ripon commended the President for adopting what it called a progressive Republican strategy. But the editorial questioned whether the President "will continue to fulfill the promise of this initiative by staying on a high course in foreign policy and by extending this approach to domestic policy (with a real shift in priorities that allows effective revenue sharing, welfare reform, and employment programs); or whether he will discredit his office, as he did in the 1970 campaign, by returning to narrow calculations of partisan advantage in exploiting the fears and prejudices of the electorate — seeking a downhill course to re-election that will more likely end in defeat." The editorial concluded: "The China initiative and the response to it. . . . give us hope, however, that Nixon has at last discovered the responsiveness of the American people to inspired Presidential leadership."

The Ripon Society has consistently criticized President Nixon's handling of the Vietnam war. It opposed the Administration's plan to deploy an ABM (antiballistic missile) system. Yet its comments on defense and foreign policy issues have not drawn as much reaction and publicity as its positions on domestic affairs, particularly in the area of civil rights and civil liberties.

Ripon operates out of small offices in Cambridge, just off Harvard Square. It occupies parts of the second and third floors of a frame building that also houses the Taj Mahal Restaurant and a shop which sells psychedelic paraphernalia. The national office is directed by Robert Behn, 29, a former assistant for urban affairs to Gov. Francis W. Sargent, R-Mass.

Behn, who became Ripon's executive director in August 1970, previously served as the organization's research director (1968-69). Ripon's other salaried employees working in the Cambridge office include two full-time secretaries and Evelyn F. Ellis and George Gilder, co-editors of the *Ripon Forum*. Miss Ellis, a graduate of Radcliff College, first joined the staff as a secretary in 1968 and served as *Forum* editor from September 1970 to June 1971, when the publication was expanded and Gilder was hired as co-editor. Gilder, 31, has been a speechwriter for Sen. Jacob K. Javits, R-N.Y., and New York Republican Governor Nelson Rockefeller. He is the co-author with Bruce Chapman of *The Party that Lost its Head*, published in 1965.

The society's policy is determined by the National Executive Committee, composed of the six national officers, Executive Director Behn and the presidents of Ripon's 14 local chapters. (See Table 8.1.) In addition to Cambridge, Ripon has chapters in Boston, Chicago, Dallas, Detroit, Hartford, Los Angeles, Minneapolis, New Haven, New York, Philadelphia, Pittsburgh, Seattle and Washington, D.C. Behn said the organization has established a provisional chapter in Portland, Ore., and expected to open chapters in Nashville, Memphis, Little Rock and New Jersey by 1972. Before chartering new groups, the society requires a prospective chapter to present a position paper on an issue of public policy, show an ability to raise funds locally and include political activities among its membership. Ripon is a young group: Few of its members are over 30. Members live in all 50 states, with more than half living outside cities with chapters. Behn said current membership figures are not available.

The *Ripon Forum*, described by Behn as the "only national magazine expressing a progressive Republican view," is sent to approximately 3,000 subscribers who pay $10 a year. In July 1971, Ripon expanded its publication of the *Forum* with the addition of a mid-month newsletter, designed to supplement the more detailed political analysis contained in the magazine.

Since its establishment in 1963, Ripon has spent about

$500,000 — a figure which Behn says demonstrates "one of the highest benefit-to-cost ratios in politics." The largest single source of funds is individual contributions; much of the remaining budget is raised through subscriptions to the *Forum* and research contracts. (Annual membership dues are $15, of which $10 goes to a *Forum* subscription.) Ripon began 1971 with a budget of $200,000, an increase of more than $80,000 over the previous year. The increase in expenditures reflects the organization's expanded publication schedule, a current membership drive and a new emphasis on political action. In the first six months of 1971, Ripon raised $84,501, including $59,040 in contributions and $7,542 in *Forum* subscriptions. Expenditures for this period totalled $67,489. In 1970, Ripon's total receipts were $113,954 — of which $80,645 was in contributions and dues — and expenses were $115,670. As an organization which does not make direct financial contributions to political candidates and does not exist primarily for the purpose of lobbying, the society is not required by the Federal Corrupt Practices Act (2 USC 241) to list its contributors with the Clerk of the House of Representatives.

In spring 1970, a group of Ripon members organized the One Percent Club to provide financial support for young, progressive Republican candidates seeking office at the federal, state or local level. Members are asked to contribute 1 per cent of their annual income, either to a specifically designated candidate through the club or to the club's general fund for distribution to selected candidates. In 1970, the fund-raising group received a total of $9,252.03 in donations from 93 persons. Of this amount, $4,673.40 was contributed directly to 51 candidates — 23 in state and local campaigns and 28 in congressional races. Another $3,100 was loaned to candidates.

The Ripon Society began in early 1971 to devote a substantial amount of its resources to expanding its membership base nationally and organizing the membership for political action. "One of the major weaknesses of the progressive wing of the

Republican Party is the absence of a cadre of people who have political experience and who know each other," Behn wrote in the society's 1971 semi-annual report.

To coordinate the membership drive and the political action program, Ripon in May 1971 hired Daniel J. Swillinger, 29, as its first full-time national political director. Two months later, it opened an office in Washington, D.C., staffed by Swillinger and one part-time secretary. Prior to joining Ripon, Swillinger was for two years counsel and research director for the Washington-based Republican political consulting firm of Bailey, Deardourff & Bowen Inc. Swillinger's primary responsibility is political organization. He travels throughout the country recruiting new members, assisting Ripon members in creating new chapters and helping progressive Republicans in states without chapters to organize themselves for political activity. Swillinger said one of his major tasks is to develop a more effective party role for GOP "moderates," who, he explained, have tended to concentrate on single candidates rather than participate in the party on a continuing basis.

In an effort to plug more Riponers into the 1972 GOP Presidential campaign, Swillinger has worked with the Nixon-organized Committee for the Reelection of the President, pinpointing Ripon talent that could be put to work in 1972 campaign. Swillinger has dealt primarily with Harry S. Flemming, a former assistant to the President who handles the committee's political work. Swillinger said Ripon's relationship with the committee is "cautious but cordial." Jeb. S. Magruder, former deputy director of communications for the executive branch who is in charge of the committee's day-to-day activities, said that he has not dealt directly with the Ripon staff, but understands they have been "most helpful" in putting the committee in touch with volunteers for the campaign.

To press its goal of an open party, Ripon has attacked the Republican Party's delegate selection process. The society on November 8, 1971, filed a complaint in the U.S. District Court for the District of Columbia asking the court to declare unconstitutional the exisiting formula for allocating delegates to the national conventions. It also sought to prevent the Republican National Committee from issuing a call to the 1972 convention under the present formula. Swillinger said party reform is essential to ensure an "open and equitable" convention in 1976—the "critical year from the progressive point of view." He said Ripon has attempted to work with the RNC, particularly on the issue of party reform, but "the initiative has always come from us—the response has always been pretty forced." Asked about the RNC's reaction to the Ripon suit, Lyn Nofziger, the committee's deputy national chairman for communications, said Ripon has once again demonstrated its preference for working "outside of the party instead of inside . . . they try to make a public case before they work it out within the family."

To demonstrate that its views are consistent with traditional Republican philosophy, Ripon has devised a system of rating the voting records of Members of Congress. Ripon contends the annual ratings issued by such groups as Americans for Constitutional Action (ACA), Americans for Democratic Action (ADA), and the AFL-CIO's Committee on Political Education (COPE) have created a belief that "the only basic cleavage in Congress is . . . the split between conservatives and liberals." The Ripon formula, introduced in March 1970, rates Members on the basis of five factors it says are central to the traditions and rhetoric of the GOP, ranging from decentralization of power at the federal level to legal and economic equality of the races. In its ratings for the 91st Congress (1969-70), Ripon utilized such issues as extending the surtax beyond its expiration date, cutting funds for the supersonic transport and guaranteed federal payments to poor families. It opposed increasing agricultural subsidies and permitting Governors to veto legal aid programs administered by the Office of Economic Opportunity. (See Table 8.2.)

The Ripon society is not without its supporters on Capitol Hill. About 30 Republican Representatives and Senators have Ripon members on their staffs. Others make use of the society's reports and position papers. At least one Senator has paid Ripon to perform research for him.

But many members, while praising Ripon's work, are quick to point out that they do not support all the society's conclusions. "The Ripon Society is providing valuable intellectual input into the Republican Party," says Sen. Marlow W. Cook, R-Ky. "While I may on occasion disagree with its position, I admire its devotion to principle and dedication to our party." Rep. Gerald R. Ford, Mich., the House minority leader, said the society makes a contribution toward having "all viewpoints within the Republican Party vigorously presented and debated." Sen. Baker, another moderate conservative, is equally unprepared to read Ripon out of the party. As he put it, "They represent as a group the thinking of some Republicans and they are entitled to be heard."

Table 8.1   Ripon Executive Committee

Policy decisions of the Ripon Society are made by the National Executive Committee, which is composed of the national officers, the national executive director and presidents of the 14 local chapters.

Howard F. Gillette Jr., 29, president. Gillette, an assistant professor of American studies at George Washington University and a former lecturer in American civilization at the University of Pennsylvania, served on the campaign staff of Gov. Nelson A. Rockefeller, R-N.Y., in 1968. He was a director of Project Pursestrings, a coalition of Ripon members and moratorium activists in support of the McGovern-Hatfield amendment to end the Vietnam war, in summer 1970. He also served as finance coordinator for John A. Nevius, 1970 GOP candidate for the District of Columbia's first non-voting delegate to the House. Gillette, who received a Ph.D. from Yale University in 1970, is Republican precinct chairman in Cleveland Park, Washington, D.C.

Paul F. Anderson, 32, chairman of the national governing board. Anderson, who was elected board chairman in August 1971, is a vice president of Booz, Allen & Hamilton Inc., a Chicago-based management consultant firm. A Republican precinct chairman in Chicago and a former White House fellow (1968-69), Anderson received an A.B. degree in electrical engineering from Notre Dame in 1959 and an M.A. in business administration from Carnegie-Mellon University in 1963. He succeeded Michael F. Brewer, who resigned as board chairman in June 1971 to work full-time on the Presidential campaign of Rep. Paul N. McCloskey, Jr., R-Calif.

Patricia A. Goldman, 29, executive committee chairman. A founding member of Ripon's Washington, D.C.,

chapter, Miss Goldman currently is a legislative counsel at the National League of Cities-U.S. Conference of Mayors. She received a bachelors degree in economics from Goucher College in 1964 and formerly was a staff member of the Joint Economic Committee and director of manpower programs at the U.S. Chamber of Commerce (1967-70). Miss Goldman assumed the committee post in October 1971, replacing Josiah Lee Auspitz, who resigned to resume his doctoral studies at Harvard University. **Howard L. Reiter,** 26, vice president. Reiter is a Ph.D. candidate and teaching fellow at Harvard University and editor of Ripon's most recent book, *Instead of Revolution* (1971). He is a former editor of the *Ripon Forum* and has contributed to *The Nation.*
R. Quincy White Jr., 38, secretary. White is a partner in the Chicago, Ill., law firm of Leibman, Williams, Bennett, Baird & Minow and president of Ripon's Chicago chapter. He graduated from Yale University in 1954 and earned a law degree from Harvard Law School in 1960. A cofounder of the Conference on Chicago Government, White was a candidate for alderman in Chicago in 1969.
Robert L. Beal, 29, treasurer. One of the founders of the Ripon Society, Beal is vice president of Beacon Construction Company, Boston, Mass., and an instructor in real estate at Northeastern University. He received an A.B. degree from Harvard College in 1963 and a MBA from Harvard Business School in 1965. Beal was cofounder of *Advance*, predecessor to the *Ripon Forum.*
Robert D. Behn, 29, national executive director. Before joining the Ripon staff as director in August 1970, Behn was assistant for urban affairs to Gov. Francis W. Sargent, R-Mass. He graduated from Worcester Polytechnic Institute and attended Har-

vard University, where he received a S.M. degree in engineering in 1965 and a Ph.D. in 1969. Behn served as Ripon's research director in 1968-69 and was editor of the society's 1968 elections analysis, *Lessons of Victory.* He served briefly as consultant to the Rand Corporation in 1966. He is a member of the State Advisory Committee to the U.S. Civil Rights Commission in Massachusetts.

Chapter presidents

Boston: Martha Reardon, executive director of Plymouth-Provincetown Celebration.
Cambridge: Joel P. Greene, student. Boston University Law School.
Chicago: R. Quincy White Jr., attorney. Partner in Leibman, Williams, Bennett, Baird & Minow.
Dallas: Neil D. Anderson, attorney. Associate at Wayne, Jaffee & Tinsley.
Detroit: Ralph J. Heikkinen, attorney.
Hartford: Stewart H. McConaughy, attorney. Partner in Shipman & Goodwin. (Nicholas Norton, Connecticut deputy commissioner of welfare, represents the chapter on the executive committee.)
Los Angeles: Michael Halliwell, professor of government. Long Beach State University.
Minneapolis: John Cairns, city councilman.
New Haven: Howard L. Draper, teaching fellow. Yale University.
New York: Werner Kuhn, professor of industrial engineering. Brooklyn Polytechnic Institute.
Philadelphia: Robert J. Moss. Bache & Company.
Pittsburgh: Leah Thayer, head resident. Chatham College.
Seattle: Tom A. Alberg, attorney. Associate at Perkins, Coie, Sone, Olsen & Williams.
Washington, D.C.: Stephen E. Herbits, student. Georgetown University Law School.

Table 8.2   Ripon Rates Members of Congress, 1969-1970

The Ripon Society's congressional ratings are based on five criteria which it contends are "central to the traditions (and the rhetoric) of the Republican Party." The ratings—on a scale of 0 to 100—favor Senators and Representatives who voted in support of the transfer of power from the Executive to Congress, to public and private local institutions and to individual citizens; an expanded free market system in national and international trade and no subsidy of inefficient business; a national economic policy aimed at correcting imbalances rather than treating symptoms through direct controls; private and multilateral initiatives in foreign policy; and legal and economic equality of the races.

Following are the Ripon ratings for the 91st Congress (1969-70). Senators were rated on the basis of 29 selected votes for the first session (1969) and 26 votes for the second session (1970). Seventeen issues were used for the 1969-70 House ratings. (House Speaker John W. McCormack did not participate in House votes.) Except where noted, Members listed were serving in the first session of the 92nd Congress, as of November 1, 1971.

Senate Ratings

Democrats	1969	1970		1969	1970
Allen, Ala	14	16	Jackson, Wash.	55	54
Anderson, N.M.	56	42	Jordan, N.C.	15	12
Bayh, Ind.	67	62	Kennedy, Mass.	80	78
Bible, Nev.	16	15	Long, La.	32	13
Burdick, N.D.	54	62	Magnuson, Wash.	55	48
Byrd, Va.	21	17	Mansfield, Mont.	64	65
Byrd, W.Va.	11	19	McCarthy, Minn. **(9)**	68	65
Cannon, Nev.	35	26	McClellan, Ark.	7	12
Church, Idaho	63	73	McGee, Wyo.	48	58
Cranston, Calif.	75	81	McGovern, S.D.	64	75
Dodd, Conn. **(4, 10)**	39	38	McIntyre, N.H.	54	46
Eagleton, Mo.	69	63	Metcalf, Mont.	60	61
Eastland, Miss.	9	4	Mondale, Minn.	79	80
Ellender, La.	31	8	Montoya, N.M.	48	65
Ervin, N.C.	19	8	Moss, Utah	60	64
Fulbright, Ark.	60	64	Muskie, Maine	67	71
Gore, Tenn. **(4)**	58	33	Nelson, Wis.	76	72
Gravel, Alaska	64	80	Pastore, R.I.	59	69
Harris, Okla.	71	82	Pell, R.I.	74	75
Hart, Mich.	82	81	Proxmire, Wis.	66	69
Hartke, Ind.	71	57	Randolph, W.Va.	45	42
Holland, Fla. **(9)**	24	8	Ribicoff, Conn.	71	91
Hollings, S.C.	17	8	Russell, Ga. **(10)**	22	6
Hughes, Iowa	71	77	Sparkman, Ala.	24	4
Inouye, Hawaii	58	69	Spong, Va.	36	33

Democrats *(cont'd)*	1969	1970		1969	1970
Stennis, Miss.	15	8	Stevenson, Ill. **(11)**	—	80
Symington, Mo.	68	61	Thurmond, S.C.	21	12
Talmadge, Ga.	4	8	Tower, Tex.	29	15
Tydings, Md. **(4)**	76	75	Williams, Del. **(9)**	59	42
Williams, N.J.	76	74	Young, N.D.	29	15
Yarborough, Tex. **(3)**	58	53			
Young, Ohio **(9)**	63	81			

Republicans

	1969	1970
Aiken, Vt.	82	75
Allott, Colo.	31	35
Baker, Tenn.	44	36
Bellmon, Okla.	42	43
Bennett, Utah	41	27
Boggs, Del.	64	54
Brooke, Mass.	90	88
Case, N.J.	86	92
Cook, Ky.	52	63
Cooper, Ky.	95	62
Cotton, N.H.	25	15
Curtis, Neb.	31	19
Dole, Kan.	50	50
Dominick, Colo.	28	50
Fannin, Ariz.	24	32
Fong, Hawaii	42	54
Goldwater, Ariz.	20	25
Goodell, N.Y. **(4)**	96	96
Griffin, Mich.	61	65
Gurney, Fla.	19	16
Hansen, Wyo.	24	27
Hatfield, Ore.	76	91
Hruska, Neb.	28	23
Javits, N.Y.	85	83
Jordan, Idaho	44	50
Mathias, Md.	89	87
Miller, Iowa	48	42
Mundt, S.D.	38	25
Murphy, Calif. **(4)**	37	32
Packwood, Ore.	72	88
Pearson, Kan.	68	54
Percy, Ill.	86	73
Prouty, Vt. **(10)**	50	58
Saxbe, Ohio	67	55
Schweiker, Pa.	86	77
Scott, Pa.	76	58
Smith, Ill. **(4)**	37	50
Smith, Maine	41	54
Stevens, Alaska	55	57

House Ratings

Democrats	1969-70
Abbitt, Va. 4	29
Abernethy, Miss. 1	18
Adams, Wash. 7	88
Addabbo, N.Y. 7	65
Albert, Okla. 3	53
Alexander, Ark. 1	40
Anderson, Calif. 17	59
Anderson, Tenn. 6	35
Andrews, Ala. 3	25
Annunzio, Ill. 7	59
Ashley, Ohio 9	82
Aspinall, Colo. 4	41
Baring, Nev. AL	18
Barrett, Pa. 1	77
Bennett, Fla. 3	47
Bevill, Ala. 7	24
Biaggi, N.Y. 24	59
Bingham, N.Y. 23	82
Blanton, Tenn. 7	25
Blatnik, Minn. 8	69
Boggs, La. 2	47
Boland, Mass. 2	73
Bolling, Mo. 5	65
Brademas, Ind. 3	82
Brasco, N.Y. 11	75
Brinkley, Ga. 3	24
Brooks, Tex. 9	43
Brown, Calif. 29 **(3)**	76
Burke, Mass. 11	50
Burleson, Tex. 17	12
Burlison, Mo. 10	53
Burton, Calif. 5	59
Byrne, Pa. 3	65
Cabell, Tex. 5	20
Caffery, La. 3	20
Carey, N.Y. 15	67
Carney, Ohio 19 **(11)**	67
Casey, Tex. 22	36
Celler, N.Y. 10	80

House Democrats (cont'd)	1969-70		1969-70
Chappell, Fla. 4	18	Garmatz, Md. 3	50
Chisholm, N.Y. 12	65	Gaydos, Pa. 20	50
Clark, Pa. 25	21	Gettys, S.C. 5	12
Clay, Mo. 1	69	Giaimo, Conn. 3	56
Cohelan, Calif. 7 (1)	81	Gibbons, Fla. 6	81
Collins, Ill. 6 (11)	67	Gilbert, N.Y. 22 (1)	71
Colmer, Miss. 5	31	Gonzalez, Tex. 20	47
Conyers, Mich. 1	67	Gray, Ill. 21	40
Corman, Calif. 22	76	Green, Ore. 3	60
Culver, Iowa 2	88	Green, Pa. 5	82
Daddario, Conn. 1 (7)	79	Griffin, Miss. 3	18
Daniel, Va. 5	24	Griffiths, Mich. 17	63
Daniels, N.J. 14	53	Hagan, Ga. 1	12
Davis, Ga. 7	24	Haley, Fla. 7	24
Dawson, Ill. 1 (9)	67	Hamilton, Ind. 9	82
de la Garza, Tex. 15	33	Hanley, N.Y. 34	67
Delaney, N.Y. 9	25	Hanna, Calif. 34	65
Dent, Pa. 21	56	Hansen, Wash. 3	67
Diggs, Mich. 13	53	Harrington, Mass. 6	87
Dingell, Mich. 16	50	Hathaway, Maine 2	65
Donohue, Mass. 4	56	Hawkins, Calif. 21	65
Dorn, S.C. 3	24	Hays, Ohio 18	38
Dowdy, Tex. 2	20	Hebert, La. 1	17
Downing, Va. 1	31	Hechler, W. Va. 4	71
Dulski, N.Y. 41	76	Helstoski, N.J. 9	82
Eckhardt, Tex. 8	71	Henderson, N.C. 3	21
Edmondson, Okla. 2	36	Hicks, Wash. 6	63
Edwards, Calif. 9	69	Holifield, Calif. 19	59
Edwards, La. 7	29	Howard, N.J. 3	76
Eilberg, Pa. 4	63	Hull, Mo. 6	38
Evans, Colo. 3	88	Hungate, Mo. 9	47
Evins, Tenn. 4	19	Ichord, Mo. 8	31
Fallon, Md. 4 (1)	50	Jacobs, Ind. 11	71
Farbstein, N.Y. 19 (1)	86	Jarman, Okla. 5	47
Fascell, Fla. 12	75	Johnson, Calif. 2	53
Feighan, Ohio 20 (1)	46	Jones, Tenn. 8	13
Fisher, Tex. 21	12	Jones, Ala. 8	19
Flood, Pa. 11	38	Jones, N.C. 1	18
Flowers, Ala. 5	25	Karth, Minn. 4	60
Flynt, Ga. 6	7	Kastenmeier, Wis. 2	76
Foley, Wash. 5	71	Kazen, Tex. 23	29
Ford, William, Mich. 15	63	Kee, W. Va. 5	31
Fountain, N.C. 2	18	Kluczynski, Ill. 5	53
Fraser, Minn. 5	82	Koch, N.Y. 17	94
Friedel, Md. 7 (1)	50	Kyros, Maine 1	65
Fulton, Tenn. 5	64	Landrum, Ga. 9	31
Fuqua, Fla. 2	12	Leggett, Calif. 4	56
Galifianakis, N.C. 4	47	Lennon, N.C. 7	18
Gallagher, N.J. 13	80	Long, Md. 2	53

House Democrats *(cont'd)*	1969-70		1969-70
Long, La. 8	6	Price, Ill. 24	59
Lowenstein, N.Y. 5 **(2)**	71	Pryor, Ark. 4	47
McCarthy, N.Y. 39 **(3)**	80	Pucinski, Ill. 11	75
McCormack, Mass. 9 **(9)**	—	Purcell, Tex. 13	23
McFall, Calif. 15	56	Randall, Mo. 4	29
McMillan, S.C. 6	0	Rarick, La. 6	18
Macdonald, Mass. 7	57	Rees, Calif. 26	76
Madden, Ind. 1	76	Reuss, Wis. 5	76
Mahon, Tex. 19	24	Rivers, S.C. 1 **(10)**	27
Mann, S.C. 4	27	Roberts, Tex. 4	18
Marsh, Va. 7 **(9)**	53	Rodino, N.J. 10	81
Matsunaga, Hawaii 1	76	Roe, N.J. 8	58
Meeds, Wash. 2	76	Rogers, Colo. 1 **(1)**	67
Melcher, Mont. 2	56	Rogers, Fla. 9	29
Mikva, Ill. 2	71	Ronan, Ill. 6 **(10)**	100
Miller, Calif. 8	56	Rooney, Pa. 15	65
Mills, Ark. 2	31	Rooney, N.Y. 14	53
Minish, N.J. 11	94	Rosenthal, N.Y. 8	75
Mink, Hawaii 2	65	Rostenkowski, Ill. 8	56
Mollohan, W. Va. 1	36	Roybal, Calif. 30	80
Monagan, Conn. 5	69	Ryan, N.Y. 20	71
Montgomery, Miss. 4	24	St. Germain, R.I. 1	69
Moorhead, Pa. 14	88	St. Onge, Conn. 2 **(10)**	71
Morgan, Pa. 26	59	Satterfield, Va. 3	29
Moss, Calif. 3	82	Scheuer, N.Y. 21	88
Murphy, N.Y. 16	59	Shipley, Ill. 23	31
Murphy, Ill. 3 **(9)**	50	Sikes, Fla. 1	20
Natcher, Ky. 2	18	Sisk, Calif. 16	44
Nedzi, Mich. 14	60	Slack, W. Va. 3	27
Nichols, Ala. 4	18	Smith, Iowa 5	63
Nix, Pa. 2	71	Staggers, W. Va. 2	50
Obey, Wis. 7	63	Steed, Okla. 4	47
O'Hara, Mich. 12	71	Stephens, Ga. 10	31
Olsen, Mont. 1 **(2)**	41	Stokes, Ohio 21	76
O'Neal, Ga. 2 **(9)**	7	Stratton, N.Y. 35	59
O'Neill, Mass. 8	69	Stubblefield, Ky. 1	24
Ottinger, N.Y. 25 **(4)**	76	Stuckey, Ga. 8	13
Passman, La. 5	38	Sullivan, Mo. 3	64
Patman, Tex. 1	21	Symington, Mo. 2	53
Patten, N.J. 15	71	Taylor, N.C. 11	29
Pepper, Fla. 11	56	Teague, Tex. 6	33
Perkins, Ky. 7	41	Thompson, N.J. 4	76
Philbin, Mass. 3 **(1,2)**	50	Tiernan, R.I. 2	76
Pickle, Tex. 10	41	Tunney, Calif. 38 **(5)**	90
Pike, N.Y. 1	76	Udall, Ariz. 2	82
Poage, Tex. 11	11	Ullman, Ore. 2	47
Podell, N.Y. 13	69	Van Deerlin, Calif. 37	71
Powell, N.Y. 18 **(1)**	75	Vanik, Ohio 22	82
Preyer, N.C. 6	50	Vigorito, Pa. 24	65

House Democrats *(cont'd)*	1969-70		1969-70
Waggonner, La. 4	24	Clawson, Calif. 23	33
Waldie, Calif. 14	71	Cleveland, N.H. 2	59
Watts, Ky. 6 **(10)**	29	Collier, Ill. 10	50
White, Tex. 16	47	Collins, Tex. 3	31
Whitten, Miss. 2	6	Conable, N.Y. 37	76
Wilson, Calif. 31	71	Conte, Mass. 1	94
Wolff, N.Y. 3	80	Corbett, Pa. 18 **(10)**	63
Wright, Tex. 12	40	Coughlin, Pa. 13	100
Yates, Ill. 9	71	Cowger, Ky. 3 **(2)**	56
Yatron, Pa. 6	59	Cramer, Fla. 8 **(4)**	35
Young, Tex. 14	21	Crane, Ill. 13	36
Zablocki, Wis. 4	59	Cunningham, Neb. 2 **(1)**	71
		Davis, Wis. 9	71
Republicans		Dellenback, Ore. 4	88
		Denney, Neb. 1 **(9)**	50
Adair, Ind. 4 **(2)**	31	Dennis, Ind. 10	63
Anderson, Ill. 16	75	Derwinski, Ill. 4	29
Andrews, N.D. 1	71	Devine, Ohio 12	35
Arends, Ill. 17	59	Dickinson, Ala. 2	35
Ashbrook, Ohio 17	18	Duncan, Tenn. 2	35
Ayres, Ohio 14 **(2)**	59	Dwyer, N.J. 12	88
Beall, Md. 6 **(5)**	64	Edwards, Ala. 1	41
Belcher, Okla. 1	35	Erlenborn, Ill. 14	71
Bell, Calif. 28	83	Esch, Mich. 2	94
Berry, S.D. 2 **(9)**	45	Eshleman, Pa. 16	59
Betts, Ohio 8	47	Findley, Ill. 20	87
Biester, Pa. 8	94	Fish, N.Y. 28	94
Blackburn, Ga. 4	29	Ford, Mich. 5	59
Bow, Ohio 16	59	Foreman, N.M. 2 **(2)**	31
Bray, Ind. 6	20	Forsythe, N.J. 6 **(11)**	100
Brock, Tenn. 3 **(5)**	44	Frelinghuysen, N.J. 5	76
Broomfield, Mich. 18	76	Frey, Fla. 5	53
Brotzman, Colo. 2	82	Fulton, Pa. 27 **(10)**	65
Brown, Ohio 7	46	Goldwater, Calif. 27	27
Brown, Mich. 3	71	Goodling, Pa. 19	29
Broyhill, N.C. 10	35	Gross, Iowa 3	29
Broyhill, Va. 10	35	Grover, N.Y. 2	41
Buchanan, Ala. 6	41	Gubser, Calif. 10	60
Burke, Fla. 10	53	Gude, Md. 8	100
Burton, Utah 1 **(4)**	53	Hall, Mo. 7	19
Bush, Tex. 7 **(4)**	54	Halpern, N.Y. 6	88
Button, N.Y. 29 **(2)**	92	Hammerschmidt, Ark. 3	41
Byrnes, Wis. 8	65	Hansen, Idaho 2	69
Camp, Okla. 6	33	Harsha, Ohio 6	29
Carter, Ky. 5	35	Harvey, Mich. 8	83
Cederberg, Mich. 10	69	Hastings, N.Y. 38	75
Chamberlain, Mich. 6	59	Heckler, Mass. 10	94
Clancy, Ohio 2	41	Hogan, Md. 5	75
Clausen, Calif. 1	44	Horton, N.Y. 36	82

House Republicans (cont'd)	1969-70		1969-70
Hosmer, Calif. 32	53	Quillen, Tenn. 1	29
Hunt, N.J. 1	50	Railsback, Ill. 19	88
Hutchinson, Mich. 4	53	Reid, Ill. 15 (9)	71
Johnson, Pa. 23	44	Reid, N.Y. 26	94
Jonas, N.C. 9	29	Reifel, S.D. 1 (9)	60
Keith, Mass. 12	71	Rhodes, Ariz. 1	75
King, N.Y. 30	36	Riegle, Mich. 7	100
Kleppe, N.D. 2 (4)	47	Robison, N.Y. 33	94
Kuykendall, Tenn. 9	41	Roth, Del. AL (5)	71
Kyl, Iowa 4	56	Roudebush, Ind. 5 (4)	25
Landgrebe, Ind. 2	31	Rousselot, Calif. 24	17
Langen, Minn. 7 (2)	53	Ruppe, Mich. 11	80
Latta, Ohio 5	56	Ruth, N.C. 8	33
Lloyd, Utah 2	59	Sandman, N.J. 2	65
Lujan, N.M. 1	67	Saylor, Pa. 22	47
Lukens, Ohio 24 (6)	31	Schadeberg, Wis. 1 (2)	44
MacGregor, Minn. 3 (4)	76	Scherle, Iowa 7	13
Mailliard, Calif. 6	69	Schmitz, Calif. 35	33
Martin, Neb. 3	33	Schneebeli, Pa. 17	76
Mathias, Calif. 18	59	Schwengel, Iowa 1	88
May, Wash. 4 (2)	59	Scott, Va. 8	29
Mayne, Iowa 6	71	Sebelius, Kan. 1	47
McClory, Ill. 12	71	Shriver, Kan. 4	69
McCloskey, Calif. 11	100	Skubitz, Kan. 5	36
McClure, Idaho 1	29	Smith, Calif. 20	38
McCulloch, Ohio 4	73	Smith, N.Y. 40	79
McDade, Pa. 10	76	Snyder, Ky. 4	27
McDonald, Mich. 19	73	Springer, Ill. 22	59
McEwen, N.Y. 31	44	Stafford, Vt. AL (12)	94
McKneally, N.Y. 27 (2)	60	Stanton, Ohio 11	94
Meskill, Conn. 6 (8)	62	Steele, Conn. 2 (11)	67
Michel, Ill. 18	53	Steiger, Ariz. 3	50
Miller, Ohio 10	53	Steiger, Wis. 6	71
Minshall, Ohio 23	44	Taft, Ohio 1 (5)	76
Mize, Kan. 2 (2)	53	Talcott, Calif. 12	65
Mizell, N.C. 5	31	Teague, Calif. 13	73
Morse, Mass. 5	88	Thompson, Ga. 5	24
Morton, Md. 1 (9)	67	Thomson, Wis. 3	63
Mosher, Ohio 13	94	Vander Jagt, Mich. 9	88
Myers, Ind. 7	41	Wampler, Va. 9	41
Nelson, Minn. 2	76	Ware, Pa. 9 (11)	33
O'Konski, Wis. 10	71	Watson, S.C. 2 (7)	7
Pelly, Wash. 1	80	Weicker, Conn. 4 (5)	92
Pettis, Calif. 33	65	Whalen, Ohio 3	88
Pirnie, N.Y. 32	65	Whalley, Pa. 12	38
Poff, Va. 6	71	Whitehurst, Va. 2	47
Pollock, Alaska AL (6)	54	Widnall, N.J. 7	88
Price, Tex. 18	25	Wiggins, Calif. 25	53
Quie, Minn. 1	76	Williams, Pa. 7	41

House Republicans (cont'd)	1969-70		1969-70
Wilson, Calif. 36	59	Wylie, Ohio 15	53
Winn, Kan. 3	53	Wyman, N.H. 1	53
Wold, Wyo. AL (4)	53	Zion, Ind. 8	47
Wyatt, Ore. 1	59	Zwach, Minn. 6	73
Wydler, N.Y. 4	80		

(1) Defeated in House primary, 1970.
(2) Defeated November 3, 1970, in House election.
(3) Defeated in Senate primary, 1970.
(4) Defeated November 3, 1970, in Senate election.
(5) Elected to Senate November 3, 1970.
(6) Defeated in gubernatorial primary, 1970.
(7) Defeated November 3, 1970, in gubernatorial election.
(8) Elected Governor, November 3, 1970.
(9) resigned or retired
(10) deceased
(11) Sworn in November 16, 1970, to fill vacancy.
(12) Appointed September 16, 1971, by Gov. Deane C. Davis, R, as interim replacement for the late Winston L. Prouty, R, pending a special primary and general election.

Source: Ripon Society, *National Journal*

9
Democratic National Committee

Since becoming Democratic national chairman, Lawrence F. O'Brien has built a record as a political fireman that nearly equals his reputation as a political organizer. As a result, the Democratic Party is alive and reasonably well—although still broke. When O'Brien assumed the chairmanship in March, 1970, the Democratic National Committee was beset by problems from all directions. It had lost the White House and could not get used to the idea. It was laboring under a $9.3-million debt with no clear prospect of solvency. The party machinery had grown sluggish. Reform was in the wind, and the old party hands were suspicious of those who would threaten their establishment.

The direction the DNC has moved in the ensuing months reflects O'Brien's view that a party out of national power should be the voice of the responsible opposition, a rallying point for the party faithful and a service organization to help party members get elected to office. It also reflects his conviction that the party needs a strong personal leader as national chairman—a role he does not find distasteful but one which is relatively new to him after more than 30 years as a behind-the-scenes political technician. Finally, it reflects the strong personal position in which O'Brien found himself when he was virtually drafted to return to Washington to lead the Democratic Party out of its mess.

O'Brien saw that electoral defeat and an economic downturn had made it impossible to wipe out the party debt in the early stages of his chairmanship. So, turning to what he felt were the two most urgent problems, aside from financing, he set out to: counteract President Nixon's domination of television, which he felt was hurting the Democrats politically and demoralizing the party down to the grass roots; and rebuild the party machinery, which had been neglected and downgraded for 15 years and had thus fallen into disrepute among Democratic politicians.

The DNC chairman also has made a considerable effort to close the communications gap between reformers and regulars, between party headquarters and Members of Congress, Governors and state chairmen. He has turned the problem of the party's debt over to Texas businessman Robert S. Strauss, DNC treasurer, and has instructed the staff not to promise more than the committee can deliver. Criticism of his performance to date is scarce. If he has not put out most of the fires, he has at least brought them under control.

When Sen. Fred R. Harris, Okla., announced his resignation as party chairman in February 1970, O'Brien quickly emerged as the leading choice for the post. Former Vice President Hubert H. Humphrey felt O'Brien was the one man who could build the necessary organization to win additional House and Senate seats in the 1970 elections and unify the badly divided party. Harris' 13-month tenure had been marked by criticism that he had been a part-time chairman and that he was using the post to further his own Presidential ambitions. After first declining the offer because he felt some party leaders did not really want him, O'Brien on March 6 accepted the unanimous call of the 110 members of the Democratic National Committee. The indecision on O'Brien's part actually strengthened his hand, giving him an independence that is rare for a party chairman.

He is the first to note the differences from his previous tenure at the DNC. Then he was managing Humphrey's 1968 Presidential campaign and closing out the office after the narrow defeat. "I've always believed in a strong national committee as a vehicle for increasing party rapport and organization," O'Brien said in an interview with *National Journal*. "There were certain things the DNC should have been doing that we did not start until we were out of power," he said, noting the reforms begun by his predecessor, Fred Harris. "He had no time to organize; it was all he could do to make sure the committee continued to function. There were some people who suggested the best answer was to dissolve the committee, but I knew this was no answer. If we didn't have a national committee, we would have to create one."

O'Brien compared the period of transition to the experiences of the Republican National Committee during the months following the 1964 elections. During those years, GOP Chairman Ray Bliss built the party organization, broadened the financial base of the party and sought to bring warring ideological factions together. Like Bliss, O'Brien has a national reputation as a "nuts-and-bolts" political technician. But he has broadened the role of party chairman to include that of party spokesman as well.

The son of Irish immigrant parents, O'Brien, 54, began organizing political campaigns in his home state of Massachusetts in 1938 at the age of 21. He successfully managed the senatorial campaigns of John F. Kennedy in 1952 and 1958 and directed the last three national Democratic Presidential campaigns. As special assistant to Presidents Kennedy and Johnson (1961-65), he was the White House link with Capitol Hill, guiding the legislative programs of the New Frontier and the Great Society in Congress. As Postmaster General (1965-68), he built a reputation as an innovator seeking to apply modern technology to moving the mails. In April 1968, when Mr. Johnson decided not to seek reelection, O'Brien resigned from the Cabinet to take a leading role in the Presidential campaign of Sen. Robert F. Kennedy. Following Sen. Kennedy's assassination, O'Brien endorsed Hubert Humphrey's candidacy, becoming campaign manager and DNC chairman after the Chicago convention. He resigned the chairmanship in January 1969 to become president of McDonnell & Company, a New York investment banking and stock brokerage firm, and left McDonnell eight months later to start his own public relations and consulting business.

O'Brien is convinced that effective use of radio and television is essential to success in modern-day politics, and thus is crucial to the future of the Democratic Party. When he returned to the committee in March 1970, O'Brien was confronted almost immediately with the problem of getting broadcast time for the party to respond to President Nixon. He felt that Mr. Nixon's frequent and effective use of television to propound his policies and to blame the Democratically controlled Congress for the nation's shortcomings was damaging the Democrats politically and demoralizing their ranks. Yet, the Columbia Broadcasting System refused to sell the DNC nationwide time to present alternatives to Nixon policies or for a fund-raising announcement. O'Brien began an intensive campaign to change the situation and secure for the Democrats exposure on national television.

O'Brien has put his own distinctive brand on DNC operations. As one of his first moves, he set about streamlining the headquarters staff that operates from the sixth floor of the four-year-old Watergate Office Building overlooking the Potomac River. "The staff structure which had existed more or less unchanged for the past 20 years was no longer capable of dealing with the political realities of the 1970s," O'Brien said. He announced a complete reorganization, setting up four operational units—the Office of the Chairman, the Office of Communications, the Office of Campaigns and Party Organization and the Office of Finance. (See Table 9.1.)

O'Brien's operating inner circle is essentially limited to four men: Stanley L. Greigg, 39, deputy chairman; William B. Welsh, 46, executive director; John G. Stewart, 36, communications director; and Joseph E. Mohbat, 33, press secretary.

Greigg, a former House Member from Iowa (1965-67), and Welsh, who was executive assistant to Harris at the DNC in 1969, assist O'Brien in developing and implementing staff projects and in managing the day-to-day operation of the headquarters. (Greigg also is head of the Office of Campaigns and Party Organization, a position he held before replacing the late Ira Kapenstein as deputy chairman in April 1971.) O'Brien appointed two men as his special assistants. Philip B. Seib, 24, who headed the "campaign '70 clearing house" set up by O'Brien to provide information and campaign techniques for involving college students in the 1970 campaign, focuses on the committee's youth programs. Seib oversees the national Democratic youth voter registration effort for 1972, and is working to organize registration drives on a nonpartisan basis. Edward E. Cubberley, 31, whose responsibilities cover a wide range of administrative duties, served as O'Brien's special assistant at the DNC in 1968.

Established party activities such as a speaker's bureau, the minorities division and women's activities are located within the Office of the Chairman. Andrew C. Muse, 43, head of the minorities division, was director of compliance at the Equal Employment Opportunity Commission before joining the committee in February 1971. Mary Lou Burg, 41, national committeewoman from Wisconsin, has been director of women's activities for the DNC since August 1970.

As head of the Office of Communications, Stewart's responsibilities include supervision of the party's public affairs audio news service and preparation of the party's two regular publications as well as special booklets. Stewart, a former legislative assistant to Vice President Humphrey, also is executive director of the Democratic Policy Council, which develops policy on a wide variety of subjects—from urban renewal to health care. Stewart's chief assistant is Mohbat, press secretary, a former reporter for the Associated Press. As O'Brien's principal spokesman, Mohbat helps write the chairman's speeches and sets up press conferences in cities where O'Brien is scheduled to make an appearance.

Under Stewart and publications director William Quinn,

the DNC has put out two new publications since O'Brien became chairman. *FACT: a Four-Letter Watchword from the DNC*, first appeared in July 1970; the first two issues featured quotes from Lewis Carroll's *Alice in Wonderland*, applied to Mr. Nixon's economic policies. Described by Stewart as "a lively commentary on the Administration's position on certain issues, with affirmative Democratic Party positions," the offset-printed newsletter is issued biweekly to 5,000 influential Democratic leaders. *National Democrat*, first issued in spring 1971, is published quarterly and goes to 35,000 persons and institutions, including libraries, schools, labor and party leaders.

In addition to the two regular publications, the DNC is putting together a series of special research studies, printed in pocket size and designed as quick election-time reference aids for candidates and others involved in the 1972 campaigns. The committee plans to print between 5,000 and 10,000 copies of each study. The studies, Stewart explained, will range in topic from a critical analysis of the Administration's law and justice policies to "key quotes" of President Nixon and Vice President Agnew.

The Office of Research, which develops the party message, is directed by David Cooper, 32, formerly a staff assistant with the Louis Harris and Mervin Field polling organizations. In charge of political research, Cooper concentrates most of his time on public-opinion sampling. The responsibility for issues research has been shifted to Stewart.

Directed by Deputy Chairman Greigg, the Office of Campaigns and Party Organization services local and state organizations with technical advice and provides services for candidates, including information on voting records and analysis of public opinion polls. Most of the nuts-and-bolts work in the office is handled by Greigg's deputy, Robert E. Moss, 31, who was a campaign coordinator in the 1968 Presidential campaigns of Robert Kennedy and Hubert Humphrey.

For the 1972 election year, Greigg's office is publishing a revised and updated edition of the party's 1970 campaign manual, the first Democratic campaign instruction book issued since 1960 when the "O'Brien Manual," which had been used successfully in John Kennedy's campaigns in Massachusetts, was applied to national politics. The techniques it details — organizing and financing campaigns, identifying the candidate's supporters and registering and activating the vote — have been widely used by candidates of both parties. Three other campaign aids have been prepared by the committee for 1972: an updated version of the 1970 campaign guide for state and local elections, a revised edition of a get-out-the-vote manual and a new publication describing techniques of voter registration.

The Office of Finance, headed by DNC Treasurer Robert Strauss, is concerned with reducing the debt and finding the money to sustain other committee operations. It is the most independent of the four divisions. O'Brien has given Strauss a free hand to go about reducing the DNC debt and to institute new fund-raising techniques. Strauss approves all requests for travel or spending by other DNC personnel — including O'Brien.

Strauss, 53, who follows the lead of O'Brien in avoiding ideological disputes, is a member of the Dallas law firm of Akin, Gump, Strauss, Hauer and Feld and is president of Strauss Broadcasting Company, which owns radio stations in Dallas, Atlanta and Tucson. Democratic national committeeman from Texas since 1958, Strauss traces his interest in politics to his law school days at the University of Texas, where his classmates included Treasury Secretary John B. Connally, former Democratic Governor of Texas (1963-69), and Rep. J. J. Pickle, D-Tex. "Bob doesn't have any particularly deep-rooted political philosophy," Pickle told *National Journal.* "He's been a working man; he's known good times and bad. He's an action man. He knows you have to put money into the party to make it run, and he knows the money-raising business."

George Bristol and Andrew Shea assist Strauss in managing the committee's finances. Bristol, 31, formerly a management consultant, is responsible for fund raising. Shea, 33, who deals with the DNC's creditors and pays the bills, practiced law before joining the committee. The DNC's direct mail fund-raising efforts are directed by Olga (Bobbie) Gechas, who joined the staff in 1969 after handling similar duties for the United Nations International Children's Emergency Fund.

Recognizing the prerogatives of Democratic congressional leaders, O'Brien does not attempt to be the only spokesman for the party. In his relationships with Democrats in Congress, he draws on his long experience on Capitol Hill, which dates back to 1949-50 when he was an aide to Rep. Foster Furcolo, D-Mass. (1949-52), whose successful 1948 campaign O'Brien had managed. O'Brien and his staff are working more closely with the House and Senate Democratic campaign committees than at any time in recent history. Both groups, which lack large staffs, financed DNC research work geared toward the November 1970 congressional elections. The DNC conducted a series of briefing sessions for Congressmen, pointing out services that would be available to them at cost for their campaigns: facilities for researching issues, taping radio spots and identifying voters through computer techniques.

In his efforts to regenerate the party organization, O'Brien has been a visible, active chairman. He has narrowly avoided public confrontations with the congressional leadership on at least two occasions. In spring 1970, 100 Democratic Congressmen signed a petition calling on former Ambassador Sargent Shriver to head a new group to promote the election of Democratic congressional candidates. O'Brien opposed the move, saying a second Democratic committee was the last thing the party needed. Receiving assurances that the Shriver operation would not be a fund-raising organization and would not get involved in policy disputes, O'Brien went along with the House and Senate majority leaders, Rep. Carl Albert, Okla., and Sen. Mike Mansfield, Mont., lending his name to a June 24 press release announcing formation of a group called "congressional leadership for the future." The release quoted O'Brien as being delighted that "we have been able to work out a method to enlist Sargent Shriver in our all-out drive this fall." (The Shriver operation went out of existence after the November 1970 elections. Shriver is now a partner in the

Washington, D.C., law firm of Fried, Frank, Harris, Shriver & Kampellman.)

O'Brien's warm relationship with Mansfield was tested again on July 7, 1970, when the Senate leader said demands for equal time to answer the President were "getting out of bounds." Since the DNC had been helping Mansfield get television time to reply to Mr. Nixon on economic policy, O'Brien felt the party needed a united front on the issue. The situation was smoothed over when the two discussed it by phone the next day. Mansfield assured O'Brien he had been talking about anti-war Senators who wanted televison time to answer Nixon statements on Cambodia and Vietnam, not about O'Brien's equal time requests.

The Democrats' financial problems result from years of neglect of fund raising, aggravated by loss of the White House in the 1968 elections. In 1960, the DNC received 70 per cent of its funds from contributors of less than $100; eight years later, 70 per cent of its resources came from donors giving more than $100. During the Kennedy and Johnson Administrations, the party was supported in the main by wealthy contributors who paid $1,000 a year for the privilege of meeting socially with the Chief Executive and other high officials of the Administration as members of the President's Club. Membership, which reached 4,000 shortly after Mr. Johnson's landslide victory in 1964, began a sharp decline the following year. The decline continued steadily until early 1968 when the President's Club was dissolved. By 1968 convention time, the party had outstanding bills totaling more than $400,000.

The Presidential campaign, plus a DNC decision in mid-1969 to take over the remaining pre-convention debts of Humphrey and Robert Kennedy, raised the debt to $9.3 million. Much of the debt is in the form of unsecured loans from wealthy donors. The largest are from Lew Wasserman, president of Music Corporation of America, and John (Jake the Barber) Factor, a California land speculator who in 1962 obtained a pardon from President Kennedy for a 1943 mail-fraud conviction. Each made 1968 loans to the Democrats of $240,000. Nineteen others loaned $100,000 each.

Because of legal prohibitions against individual loans or donations of more than $5,000 to a single campaign committee, the transactions were made in multiples of $5,000 or less to national, state and local organizations. Most of the loans came in the fall when the Democrats attempted to match the huge television expenditure supporting the Nixon-Agnew ticket. Making radio and television payments in advance, the Democrats spent $7.1 million. The Republicans spent $12.1 million.

Strauss has pledged that all creditors will be paid, a contrast to the common practice among defeated candidates of negotiating settlements. The treasurer contends negotiated settlements are unfair and illegal, particularly when the creditors are airlines and telephone companies which are regulated by government agencies. Among the DNC debts are $1.5 million owed to telephone companies; $1 million to American Airlines and another half-million dollars to other carriers; about $1 million to hotels; and $750,000 for supplies at the 1968 Chicago convention. The committee has delayed immediate payment of its debt, applying its financial resources to daily operational expenses, financing of the 1972 national convention and getting the party machinery in motion to support the Democratic Presidential nominee. Bristol, assistant to Strauss, told *National Journal* in July 1971 that the DNC plans to "take a hard look" at the debt situation "around the first of the year (1972)." "If we can win the White House, we'll have the political muscle to raise the money to pay off our debts and get the party back on sound ground financially," he said.

Since his appointment as party treasurer, Strauss has instituted economy measures at the DNC, such as calling in credit cards which staff members had used for travel and entertainment. He also has set in motion several fund-raising devices. In March 1970, Strauss asked 1,000 wealthy contributors to give $100 a month each for the remaining nine months of 1970 to provide operating funds for the DNC and to finance special mass-mailings. The appeal produced 400 monthly $100 contributors. In April 1970, he staged a $50-a-person fund-raising party, inviting some 300 former Cabinet members and other high officials from previous Democratic administrations. The proceeds from the dinner—approximately $1 million—gave the DNC "some breathing room" to begin developing plans and programs for 1972, Bristol said. (Although the committee had been operating in the black for some weeks prior to the April dinner, its funds were absorbed by daily operating expenses, leaving no margin for planning or instituting new programs.) In 1971, the DNC organized the "$72-a-Month Sponsors Club," which, Bristol said, had an initial mailing list of between 5,000 and 7,000 new names. The committee's fund-raising efforts have enabled it to support a $150,000-a-month office operation. Reports on file with the Clerk of the House of Representatives for the first eight months of 1971 show total receipts of $1,134,766.74 for the DNC, and expenditures of $1,124,343.29.

Strauss' major concern is broadening the financial base of the party, primarily by increasing the number of small contributors who will give to the party on a regular basis. Bristol described the long-range financial plan for 1972 as two-fold: finance the national convention, specifically without adding new debts to the $9.3 million already owed, and expand the program of direct-mail solicitation. Bristol said the committee is working toward a "good solid list of small contributors" by the July convention and is planning a mass-mailing immediately after the convention's selection of a candidate. (According to Bristol, the DNC by August 1970 had 65,000 names of contributors on file. The committee will continue to test and build this list for the post-convention mailing.)

O'Brien feels a solution to the DNC financial problem is "the first order of business," a necessity for the survival of the two-party system. O'Brien thinks legislation is needed to provide a method for public support of campaigns, such as the 1965 proposal to permit taxpayers to check off a $1 contribution to their political party on their income tax forms. He also emphasizes the need for enactment of campaign-spending reform legislation before the 1972 elections. "Trying to look down the long road, I see the Democratic Party priced out of existence," O'Brien said. The Republicans, he said, were "outspending" the Democrats "five-to-one" in 1970.

In his August 1971 statement outlining the party's strategy for the next 12 months, the DNC chairman said the various fund-raising projects undertaken by the committee "have success-fully brought the DNC through a most difficult financial period." O'Brien added that "despite the unprecedented out-pouring of Republican money that can be expected in the '72 campaign, the Democratic Party will be prepared to take its candidate and its case directly to the American people. We do not intend to lose the '72 election by default . . . we intend to win by laying the financial foundations in the next twelve months for the Democratic nominee to wage a vigorous and victorious campaign."

When O'Brien became chairman in March 1970, the Demo-cratic National Committee had plans under way to buy time on the three television networks for a program refuting the Nixon Administration's record. It hoped to cap a half-hour program with an appeal for funds. The Columbia Broadcast-ing System, however, declined to sell the time, citing a long-standing policy of restricting political programs to the weeks immediately preceding an election. O'Brien told his staff to look into all possibilities for getting the Democrats exposure on national television. Outside of a one-hour response to the State of the Union address, there had been no TV program devoted to opposition party views during Mr. Nixon's first 16 months in office.

After the President's nationally televised speech April 30, 1970, explaining his decision to move American troops into Cambodia, O'Brien sent telegrams to the presidents of the three television networks asking for live coverage of an O'Brien speech in Milwaukee on May 9. John Stewart, DNC

communications director, said the request was not "overly
presumptuous" because Administration spokesmen had been
"blanketing" network news and talk shows in an effort to rally
support for the President's new policies in Southeast Asia.
Stewart called the O'Brien move "the first attempt by the opposition party to reach the American people with a coherent
and comprehensive analysis of the Cambodian decision as
well as a detailed critique of the Vietnamization program as
advocated by President Nixon." All three networks rejected
O'Brien's contention that coverage of his speech should be
allocated under the "fairness doctrine" of the Federal Communications Commission (FCC). The American Broadcasting
Company decided to cover the speech live and in full as a
"newsworthy event," although only 45 of the network's 160
affiliates and the five stations it owns picked up the program.
CBS and the National Broadcasting Company gave limited
radio and television coverage of the speech during weekend
news programs.

In its next move toward opening up television, the DNC on
May 19, 1970, filed a request with the FCC, asking for a declaratory ruling governing the sale of radio and television time
to political groups. Through its counsel, Joseph A. Califano
Jr., the committee asked that broadcasters—networks and individual stations—be denied the authority to refuse to sell
time to "responsible entities such as the DNC" to comment on
public issues or to solicit funds. "A political organization seeking the attention and support of potential small contributors
must have access to the broadcast media," said Califano, who
served as President Johnson's chief assistant for domestic
programs (1965-69). "Television has brought the Vietnam war,
racial strife and student disorder into every living room in
America with consequences for our society we cannot fully
perceive. It is only through this medium that an effective nationwide campaign such as the DNC proposes can be
launched."

NBC already had agreed to sell time to the Democrats. In
its reply to the FCC, ABC indicated it would change its policy.
CBS opposed the petition but on June 22 CBS President Frank

Stanton, in a telegram to O'Brien, offered the Democrats 25 minutes of free prime time to present its views. Stanton said the offer was "in keeping with the long-standing CBS policy to achieve fairness and balance in the treatment of public issues, including the disparity between Presidential appearances and the opportunities available to the principal opposition party." CBS said it would also permit the DNC to purchase spot announcements, up to one minute in length, for fund-raising purposes. Two weeks later, on July 7, CBS presented "The Loyal Opposition," which featured O'Brien seated before a television set watching taped excerpts from Mr. Nixon's past speeches and commenting on the Administration's performance. CBS declined to sell network time for a fund-raising spot, but the Democrats bought 30-second and 60-second time segments to follow the program in 15 major markets.

On August 5, 1970, the FCC ruled on the DNC's May 19 request for a declaratory ruling on the sale of radio and television time to political groups for fund raising or comment on public issues. The commission said broadcasters "may not arbitrarily refuse" to sell political parties time for fund-raising appeals. The FCC denied, however, the DNC's contention that such groups should be allowed to purchase time for comment on public issues. (The U.S. Court of Appeals for the District of Columbia August 3, 1971, upheld the DNC's position, ruling that radio and television stations cannot, as a general policy, refuse to sell time for discussion of controversial public issues. The court said a "flat ban" on editorial advertising violates the 1st Amendment. It left to the discretion of the broadcaster the decision of which advertisements would be accepted, and said the commission could require that the opposition must be given response time, free of charge if necessary. The DNC interpreted the decision to mean that the FCC is responsible for setting down guidelines for broadcasters. The FCC voted October 22 to appeal the case to the Supreme Court.)

The DNC's legal action, along with the showing of the July 7, 1970, CBS program, brought a loud response from the GOP and touched off spirited debate within Congress and the industry. Before the CBS program, "The Loyal Opposition," appeared on the air, the Republican National Committee had mounted a counterattack. Rogers C. B. Morton, then RNC chairman and now Interior Secretary, sent a telegram to Stanton accusing the network of delegating its "journalistic judgment" by giving the DNC full control of the broadcast. Morton called the show "an unprecedented, inaccurate, personal attack on the President," and demanded equal time for response by the Republican National Committee. CBS refused, and the RNC on July 13 filed a petition against the network with the FCC.

Stanton defended the network decision, citing "a very pronounced increase in the use of prime time (6:30-10 p.m.) by the President." He said that during the first 18 months of their administrations, President Eisenhower made three prime time network appearances; President Kennedy appeared four times; President Johnson, seven times; and President Nixon, 14 times. In remarks to the Broadcast Editorial Conference in Park City, Utah, on July 10, Stanton applauded the increased use of the media by Mr. Nixon, adding that the CBS offer of time to "the party out of executive power" was made "to minimize the risk of imbalance and to treat opposing views on public issues fairly." Simultaneously, Senate Republican Whip Robert P. Griffin of Michigan and three GOP colleagues were denouncing the CBS action of giving free time for "an unprecedented blatantly partisan political program." Rep James T. Broyhill, R-N.C., a member of the Communications Subcommittee of the House Commerce Committee, accused the network of conspiring with the Democrats "to help them raise money."

At a July 17 press conference announcing the party's FCC action, Morton said only Congress should respond to remarks by the President, and he accused Stanton of becoming a "deputy chairman of the Democratic National Committee." He contended that presentation of a so-called public service program, followed by a "pitch for funds," was "an unhygienic way to play pool." Morton noted that Senate Majority Leader Mike Mansfield—the first Democratic spokesman to ask for and receive time from the networks (he was given a half-hour on NBC and ABC to rebut the President's June 17, 1970, economic address)—had told newsmen that demands for equal

time were "getting out of bounds." On August 14, 1970, the
FCC upheld the RNC petition against CBS and ordered the
network to make time available to the committee or to a partisan Republican spokesman "to answer matters raised in the
DNC broadcast." When the FCC refused to reconsider its decision, the Democrats and CBS turned to the court of appeals
which agreed to consider the case. Arguments were heard
September 24, 1971.

Continuing to press its case for access to free television
time, the DNC in spring 1971 asked all three major networks
for time to respond to three separate television appearances
made by Mr. Nixon. O'Brien sent response-time requests to
NBC following Barbara Walters' two-hour interview with
Mr. Nixon on the Today Show March 15; to ABC following
Howard K. Smith's one-hour interview with the President
March 22; and to NBC, ABC and CBS following the President's
April 7 address to the nation on the Indochina war. The
first two requests were denied, and only ABC agreed to grant
the DNC time to respond to the President's April 7 message.
(The ABC program, "Indochina: Another View," was aired
April 22 and featured O'Brien and six Democratic Senators, all
declared or undeclared contenders for the 1972 Presidential
nomination, expressing their views on the war.)

In mid-April, the DNC filed complaints with the FCC against
the networks which refused to grant response time. The commission's delay in acting on the complaints prompted the DNC
on August 11 to ask the appeals court to step in and "treat
the commission's failure to act" as a "final order denying the
relief sought." The committee requested the court to schedule
a full hearing or order the FCC to rule on its complaints within
10 days. On August 20, before the court had taken any action,
the FCC ruled on the DNC complaints, denying all four. (On
the same day, the commission denied a request by the Republican National Committee for response time to the Democrat's April 22 presentation on ABC. Lyn Nofziger, the RNC's
deputy national chairman for communications, told National
Journal the RNC will appeal the decision.) Charles H. Wilson
Jr., a member of the Washington, D.C., law firm of Williams,
Connolly & Califano who serves with Califano as counsel for

the DNC, said the DNC has amended its August 11 petition and asked the court to review the FCC's denial of the committee's complaints against the networks.

In addition to response-time requests, the DNC is seeking to achieve its goal of "fairness and equity for the major opposition party in the area of television and politics" through a general FCC ruling on the obligations of broadcasters under the fairness doctrine. In May 1970, the FCC announced it would spell out broadcast licensees' obligations under the fairness doctrine and asked interested parties to file their views and comments. On June 22, the committee responded, requesting the FCC to broaden the fairness doctrine to require networks and individual stations to seek out responsible persons or groups to present "significant contrasting viewpoints" each time the President appears on television. Califano said in his brief: "We submit that virtually every time the President addresses the nation or appears at a press conference — whether speaking as Chief Executive on legislative or economic matters, Commander-in-Chief on military operations or new weapons systems or the head of his party on issues or candidates in a forthcoming election — he expresses his self-interested viewpoint on controversial issues of current public interest."

One year later, on June 9, the FCC announced it was undertaking "a broad-ranging inquiry into the efficacy of the fairness doctrine and other commission public interest policies, in the light of current demands for access to the broadcast media to consider issues of public concern." The FCC subsequently denied a DNC request that it separate from its overall review of fairness policies the issues outlined in its May 1970 proceeding. On September 15, the DNC petitioned the court of appeals for a review of the FCC decision. Wilson told *National Journal* the DNC views the commission's decision as an effort to delay the resolution of broadcasters' obligations until after the 1972 Presidential campaign is underway. "There is no way they (the FCC) can decide the issue between now and July (1972), the critical period before next August when the President will become a candidate for reelection," said Wilson.

In his August 1971 party strategy statement, DNC Chairman

O'Brien termed the committee's efforts to secure free broadcast time in response to Presidential appearances "of vital
importance to a proper functioning of a democratic system of
government." O'Brien said: "Recent political campaigns have
starkly demonstrated the severe strain that paid political
broadcasts can place on any party's financial resources. If
free time is denied the party out of power to respond to the
President, that party can exercise its right to answer the President only at the risk of financial collapse."

The chaos and divisiveness that erupted at the 1968 Democratic National Convention in Chicago produced a demand
from large numbers of dissident Democrats for changes in
party procedures. While the focus in Chicago was on the
manner of selecting delegates, at the heart of the debate was
the structure of each state organization and the limited participation in affairs of the party that is common in most states.

On August 26, 1968, the convention adopted the majority report of the credentials committee calling for "a meaningful
and timely opportunity" for all Democratic voters to participate in future conventions. The following day the minority report of the rules committee was adopted, calling for a "full
and timely opportunity" to participate. The DNC was directed
to establish a commission to help state parties meet these requirements. The convention adopted another resolution directing the chairman to appoint a rules commission to make
recommendations for the 1972 convention, to avoid a repeat
performance of the 1968 event. (See Table 9.3.)

In early 1969, Chairman Harris appointed two commissions
to carry out these reforms, naming Sen. George S. McGovern
of South Dakota and Rep. James G. O'Hara of Michigan as
chairmen. McGovern, who resigned as chairman of the Commission on Party Structure and Delegate Selection in January
1971 after declaring his candidacy for President, was succeeded by Rep. Donald M. Fraser, D-Minn., a former chairman of the House Democratic Study Group (1969-70). (The

28-member commission headed by Fraser is part of the two-pronged effort to reform party procedures. A parallel Commission on Rules, headed by O'Hara, is dealing with procedures at the convention.) (See Table 9.2.)

When the reform commission was getting under way in early 1969, Sen. McGovern said that "there has never been a political party which, when confronted with the choice of reform or death, has chosen reform." He hoped the Democrats would break with that tradition. In an effort to do so, the commission produced 18 specific changes in party rules and practices which, it said, must be met before a state's delegation could be seated at the 1972 Democratic National Convention. These changes are keyed directly to abuses that the commission and its staff identified in the 1968 delegate-selection process. They fall into three broad categories: procedural irregularities, discrimination and inadequate party structures.

The commission found that no written party rules existed in at least 10 states and that rules in many other states were so vague regarding the selection of convention delegates as to frustrate anyone who might want to run a challenge slate of delegates. It also found wide use of the "unit rule," a century-old practice by which a majority of a delegation can bind a dissenting minority to vote in accord with the wishes of the majority. (In 1968, the controversial unit rule was employed in one form or another at party meetings in at least 15 states. In addition, two states, Massachusetts and Oregon, bound their delegations to vote for the candidate who received the most votes in state Presidential preference polls regardless of each delegate's personal preference.) The commission's guidelines require states to adopt written rules and open systems in the selection of delegates to the party's 1972 convention. They also ban the unit rule.

The commission found that only 5.5 per cent of the 1968 delegates were black, although blacks constitute 11 per cent of the total population and an even higher percentage of Democratic voters. According to the commission, 85 per cent of the blacks who voted in 1968 cast their Presidential ballots for Hubert Humphrey. (An exception to the 1968 pattern was Mississippi, where 50 per cent of the convention delegates were black, against a 42-per cent black population. The exception resulted from a convention vote to seat a delegation led by Aaron E. Henry, instead of an all-white Mississippi delegation.)

The 1968 convention also had very few younger persons as delegates: 16 delegations had no voting members under the age of 30 and another 13 had only one delegate from that age group. In eight state delegations, the average age was more than 50. As an afterthought, prompted by Sen. Birch Bayh, D-Ind., the commission also sought to deal with discrimination against the seating of women at the 1968 convention, where they comprised only 13 per cent of the voting delegates. The commission's guidelines insist that these groups be represented in "reasonable" ratios at the 1972 convention, but they set no formula or quota that must be met. As McGovern said in an interview: "The way we got the quota thing through was by not using the word 'quotas.' We couldn't have gotten quotas."

Also covered by the commission's reform efforts were practices that were not intentionally discriminatory but still had the effect of limiting access to the delegate-selection process. The commission noted that, one way or another, 38 per cent of the delegates who cast votes at the 1968 convention were named before former Sen. Eugene J. McCarthy, D-Minn. (1959-71), announced his Presidential candidacy on November 30, 1967. By March 31, when President Johnson announced that he would not seek another term, all but 12 of the states had begun their formal delegate-selection process. The commission's guidelines assert that all delegates must be picked in 1972.

The commission also found that in about one-fifth of the states, some or all of the delegates were being selected by party committees. In many cases, the committees met in what were described as conventions, although, in reality, attendance at the meetings was limited to party officers. These practices also have been curbed in the guidelines.

The following is a summary of the 18 requirements—known as guidelines—for the selection of delegates to the 1972 Democratic National Convention, as adopted by the party's reform commission:

- Adopt explicit written party rules governing delegate selection.
- Adopt procedural rules and safeguards for the delegate-selection process that would: forbid proxy voting; ban the use of the unit rule; require a quorum of not less than 40 per cent at all party committee meetings; remove all mandatory assessments of delegates to the national convention; limit mandatory fees to no more than $10 and delegate petition requirements to no more than 1 per cent of the Democratic vote; ensure, except in rural areas, that party meetings are held on uniform dates in public places; and ensure adequate public notice of all party meetings involved in the delegate-selection process.
- Seek a broader base for the party through: adding to state party rules anti-racial-discrimination standards; encouraging representation on the state's delegation to the convention of minority groups, young people and women in a reasonable relationship to their presence in the state's population; and allowing all persons 18 years of age or older to participate in all party affairs.
- Make the following changes in the delegate-selection process: select alternates in the same manner as delegates; ban designation of ex-officio delegates; conduct the entire process of delegate selection within 1972; select no less than 75 per cent of the total delegation at conventions at a level no higher than congressional districts, and follow apportionment formulas; apportion all non-at-large delegates to the convention on a representation basis that gives equal weight to population and Democratic voting strength based on the previous Presidential election; designate procedures by which delegate slates are prepared and may be challenged; and select no more than 10 per cent of the delegates by the state committee.

Guidelines to reform delegate selection imply profound

changes in the political life of the state Democratic Parties. Many have been slow to adjust their rules to comply. Two major reasons exist for the spotty performance. In some states the necessary changes must be approved by the legislature, dominated either by Republicans hostile to a democratized opposition, or by Democrats reluctant to make the revisions, or by a coalition of Democrats and Republicans who are un-enthusiastic about reform. In other states, there have been paralyzing disagreements over how to implement the guide-lines within the party.

While Democratic leaders such as Humphrey maintain that "you can't make quantum jumps overnight," many state party chairmen have expressed fear of a credentials challenge if they fail to make a "good-faith effort" to get in line with the new national rules. Dr. Elmer C. Baum, Texas state Demo-cratic chairman, voiced a position held by many of his party colleagues in other sections of the country. Speaking of his state's 130 delegates, he told *National Journal:* "Certainly, we want to be seated. We will comply." Richard J. Hughes, the New Jersey national committeeman, said, "We wouldn't think of not meeting the guidelines for fairness."

With 271 delegates, one-fifth of the total needed for Presi-dential nomination, California's Democratic Party represents a powerful force at the 1972 convention. Leading Democrats there wrestled with the guidelines for months, and their maneuvering brought O'Brien nearly to the point of exaspera-tion. "It's our biggest problem," he said.

California will be the only big state coming to the con-vention with all its delegates committed to a single candidate on the first ballot. This is because California has a "winner-take-all" Presidential preference primary that makes the state the largest single delegate lode in the nation. The reform com-mission opposed in principle winner-take-all primaries. But its members chose not to decree that states must do away with them. (The only other state with a similar primary procedure is McGovern's own, South Dakota.) Instead, the commission merely "urges" states to abandon the device. It suggested an alternative allowing any Presidential candidate receiving more than 15 per cent of the primary vote to be assigned a proportional share of the delegates at the national nominating convention.

California party leaders flatly refused to end the practice. "Everyone agreed on winner-take-all," said Stephen Reinhardt, California's Democratic national committeeman. "There isn't a chance of a snowball in hell that we will change this," said M. Larry Lawrence, Southern California state chairman. "We like the power and strength . . . California is going to be the dominant force at the convention." Since the Democratic leadership was immovable on the issue, and since the commission did not require termination of winner-take-all primaries, Californians were given permission to continue the system, assured that there would be no credentials challenge on that issue.

The rules changes imposed by the reform commission have had a clear impact on the South. In many states below the Mason-Dixon line, delegates to past conventions were often chosen by the state chairman and the Governor, after consultation with the Presidential candidate of their choice. "That's the way it was always done," said Charles Kirbo, chairman of the Georgia Democratic Party. "That's the end of that," he said. "The way you used to be able to set up delegates, the wheeling and dealing of the past is over," said Jon Moyle, Florida state chairman. Even in Alabama, long known for its all-white delegations, Democrats have written new party rules which wipe out the old procedure of choosing delegates through a decision by the state party's executive committee. The new rules require delegate selection to begin at the lowest "practical" community unit, ensuring blacks an opportunity to participate in the process.

Not all Southern states rushed to conform, and there were signs of rebellion elsewhere. In Louisiana, J. Marshall Brown, the national committeeman, described McGovern as a "jerk" and a "knucklehead." Louisiana has "done what we can to comply," said Brown. He added: "I always took the position that the McGovern Commission was not binding." In Maryland, National Committeeman Dale Anderson refused to stand in awe of the reform effort. "They (the DNC) don't have as much of a club over us as they think," he said. "The Democratic Party cannot dictate. I have never been in favor of McGovern." James Ronan, Democratic state chairman in Illinois, was in the Brown-Anderson camp. "I question the right of the previous convention to set the rules of the 1972 convention," he said.

In Michigan, the reluctance to change was located in the state legislature, rather than among party leaders. Although State Chairman James M. McNeely tried for three years to push election reform bills through the state legislature, there was little affirmative action in either chamber even after the DNC approved the reform commission guidelines. The legislature was also the scene of trouble in New York. There, Republicans control both houses as well as the Governor's office. To meet the guidelines, New York must pass a law that requires each delegate candidate in the Presidential primary to list his preference or state that he is uncommitted. The legislature adjourned for the year on June 9, 1971 without enacting a bill that would require this change on the ballot. John F. English, the top political aide for Sen. Edmund S. Muskie, D-Maine, said Gov. Nelson A. Rockefeller opposed the bill. He said Rockefeller wants to keep his own Republican Presidential options open for 1972, and he fears he would be foreclosed from this if delegates are forced to state their preferences on the ballot.

The guidelines were adopted by the party's reform commission November 19, 1969; only nine states were certified in full compliance as of July 16, 1971. Five states had unofficially complied with the guidelines, but were awaiting final official party ratification. Fraser has expressed satisfaction with progress towards reform across the nation. But some other commission members are not so optimistic. These dissidents contend that the Democratic National Committee is far from enthusiastic about forcing state-by-state adherence to the new rules. Moreover, one former commission staff man was so disappointed with the DNC's enforcement attitude that he set up his own organization, supported by several Democratic money men, to bring suit against non-complying state parties. But Chairman O'Brien told *National Journal* he did not intend to let up in his effort to effect reforms and was determined to have a minimum of 40 states in compliance by the end of 1971.

Anticipating that many states would balk at being told by a commission that they must reform their delegate-selection machinery, the reform group took the position that its word was party law. "Our position from the start was that we were the creature of the 1968 convention and that only the 1972 convention could negate what we had done," said Robert W. Nelson, the commission's staff director.

The group was also armed with a legal opinion from DNC counsel Califano which held that the commission's guidelines were binding in the states' Democratic Parties unless they were rescinded by the 1972 convention. Nelson said he also counted on momentum building for reform as a number of states, taking cue from the commission, set up reform commissions of their own. Maine, Alabama, North Carolina, Iowa and Minnesota Democratic Parties all set up reform commissions at the same time that the McGovern group was preparing its proposals.

As a follow-up to the strategy worked out in advance of the approval of the guidelines, McGovern decided to send "compliance letters" to each state and territory. These lengthy and gently worded communications dated February 27, 1970 — three months after the rules were approved by the commission — notified the party chairmen, national committeemen and committeewomen that they were out of compliance with the guidelines and cited which rules each state and territorial party had failed to meet. "We are prepared to offer you whatever technical assistance you may need," McGovern wrote to party officials. Several reminders were sent to the states, and Nelson has kept in telephone contact with state leaders. In some cases, he has traveled to state party meetings to discuss methods of complying with the guidelines, but these trips are made only at the invitation of the state party. "I would not describe my work as enforcement," Nelson said. "Our job is to aid the states. We're not acting as an enforcement agency."

Nelson's attitude and McGovern's soft words troubled several members of the reform commission. Most vocal in their complaints were William Dodds, director of the Community Action Department of the United Auto Workers of America, and David Mixner, a staff assistant for Common Cause in Denver. "The letters mean nothing," said Dodds. "We did a great job on substance and ideology, but because of a lack of money we didn't follow up as effectively as we should have," he said in an interview.

The union official placed some of the blame on O'Brien. "I wish he were more enthusiastic," said Dodds. However, he also criticized himself and other commission officials for failing to work harder for compliance. "I should be in the states and make sure they're doing the work," he said. Dodds said he understood that commission members McGovern and Sen. Harold E. Hughes, D-Iowa, could not push reform very hard any more. "Their quest for the Presidency has had an erosive effect on their follow-through," he said. Taking a similar view, Mixner leveled his criticism primarily at Nelson. "He has not been agressive at all. I am very disappointed. But O'Brien and the commission share the blame." If enforcement activities continue to lag, "the likelihood of an interior Chicago is high," he said.

Even less impressed with DNC enforcement activities was Kenneth A. Bode, the former research director of the commission. Bode, who has been involved in political reform since 1968, became concerned in 1970 that the commission guidelines would not be carried out. Bode interested several well-known Democratic contributors in a proposal that an outside organization be established and push for compliance. He soon had $35,000 to start his enforcement project.

Bode's patrons were: Philip M. Stern, president of the Philip M. Stern Family Fund in Washington ($10,000); Martin H. Peretz, assistant professor of social studies at Harvard, who is independently wealthy ($10,000); Edgar M. Bronfman, president and director of Joseph E. Seagram & Sons Inc., New York, and a contributor to the Humphrey Presidential campaign

($5,000); Stanley K. Sheinbaum, writer and economist, New York ($5,000); Arthur Cohen, New York businessman ($2,500); and Philip J. Levin, who is also in business in New York ($2,500). In addition Joseph L. Rauh Jr., a Washington lawyer prominent in Democratic national politics, agreed to serve as Bode's legal counsel. Rauh has had first-hand experience with party reform. In 1964, he represented the Mississippi Freedom Democratic Party in its seating challenge against the regular all-white Democratic delegation. The challengers won two at-large seats at the convention. (Rauh and Bode also are members of the Americans for Democratic Action 1972 Convention Task Force, organized to oversee delegate selection and national convention procedures in the Democratic and Republican Parties.)

The Bode organization, called Center for Political Reform, opened its doors in a converted fieldstone town house near Dupont Circle in Washington January 1, 1971. Its principal activity is tracking state compliance with commission rules and organizing reform-minded groups in the states to work for the cause. "I want the nutcutting to start now," Bode said. He said every state Democratic Party failing to implement the guidelines will be challenged. "We will bring a suit in any state before giving it up. I don't trust O'Brien." Bode's aim is "to start a liberal, independent constituency." Bode said: "The lack of aggressive enforcement by the DNC leaves open the possibility for development of such a constituency."

Both O'Brien and Fraser denied they are lax on enforcement. In interviews, each of them said he would take it upon himself to see that the states complied. O'Brien made his feelings clear in a March 19, 1971, letter to state party officials concerning reform efforts by outside groups. In the letter, O'Brien discounted the Bode organization without mentioning it by name. O'Brien told the party leaders, some of whom had asked about the reform groups, including the Center for Political Reform, that the groups "have no official status or relationship to the officially created reform commissions or the Democratic National Committee."

The DNC chairman was critical of the reform commission

for inaction on the rules. He said that, "on a staff basis, we (the DNC) don't have the horses" to keep in steady consultation with the states. "I'm in no goddamn position to put 50 people on this payroll," he said. O'Brien said he had seen the commission's job as two phases. Developing the guidelines was "stage one." As "stage two," he proposed that "commission members move in state by state. I proposed originally that each member of the commission work in a state or a series of states on compliance."

However, "that probably wasn't realistic from the outset," said O'Brien. Some commission members are running for President, some are working for other candidates. And a few lack sufficient personal funds or time to devote to enforcement. Convinced that the commission members will not make the compliance drive, which he equated with "a national effort comparable to a Presidential campaign," O'Brien said: "It's obvious to me we're going to have to do it." He pointed to himself. "I'll get it done," he said. By August 1971, O'Brien had worked out a plan under which volunteers would be made available by the DNC to go into states and help them work out reforms. (O'Brien said the DNC had already spent over $292,000 in support of party reform.) As for the states that fail to comply, O'Brien warned: "They are really gambling. They may not be seated."

Unlike O'Brien, Fraser welcomed Bode's participation. "I myself am delighted he's operating," he said. Fraser also said O'Brien is "committed to the whole idea of reform. His commitment is very deep and very real." Nevertheless, Fraser continued, it is the commission's job to obtain compliance. On March 1, two months after taking over the commission, Fraser sent state chairmen an accounting of where each state stood on the path towards compliance. His next official action was to praise Democratic Party leaders across the country May 28, saying, "By and large state party leadership has responded with vigor and determination." He also expressed disappointment with parties in Connecticut, Delaware, Michigan and Washington for moving too slowly in implementing reform. He said that since the DNC has endorsed the guidelines, "there is real muscle behind us." Now, he said, enforcement should come "from the commission office." "We're going to fall short clearly in some of the states," Fraser added. He said he would be in telephone contact with states lagging behind in guideline adherence. Told of O'Brien's insistence on enforcing the guidelines himself, Fraser was silent for a moment, then said: "That's a plus for us."

Former Chairman McGovern also welcomed Bode's reform efforts. "The vehicle for forcing compliance is having a challenge slate in a position to go, you see," he said. "What people like Bode can do is to alert reform-minded Democrats to watch the delegate-selection process and be prepared to come in with a challenge slate if the one that is picked is out of compliance." McGovern said that he was "pleasantly surprised the way the national chairman and the Democratic National Committee are going in behind the guidelines."

O'Brien recognizes that there is a lack of men and money to enforce the commission's handiwork. Nevertheless, he has vowed to carry the reforms through, largely by his own selling efforts. "I think it will have a dramatic effect on the tone of the convention," O'Brien said in an interview. "It's the greatest goddamn change since (the advent of) the two-party system."

A June 1971 survey by the Democratic National Committee, which was made available to *National Journal,* showed that more than 70 per cent of the states had yet to comply with the commission's guidelines regarding racial minority representation at the 1972 convention. More than 75 per cent of the states had failed to comply with another key guideline that requires state party officials to prepare and issue written rules for the selection of convention delegates.

Despite these shortcomings, many Democratic politicians interviewed by *National Journal* remained impressed with the scope of the prospective reforms. All of the declared and undeclared Presidential candidates in the party publicly have said that they will be substantially carried out in 1972. "All the press has done during all these months is to indicate that it can't happen, and it *has* happened," said Sen. Hughes. "There

would be a split in the Democratic Party right now without
the commission and without Richard Nixon," a top political
adviser to one of the Democratic Presidential hopefuls said.
"As it is, you hear almost no third-party talk."

A study of U.S. political parties by John S. Saloma III and
Frederick H. Sontag, commissioned by the Twentieth Century
Fund and still unpublished, states: "Never on such a scale and
in such detail has a major American party attempted to set
national standards for its state parties." The authors conclude
that the reform commission has drafted "what is in effect a
new constitution for the Democratic Party."

A mid-1970 *National Journal* survey of more than two dozen
Democratic leaders—Senators, Representatives, Governors,
state chairman, committeemen and committeewomen—brought
forth near-unanimous praise for O'Brien's leadership of the
DNC. Many of those questioned said they had no criticism of
O'Brien's predecessor, Fred Harris. "I doubt if anybody could
have done too much after the despair of 1968," said a Senate
aide who asked that his name not be used. "Now it looks as
if Nixon is vulnerable, and the Democrats see things looking
up again." Spokesmen for leading Presidential candidates
agreed that O'Brien has become an effective party spokesman
and a unifying force without trying to become the Democrats'
only voice.

"Can you imagine Ed Muskie or Ted Kennedy or Mike
Mansfield relinquishing their positions as party spokesman?"
asked former Muskie press aide Robert Shepherd, now press
aide to Gov. Kenneth M. Curtis, D-Maine. "There is a sense
of confidence in Larry personally, in his abilities to organize,
to make the party a viable institution and to make it something besides a debt-ridden, splintered organization." The
knowledge that "Larry's not running for anything" clearly
adds to his stature as chairman, in the opinion of office-
holders and those concerned with getting Democrats elected.

Even when he does not follow their advice, party officials

feel they have been consulted on major matters of DNC policy. "I sometimes had the feeling that things were going on behind my back before," said Robert S. Vance, state chairman of Alabama. "I don't have that feeling now. . . . When he deals with a state chairman, he understands what the chairman's problems are." "He's doing a fine job under extremely difficult financial circumstances," said John C. Mitchell of Omaha, then Nebraska state chairman and president of the Democratic State Chairman's Association. "I've heard no complaints from any (state chairmen). Our relationship is excellent." Mrs. Mildred Jeffrey of Detroit, national committeewoman from Michigan, said O'Brien and DNC Treasurer Strauss are doing an excellent job "keeping the doors open." "Larry has given a feeling and a sense of direction (to the party). His skills as a professional politician are creating the impression across the country that there is a Democratic National Committee," said Mrs. Jeffrey, who is national community relations director for the United Auto Workers and an outspoken advocate of party reform.

Table 9.1   Key Staff at Democratic Headquarters

Following are the key staff personnel who work with Chairman Lawrence F. O'Brien and Treasurer Robert S. Strauss at the Democratic National Committee headquarters. (See pp.227, 231 for O'Brien and Strauss biographies.)

William B. Welsh, 46, executive director, was executive assistant to DNC Chairman Fred R. Harris in 1969. He served as administrative assistant to Vice President Humphrey (1967-68) and held a similar position with Sen. Philip A. Hart of Michigan (1959-67). A native of Kentucky and a graduate of Berea College, Welsh came to Washington in 1952 as legislative assistant to the late Sen. Herbert H. Lehman of New York (1949-57).

Stanley L. Greigg, 39, is deputy to O'Brien and director of the Office of Campaigns and Party Organization. He serves as liaison with Democratic Senators, Representatives and state party organizations. A former Member of Congress from Iowa (1965-67), Greigg has also been a college dean and mayor of Sioux City. He was a director of the office of regional administration of the Post Office Department (1967-68), leaving to coordinate the Humphrey-Muskie campaign in Northern California.

Philip B. Seib, 24, is a special assistant to the chairman. Seib, who concentrates primarily on youth activities and oversees the committee's youth voter registration effort for 1972, is a graduate of Princeton

University where he was president of the student body. He directed the "campaign '70 clearing house," a program set up by O'Brien to involve college students in the 1970 campaign.

Edward E. Cubberley, 31, was named special assistant to the chairman in June 1971. A native of Trenton, N.J., Cubberley graduated from Rutgers University in 1961 and earned his law degree from the university in 1964. He was assistant treasurer of the national campaign committee for Robert F. Kennedy's 1968 Presidential campaign and a special assistant to O'Brien at the DNC during the Humphrey-Muskie campaign in 1968. Before returning to the committee in 1971, Cubberley was in private law practice in Washington, D.C.

John G. Stewart, 36, is director of the Office of Communications. He was a legislative assistant to Vice President Humphrey, before becoming executive director of the Democratic Policy Council in 1969. He has a Ph.D. in political science from the University of Chicago.

Joseph E. Mohbat, 33, press secretary, formerly worked for the Associated Press in Chicago and Washington. A former Nieman Fellow in journalism (1966-67), he is a graduate of Middlebury College (Vt.).

Joseph A. Califano Jr., 39, general counsel, was chief domestic aide to President Johnson (1965-69). He is now a partner in the Washington, D.C., law firm of Williams, Connolly & Califano. Since October 1969, he has been co-chairman of the DNC's committee on national priorities.

Mary Lou Burg, 41, vice chairman and national committeewoman from Wisconsin, directs women's activities and other programs at the DNC. Miss Burg formerly managed a radio station in Jackson, Wis., a Milwaukee suburb.

Dorothy Vredenburgh Bush, 54, secretary of the DNC since 1944, calls the role of the states at each Democratic National Convention. A native of Mississippi, she is married to former ICC Chairman John W. Bush.

George Bristol, 31, assistant to the treasurer, is concerned with fund raising. A native of Denton, Tex., and a graduate of the University of Texas, Bristol worked for two Texas Congressmen and was a management consultant.

Andrew Shea, 33, assistant to the treasurer, is a lawyer who deals with the DNC's many creditors and pays current bills. A native of St. Paul, Minn., and a law graduate of George Washington University, he worked in his father's professional fundraising firm and practiced law before joining the DNC in 1969.

Robert E. Moss, 31, serves under Greigg as deputy director of the Office of Campaigns and Party Organization. He received an A.B. degree from the University of the Pacific in 1963 and a law degree from the University of California at Berkeley in 1966. In 1968, he was northern California coordinator of the "get out the vote" program for Robert Kennedy in the Democratic Presidential primary and San Francisco campaign manager for the Humphrey-Muskie campaign.

Olga (Bobbie) Gechas is in charge of direct mail fund-raising activities. She came to the DNC in August 1969, after directing similar activities for the United Nations International Children's Emergency Fund in New York, including promotion of UNICEF Christmas cards.

David Cooper, 32, director of political research, has previous experience with the Louis Harris and Mervin Field polling organizations. Born in Chicago, Ill., he is a graduate of the University of Southern California.

William Quinn, 32, director of publications, joined the committee in 1970. A native of Chicago, Ill., and a graduate of Howard University (Washington, D.C.), he previously worked for *Playboy, Down Beat* and *Muhammad Speaks* publications.

Richard J. Murphy, 41, is director of the 1972 national convention activities. Murphy, named to the post in June 1971, is a native of Baltimore, Md., and a graduate of the University of North Carolina. He was assistant postmaster general for personnel in the Kennedy and Johnson Administrations and executive director of the DNC's Young Democratic Division from 1956 to 1961. Murphy was the DNC's New York representative for the Humphrey-Muskie campaign in 1968.

Andrew C. Muse, 43, was appointed director of the minorities division in February 1971. Muse, named direc-

tor with the unanimous recommendation of the Congressional Black Caucus, was director of compliance at the Equal Employment Opportunity Commission. A native of Danville, Va., he received his law degree from Lincoln University School of Law in St. Louis, Mo.

Robert W. Nelson, 49, staff director of the Commission on Party Structure and Delegate Selection since 1969, is in charge of tracking Democratic delegate-selection reform for the 1972 national convention in the 55 states and territories. He was administrative assistant (1956-60) to Sen. George S. McGovern, D-S.D., while McGovern was in the House, and worked for the Interior Department from 1961 to 1969.

Table 9.2   DNC Reform Commission Membership

The following are the 28 members of the Democratic Party's Commission on Party Structure and Delegate Selection:

Rep. Donald M. Fraser, Minnesota (chairman).

Sen. Harold E. Hughes, Iowa (vice chairman).

I. W. Abel, President, United Steelworkers of America.

Sen. Birch Bayh, Indiana.

Samuel H. Beer, professor of government, Harvard University; national chairman of Americans for Democratic Action (1959-62).

Bert Bennett, chairman of the Democratic executive committee of North Carolina (1960-63).

Warren M. Christopher, deputy attorney general (1967-69).

Leroy Collins, Governor of Florida (1955-60).

Will D. Davis, chairman of the Democratic executive committee of Texas (1965-70).

William Dodds, director, Community Action Department, United Auto Workers.

Frederick G. Dutton, executive director, Robert F. Kennedy Memorial Foundation; special assistant to President Kennedy (1961).

John F. English, national committeeman from New York; national political coordinator for Sen. Edmund S. Muskie, Maine.

Peter Garcia, deputy director of the Community Action Program of Pulare County, Calif. (1965-67).

Earl G. Graves, president of Earl Graves Associates, New York, N.Y.

Aaron E. Henry, chairman, Democratic state committee of Mississippi; member of the national boards of directors, National Association for the

Advancement of Colored People (NAACP) and Southern Christian Leadership Conference.

John Jay Hooker, practicing attorney, unsuccessful candidate for Governor of Tennessee in 1970.

Patti Knox, vice chairman, Democratic state central committee of Michigan.

Louis E. Martin, publisher, *Chicago Daily Defender;* deputy chairman of the Minorities Division, Democratic National Committee (1961-68).

Oscar H. Mauzy, Texas state senator, Dallas.

Sen. George S. McGovern, South Dakota.

George Mitchell, national committeeman from Maine; chairman of the Democratic state committee of Maine (1966-68).

David Mixner, codirector of the Vietnam Moratorium Committee (1969-70); staff assistant, Common Cause, Denver, Colo.

Katherine G. Peden, state commissioner of commerce (1963-67) of Kentucky.

Albert A. Pena Jr., county commissioner, Bexar County, Tex.

Gov. Calvin L. Rampton, Utah.

J. Austin Ranney, professor of political science, University of Wisconsin; editor of the *American Political Science Review.*

Sen. Adlai E. Stevenson III, Illinois.

Carmen H. Warschaw, national committeewoman from California.

Table 9.3   A Four-Year Path to Reform

Efforts to reform delegate-selection procedures within the Democratic Party began shortly before the 1968 Democratic National Convention in Chicago. The chronology below summarizes the steps that have been taken, leading up to the 1972 convention:

1968

August 4: Harold E. Hughes, then Governor of Iowa, formed an ad hoc commission on delegate-selection procedures.

August 27-28: The Democratic National Convention, meeting in Chicago, passed resolutions calling for the creation of a national commission to study the party's delegate selection.

1969

January 14: The Democratic National Committee directed its chairman, Sen. Fred Harris, D-Okla., to create the Commission on Party Structure and Delegate Selection.

February 8: Harris announced formation of the commission and named Sen. George S. McGovern, D-S.D., chairman of the 28-member body.

February 24: The process of forming the commission staff began with the hiring of Robert W. Nelson as director.

March 1: The commission held its first meeting. (As with all subsequent sessions, the meeting was open to the public.)

April 25: The commission held the first of 17 field hearings, taking testimony on delegate-selection problems.

July 10: The field hearings ended.

November 18-19: The commission approved 18 guidelines and forwarded them to the 55 state and territorial parties.

1970

February 27: McGovern mailed to each state and territorial party a "compliance letter," explaining what each must do to adhere to the guidelines.

April 28: *Mandate for Reform* was published. This was a 63-page formal report to the Democratic National Committee that lists the changes adopted by the McGovern Commission and cites reasons for the recommended changes.

May 18: Joseph A. Califano Jr., counsel to the Democratic National Committee, issued an opinion that the McGovern guidelines are not recommendations, but rules that must be complied with before the 1972 convention.

1971

January 7: Harris' successor as national chairman, Lawrence F. O'Brien, named Rep. Donald M. Fraser, D-Minn., commission chairman. Fraser, who had served on the commission, succeeded McGovern, who resigned as chairman (but kept his commission seat) after declaring his candidacy for President.

February 19: The Democratic National Committee, meeting in Washington, approved all commission guidelines and made them part of the call to the 1972 convention. National committeemen and committeewomen also voted that they be seated automatically as convention delegates, in contravention to the McGovern Commission's guidelines.

March 1: Fraser mailed reminders to all states and territories, noting where each stood on the path to reform.

May 28: Fraser announced that he was satisfied that all but a handful of states were moving toward reform with "vigor and determination."

This report on the Democratic National Committee is a compilation of several reports which appeared in National Journal *in 1970-71. Contributions were made by Jonathan Cottin, Andrew J. Glass and Neal Gregory.*

10

Common Cause

ANDREW J. GLASS

Common Cause, the citizens lobby which in September 1971 celebrated its first birthday and enrolled its 200,000th member, intends to have an important role in shaping the issues of the 1972 Presidential campaign. John W. Gardner, who created Common Cause as a nonpartisan third force in public life, said its future growth may depend on whom the Democrats and Republicans select to lead them in 1972. "If we have two candidates that turn a lot of people off, we'll get more members," Gardner predicted.

In Common Cause, Gardner has clearly tapped a vein of discontent in society. Attracting a cadre of top professionals to his side, he has sought, by waging a kind of establishment populism, to hasten the end of American military involvement in Vietnam and to open the elective and governing process to broader participation. But, as Common Cause has grown beyond his expectations, he has aimed to keep its focus narrow—both as a lobby and as a movement—and to keep its goals within achievable range. "It's perfectly clear that our efforts to end the war have put about as much pressure on President Nixon as they have on Congress," Gardner said in an interview. "Any major effort spills over and affects him."

Gardner's movement was strengthened in March 1971, when Jack T. Conway, who has roots in the industrial union movement, joined him as president. "We had a long series of discussions about what we really believed," Conway recalled. "And I concluded he was for real." Conway said he wanted from Gardner "a commitment to organize around issues that could be serious enough to pull the house down. When you commit yourself to a battle, do you begin to check as soon as you see what the consequences are? I wanted to make sure that I wasn't going to be getting into a powder-puff atmosphere where a call from the White House or a call from somebody turns things off. I have lived in that environment on other occasions and I don't have any interest in that." Gardner and Conway have seen other citizens movements atrophy; as they won the issues they were fighting for, they faded from the scene. Both men are determined that will not happen to Common Cause.

Conway said Common Cause is considering whether it should develop a set of "candidate standards" and whether, as a further step, it should endorse candidates who meet those standards. "We may be forced to move in this direction, or we may move out of choice," Conway said. Gardner said, "We cannot endorse candidates; that's out. But obviously, when you come out for legislation, you are by implication setting a standard against which your members may judge a candidate."

Yet, amid all the good works, there is a hint of unconscious arrogance. There is a feeling that because their cause is manifestly just, it need not stand the kind of rigorous ethical test that Common Cause would be the first to apply in an effort to expose pursuits more selfish and ignoble than their own. For example, in 1970 Common Cause hired M. Carl Holman, president of the Urban Coalition, which Gardner had headed, as a $7,200-a-year part-time consultant. Holman advised Gardner on how to improve relations with the black community— advice that often went unheeded. But the arrangement with Holman was not reported in quarterly filings with the Clerk of the House of Representatives, required under the 1946 Federal Regulation of Lobbying Act (60 Stat 839). ("As a matter of propriety, he should have been listed," said Lowell R. Beck, executive director of Common Cause.) Holman dropped his consulting role in August 1971.

Gardner declined to disclose the sources of his income. It was pointed out to him that his refusal appeared inconsistent with his stand against financial secrecy in lobbying operations and exposed him to conflict-of-interest suspicions. He then prepared a statement which reviewed his income in broad terms. But he did not disclose his stock holdings, other than to report that dividends account for a sixth of his income.

A Democratic Party official eased back in his chair, chuckled quietly and said: "John Gardner is a Republican. But he has the Arthur Goldberg view of politics, which is that they should be elected to high office by acclamation. Unfortunately, it never works that way." A half-mile away, and a day later, Gardner, in shirtsleeves, leaned forward on the edge of his chair and replied to the allegation that he is seeking to build in Common Cause a base to run for the Presidency—or perhaps a base to run someone else.

"It's easier to believe that I have no political ambitions if you understand the potential of what I'm doing here," he said. "If you don't understand that, then it's a mystery. What in Heaven's name is that guy doing, they must be asking themselves. . . . But if you take my point of view, I believe we are at something much deeper and much more fundamental than anything that could possibly happen in the 1972 Presidential elections."

Gardner has come under attack from both ends of the political spectrum. An unsigned article in the July 10, 1971, issue of *Human Events* said: "Gardner's Common Cause has a sweetheart contract with corporate liberalism—and the diminution of establishment power can never take place so long as the establishment's 'house rebel' is leading the rebellion." An October 20, 1969, column by Nicholas von Hoffman in the *Washington Post* begins: "People say, 'Don't write anything bad about John Gardner. He's on our side. Leave him alone and stick to attacking the baddies.'" Nonetheless, von Hoffman concludes that Gardner is "a scared man in a world incomprehensibly falling away from him and his social order."

Gardner, 59, was born in Los Angeles. He earned his bachelor's and master's degrees at Stanford University and a doctorate in psychology at the University of California. Before World War II, Gardner came East to teach at the Connecticut College for Women and then at Mount Holyoke College. In 1943, Gardner joined the Marines. He served in Washington, Italy and Austria as an officer in the Office of Strategic Services—the forerunner of the Central Intelligence Agency. In 1946, Gardner joined the Carnegie Corporation, a philanthropic foundation established by steelmaker Andrew Carnegie. He became its president in 1955. President Johnson named Gardner Secretary of Health, Education and Welfare in July 1965. He served for 32 months (*Human Events* described him as the "Good German" in the Johnson Cabinet) until a dispute over HEW funding caused him to resign.

Gardner became chairman of the National Urban Coalition. The coalition was formed in response to the black urban riots of the 1960s and was largely funded at the national level by the Ford Foundation. The concept called for bringing together leaders in business, government, labor and the minority community to seek social and economic reforms. But Gardner found the coalition a limited tool. Seeking to circumvent the federal income tax laws, which bar the coalition from lobbying, Gardner formed the Urban Coalition Action Council, which lobbied, among other things, against the confirmation of G. Harrold Carswell, then of the 5th Circuit Court of Appeals, to the Supreme Court and for minority hiring quotas in government construction contracts.

In August 1970, Gardner converted the Action Council into Common Cause. The key change was his bid for a membership base—and the potential of broad financing that the new base represented. Several business leaders on the Action Council declined to go along. Among those who resigned from the reconstituted board were James M. Roche, chairman of General Motors Corporation; H. I. Romnes, chairman of American Telephone & Telegraph Company; David Rockefeller, chairman of the Chase Manhattan Bank; Ben W. Heineman, president of Northwest Industries Inc., parent company of the Chicago and North Western Railway Company; and Edgar F. Kaiser, chairman of Kaiser Industries Corporation. George Meany, president of the AFL-CIO, who had opposed Gardner's stand on minority hiring in construction, and Richard J. Daley, mayor of Chicago, also left. But such stalwart supporters as John V. Lindsay, mayor of New York, remained on Gardner's board.

Gardner now earns about $50,000 a year, with speaking fees and royalties accounting for half the total. Harper & Row published *Excellence* (1961), *Self-Renewal,* (1964), and *No Easy Victories* (1970). W. W. Norton published *The Recovery of Confidence* (1970). Gardner said about a third of his income comes from consulting fees, "now chiefly" from Carnegie and the Mellon Foundation. He planned to resign at the end of 1971 as a director of American Airlines and Time Inc.

"I don't think anybody is a close friend of John Gardner," said David M. Thompson, secretary-treasurer of the National Urban Coalition. "In many ways, he's very aloof. But in other ways, he can be quite warm. I visited 375 corporations last year (1970), mostly at the chief executive officer level. In practically every case, the first question was: 'How is John?' They spoke eloquently many times about how much they admire the man. They spoke of how much they disagreed with him in terms of his position but they ended up by saying, 'Thank God, we've got a John Gardner in this society.' "

Thompson said Gardner's ability as an administrator "is probably the most common concern people have." But he called Gardner "probably the most intelligent man I've ever dealt with." A foundation official who has known Gardner for many years took a more restrained view. "He's a complex man, difficult to explain," the official said. "There are those who admire him as a man of the Second Coming. But there are others who, without contesting his charisma, remain concerned about what he really accomplishes."

In an August 1971 interview with *National Journal*, Gardner spoke of the role a public interest lobby plays and the reasons Common Cause was founded:

"We are going more and more into the kind of issue that isn't going to be settled easily. When you're talking about the gut questions of who holds power and how deep are the defenses that prevent somebody else from getting power, you are talking about final questions over which people will fight to the death. Matters like seniority, lobbying controls, campaign spending, exposure of conflict of interest get right to the heart of how the power structure maintains itself. . . . No President has really tackled these questions—questions that deal with how power is distributed. They do not intervene in these arrangements. They make their accommodations in the course of campaigning with the interests that would have no change.

"I believe we're working in a territory that no politician can work. They can't afford to. It's too close to the bone. This campaign spending business, you know, is right at the heart of politics. Some of the things we are going to be saying about money and secrecy in the next few months are things that no politician can say. . . . If Common Cause continues to exhibit vitality through the Administrations of three or four Presidents, I think we will be unpopular with every one of them. You don't tee off on a President and spend a lot of time at White House dinners. It just doesn't work that way. . . . I've been concerned about institutional change for the last 20 years, and I don't think there was a time when I thought less about it than when I was Secretary (of Health, Education and Welfare). I had to try to gain yards in terms of the way the game is played. I couldn't think about some other way of doing it. I had to get my appropriations. I had to get my bills passed—and fight, fight, fight. . . .

"You have to understand that for a public interest lobby the most important weapon is public information. It isn't like a special-interest lobby, which wants to keep most things quiet. The public interest lobby wants to tell the story and tell it big. With (congressional) seniority, for example, we got the story out and into the papers. That affects the President and the executive branch as much as it does Congress. And it affects the people back home. . . . We succeeded in bringing the issue to public notice, which nobody believed we could do. . . .

"Ninety-five per cent of the people are being victimized — not 5 per cent, not 10 per cent, not just the poverty level. I am paying more for products, I am paying more for services, I am paying more for my utilities — all as a result of inadequate regulation of our public bodies — than I ought to be paying. If there is anything I have learned in the past year, it is that this discontent — this sense of being 'had' — runs right through the American people. The sense of being dispossessed and separated from the decisions governing your own lives is not limited to the black, the poor and the young. It's the average American. It's even the upper-middle-class American. We want to clean up the courts because any average American who gets in there just gets driven crazy.

"But there is hardly an issue where a malfunction of government occurs that doesn't hit the poor harder. You know, if it isn't working, the poor get it in the neck quicker. So just in the normal course of events, we're serving the poor. If the courts are clogged, the affluent can follow alternative routes. They can hire an expensive lawyer. . . . The weight of officialdom lies much more heavily on the poor. First, there is the number of times they must deal with an official in the course of their lives. Second, there is the extent to which that official can control what they do. And, third, there is a lack of alternative routes and resources. . . .

"I don't see where John (D.) Rockefeller (III) is going to benefit if and when the society goes down. Do you really believe he's going to benefit by the society disintegrating? And, you know, we didn't pick up 200,000 John Rockefellers. There's a rather small percentage of any segment of the population or of any group that's committed to the public interest. Maybe 5 per cent. And I don't know that it varies with whatever group you're talking about. Doctors? Most of them (are) not at all conscious of community needs. But a certain percentage of doctors are just absolutely clear that if the medical profession doesn't serve the community, it's in trouble. . . . It's exactly the

same with businessmen. Most businessmen are selfishly motivated, but there's a percentage that just naturally sees it an-
nother way. I think it's something in their character and personal upbringing that makes them see the larger community.
So I think the (Tom) Watsons and the Rockefellers are caught
in that." (Thomas J. Watson Jr. is chairman of International
Business Machines Corporation; John D. Rockefeller III is
chairman of the Rockefeller Foundation.)

In its first year, Common Cause for the most part looked in-
ward. It built its name, its membership rolls and its staff expertise. Now, Common Cause is beginning to push outward.
It has opened its policy board to elected newcomers. And it is
creating a national field organization. (See Chart 10.1.) The
election, which was completed in November 1971, and the field
campaign also should give Gardner and his top staff a better
idea of who belongs to Common Cause, why they have joined
and in what direction they seek to move.

Conway characterizes the membership as "highly intelligent,
highly educated, highly professional, highly white, highly
suburban or small town." Other Common Cause staffers who
have dealt directly with members offer similar descriptions.
Mitchell Rogovin of the Washington, D.C., law firm of Arnold
& Porter, who is the counsel to Common Cause, said the membership is "white, middle-class, intelligent and educatable."
"This isn't a race-and-poverty group. It doesn't have a ground-
swell. And it doesn't have muscle in terms of Presidential
elections," he said.

Conway, who is ultimately responsible for the organizing
drive, put it this way: "These are people who, no matter what
their circumstances, feel that they have a stake in the system,
and they are worried about it. They want to do what they can,
through some personal organization or activity, to get ahold
of it again and make it work. They are not radical, but they
are concerned enough to support anything that's reasonable,
that will produce results. . . . You'll find that this is not a mem-

bership that has other organizations that theoretically also represent them. You don't find people who are union members as activists in Common Cause, anymore than you find representatives of farm groups or so on. You find individuals who may be union members but who don't look to their union anymore." (See Table 10.2.) Conway's analysis is being supplemented by a scientific canvass of the membership. The purpose is to seek members' views on issues and to be able to project what the second-year renewal rate will be. The telephone survey is being conducted by the New York-based polling firm of Daniel Yankelovich Inc.

The 39-member Common Cause governing board, for the most part hand-picked by Gardner, reconstituted itself after the first year. About 193,000 ballots were mailed to members of record as of August 1, 1971; they had to be returned by September 10 to be counted. After consultations, a nominating committee chose 30 names from which the membership could pick new directors. A folder that accompanied the ballot said: "Although the list includes some prominent Americans, national eminence was not a criterion. Rather, the committee sought evidence that the nominee was an active, effective leader, dedicated to citizen action."

The committee's choices included Elly M. Peterson, the Republican national committeewoman for Michigan and a former assistant chairman of the Republican National Committee (1963-64, 1969-71); Betty Furness, former chairman of the New York State Consumer Protection Board (1970-71); Josiah A. Spaulding, a Massachusetts attorney who ran unsuccessfully for the Senate in 1970 as a Republican against Sen. Edward M. Kennedy; Walter A. Haas Jr., chairman of Levi Strauss and Company, and a trustee of the Ford Foundation; Raymond A. Lamontagne, president of Washington-based Development Technologies Inc., and a former counsel to John D. Rockefeller III (1964-68); Wilbur J. Cohen, dean of the school of education at the University of Michigan, who succeeded Gardner as HEW Secretary (1968-69); and Gardner.

In addition to the 30 official nominees, the ballot listed 42 candidates who were nominated by petitions signed by at least

10 Common Cause members. Of the 72 nominees, the 20 receiving the most votes were elected to three-year terms. Each year, another 20 directors will be picked by the board to serve one-year terms. Thus, for the first year of the election plan, the elected directors constitute a minority on the board. But Conway envisions the time when "our organization will reflect the leadership inputs of these new people." (See Table 10.1.)

As matters stand, Gardner, Conway and the inner circle of policy-making aides retain a relatively free hand in their operations. The board has yet to set aside a major policy decision taken by Gardner and his staff. Rogovin recalled a board meeting at which Vernon E. Jordan Jr., executive director of the United Negro College Fund Inc., questioned the wisdom of intervening against the Treasury Department's plans to revise depreciation allowances. Jordan thought the drive would sap strength from another prime Common Cause concern, passage of welfare-reform legislation (HR 1). As the controversy continued, Gardner sat silently. "John was letting the board argue it out," Rogovin said. "But I got very nervous." Finally, Leonard Woodcock, president of the United Auto Workers, told Jordan that "the $4 billion they want to give away is your appropriations." That settled the argument. Afterwards, when Rogovin asked Gardner why he didn't intervene, Gardner said: "Every board likes to wrestle with an issue once in a while. I knew how it would come out."

Conway said: "When I got here (in late March 1971), we had 100,000 members and no notions about what to do"—aside from an already functioning lobbying effort on Capitol Hill. Conway observed that the task of relating a professional lobbying organization to a field constituency has defied almost all groups:

"There's always a jealous separation between the political work of an organization and the legislative work. Invariably, the legislative guy is moaning and groaning because the guy he has carefully developed and nurtured for his specialized reasons doesn't sit well with the people out in the district because he's a rotten old son-of-a-bitch who does the wrong

things on most other issues. The fact that he's right on the
narrow issues makes the legislative guy very protective. The
problem is how to put together an articulate constituency
which is issue-oriented with a legislative operation in Washington which is, by its very nature, only able to take on a certain number of battles. What I did is to cut through all of the
differences of opinion on how to organize by simply saying
that, in any event, we couldn't afford to do what everyone was
suggesting. The only thing we could afford to do was to take
our first mission—which is to be a citizens lobby on the Hill
in Washington—and to take three or four issues that we are
working on and work out some 'target' districts."

The primary intent is to create what Conway calls "a legislative response mechanism" that will reinforce lobbying efforts
on Capitol Hill. Conway said the 100 "target" districts were
chosen without following any over-all plan. But, he said, they
do reflect such things as whether the Member is on a committee with jurisdiction over an issue that Common Cause wants
to pursue; whether the district is politically marginal; whether
the Member is especially intelligent or influenceable; and
whether the Member is a potential leader in the House.

The field network, based in many districts on a telephone
chain, will be organized without the issuance of any formal
charters or the formation of any regional, state or local chapters. "Since we're not issuing charters, we don't have any
charters to revoke," Conway said. The new structure is being
put together by a veteran Washington lobbyist, David Cohen,
who is director of field organization for Common Cause. By
September 1971, small field offices had been opened in San
Francisco, Denver, New York and Boston. Cohen said Common Cause plans to open four more offices—one each for the
industrial Midwest, the Plains states, the South and the Border
states.

In the meantime, Common Cause is conducting two programs to gain further experience in how it should organize in
the field. One program, known as the voting rights project,
is aimed at identifying obstacles to registration and devising
means to overcome them on a state-by-state basis. The task

force assembling the voting rights project is headed by Mrs. Anne Wexler, 1968 organizer for former Sen. Eugene J. McCarthy, D-Minn. (1959-71), and campaign manager for Joseph D. Duffey, a Democrat who ran unsuccessfully for the Senate from Connecticut in 1970. The drive headed by Mrs. Wexler is directed specifically against restricted registration periods and hours, early filing deadlines, lengthy residence requirements and closed delegate-selection processes for political nominating conventions.

The other program, known as the Colorado project, is aimed at promoting basic changes in the mechanics of state legislatures, which, Cohen said, "are now shrouded in secrecy." The project is headed by David Mixner, a 1968 McCarthy organizer and a member of the Democratic Party's Commission on Party Structure and Delegate Selection. Mixner lobbied for two "right to know" bills in the Colorado state legislature. One required lobbyists to register with a state official and to disclose expenses, companies and interests they represent, as well as the legislation in which they are interested. The other bill required state legislators, elected officials and judges to file periodic statements disclosing their financial interests. Despite an extensive lobbying campaign, in which many of the 3,475 members of Common Cause who live in Colorado were contacted, the legislature failed to vote on either of the bills.

"I had no idea that we could operate in the states as easily as we have," Gardner said. "We've found it's quite possible to lobby there because there hasn't been very much citizen lobbying in the states up to now, and the legislators are quite struck with the citizen voice suddenly appearing."

The following persons play major roles in shaping policy at Common Cause as members of John Gardner's staff:

• Jack Conway, 53, stepped into a newly created position as president of Common Cause. Conway, a Democrat, is a tough-minded administrator with broad experience both in government and in pressure groups that affect federal policy. Yet he shares with Gardner a deep idealistic streak. During part of World War II, Conway worked at a General

Motors plant in Melrose Park, Ill., and later in the war he served in the U.S. Merchant Marine. He bristles at any suggestion that Common Cause is an elitist organization.

In 1946, Conway became administrative assistant to the late Walter P. Reuther, then president of the United Auto Workers. He held the position until 1961, when he was named deputy administrator of the Housing and Home Finance Agency, which later became the HUD Department. In 1963, he resigned to become executive director of the Industrial Union Department of the AFL-CIO, then a Reuther stronghold in the labor movement. He left for a year to serve as deputy director of the Office of Economic Opportunity. In 1968, Conway resigned from the IUD and founded the Center for Community Change, a tax-exempt organization aimed at bolstering community groups composed of the poor. It is funded largely by the Ford Foundation.

- Lowell Beck, 37, served as executive director of the Urban Coalition Action Council from its inception in 1968 and retains the same title in Common Cause. Beck said he strongly favored Conway's appointment over him and probably would have resigned had Conway not taken the job. Beck is a Republican. From 1959 to 1968, Beck worked for the American Bar Association. He served as associate director of the ABA's Washington office (primarily a lobbying job on Capitol Hill) and as director of public service activities at the ABA headquarters in Chicago.

- Tom Mathews, 50, is special assistant to Gardner for public relations. A veteran San Francisco newspaperman, Mathews helped organize the Peace Corps and became its first director of public information. In 1968, he ran the Washington press office for the Presidential campaign of the late Sen. Robert F. Kennedy, D-N.Y. (1965-68). After Kennedy's death, Mathews worked in public relations in New York on such projects as the Lincoln Center for the Performing Arts. Gardner brought Mathews into the National Urban Coalition as his spokesman. Mathews followed Gardner to Common Cause.

- David Cohen, 34, was named in July 1971 as director of field organization. He is well known and highly regarded on Capitol Hill as a former lobbyist for the Americans for Democratic Action (ADA) and for the Industrial Union Department of the AFL-CIO. In 1968, Conway hired Cohen as associate director for field operations at the Center for Community Change, where he continued his lobbying role. He remains a vice-chairman of ADA.

- Robert E. Gallamore, 30, director of policy development, joined the National Urban Coalition in 1970 after working for the Bureau of the Budget and the Department of Transportation. He has a doctorate in economics and political science from Harvard.
- John Lagomarcino, 35, director of legislation, was a lawyer in Arizona and Iowa until 1966, when he joined the Department of Health, Education, and Welfare to work in the Civil Rights Division of the general counsel's office. He was formerly deputy executive director of the Urban Coalition Action Council.
- Robert Meier, 55, secretary-treasurer, served as an assistant to the HEW Secretary from 1962 to 1968 after previous service as a personnel officer and finance administrator in federal and local government.
- Georgianna F. Rathbun, 50, edits the monthly *Report from Washington*. She was legislative editor of *Congressional Quarterly* for 15 years and joined the Urban Coalition Action Council in 1968.

In early September 1971, Common Cause went back to its members to ask them to sign on for another year. "On the first time around, a 50-per cent renewal would be very satisfactory," said Meier, secretary-treasurer. "Anything more than 50 per cent would be great. Anything less than that would range from disappointing to (raising) a question over whether we are responding to what our members really feel like." The first-year membership drive well exceeded original targets set by Gardner and his staff. The initial goal, 100,000 members by the end of the first year, was reached in 23 weeks. On September 1, membership passed 200,000, with about 5,000 new members being enrolled each week.

All operations are funded by membership dues or through contributions. Dues currently account for 77 per cent of total income. (An initial $10,000 loan from the United California Bank was repaid in nine months; Common Cause is now debt-free.) Dues and contributions are not tax-deductible because Common Cause lobbies, but the organization itself is tax-exempt under section 501 (c) (4) of the Internal Revenue Code. During its first 12 months, Common Cause raised $3,217,297, of which $2,442,832 was in dues and $774,465 was in contributions.

Gardner originally planned to raise $500,000 in "start-up" capital that would be used until dues could begin to carry Common Cause expenses. As it turned out, by the time $250,000 was raised, the membership campaign had secured financial stability. Most of the larger contributors were approached directly by Gardner. Many of them are men and women with whom Gardner has worked in his career as a foundation executive and with whom he worked later as chairman of the Urban Coalition and its Action Council. In the first year, 5.6 per cent of the total income was raised through gifts of $1,000 or more. Only one contributor in this class serves on the Common Cause governing board. He is Andrew Heiskell, board chairman of Time Inc., and a long-time Gardner friend, who gave $10,000. In September 1971, Common Cause received its first foundation grant—$40,000 from the Stern Family Fund—which was earmarked, under terms of the grant, for the voting rights campaign.

The following persons and corporations have contributed $6,000 or more to Common Cause since July 1, 1970: Arlen Properties Inc. (now Arlen Realty and Development Corporation, Long Island City, N.Y., ($35,000—$10,000 of which was a personal contribution by Arthur N. Levien, then president of Arlen Properties, currently chairman of Arlen Realty); Helen W. Buckner, New York, N.Y., ($7,500); Joseph W. Drown, Bel Air, Calif., self-employed (real estate and oil) ($10,000); Ford

Motor Company, Dearborn, Mich., ($10,000); Walter A. Haas Jr., San Francisco, Calif., president, Levi Strauss and Company, and his cousin, Madeleine Haas Russell ($6,000 each); Arthur A. Houghton Jr., New York, director, Corning Glass Works ($10,000); Andre Meyer, New York, N.Y., senior partner, Lazard Freres and Company ($10,000); Max Palevsky, Los Angeles, Calif., chairman, Xerox Data Systems, director, Xerox Corporation ($21,000); John D. Rockefeller III, New York, N.Y., chairman, Rockefeller Foundation ($25,000); Norton Simon, Los Angeles, Calif., president, Norton Simon Foundation ($6,280.42); Iphigene Ochs Sulzberger, New York, N.Y., director, The New York Times Company ($11,000).

An initial test mailing in August 1970 placed some membership cards at $10 a year and some at $15. The $15 mailing, surprisingly, drew not only more money but more members as well. Consequently, dues were pegged at $15. Carl Holman initially argued against the flat $15 rate. Holman recalled: "I predicted that it would be relatively easy to get a lot of people to pay their $15, but that it was almost automatically going to cant the organization in such a direction that it would be very difficult for them to get some of the very people Gardner was most interested in — the black, the young, the poor."

In an interview, Gardner defended his decision to set dues at $15. "You know what the average dues are for the (National Welfare Rights Organization)?" he asked. "Thirteen bucks. You're not going to run a national organization on just nothing. Look at the unions. Look at dues generally." Nevertheless, Meier reported that Common Cause is considering a reduced student rate. Currently, students and others who send less than $15 are still enrolled if they assert they cannot afford more. But this policy is not publicized.

Of each $1 raised, Common Cause plows back about 35 cents to seek new members. About two-thirds of all expenses in the membership hunt go into the direct-mail campaign. Since the initial test mailing in 1970, Common Cause has sent out 6.5 million direct solicitations. (The 6.5 million included what Meier called "an unfortunate number" of duplications.) About 110,000 persons, or 1.7 per cent of the total mailing responded by joining up—a rate that professional mailers regard as above average. "It costs about $6.50 to sign up a new member," Meier said. "That's why we're so much looking forward to renewals, where the cost is at most $2."

Gardner's four-page "Dear Friend" solicitation letters, much of which he composes himself, are viewed as unorthodox by professionals, who prefer shorter and punchier formulas in their direct-mail campaigns. Guy Yoltan, the second of three direct-mail specialists who were successively hired by Common Cause in its first year, told *Advertising & Sales Promotion* in July 1971 that "Gardner has hit a responsive chord in one helluva lot of people, and all the professional dressing in the world would probably not have done any better." For the most part, Common Cause buys its mailing lists from list brokers. But Common Cause will not sell its own list, although it will swap lists with other organizations when they are available. After being widely criticized for one such swap with the Democratic National Committee in March 1971, Common Cause instituted a policy of not exchanging lists with political parties or campaign groups.

The success of the direct-mail campaign, and of the companion advertising campaign, enabled Common Cause to accumulate a cash reserve of about $400,000. First year operations cost $2.8 million, of which $1.2 million was earmarked for the membership drive. Another $1.2 million was spent on "program operations" and $400,000 on such special projects as a half-hour television show on the war in Vietnam ($120,000), filmed by Guggenheim Productions Inc.; the successful attempt to put the 18-year-old vote through 38 state legislatures as a constitutional amendment; and the voting rights project.

Of total expenses in the first year, about 21 per cent went for salaries; 25 per cent for lobbying activities; 25 per cent for mailings, including the handsomely printed *Report From Washington*; 15 per cent for rent and office expenses; and 15 per cent for field organization. After the wall-to-wall carpets and other furnishings in the Common Cause offices had been described in several articles, Tom Mathews, Gardner's public relations aide, became concerned. Subsequently, there has been an effort, in the words of one staff member, to "deposh the place." The current atmosphere is comfortable but somewhat informal.

Gardner has an expense account but draws no salary. Conway earns $45,000 a year. Four top professional staff members receive between $30,000 and $35,000, and most of the remaining professionals on the 60-member staff make about $20,000. The average staff salary is $10,000. Common Cause is operating under a second-year budget of $3.8 million, an increase of 36 per cent over the first year. In the new budget, program operations have been doubled, to $2.5 million. Another $1.3 million will be spent soliciting new members. Meier said the budget would work if membership rose to 250,000 over the year.

The credibility of Common Cause as a bipartisan organization is one of the most sensitive issues facing the citizens lobby. Conway, a lifelong Democrat, said "When I got into the boat, it rocked, there's no doubt about it. I was very conscious of this. That's one of the reasons why I didn't arrive with any particular splash." A week after Conway arrived at Common Cause, Monday, the weekly house organ of the Republican National Committee, published an article entitled, "Just How Nonpartisan is the 'Nonpartisan' Common Cause." The article included a Monday poll of Common Cause's executive committee, which showed Democrats out-numbering Republicans 11-6. One director said she was an independent, and the remaining director was not reached. Gardner was described in the article as "a nominal Republican (who) ... has become a purveyor of the radical Democratic line on virtually every issue."

In resuming the assault against Common Cause in May 1971, Monday complained that Matt Reese and Associates, a Washington-based political consulting firm, had been hired by Common Cause to aid in its campaign for a U.S. withdrawal from Indochina by the end of 1971. Reese is a former director of operations for the Democratic National Committee (1961-65). His firm received $19,867.11 to set up a telephone network for the antiwar campaign, according to records filed with the Clerk of the House.

Sen. Robert Dole, of Kansas, the Republican national chairman, on February 24, 1971, labeled Gardner's criticism of President Nixon's Vietnam policies "political efforts to gain headlines" and called them "bitterly divisive." Asked about the series of attacks on Gardner and Common Cause, a top-ranking GOP official said privately: "Things are strained with Mr. Gardner because while he alleges to support us in some areas, he has been less than kind in other areas, such as Vietnam, the national defense and SST. And, in the process, he has made some rather snide remarks about the President."

Gardner has not sought a meeting with the President since Mr. Nixon took office; neither has the White House moved on its own initiative to invite Gardner over. Nevertheless, in an interview, Gardner said that he has "far better relations with *parts* of the Administration than have ever come out." Referring to his "right-wing critics," Gardner said: "It would hurt their case if they were honest and said that I work very closely with Elliot Richardson; that we collaborated intimately on Nixon's welfare-reform measures; that I've worked very closely with George Shultz on the Philadelphia Plan and that I was very helpful to him then, and that I testified more recently on federal reorganization and that he felt it was very helpful as well. They don't mention that I've worked very closely with Len Garment and Pete Peterson and that George Romney is an old friend and that I've worked with him. These things just kind of get left out. But we feel it is essential that we not develop a habit of anti-Administration action. We want to work with any part of this Administration we can when they're going in our direction. . . . The distances have arisen because there are some policies we just can't accept." (Elliot L. Richardson is Secretary of Health, Education, and Welfare; George P. Shultz, director of the Office of Management and Budget, served previously as Secretary of Labor, where he supported the Philadelphia Plan as a means of hiring more minority group construction workers; Leonard Garment is a special consultant to the President; Peter G. Peterson is an assistant

to the President for international economic affairs; George
W. Romney is secretary of Housing and Urban Development.)

Lowell Beck, who is also a Republican, raised the same
theme. He said: "We certainly are not anti-Nixon. But the
Administration makes it awfully difficult for us. For one thing,
you never know whom to deal with in the Administration. . . .
And you never know where the next holdup is going to be."
Conway is determined to preserve as much of a bipartisan
image as possible. As he put it: "I've tried in everything that
I've done here to either maintain a bipartisan balance where
it existed or to achieve one where it hasn't. This is a conscious
policy. And any structures that we build in the congressional
districts and the states, the same thing holds true."

During Gardner's trips outside Washington, the small advance team that goes in ahead of his visits now makes it a
policy to make appointments for him with leading Democratic
and Republican figures in the state. But the credibility problem remains unsettled—even within the Common Cause
staff. One staff member, Pamela Curtis, a former aide to Mrs.
Peterson at the Republican National Committee, said: "Some
of their attacks are justified. If you are setting up to be
bipartisan, you have to really do it. There are a lot of people
here who have very strong Democratic credentials."

The Nixon staff does not berate Common Cause quite as
sharply as Dole and his aides do. However, within the White
House, Common Cause is widely regarded as a hostile force.
One aide to the President, who asked not to be quoted by
name, said: "They are going to find it very difficult to maintain that non-partisan image because they have nearly always
come down against us. Would it have been that difficult for
them to pick an issue on which they could have supported us?
For instance, what about revenue sharing? They are no factor
there whatsoever. But I suppose it would have cost them something to go in heavily. It would cost them with the powers in
their left-of-center group."

Another White House aide grudgingly gave Common Cause
high marks for the way in which the lobby organized on the
antiwar issue in the House. The aide, who asked not to be

quoted by name, said: "They employed some tactics that were interesting from a lobbying standpoint. And because they were new, they weren't easily detected by House Members and their staffs. You have to remember that contact on the district level is new for most of these guys. They are dealing in the field with third- and fourth-level congressional assistants who, whenever they get a dozen calls a day on the same subject, are apt to put in a panic call to Washington. By the time it reaches the Hill office, it gets to be 50 calls instead of 12. By the time it gets to the Congressman, it's even more. And the next thing you know, he's walking around the House floor telling everybody that he's had 100 calls. On the war issue, they were probably responsible for turning 20 to 25 House votes—or at least partly responsible. On SST, they may have been a marginal factor in what was, after all, an awfully close vote. On welfare reform, they have been very ineffectual and only half-heartedly into it."

Ties between Democratic Party officials in Washington and Common Cause, while not close, are far less hostile than with their Republican counterparts. "I think quite a lot of people around here are members of Common Cause," a top aide at the Democratic National Committee said. "I think there's a feeling around here that so far they haven't done anything particularly. But they are obviously into an important political strain that affects the two parties." The official also said that the party's efforts at internal reform reflect in part pressures raised by Common Cause. Regarding legislation, he said: "At least 90 per cent of the time when they are active on Capitol Hill, they are working for things that we should be for also."

Of the nine Senators who belong to Common Cause, only two are Republicans: Jacob K. Javits, N.Y., and Charles H. Percy, Ill. The Democratic members are Sens. Birch Bayh, Ind., Lawton Chiles, Fla., Edward M. Kennedy, Mass., Edmund S. Muskie, Maine, Claiborne Pell, R.I., Adlai E. Stevenson III, Ill., and John V. Tunney, Calif. There are also 24 House Members who belong to Common Cause, 19 Democrats and five Republicans.

Although Common Cause concentrated its efforts on the House in its first year of operation, it has not established effective links with either House Speaker Carl Albert, Okla., or Majority Leader Hale Boggs, La. (The No. 3 man in the House Democratic hierarchy, Rep. Thomas P. O'Neill Jr., Mass., was the chief Democratic sponsor of an antiwar "statement of purpose" pushed in spring 1971 by Common Cause.) Gary G. Hymel, administrative assistant to Boggs, said: "I remember during the 18-year-old vote—that's the first one they cooked up—some girl kept calling here and asking if she could write a speech. He (Boggs) was for it anyhow. Of course we didn't use it. They didn't work on it with the leadership. They seem to be working from underneath rather than from the top. We never have contacted them to get mobilized to help us as we do with labor or with the NAACP (National Association for the Advancement of Colored People)."

Common Cause strives to work in tandem with specialized lobbying groups whenever their interests coincide. "I'm glad they're here," said Marvin Caplan, legislative representative for the Industrial Union Department of the AFL-CIO. "Often our objectives differ from theirs. But, at times, they are quite complementary."

The alliances forged by Common Cause are sometimes unplanned. Thus, on the SST battle, Common Cause intervened only after the Washington office received a tide of mail and telephone calls urging action against the appropriation. Beck reported: "At that point, Friends of the Earth came to see us. We asked how we could be most helpful. We took their list of Congressmen and made calls." On the antiwar issue, Common Cause took a different tack. It opened an office near the Capitol that ultimately served as a base for some 100 peace groups during the height of the campaign that followed the U.S. military intervention in Laos. "That's where we put our chips," Beck recalled. "We gave the peace groups a logistical base to work with. But we did not attempt to manage the peace movement. That would have been absolute folly."

Not all relationships with similar-minded lobbies are as smooth as Common Cause would like them to be. For example, Gardner is aware of private criticism by Ralph Nader that Gardner has "pulled his punches" and declined to make an all-out effort on such issues as the protection of the environment and unfair dealings by industry to consumers. Gardner rejects the charge and, in effect, turns the other cheek. As he put it in an interview: "I think what we're at is so big that we're not only going to need all the organizations we have, we're going to need a lot more. . . . Look at the thing on environment. We're immensely interested in environment. But how much are we going to be able to do on environment when we're working on the war, on campaign spending and on a lot of other things? It is tragic that the environment groups fight each other. The fact that they exist means that when we go on an SST issue we're working with a lot of allies. They know the subject better than we do. And we take their orders."

Until Common Cause came on the Washington scene, most of the effective lobbying that was done on Capitol Hill was related—implicitly or directly—to the promise of future campaign contributions (or the threat of withholding contributions). Gardner is seeking to prove that a general-purpose lobbying organization can be effective without at the same time providing a direct financial payoff at election time.

Common Cause has stirred the animosity and jealousy of other lobbying groups with similar interests. The main reason for the resentment is that Common Cause, to keep growing, has had to show results to members and prospective members. And, in publicizing its accomplishments, Common Cause often has neglected to acknowledge that its lobbying role on such issues as the SST and campaign spending was either peripheral or late in coming.

In its first year of operation, Common Cause focused its attention on the following issues:

Common Cause lobbied on behalf of the campaign-spending bill (S 382) that passed the Senate August 5, 1971, by an 88-2 vote. It will make a major effort in the House to seek enactment of a companion reform bill. The organization also filed suit January 11, 1971, in the U.S. District Court for the District of Columbia to enjoin the Democratic, Republican and Conservative Parties from violating campaign contribution laws. The major purpose of the suit is to force political parties to observe the spirit of existing restrictions on campaign contributions and spending.

Lloyd N. Cutler, a partner in the Washington, D.C., law firm of Wilmer, Cutler and Pickering, is acting as Common Cause's attorney in the suit. Joseph A. Califano Jr., counsel to the Democratic National Committee and a partner in the Washington law firm of Williams, Connolly & Califano, is serving as chief defense lawyer for the Democrats. Califano, a one-time special assistant to President Johnson (1965-69), is a member of Common Cause. On August 23, Judge Barrington J. Parker denied motions to dismiss the suit, ruling that the court had jurisdiction to consider the case and that Common Cause had legal standing to bring the action.

When the 92nd Congress convened in January 1971, Common Cause mounted its first major campaign—directed against the seniority system which prevails in the House. It also endorsed a Senate move to enable itself to choke off filibusters by liberalizing Rule XXII. The Senate move was unsuccessful. The organization lobbied for automatic open votes in the selection of House committee chairmen; for the removal of three committee chairmen, Reps. William M. Colmer, D-Miss. (Rules); W. R. Poage, D-Tex. (Agriculture); and John L. McMillan, D-S.C. (District of Columbia); and for stripping seniority from the five members of the Mississippi delegation in the House. None of these proposals were approved.

Common Cause supported legislation to grant the Equal Employment Opportunity Commission wider powers to curb job discrimination against minority groups and women. In September 1971, the House considered a bill (HR 1746) to increase the EEOC's powers. The main point of contention dealt with granting the EEOC power to issue cease-and-desist orders. The House passed an amended version of the bill that provided court enforcement powers instead of cease-and-desist authority and did not broaden the EEOC's jurisdiction.

Common Cause lobbied for legislation to establish a policy of public-service employment. A compromise bill was signed into law July 12, 1971 (85 Stat 146). Common Cause also has testified on behalf of retention of the Office of Economic Opportunity and against efforts by the Administration to strip the anti-poverty agency of some of its functions (HR 40 and S 397).

The organization joined with conservation groups in the successful effort to end federal subsidies for a supersonic commercial transport (HR 8190). Acting independently of the Coalition Against the SST, Common Cause focused on 80 "target" congressional districts and 17 "target" states for action by its membership. It claimed success in 49 districts and 11 states. Common Cause has joined in a legal challenge to the Treasury Department's proposed regulations that would liberalize depreciation rates. In testifying at a departmental hearing, it argued that the new regulations would have the effect of granting tax write-offs of $3 billion to $5 billion to a segment of industry without congressional approval.

The principal activity of Common Cause on Capitol Hill was to generate support for a complete withdrawal of U.S. forces from Indochina by the end of 1971 (S 376 and HR 4100). It concentrated its efforts in the House. In spring 1971, Common Cause mounted a campaign to induce House Members to sign either of two "statements of purpose," pledging themselves to strive for withdrawal from Vietnam by the end of the year. A Republican version, circulated by Rep. Charles A. Mosher, Ohio, received 21 signatures by June 16, and a Democratic statement, circulated by Rep. O'Neill, received 121 signatures by the same date.

On June 17, the House rejected, on a recorded teller vote of 158-254, an amendment by Reps. Lucien N. Nedzi, D-Mich., and Charles W. Whalen Jr., R-Ohio, to bar use of any funds authorized by the fiscal 1972 military procurement bill (HR 8687) for use in Indochina after December 31, 1971, or some

other date during fiscal 1972 that the President might recommend. Only 23 Republicans supported the amendment. But
Fred M. Wertheimer, the chief Common Cause lobbyist against
the war, said that "very significant advances did take place . . .
among more conservative members of both parties."

Wertheimer's main assignment when Congress resumed
work September 8 was an effort in behalf of the antiwar
amendment of Sen. Mike Mansfield, D-Mont., to the selective
service bill (HR 6531). The amendment, which established a
nine-month deadline for withdrawal of troops from Indochina,
was passed by the Senate June 24, 1971, by a 72-16 vote, but
was substantially weakened in conference. As a result, Mansfield introduced a stronger amendment to HR 8687, establishing a six-month deadline for withdrawal of U.S. troops, subject to release of American prisoners of war, and declaring it
U.S. policy to terminate military operations in Indochina at
the earliest practicable date. The Senate passed the Mansfield amendment September 30 by a vote of 57-38.

Common Cause lobbied for congressional approval and
ratification by state legislatures of the 26th Amendment, which
permits persons between 18 and 21 to vote in all elections.
The welfare reform bill (HR 1) that passed the House June
22, 1971, was backed by Common Cause. Chairman Gardner
worked with HEW Secretary Richardson on the measure.
Common Cause will seek two changes in the Senate. One
would prevent states from paying less to welfare recipients
than they now pay. The other would provide larger benefits.

After a year of rapid growth, Common Cause has found its
own individual style as a citizen's movement. The Common
Cause agenda has been well refined. It calls for waging
limited warfare on selected battlefields—both in Washington
and, where the targets are tempting, throughout the country.
Gardner is comfortable with this approach and, so far as anyone can tell, so is his constituency.

"We aren't going to be effective if we take only the problems of the blacks and minorities," said Lowell Beck, executive director of Common Cause. "We have to keep our target areas small. The main issues will continue to be the war, opening up the system and making it honest, and tax reform. The 'B' issues will be health, environment and no-fault insurance. But we will not speak out on everything. We have been silent, for example, on education and housing."

The continued silence of Common Cause on some issues and the familiar, easy relationship between John Gardner and his movement and the upper-middle class have led to a polarization with more radical forces in the society. "They are just not prepared to lead a broader constituency," said a former consultant to Common Cause, who asked that his name not be used. "They could have transformed Common Cause into an antiwar organization. It might have ended the war, but it would have hurt the organization. It would have been an interesting trade-off."

Black militants have been equally put off by Common Cause. While Gardner was forging his new lobby, he attended several meetings in New York, arranged by Carl Holman, with black leaders. Gardner's main purpose was to discuss why Common Cause would make a fight on the seniority issue in the House. But the blacks thought the main purpose should be to tell Gardner how he could make his lobby more relevant to them and the poor inner-city blacks whom they sought to represent. Tom Mathews, Gardner's press aide, recalled that "Gardner argued it very forcibly and argued it against the kind of put-down that you get from angry, intelligent, minority members. It was a reverse kind of education; it was they who were being educated by Gardner." There was no follow-through with the black leadership. But, Mathews said, "We didn't want their follow-through. We just wanted them to think about what this meant to them."

Later in the year, Gardner set up a private meeting between HEW Secretary Richardson and leaders of welfare groups throughout the country to discuss the pending welfare reform legislation—the Administration's family assistance plan. But George A. Wiley, executive director of the National Welfare

Rights Organization, insisted that a large group of welfare
mothers, whom he had called to Washington at the same time,
also be allowed to attend the meetings with Richardson. Again,
Mathews recalled what happened: "We offered them up to a
dozen slots. Wiley said no dice. The meeting was then can-
celed (by Richardson and Gardner). Wiley was both angry
and chagrined because what happened was that he blew the
meeting. But we took the blame; we didn't lay it on him. If
you are on their side of the fence, it is timidity or sellout or
worse. But you can't be all things to all people and our credibility is better maintained by common sense and restraint
than it is by going down some side street with a wild ally."
In working to reform the system, there has never been any
question as to what side of the fence Common Cause is on.

Table 10.1   Common Cause Governing Board

The following 39 members of Common Cause are on the organization's governing board, which makes the policy decisions:

Joseph H. Allen,* president, McGraw-Hill Publications, New York, N.Y.

Arnold Aronson,* secretary, Leadership Conference on Civil Rights, New
York, N.Y.

Monsignor Geno Baroni, director, Center for Urban Ethnic Affairs, Washington, D.C.

Lucy Wilson Benson,* president, League of Women Voters of the United
States, Washington, D.C., and Amherst, Mass.

Richard Blumenthal, student, Yale Law School, New Haven, Conn. Former
White House staff assistant, Urban Affairs Council (1969-70).

Humberto Cintron, chairman, Concerned Citizens of East Harlem Inc., New
York, N.Y.

Wilbur J. Cohen, dean, School of Education, University of Michigan, Ann
Arbor, Mich.

Paul R. Ehrlich, professor of biology, Stanford University, Stanford, Calif.

Betty Furness, consumer protection consultant, Hartsdale, N.Y.

John W. Gardner,* chairman, Common Cause, Washington, D.C.

The Most Rev. George H. Guilfoyle,* Bishop, Diocese of Camden, N.J.

LaDonna Harris, president, Americans for Indian Opportunity, Washington,
D.C.

Dorothy I. Height, president, National Council of Negro Women Inc., New
York, N.Y., and Washington, D.C.

Andrew Heiskell,* board chairman, Time Inc., New York, N.Y.

Aileen C. Hernandez,* Western representative, National Committee Against
Discrimination in Housing, San Francisco, Calif.

Mrs. Christian A. Herter Jr., Washington, D.C.

Rev. **Jesse Jackson,** national director, Operation Breadbasket-Southern Christian Leadership Conference, Chicago, Ill.

Howard W. Johnson, chairman of the corporation, Massachusetts Institute of Technology, Cambridge, Mass.

Barbara Greene Kilberg, attorney, Arnold & Porter, Washington, D.C.

Margot Coffin Lindsay, co-chairman, WBZ Call for Action, Lincoln, Mass.

Ruby Grant Martin, fellow, Washington Research Project, Washington, D.C.

Martin Meyerson,* president, University of Pennsylvania, Philadelphia, Pa.

Herbert S. Miller, deputy director, Institute of Criminal Law and Procedure, Georgetown University Law Center, Washington, D.C.

Grace Olivarez, executive director, Food for All Inc., Phoenix, Ariz.

Susan V. Paris, founder, Vermont Project for Public Interest Law, Bennington, Vt.

James W. Rouse, president, The Rouse Company, Columbia, Md.

Bayard Rustin,* executive director, A. Philip Randolph Institute, New York, N.Y.

Howard D. Samuel, vice president, Amalgamated Clothing Workers of America, New York, N.Y.

Henry Santiestevan, executive secretary, La Raza, a Mexican-American action group, Phoenix, Ariz.

Rabbi Solomon J. Sharfman, president, Synagogue Council of America, New York, N.Y.

Mark R. Shedd, superintendent of schools, Philadelphia, Pa.

Asa T. Spaulding, consultant, Durham, N.C.

Fortney H. Stark Jr., president, Security National Bank, Walnut Creek, Calif.

Michael H. Walsh, staff attorney, Defenders Program of San Diego Inc., San Diego, Calif.

Cynthia C. Wedel,* president, National Council of Churches, New York, N.Y.

John H. Wheeler, president, Southern Regional Council, Durham, N.C.

Harold Willens, national chairman, Businessmen's Educational Fund, Los Angeles, Calif.

Leonard Woodcock,* president, United Auto Workers, Detroit, Mich.

Jerry Wurf, president, American Federation of State, County and Municipal Employees, Washington, D.C.

*executive committee

The following persons served on the Common Cause board from September 1970 to December 1971, when their terms expired:

Albert E. Arent, partner in the law firm of Arent, Fox, Kintner, Plotkin & Kahn, Washington, D.C.

State Sen. Joseph J. Bernal, D-San Antonio, Tex.

State Rep. Julian Bond, D-Atlanta, Ga.

James E. Cheek, president, Howard University, Washington, D.C.

Kenneth B. Clark, president, Metropolitan Applied Research Center, New York, N.Y.

Dr. Hector P. Garcia, Corpus Christi, Tex.

Ernest Green, director, Joint Apprenticeship Program, New York, N.Y.

Mayor Richard G. Hatcher, D-Gary, Ind.

Vivian W. Henderson, president, Clark College, Atlanta, Ga.

Vernon E. Jordan Jr., executive director, United Negro College Fund Inc., New York, N.Y.

Joseph D. Keenan, international secretary, International Brotherhood of Electrical Workers, Washington, D.C.

Mayor John V. Lindsay, D-New York, N.Y.

Donald S. MacNaughton, chairman and chief executive officer, Prudential Insurance Company of America, Newark, N.J.

Carl B. Stokes, former Democratic mayor of Cleveland, Ohio (1967-71).

Martin Stone, president, Monogram Industries Inc., Los Angeles, Calif.

James H. J. Tate, former Democratic mayor of Philadelphia, Pa. (1962-71).

Andrew J. Young Jr., executive director, Community Relations Commission, Atlanta, Ga.

Table 10.2   Common Cause Membership: Uncommon Names

The following 19 prominent persons are among the 200,000 Americans who joined Common Cause in its first year (1970-71):

Gardner Ackley, professor of political economy, University of Michigan, Ann Arbor; U.S. Ambassador to Italy (1968-69), member, Council of Economic Advisors (1962-68) and its chairman (1964-68).

Winthrop W. Aldrich, U.S. Ambassador to Great Britain (1953-57), chairman, Chase Manhattan Bank, New York (1934-53).

Herbert Brownell, member, law firm of Lord, Day and Lord, New York, N.Y.; U.S. Attorney General (1953-57).

Joseph A. Califano Jr., member, law firm of Williams, Connolly and Califano, Washington, D.C.; special assistant to President Johnson (1965-69).

Ramsey Clark, member, law firm of Paul, Weiss, Goldberg, Rifkind, Wharton, and Garrison, New York, N.Y.; U.S. Attorney General (1967-69).

Henry Steele Commager, author, professor of history, Amherst College, Mass.

Thomas G. Corcoran, member, law firm of Corcoran, Foley, Youngman and Rowe, Washington, D.C.; assistant to U.S. Attorney General (1933-40).

Lloyd N. Cutler, member, law firm of Wilmer, Cutler and Pickering, Washington, D.C.; executive director, Commission on Causes and Prevention of Violence (1968-69).

S. I. Hayakawa, president, San Francisco State College, San Francisco, Calif.

Barbara Laird, wife of Defense Secretary Melvin R. Laird, Washington, D.C.

Sol M. Linowitz, chairman, National Urban Coalition, Washington, D.C.; U.S. Ambassador to Organization of American States (1966-69), chairman, Xerox Corporation (1966).

Robert S. McNamara, president, World Bank, Washington, D.C.; Secretary of Defense (1961-67).

David Packard, deputy secretary of defense, Washington, D.C.

Gov. Nelson A. Rockefeller, R, of New York.

John D. Rockefeller III, chairman, Rockefeller Foundation, New York.

Gov. Francis W. Sargent, R, of Massachusetts.

Gloria Steinem, journalist; member, policy council, National Women's Political Caucus, New York, N.Y.

Stewart L. Udall, board chairman, Overview Corporation, Washington, D.C.; Secretary of the Interior (1961-69).

Thomas J. Watson Jr., chairman, International Business Machines Corporation, Armonk, N.Y.

Chart 10.1

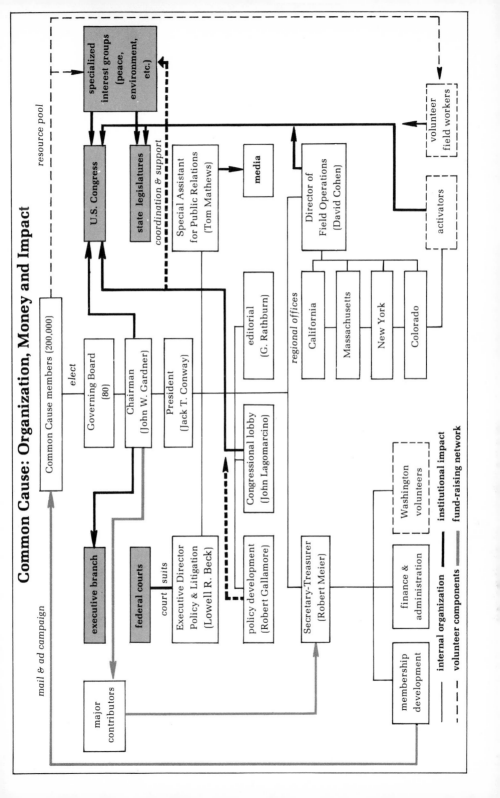

Common Cause: Organization, Money and Impact

resource pool

specialized interest groups (peace, environment, etc.)

U.S. Congress

state legislatures

coordination & support

Special Assistant for Public Relations (Tom Mathews)

media

volunteer field workers

activators

Director of Field Operations (David Cohen)

editorial (G. Rathburn)

regional offices

California

Massachusetts

New York

Colorado

Common Cause members (200,000)

elect

Governing Board (80)

Chairman (John W. Gardner)

President (Jack T. Conway)

Congressional lobby (John Lagomarcino)

mail & ad campaign

executive branch

federal courts

court suits

Executive Director Policy & Litigation (Lowell R. Beck)

policy development (Robert Gallamore)

Secretary-Treasurer (Robert Meier)

Washington volunteers

finance & administration

membership development

major contributors

— **internal organization**

— **institutional impact**

— **fund-raising network**

internal organization

volunteer components

APPENDIX I

1970 Reports of Political Committees

Associations and committees which receive contributions and distribute funds to influence elections in two or more states are required by federal law to file statements of receipts and expenditures with the Clerk of the House of Representatives.

A section of the Federal Corrupt Practices Act (2 USC 244) requires quarterly statements from the committees in non-election years and two statements around election time in addition to the quarterly statements in election years.

Listed below are the 193 committees which filed statements with the House clerk in calendar year 1970 and their reported receipts and expenditures. It is common practice for political committees to gather funds in off-election years for use in election years. In many instances, this practice accounts for discrepancies that may appear in receipts and expenditures. Committees whose receipts include funds transferred from other political committees have an additional listing in the table for "adjusted receipts"—total receipts less identifiable transfers from other groups.

The final 1970 report was due on January 1, 1971. Committees which had not filed complete 1970 reports as of February 10, 1971, are identified in the list by asterisks.

POLITICAL COMMITTEES

DEMOCRATIC PARTY

(Total Expenditures:
$4,266,531.07)

Commission on Party Structure and Delegate Selection, Democratic National Committee, 2600 Virginia Ave. NW, Washington, D.C. 20037. Robert W. Nelson, treasurer.

Receipts: $21,567.75
Adjusted receipts: $18,567.75
Expenditures: $23,472.87

Committee for National Unity, 1812 N St. NW, Washington, D.C. 20036. Raymond J. Rasenberger, treasurer.

Receipts: $64,694.98
Expenditures: $15,200.68

Committee for Ten, 1826 Jefferson Pl. NW, Washington, D.C. 20036. John R. Wagley, treasurer.

Receipts: $4,096.82
Expenditures: $12,025.19

Congressional Leadership for the Future, 1701 K St. NW, Suite 1203, Washington, D.C. 20006. Harold H. Flickinger, administrative officer.

Receipts: $65,686.00
Expenditures: $63,734.18

Democratic Congressional Campaign Committee, B357 Rayburn House Office Building, Washington, D.C. 20515. Jess Larson, treasurer.

Receipts: $441,870.17
Expenditures: $403,762.65

Democratic National Congressional Committee, B357 Rayburn House Office Building, Washington, D.C. 20515. Jess Larson, treasurer.

Receipts: $16,857.21
Expenditures: $212,479.10

Democratic National Committee, 2600 Virginia Ave. NW, Washington, D.C. 20037. Robert S. Strauss, treasurer.

Receipts: $1,599,401.36
Adjusted receipts: $1,417,688.95
Expenditures:$1,617,592.99

1970 Democratic National Gala Committee, Democratic National Committee, 2600 Virginia Ave. NW, Washington, D.C. 20037. Robert S. Strauss, treasurer.

Receipts: $164,239.00
Expenditures: $164,239.00

1970 Democratic National Gala Committee—Florida, Democratic National Committee, 2600 Virginia Ave. NW, Washington, D.C. 20037. Robert S. Strauss, treasurer.

Receipts: $14,460.00
Expenditures: $14,260.00

Democratic Senatorial Campaign Committee, 130 Old Senate Office Bldg., Washington, D.C. 20510. Eiler C. Ravnholt, secretary-treasurer.

Receipts: $482,701.54
Expenditures: $628,670.63

Democratic Study Group 1970 Campaign Fund, 2331 Barbour Rd., Falls Church, Va. 22043. Marti Conlon, agent.

Receipts: $182,793.43
Expenditures: $146,986.47

Let It Be Committee, 2600 Virginia Ave. NW, Washington, D.C. 20037. Kathy Slosky, secretary to the chairman.

Receipts: $3,617.50
Expenditures: $3,195.13

National Democratic Policy Council, 2600 Virginia Ave. NW, Washington, D.C. 20037. Robert S. Strauss, treasurer.

Receipts: $56,920.77
Adjusted receipts: $17,350.00
Expenditures: $67,499.54

Nineteen Seventy (1970) Campaign Fund, P.O. Box 2446, Washington, D.C. 20013. Carol Valverde, treasurer.

Receipts: $874,955.90
Expenditures: $846,396.86

Project '70 Committee, 2600 Virginia Ave. NW, Washington, D.C. 20037. Robert S. Strauss, treasurer.

Receipts: $7,980.00
Expenditures: $12,980.00

Reform DNC Committee, Democratic National Committee, 2600 Virginia Ave. NW, Washington, D.C. 20037. Robert S. Strauss, treasurer.

Receipts:$21,855.89
Expenditures: $20,685.78

Victory '72 Committee, 2600 Virginia Ave. NW, Washington, D.C. 20037. Robert S. Strauss, treasurer.

Receipts: $5,000.00
Expenditures: $9,500.00

Young Democratic Operating Committee, 2600 Virginia Ave. NW, Washington, D.C. 20037. Kathy Slosky, secretary to the chairman.

Receipts: $4,000.00
Adjusted receipts: $0
Expenditures: $3,850.00

REPUBLICAN PARTY
(Total Expenditures: $13,076,515.25)

Committee of Nine, The First National Bank of Washington, Washington, D.C. 20004. Tudor Whiton, treasurer.

Receipts: $500.00
Expenditures: $5,912.19

D.C. Republican Committee 1970 Dinner, 1625 Eye St. NW, Washington, D.C. 20006. Henry K. Willard, chairman of finance.

Receipts: $137,083.00
Expenditures: $137,083.00

Institute for Republican Studies, 1000 Vermont Ave., Washington, D.C. 20005. John A. Nevius, treasurer.

Receipts: $4,610.00
Expenditures:$4,959.29

National Federation of Republican Women, 3000 Overridge Dr., Ann Arbor, Mich. 48104. Ruth J. Hobbs, treasurer.

Receipts: $70,764.42
Expenditures: $87,570.09

National Republican Congressional Committee, 412 Congressional Hotel, Washington, D.C. 20003. Gen. George Olmstead (U.S. Army Reserve, ret.), treasurer.

Receipts: $2,492,729.55
Adjusted receipts: $2,490,179.55
Expenditures: $2,796,194.82

National Republican Senatorial Committee, The First National Bank of Washington, Washington, D.C. 20004. Joseph R. Fitzpatrick, treasurer.

Receipts: $1,520,222.64
Adjusted receipts: $1,270,222.64
Expenditures: $1,255,824.07

Nixon-Agnew Campaign Committee, 310 1st St. SE, Washington, D.C. 20003. Raymond T. Underwood Jr. assistant treasurer.

Receipts: $3,625.53
Expenditures: $17,647.79

Republican Campaign Committee, 310 1st St. SE, Washington, D.C. 20003. Ruth W. Clark, assistant treasurer.

Receipts: $703,805.01
Expenditures: $696,046.02

Republican Candidates Committee, 412 Congressional Hotel, Washington, D.C. 20003. J.R.Gorman, treasurer.

Receipts: $2,550.00
Expenditures: $2,550.00

Republican Congressional Boosters Club, 310 1st SE, Washington, D.C. 20003. William J. Schuiling, treasurer.

Receipts: $874,774.24
Expenditures: $1,297,227.00

Republican National Committee, 310 1st St. SE, Washington, D.C. 20003. John M. Christie, treasurer.

Receipts: $2,955,597.49
Expenditures: $2,974,158.59

Republican National Finance Advisory Committee, 412 Congressional Hotel. Washington, D.C. 20003. Fred L. Dixon, treasurer.

Receipts: $166,578.49
Expenditures: $194,763.40

Republican National Finance Committee, 310 1st St. SE. Washington, D.C. 20003. Raymond T. Underwood Jr., assistant treasurer.

Receipts: $2,589,886.28
Adjusted receipts: $2,541,886.28
Expenditures: $2,980,308.27

Republican National Finance Operations Committee, 310 1st St. SE, Washington, D.C. 20003. Raymond T. Underwood Jr., assistant treasurer.

Receipts: $286,227.91
Expenditures: $553,306.22

Republican Victory Committee, 310 1st St. SE., Washington, D.C. 20003. Janet Riccio, assistant treasurer.

Receipts: $30,698.00
Expenditures: $21,299.41

RN Associates, 310 1st St. SE, Washington, D.C. 20003. Mildred Bighinatti, assistant treasurer.

Receipts: $17,000.00
Expenditures: None reported

United Republican Finance Committee of San Mateo County, 231 2nd Ave., San Mateo, Calif. 94401. Mrs. Junius Cary, treasurer.

Receipts: $50,269.88
Expenditures: $50,654.09

MISCELLANEOUS
(Total Expenditures: $1,870,307.53)

American Conservative Union, 328 Pennsylvania Ave. SE, Washington, D.C. 20003. Lammot Copeland, Jr., treasurer.

Receipts: $319,757.58
Expenditures: $355,715.76

Americans for Constitutional Action, 955 L'Enfant Plaza North, SW, Washington, D.C. 20024. Edward G. Orbann, treasurer.

Receipts: $138,475
Expenditures: $188,875

Conservative Victory Fund, 328 Pennsylvania Ave. SE, Washington, D.C. 20003. Lammot Copeland Jr., treasurer.

Receipts: $427,753.17
Expenditures: $412,852.43

Council for a Livable World, 12 Howard St., Cambridge, Mass. 02139. Jane M. O. Sharp, associate director.

Receipts: $211,055.31
Expenditures: $214,626.47

National Committee for an Effective Congress, 10 East 39th St., New York, N.Y. 10016. Stacey Feiner.

Receipts: $669,736.03
Expenditures: $695.501.43

BUSINESS, PROFESSIONAL
(Total expenditures: $3,238,011.22)

Action Committee for Rural Electrification, P.O. Box 19066. Washington, D.C. 20036. Paul Ogier, treasurer.

Receipts: $101,618.90
Expenditures: $131,068.48

Agricultural Cooperative Trust, 30 F St. NW, Washington, D.C. 20001. Patrick B. Healy, chairman.

Receipts: $10,871.00
Expenditures: $6,700.00

Agricultural and Dairy Education Political Trust, P.O. Box 1837, S.S. Station, Springfield, Mo. 65805. William A. Delano, trustee.

Receipts: $10,034.07
Expenditures: $9,601.00

American Dental Political Action Committee, 4240 Fordham Rd. NW, Washington, D.C. 20016. C. Willard Camalier Sr., treasurer.

Receipts: $1,651.00
Expenditures: $300.00

American Insurance Men's Political Action Committee, P.O. Box 366, Yankton, S.D. 57078. Lenard Ludwig, treasurer.

Receipts: $3,160.96
Expenditures: $3,949.41

American Medical Political Action Committee, 520 North Michigan Ave., Chicago, Ill. 60611. Dr. George J. Lawrence Jr., chairman.

Receipts: $448,423.27
Expenditures: $693,412.80

American Nursing Home Education and Political Action Committee, P.O. Box 93, Alexandria, Va. 22313. John K. Pickens, treasurer.

Receipts: $28,548.70
Expenditures: $19,355.54

Bankers Action Now Committee,* 50 W. Broad St., Columbus, Ohio 43215. Lawrence J. Burns, secretary-treasurer. (1970 report filed through Oct. 31.)

Receipts: $24,355.00
Expenditures: $32,019.97

Bankers Congressional Committee, 1000 Connecticut Ave. NW, Suite 500, Washington, D.C. 20036. Louis C. Paladini, treasurer.

Receipts: $3,145.00
Expenditures: $2,410.00

Bankers Political Action Committee, P.O. Box 838, East Lansing, Mich. 48823. Ralph L. Stickle.

Receipts: $205,428.19
Expenditures: $85,795.10

Bus Industry Public Affairs Committee, P.O. Box 2022, Washington, D.C. 20013. James T. Corcoran, secretary-treasurer.

Receipts: $1,492.50
Expenditures: $2,268.90

Business-Industry Political Action Committee, 1747 Pennsylvania Ave. NW, Washington, D.C. 20008. Robert L. Humphrey, president.

Receipts: $302,553.54
Adjusted receipts: $301,504.39
Expenditures: $539,156.62

Business-Industry Political Action Committee of New York, 280 Park Ave., New York, N.Y. 10017. Robert H. Brome, treasurer.

Receipts: $6,049.15
Adjusted receipts: $1,049.15
Expenditures: $6,049.15

Canners Public Affairs Committee, 1101 Waverley Way, McLean Va. 22101. Robert B. Heiney, treasurer.

Receipts: $5,139.00
Expenditures: $4,707.20

Citizens Committee for Improved Government,* 225 S. Washington Blvd., Hamilton, Ohio 45013. R. A. Weiser, treasurer, (1970 report filed through Oct. 31.)

Receipts: $2,200.00
Expenditures: $1,900.00

Committee for Action, P.O. Box 519 14446 Sunset Highway. Bellevue, Wash. 98009. Carl W. Erickson, treasurer.

East
Receipts: $29,158.00
Expenditures: $37,791.03

Midwest
Receipts: $39,615.00
Expenditures: $58,491.03

South
Receipts: $45,368.00
Expenditures: $36,041.03

West
Receipts: $54,922.00
Expenditures: $53,391.03

Committee for American Principles, P.O. Box 34437, Bethesda, Md. 20034. Ellis E. Meredith, treasurer.

Receipts: $10,230.00
Expenditures: $10,144.74

Committee of Automotive Retailers, P.O. Box 19169, Washington, D.C. 20036. Frank E. McCarthy, secretary-treasurer.

Receipts: $2,699.00
Expenditures: $6,683.26

Committee on American Leadership, P.O. Box 19289, Washington, D.C. 20036. John B. Howerton, treasurer.

Receipts: $10,158.00
Expenditures: $12,058.54

Communications Political Action Committee, P.O. Box 83, Franklin Station, Washington, D.C. 20044. William S. Kingman, chairman.

Receipts: $7,555.00
Expenditures: $10,607.42

Construction Equipment Political Action Committee, 3600 M St. NW, Washington, D.C. 20007. George W. Gagel, treasurer.

Receipts: $1.08
Expenditures: $292.75

Effective Government Association, 1629 K St. NW, Suite 5071, Washington, D.C. 20006. Charles W. Dougherty, treasurer.

Receipts: $19,760.00
Expenditures: $25,468.00

Fed Pac, P.O. Box 35333, Airlawn Station, Dallas, Tex. 75235. Dr. Cleo M. Miller, treasurer.

Receipts: $4,793.00
Expenditures: $4,102.97

Food Processors Public Affairs Committee, 21 Cobb Terrace, Rochester, N.Y. 14620. W. T. Tyler, treasurer.

Receipts: $2,811.50
Expenditures: $4,644.12

Forest Products Political Education Committee, 9100 River Rd., Potomac, Md. 20854. Henry Baler, secretary-treasurer.

Receipts: $28,150.59
Expenditures: $26,394.29

Freezers Political Action Committee, 901 South Carey St., Baltimore, Md. 21223. Edward L. Morin, treasurer.

Receipts: $396.50
Expenditures: $896.69

Home Furnishings Political Committee, 1025 Vermont Ave. NW, Suite 1109, Washington, D.C. 20005, Spencer A. Johnson, treasurer.

Receipts: $2,954.94
Expenditures: $2,877.35

Indiana Medical Political Action Committee. 502 W. 2nd St., Seymour, Ind. 47274. Dr. J. M. Black.

Receipts: $74,143.00
Expenditures: $86,064.10

Life Underwriters Political Action Committee. 525 20th St. NW, Washington, D.C. 20006. James W. Wood, secretary-treasurer.

Receipts: $35,351.06
Expenditures: $43,855.00

Lone Star Executives' Voluntary Political Fund. One Greenwich Plaza, Greenwich, Conn. 06830. C. C. Burns, treasurer.

Receipts: $9,116.05
Expenditures: $7,200.00

Maritime Action Committee, 815 16th St. NW, Suite 501, Washington, D.C. 20006. Peter M. McGavin, treasurer.

Receipts: $83,000.00
Expenditures: $95,646.30

Motel Development Committee,* 1025 Vermont Ave. NW, Suite 1100. Washington, D.C. 20005. Kenneth H. Layer, secretary-treasurer. (1970 report filed through June 10.)

Receipts: $2,865.00
Expenditures: $2,476.78

National Audio-Visual Association Inc., 3150 Spring St., Fairfax, Va. 22030. T. M. White, executive vice-president.

Receipts: $720.00
Expenditures: $770.00

North Street Good Government Group, 2650 Virginia Ave. NW, Suite 1116, Washington, D.C. 20037. Herbert M. Cleaves, treasurer.

Receipts: $7,459.50
Expenditures: $6,800.00

Political Action Committee of Cable Television, 1534 28th St. NW, Washington, D.C. 20007, Alan Raywid, secretary-treasurer.

Receipts: $17,057.78
Expenditures: $30,001.63

Political Action for Cooperative Effectiveness, 888 17th St. NW, Suite 700, Washington, D.C. 20006. Richard T. O'Connell, treasurer.

Receipts: $10,161.38
Expenditures: $18,739.83

Public Affairs Committee of Savings Associations, P.O. Box 797, Harrisburg, Pa. 17108. Robert B. Rosenberger, secretary-treasurer.

Receipts: $23,181.50
Expenditures: $16,882.23

Real Estate Political Education Committee, 120 East Market St., Indianapolis, Ind. 46204. Fred C. Tucker, Jr., treasurer.

Receipts: $26,374.56
Expenditures: $17,729.19

Restaurateurs Political Action Committee, 228 N. LaSalle St., Suite 2219, Chicago, Ill. 60601. Ralph Lewy, treasurer.

Receipts: $33,935.00
Expenditures: $71,683.13

Savings Association Political Education Committee, National Permanent Federal Savings and Loan, 1400 G St. NW, Washington, D.C. 20005. John W. Stadtler, treasurer.

Receipts: $70,800.50
Expenditures: $88,281.24

Savings Association Public Affairs Committee of Michigan, P.O. Box 364, Lansing, Mich. 48902. Robert E. Clark, treasurer.

Receipts: $9,382.00
Expenditures: $11,576.46

Savings Bankers Non-Partisan Political Action Committee, P.O. Box 3871, Grand Central Station, New York, N.Y. 10017. Edgar T. Hussey, treasurer.

Receipts: $4,353.00
Expenditures: $4,271.87

SCRAP Political Action Committee, 6210 Hardy Drive, McLean, Va. 22101. Charles D. Hoffman, executive secretary.

Receipts: $4,350.00
Expenditures: $6,263.83

Securities Industry Campaign Committee, P.O. Box 19188, Washington, D.C. 20036. Richard O. Scribner, secretary-treasurer.

Receipts: $65,555.00
Expenditures: $59,396.73

Shoe Manufacturers Good Government Committee, Brown Shoe Company, St. Louis, Mo. 83105. W. L. Hadley Griffin, trustee.

Receipts: $11,850.00
Expenditures: $6,750.00

Telephone Education Committee Organization, 1000 Connecticut Ave. NW, Suite 601, Washington, D.C. 20036. David C. Fullarton, assistant treasurer.

Receipts: $6,272.00
Expenditures: $4,679.62

Transportation Political Education League, 15401 Detroit Ave., Cleveland, Ohio, 44107. John H. Shepherd, secretary-treasurer.

Receipts: $414,014.08
Expenditures: $283,821.00

Truck Operators' Non-Partisan Committee, P.O. Box 12006, Washington, D.C. 20005. Frank L. Grimm, treasurer.

Receipts: $36,169.50
Expenditures: $38,522.91

Trust for Agricultural Political Education, P.O. Box 32287, San Antonio, Tex. 78216. Robert O. Isham, treasurer and trustee.

Receipts: $535,422.95
Expenditures: $368,851.15

Trust for Special Political Agricultural Community Education, 508 Portland Federal Building, 200 W. Broadway, Louisville, Ky. 40202. J. E. Mueller, trustee-treasurer.

Receipts: $111,786.74
Expenditures: $123,669.80

Wisconsin Bankers Political Action Committee, c/o Farmers State Bank of Manawa, Manawa, Wis., 54949. Myrle G. Hales, secretary-treasurer.

Receipts: $19,667.50
Expenditures: $15,500.00

LABOR

(Total Expenditures: $5,701,045.08)

Active Ballot Club, Retail Clerks International Association, Suffridge Building, Washington, D.C. 20006. James L. Huntley, field director.

Receipts: $143,501.03
Expenditures: $188,187.96

Amalgamated Clothing Workers, AFL-CIO Political Education Committee, * 73 Tremont St., Boston, Mass. 02108. Diana Nunes, treasurer. (1970 report filed through Oct. 31.)

Receipts: $2,972.00
Expenditures: $5,000.00

Amalgamated Clothing Workers of America. Chicago Joint Board Political Action Committee, 333 S. Ashland Blvd., Chicago, Ill. 60607. A. J. Lifton treasurer.

Receipts: $19,947.43
Expenditures: $12,767.00

Amalgamated Clothing Workers of America, Committee on Political Education, Cincinnati Joint Board 35 E. 7th St., Suite 500, Cincinnati, Ohio 45202. Joseph Eisen, treasurer.

Receipts: $1,811.77
Expenditures: $600.00

Amalgamated Clothing Workers of America, Local 169, 33 W. 14th St., New York, N.Y. 10011. David Shaw, secretary-treasurer.

Receipts: $2,707.00
Expenditures: $3,850.00

Amalgamated Clothing Workers of America, Midwest Regional Political Action Committee, 333 S. Ashland Boulevard, Chicago, Ill. 60607. A. J. Lifton, treasurer.

Receipts: $6,317.24
Expenditures: $6,094.00

Amalgamated Clothing Workers of America, Political Action Fund, Southwest Regional Joint Board, 1627 Locust St., St. Louis, Mo. 63103. Vera Heisler, treasurer.

Receipts: $14,679.36
Expenditures: $14,679.36

Amalgamated Meat Cutters and Butcher Workmen,* 2800 N. Sheridan Rd., Chicago, Ill. 60657. Patrick E. Gorman, secretary-treasurer. (1970 report filed through Oct. 23.)

Receipts: $110,081.35
Expenditures: $167,375.75

Amalgamated Political Education Committee, 15 Union Sq., New York, N.Y. 10003. Frank Rosenblum, treasurer.

Receipts: $89,676.66
Expenditures: $82.048.88

American Federation of Musicians Political Fund, 220 Mt. Pleasant St., Newark, N.J. 07104. Stanley Ballard, treasurer.

Receipts: $22,298.18
Expenditures: $27,899.44

Atlanta Democratic, Republican, Independent Voter Education Committee (DRIVE) #728, 2540 Lakewood Ave. SW, Atlanta, Ga. 30315. Samuel L. Jones, treasurer.

Receipts: $7,795.00
Expenditures: $10,804.75

Boilermakers-Blacksmiths Legislative Education Action Program. 8th and State Ave., Suite 565, Kansas City, Kan. 66101. H. E. Patton, international secretary-treasurer.

Legislative education fund
Receipts: $65,122.39
Expenditures: $41,893.45

Campaign assistance fund
Receipts: $17,941.87
Expenditures: $27,100.00

Brotherhood of Maintenance of Way Political League, 12050 Woodward Ave., Detroit, Mich. 48203. B. L. Sorah Jr., treasurer.

Receipts: $27,705.70
Expenditures: $7,470.74

Building and Construction Trades Department, AFL-CIO, Political Education Fund, 815 16th St. NW, Suite 603, Washington, D.C. 20006. Walter J. Mason, director.

Receipts: $28,820.00
Expenditures: $36,684.48

Carolina DRIVE Chapter No. 1, c/o Ren Drum Pepper Building, Suite 206, Winston Salem, N.C. 27101. B. D. Blevins, treasurer.

Receipts: $9,425.00
Expenditures: $11,497.04

Carpenters Legislative Improvement Committee, 101 Constitution Ave. NW, Washington, D.C. 20001. James F. Bailey, representative.

Receipts: $90,224.18
Expenditures: $139,886.69

Chauffeurs, Teamsters and Helpers*, P.O. Box 1155, 2116 5th Ave., Rock Island, Ill. 61201. Vernie H. Ervin, secretary. (1970 reports filed through Nov. 3.)

Receipts: none
Expenditures: $3,550.00

Clothing Workers Political Committee for Eastern Pennsylvania, 803 Hamilton St., Room 403, Allentown, Pa. 18101. Alfred Hanna, treasurer.

Receipts: $3,285.00
Expenditures: $2,742.65

Colorado Wyoming DRIVE #54, 3245 Eliot St., Denver, Colo. 80211. Harry Bath, treasurer.

Receipts: $7,501.50
Expenditures: $4,972.45

Committee for Good Government, 8000 East Jefferson Ave., Detroit, Mich. 48214. Arthur M. Miller, secretary-treasurer.

Receipts: $52,352.00
Expenditures: $68,848.63

Committee on Political Education, AFL-CIO, 815 16th St. NW, Washington, D.C. 20006. Alexander E. Barkan, national director.

Receipts: $803,594.32
Expenditures: $969.328.10

Communications Workers of America, Individual Contributions Fund, 1925 K St. NW, Washington, D.C. 20006. Glenn E. Watts, secretary-treasurer.

Receipts: $36,638.56
Expenditures: $84,897.01

Connecticut Committee on Political Education,* 9 Washington, Ave., Hamden, Conn. 06518. Joseph C. Bober, treasurer. (1970 report filed through Nov. 4.)

Receipts: $16,345.05
Expenditures: $15,940.59

Democratic, Republican, Independent Voter Education Committee (DRIVE), International Brotherhood of Teamsters, Chauffeurs, Warehousemen, and Helpers, 25 Louisiana Ave. NW, Washington, D.C. 20001. Carlos Moore, executive director.

Receipts: $104,084.49
Expenditures: $170,790.42

Democratic, Republican, Independent Voter Education Committee (DRIVE) 42,* 1616 W. 9th St. Rm. 504, Los Angeles, Calif. 90015. Joseph Caramagno, secretary-treasurer. (1970 report filed for the period Oct. 29-Dec. 1.)

Receipts: $4,897.00
Expenditures: $1,124.43

DRIVE 619 Committee, 1000 A Washington St., Manitowoc, Wis. 54220. Alvin E. Keeman, treasurer.

Receipts: None reported
Expenditures: $0.06

DRIVE Chapter No. 90, 2425 Delaware, Des Moines, Iowa 50317. Edgar C. Hartz, treasurer.

Receipts: $920.00
Expenditures: $761.50

DRIVE Chapter No. 238, P.O. Box 909, 5110 J St. SW, Cedar Rapids, Iowa 52404. Harry J. Wilford, secretary-treasurer.

Receipts: $478.51
Expenditures: $481.44

DRIVE Chapter No. 650 Political Division, 506 6th St., Waterloo, Iowa 50701. Melvin C. Jensen, treasurer.

Receipts: none
Expenditures: $270.00

DRIVE Chapter No. 667, 796 E. Brooks Ave., Memphis, Tenn. 38116. J.V. Pellicciotti, secretary-treasurer.

Receipts: $6,090.50
Expenditures: $8,241.50

DRIVE Local 218, 304 Washington St., Burlington, Iowa 52601. Rex L. Conn, treasurer.

Receipts: $459.51
Expenditures: $703.15

DRIVE Local 745, 1007 Jonelle, Dallas, Tex. 75217. W.L. Piland, secretary-treasurer.

Receipts: $17,469.38
Expenditures: $18,768.22

DRIVE No. 525, 830 E. Broadway, Alton, Ill. 62002. William Doty, treasurer.

Receipts: none
Expenditures: $670

DRIVE No. 568, P.O. Box 7805, Shreveport, La. 71107. Lester C. Sanders, treasurer.

Receipts: $100
Expenditures: None reported

DRIVE Political Fund Chapter 886, 716 S.W. 3rd, Oklahoma City, Okla. 75125. H.L. McDaniel, secretary-treasurer.

Receipts: $10,387.00
Expenditures: $13,625.65

DRIVE, Teamsters Local 373 Political Fund, P.O. Box 6268, Fort Smith, Ark. 72901. Hoyle Sallis, secretary-treasurer.

Receipts: $675.00
Expenditures: $1,577.50

Engineers Political and Education Committee, 1125 17th St. NW, Washington, D.C. 20036. N. J. Carman, general secretary-treasurer.

Receipts: $6,231.50
Expenditures: $1,163.82

Firemen and Oilers Political Committee, International Brotherhood of Firemen and Oilers, 200 Maryland Ave. NE, Washington, D.C. 20028. John J. McNamara, treasurer.

Receipts: $14,172.95
Expenditures: $12,420.47

Industrial Union Department, AFL-CIO Voluntary Funds, 815 16th St. NW, Washington, D.C. 20006. Jacob Clayman, administrative director.

Receipts: $29,687.60
Expenditures: $29,776.00

International Brotherhood of Electrical Workers Committee on Political Education, 1200 15th St. NW, Washington, D.C. 20005. Joseph D. Kennan, treasurer.

Individual contributions fund
Receipts: $58,701.20
Expenditures: $81,473.50

Education fund
Receipts: $10,600.00
Expenditures: $12,250.00

International Brotherhood of Painters and Allied Trades Political Action Together Program,* 217-19 N. 6th St., Lafayette, Ind. 47901. O.T. Satre, general secretary-treasurer. (1970 reports filed through Mar. 31.)

Political fund
Receipts: $1,077.50
Expenditures: $2,420.00

Educational fund
Receipts: $4,236.50
Expenditures: $4,953.90

International Brotherhood of Teamsters, Chauffeurs, Warehousemen, and Helpers of America*, The Hotel Governor, 418 E. Jefferson St., Springfield, Ill. 62701. W. V. Hughes, executive secretary. (1970 report filed for period of Oct. through Nov. 2.)

Receipts: none
Expenditures: $1,550

International Chemical Workers Union, Labor's Investment in Voter Education, Individual Contribution Fund,* 1655 West Market St., Akron, Ohio 44313. Dan W. Richards, accountant. (1970 report filed through Oct. 30.)

Receipts: $7,227.74
Expenditures: $6,700.00

International Ladies' Garment Workers' Union, 1970 Campaign Committee, 1710 Broadway, New York, N.Y. 10019. James Lipsig, treasurer.

Receipts: $834,659.91
Expenditures: $692,109.12

International Typographical Union Political Committee, P.O. Box 2341, Colorado Springs, Colo. 80901. William R. Cloud, secretary-treasurer.

Receipts: $3,783.00
Expenditures: $8,091.50

Laborers Political League, 905 16th St. NW, 5th floor, Washington, D.C. 20006. W. Vernie Reed, treasurer.

Receipts: $150,297.73
Expenditures: $145,006.60

Labor's Non-Partisan League, 900 15th St. NW, Room 203, Washington, D.C. 20005. Leonard Gazenski, treasurer.
Receipts: $32,495.90
Expenditures: $19,866.75

Local DRIVE 949, 3520 Montrose Blvd., Suite 202, Houston, Tex. 77006. R. B. Moon, treasurer.

Receipts: None reported
Expenditures: None reported

Machinists Non-Partisan Political League, 1300 Connecticut Ave. NW, Washington, D.C. 20036. W. G. Flinn, secretary-treasurer.

Educational fund
Receipts: $301,935.68
Expenditures: $318,979.80

General fund
Receipts: $256,872.39
Expenditures: $404,030.21

Marine Engineers Beneficial Association Political Action Fund (AFL-CIO), Pacific Coast District (District No. 1), 17 Battery Place, Room 1930, New York, N.Y. 10004. Leon Shapiro, treasurer.

Receipts: $126,272.43
Expenditures: $105,022.98

Retirees' Group
Receipts: $224,616.80
Expenditures: $294.312.93

Marine Engineers Beneficial Association Political Action Fund (AFL-CIO), District 2, 650 4th Ave., Brooklyn, N.Y. 11232. John F. Brady, treasurer.

Receipts: $60,495.00
Expenditures: $70,193.10

National Maritime Union, Fighting Fund*, 36 7th Ave., New York, N.Y. Shannon J. Wall, treasurer. (1970 report filed for period of June 21, 1969 to Nov. 30, 1970.)

Receipts: $187,705.32
Expenditures: $27,150.00

New York Joint Board, Committee on Political Education, 31 W. 15th St., New York, N.Y. 10011. Samuel Masler, secretary.

Receipts: None reported
Expenditures: None reported

New York Joint Board Political Action Fund, 31 West 15th St., New York, N.Y. 10011. Louis Hollander, president.

Receipts: none reported
Expenditures: $1,152.80

Ohio DRIVE, 2070 E. 22nd St., Cleveland, Ohio 44115. John I. Felice Jr., secretary-treasurer.

Receipts: $112,631.35
Expenditures: $104.505.34

Oil, Chemical, and Atomic Workers International Union, P.O. Box 2812, Denver, Colo. 80201. B. J. Schafer, secretary-treasurer.

Receipts: $48,190.10
Expenditures: $48,478.96

Political Action Committee of the Joint Board of Shirt, Leisurewear, Robe, Glove and Rainwear Workers' Union,* 111 E. 15th St., New York, N.Y. 10003. Charles J. Garrahan, treasurer. (1970 report filed through Oct. 31.)

Receipts: $2,544.00
Expenditures: $2,623.50

Political Information League of Teamsters,* 435 S. Hawley St., Toledo, Ohio 43609. Paul Steinberg, president. (1970 report filed through Dec. 14.)

Receipts: $1,700.00
Expenditures: $1,700.00

Railway Clerks Political League, 716 Railway Labor Building, 400 1st St. NW, Washington, D.C., 20001. D. J. Sullivan, secretary-treasurer.

Receipts: $85,861.23
Expenditures: $86,448.76

Railway Labor's Political League-BLF & E Division, 15401 Detroit Ave., Cleveland, Ohio, 44107. R. R. Bryant, treasurer.

Receipts: $26,832.27
Expenditures: $47,070.00

Rural Political Education Committee, P.O. Box 387, Denver, Colo., Kenneth L. Motz, treasurer.

Receipts: $1,849.00
Expenditures: $3,177.28

Seafarers International Union of North America, AFL-CIO, Committee on Political Education, 675 4th Ave., Brooklyn, N.Y. 11232. Al Kerr, secretary-treasurer.

Receipts: $21,842.00
Expenditures: $30,037.57

Seafarers International Union of North America, AFL-CIO, Political Activity Donation, 675 4th Ave., Brooklyn, N.Y. 11232. Al Kerr, secretary-treasurer.

Receipts: $302,431.17
Expenditures: $422,649.92

Sheet Metal Workers' International Association Political Action League,* 1000 Connecticut Ave. NW, Washington, D.C. 20036. David S. Turner, treasurer. (1970 report filed through Nov. 30.)

Receipts: $26,387.28
Expenditures: $26,683.07

Teamsters Joint Council No. 13, 300 S. Grand Ave., St. Louis, Mo. 63103. Dale Ferris, treasurer.

Receipts: None reported
Expenditures: $8,482.36

Teamsters Local Union No. 688*, 300 Grand Blvd., St. Louis, Mo. 63103. J. Thanous, secretary-treasurer. (1970 report filed through Oct. 26.)

Receipts: None reported
Expenditures: $47,283.29

Tennessee Joint Council of Teamsters No. 87, 125 57th St. N, P.O. Box 4508, Birmingham, Ala. 35206. G. Sam Webb, treasurer.

Receipts: $7,550.00
Expenditures: $13,714.00

Texas Conference of Teamsters, 6162 E. Mockingbird, Suite 212, Dallas, Texas 75214. (No signator on the report.)

Receipts: $5,477.16
Expenditures: $4,075.00

Textile Workers Union of America, 99 University Place, New York, N.Y. 10003. Sol Stetin, general secretary-treasurer.

Receipts: $22,023.65
Expenditures: $29,124.16

United Auto Workers, Committee on Political Education,* 8000 E. Jefferson, Detroit, Mich. 48214. Emil Mazey, secretary-treasurer. (1970 report filed through Aug. 31.)

Receipts: $267,709.73
Expenditures: $81,567.19

United Federation of Teachers Political Action Committee, 54 East 21st St., New York, N.Y. 10010. Ray Frankel, treasurer.

Receipts: $11,845.97
Expenditures: $10,664.20

United Plant Guard Workers of America, Political Action Committee, 14214 East Jefferson, Detroit, Mich. 48215. Ray C. Hildebrandt, secretary-treasurer.

Receipts: $2,227.86
Expenditures: $4,163.00

United Rubber, Cork, Linoleum and Plastic Workers of America, AFL-CIO, 87 South High St., Akron, Ohio 44308. Peter Bommarito, president.

Receipts: None reported
Expenditures: $31,440.00

United Steelworkers of America Voluntary Political Action Fund, 1500 Commonwealth Building, Pittsburgh, Pa. 15222. Walter J. Burke, secretary-treasurer.

Receipts: $226,323.16
Expenditures: $307,401.16

PEACE

(Total Expenditures: $536,602.45)

Boston Lawyers' Vietnam Committee Campaign Fund, 73 Tremont St., Room 344, Boston, Mass. 02108. L. Scott Harshbarger, treasurer.

Receipts: $10,176.13
Expenditures: $17,113.81

Congressional Action Fund, P.O. Box 8108, Washington, D.C. 20024, Sharon Rulzick, secretary-treasurer.

Receipts: $42,376.19
Expenditures: $36,200.00

Congressional Peace Campaign Committee, 3003 Van Ness St. NW, Washington, D.C. 20008. Edith J. Miller, treasurer.

Receipts: $47.54
Expenditures: $1,348.44

Fund for New Priorities in America,* 415 Lexington Ave., New York, N.Y. 10017. Eli J. Sagen, vice chairman. (1970 report filed through Oct. 20.)

Receipts: $104,550.00
Expenditures: $49,650.00

Lawyers Committee for Effective Action to End the War,* One Chase Manhattan Plaza, New York, N.Y. 10005. Carol Bellamy, chairman. (1970 report filed through Oct. 31.)

Receipts: $69,854.03
Expenditures: $67,970.58

Metamorphosis: The Committee for a Peace Congress,* 330 3rd Ave., Apt. 6-K, New York, N.Y. 10010. Stephen H. Schwartz, treasurer. (1970 report filed through Nov. 4.)

Receipts: $14,755.18
Expenditures: $11,156.62

Peace Candidates Fund*, P.O. Box 2446, Washington, D.C. 20013. Carol Valverde, treasurer. (1970 report filed through Oct. 23.)

Receipts: $1,497.64
Expenditures: $989.95

Peace Commencement Fund, 386 Riverway, Apt. No. 4, Boston, Mass. 02115. Robert L. Kirkman.

Receipts: $75,132.93
Expenditures: $75,132.93

Peace Elections Desk, 3710 Raymond St., Chevy Chase, Md. 20015. Mary Meehan.

Receipts: $1,056.63
Expenditures: $1,056.63

Peace Votes, Box 2700, Washington D.C. 20013. Jeff Lerner, co-chairman.

Receipts: $262.50
Expenditures: $262.50

Task Force for Peace, P.O. Box 48458, Los Angeles, Calif. 90048. Stanley M. Gortikov, chairman, treasurer.

Receipts: $46,424.86
Expenditures: $46,252.79

Universities National Anti-War Fund, Box 800, Cambridge, Mass. 02139. Allan Robinson, treasurer.

Receipts: $233,770.94
Expenditures: $229,468.20

OTHERS

(Total Expenditures: $727,245.34.)

Christian Nationalist Crusade, P.O. Box 27895, Los Angeles, Calif. 90027. E. M. Smith.

Receipts: $356,812.94
Expenditures: $297,864.58

Employment Education Committee*, 402 Frick Bldg., Pittsburg, Pa. 15219. Richard Edwin, treasurer. (1970 report filed for period of Oct. 31, 1968, to Aug. 31, 1970, and for period of Sept. 1, 1970, to Oct. 31, 1970.)

Receipts: $200.00
Expenditures: $200.00

Federalist Campaign Fund, P.O. Box 4936, Washington, D.C. 20008. Illene M. Harrison, secretary-treasurer.

Receipts: $7,310.90
Expenditures: $7,310.90

Fund for Good Government, 20 Pine St., New York, N.Y. 10015. Raymond F. Adams, treasurer.

Receipts: $12,139.00
Expenditures: $13,580.00

Government Improvement Group*, P.O. Box 19094, Washington, D.C. 20036. James E. Mack, treasurer. (1970 report filed for period June 1 through Oct. 29.)

Receipts: $8,514.00
Expenditures: $15,718.00

INA Political Action Committee, P.O. Box 7124, Benjamin Franklin Station, 12th and Pennsylvania Ave. NW, Washington, D.C. 20044. Bertram C. Dedman, treasurer.

Receipts: $9,535.00
Expenditures: $9,177.20

Indiana Friends of Rural Electrification, R.R. 1, Gosport, Ind. 47433. M. John Stierwalt, treasurer. (1970 report filed for period of Nov. 1, 1968 to Oct. 29, 1970.)

Receipts: $17,473.54
Expenditures: $17,406.40

League of Conservation Voters, 917 15th St. NW, Washington, D.C. 20005. Joe Browder, treasurer.

Receipts: $77,107.68
Expenditures: $76,010.53

National Association of PRO America, P.O. Box 649, Littlefield, Tex. 79339. Mrs. Charles E. McLean, treasurer.

Receipts: $4,908.31
Expenditures: $2,640.13

National States Rights Party, P.O. Box 6263, Savannah, Ga. 31405. Peter L. Xavier, treasurer.

Receipts: $39,432.55
Expenditures: $40,298.14

The Public Interest Committee, c/o Robert N. Thurston, 345 Merchandise Mart, Chicago, Ill. 60654. Sam H. Flint, treasurer.

Receipts: $9,427.00
Expenditures: $9,405.65

Riverside Civic Association, Room 2101, 1000 Lake Shore Dr., Chicago, Ill. 60611. H. J. Nord, treasurer.

Receipts: $4,025.00
Expenditures: $2,853.15

United Congressional Appeal, P.O. Box 1902, Washington, D.C. 20013. Clara Sandahl, treasurer.

Receipts: $87,127.00
Expenditures: $106,235.33

United Republicans of America, 415 2nd St. NE, Washington, D.C. 20013. Wainwright Dawson Jr., executive director.

Receipts: $83,172.43
Expenditures: $81,711.28

Volunteers for Better Government, P.O. Box 1007, Kingsport, Tenn. 37662. C. A. Ross Jr., secretary-treasurer.

Receipts: $33,345.27
Expenditures: $26,035.96

Young America's Campaign Committee, 2130 Brooks Drive, Apt. 522, Suitland, Md. 20028. Randal Cornell Teague, chairman and acting treasurer.

Receipts: $21,634.73
Expenditures: $20,798.09

THE STATUTORY REQUIREMENT

Following are excerpts from the Federal Corrupt Practices Act (2 USC 241 et seq.), which requires political committees to report receipts and expenditures.

"The term 'political committee' includes any committee, association or organization which accepts contributions or makes expenditures for the purpose of influencing or attempting to influence the election of candidates . . . (1) in two or more states, or (2) . . . if such committee . . . is a branch or subsidiary of a national committee, association or organization. . . . "

"The treasurer of a political committee shall file with the Clerk . . .
"1. The name and address of each person who has made a contribution . . . of $100 or more . . . ;
"2. The total sum of the contributions . . . ;
"4. The name and address of each person to whom an expenditure . . . of $10 or more has been made . . . ;
"5. The total sum of all expenditures made by or on behalf of such committee . . . . "

APPENDIX II

Final Returns for 1970 Elections

Democrats polled 54.7 per cent of the major-party votes in the 1970 House elections, increasing their majority from 246-189 to 255-180. A *National Journal* compilation of official 1970 election returns also revealed that Democrats received 56.8 per cent of the major-party votes in the 35 Senate races and 51.1 per cent in the 35 Governors' elections. (See Tables 1 and 2.)

The Democratic percentage for House voting was up from 51.1 in 1968 and 51.3 in 1966. Democrats have registered a majority of major-party House votes in each election since 1946. The Democrats also reduced their number of "marginal" districts—those won by less than 55 per cent of the vote—from 38 to 29, while the number of Republican marginal districts increased from 25 to 31. National interest groups often focus their campaign efforts on marginal districts. These districts also indicate areas where redistricting might cause shifts of party power.

In the Senate, the Democrats' majority decreased from 57-43 to 55-45 as a result of the election. The party's 56.8 per cent of the major-party votes also represented a decline from the 57.2 per cent it recorded in 1964, when virtually the same seats were at stake. The gubernatorial party balance shifted from 32 Republicans and 18 Democrats to 29 Democrats and 21 Republicans.

The voter turnout of 54,753,755 for House elections compared with 51,303,647 in 1962 and 52,881,673 in 1966—the last two mid-term elections. The 1970 House turnout was 45.4 per cent of the 120,701,000 estimated by the Census Bureau as eligible to vote. The percentage of eligible voters who participated in the 1962 elections was 47.0; in 1966, it was 45.6. (The Census Bureau reported December 24, 1970, that 54.6 per cent of those eligible had voted in the 1970 elections—indicating a total vote of 65,888,000. Some persons may have voted for Senators or Governors but not House Members. However, Census surveys often indicate votes higher than those actually recorded.)

(*National Journal* researchers Patrick McMahon, Susan Mueller and Monica Benderly compiled these election returns. Incumbents are designated by asterisk (*); in some instances, candidates ran on more than one party ticket.)

Table 1   Vote totals, 1970 election *

	House votes	pct.	Senate votes	pct.	Governors votes	pct.
Democrats	29,226,547	53.4	25,435,301	52.3	21,467,828	49.6
Republicans	24,198,137	44.2	19,336,375	39.7	20,557,966	47.5
others	1,329,071	2.4	3,844,080	8.0	1,239,977	2.9

* The vote totals do not include votes for unopposed candidates in Arkansas and Florida, where uncontested races are not tabulated. The Democratic and Republican vote totals do not include votes cast on minor party tickets for candidates in New York running under two or more party labels.

Table 2   Major-party percentages

	House of Representatives † overall	East	Mid-west	South	West	Senate	Governor
Democrats	54.7	53.6	51.7	64.8	51.9	56.8	51.1
Republicans	45.3	46.4	48.3	35.2	48.1	43.2	48.9

† In this breakdown, the East is a 12-state region extending through Maryland, Pennsylvania and West Virginia; the Midwest is a 12-state area extending south through Kansas, Missouri, Indiana and Ohio; the South includes 13 states; and the West includes Montana, Wyoming, Colorado, New Mexico and the nine states farther west.

ALABAMA

AC—Alabama Conservative Party
Ind—independent
NDPA—National Democratic Party of Alabama
P—Alabama Prohibition Party
W—Whig Party

Governor

George C. Wallace, D	637,046	74.5
John Logan Cashin, NDPA	125,491	14.7
A. C. Shelton, Ind	75,679	8.9
Jerome B. Couch, P	9,705	1.1
Menter G. Walker Jr., Ind	3,534	0.4
John Watts, W	3,497	0.4

Wallace plurality: 511,555

U.S. Representative (by district)

1 (Southwestern counties, Mobile)

Jack Edwards, R*	63,457	60.6
John C. Tyson, D	27,457	26.2
Noble Beasley, NDPA	13,798	13.2

Edwards plurality: 36,000

2 (South Central counties, Montgomery)

William L. Dickinson, R*	62,316	61.4
Jack Winfield, D	25,966	25.6
Percy Smith Jr., NDPA	13,281	13.1

Dickinson plurality: 36,350

3 (Southeastern counties, Dothan)

George W. Andrews, D*	70,015	89.1
Detroit Lee, NDPA	8,537	10.9

Andrews plurality: 61,478

4 (East central counties, Anniston)

Bill Nichols, D*	77,701	83.7
Glenn Andrews, R	13,217	14.2
Wilpha Harrel Jr., NDPA	1,903	2.1

Nichols plurality: 64,484

5 (West central counties, Tuscaloosa)

Walter Flowers, D*	78,368	75.9
T. Y. Rogers, NDPA	24,863	24.1

Flowers plurality: 53,505

6 (Birmingham)

John Buchanan, R*	50,060	60.1
John C. Schmarkey, D	31,378	37.7
Dan C. Moore, AC	1,900	2.3

Buchanan plurality: 18,682

7 (North central counties, Gadsden)

Tom Bevill, D*	87,797	100.0

8 (Northern counties, Huntsville)

Robert E. Jones, D*	76,413	84.8
Ken Hearn, AC	7,599	8.4
Thornton Stanley, NDPA	4,846	5.4
Thomas Lee Harris, Ind	1,200	1.3

Jones plurality: 68,814

ALASKA

AIP—American Independent Party

Governor

William A. Egan, D	42,309	52.4
Keith H. Miller, R*	37,264	46.1
Ralph Milton Anderson, AIP	1,206	1.5

Egan plurality: 5,045

Senator

Ted Stevens, R*	47,908	59.6
Wendell P. Kay, D	32,456	40.4

Stevens plurality: 15,452

U.S. Representative (at large)

Nicholas J. Begich, D	44,137	55.1
Frank H. Murkowski, R	35,947	44.9

Begich plurality: 8,190

ARIZONA

AIP—American Independent Party

Governor

Jack Williams, R*	209,356	50.9
Raul H. Castro, D	202,053	49.1

Williams plurality: 7,303

Senator

Paul J. Fannin, R*	228,284	56.0
Sam Grossman, D	179,512	44.0

Fannin plurality: 48,772

U.S. Representative (by district)

1 (Parts of Maricopa County, Phoenix)

John J. Rhodes, R*	99,706	68.5
Gerald A. Pollock, D	45,870	31.5

Rhodes plurality: 53,836

2 (Southern counties, Tucson)

Morris K. Udall, D*	86,760	69.0
Morris Herring, R	37,561	29.9
Cliff (Tamale) Thomallo, AIP	1,357	1.1

Udall plurality: 49,199

3 (Northern counties, part of Maricopa County)

Sam Steiger, R*	81,239	62.1
Orren Beaty, D	49,626	37.9

Steiger plurality: 31,613

ARKANSAS

AIP — American Independent Party
X — Votes not tabulated: no contest

Governor

Dale Bumpers, D	375,648	61.7
Winthrop Rockefeller, R*	197,418	32.4
Walter L. Carruth, AIP	36,132	5.9

Bumpers plurality: 178,230

U.S. Representative (by district)

1 (Eastern counties, Memphis suburbs)

Bill Alexander, D*	X	100.0

2 (North central counties, Little Rock)

Wilbur D. Mills, D*	X	100.0

3 (Western counties, Fort Smith)

John Paul Hammerschmidt, R*	115,532	66.7
Donald Poe, D	57,679	33.3

Hammerschmidt plurality: 57,853

4 (Southern counties)

David Pryor, D*	X	100.0

CALIFORNIA

AIP — American Independent Party
P&F — Peace and Freedom Party

Governor

Ronald Reagan, R*	3,439,664	52.8
Jess Unruh, D	2,938,607	45.1
Richardo Romo, P&F	65,954	1.0
William K. Shearer, AIP	65,847	1.0

Reagan plurality: 501,057

Senator

John V. Tunney, D	3,496,558	53.9
George Murphy, R*	2,877,617	44.3
Charles C. Ripley, AIP	61,251	0.9
Robert Scheer, P&F	56,731	0.9

Tunney plurality: 618,941

U.S. Representative (by district)

1 (Northern coastal counties)

Don H. Clausen, R*	108,358	63.4
William M. Kortum, D	62,688	36.6

Clausen plurality: 45,670

2 (Northeastern and central counties)

Harold T. Johnson, D*	151,070	77.9
Lloyd E. Gilbert, R	37,223	19.2
Jack R. Carrigg, AIP	5,681	2.9

Johnson plurality: 113,847

3 (Sacramento)

John E. Moss, D*	117,496	61.6
Elmore J. Duffy, R	69,811	36.6
Allen E. Priest, AIP	3,554	1.9

Moss plurality: 47,685

4 (North Central Valley counties, Vallejo)

Robert L. Leggett, D*	103,485	68.0
Andrew Gyorke, R	48,783	32.0

Leggett plurality: 54,702

5 (Eastern San Francisco)

Phillip Burton, D*	76,567	70.8
John E. Parks, R	31,570	29.2

Burton plurality: 44,997

6 (Western San Francisco, lower Marin County)

William S. Mailliard, R*	96,393	53.4
Russell R. Miller, D	84,255	46.6

Mailliard plurality: 12,138

7 (Berkeley, part of Oakland)

Ronald V. Dellums, D	89,784	57.3
John E. Healy, R	64,691	41.3
Sarah Scahill, P&F	2,156	1.4

Dellums plurality: 25,093

8 (Part of Alameda County, part of Oakland)

George P. Miller, D*	104,311	69.0
Michael A. Crane, R	46,872	31.0

Miller plurality: 57,439

9 (Parts of Alameda, Santa Clara counties, San Jose)

Don Edwards, D*	120,041	69.1
Mark Guerra, R	49,556	28.5
Edmon V. Kaiser, AIP	4,009	2.3

Edwards plurality: 70,485

10 (Part of Santa Clara County, Palo Alto)

Charles S. Gubser, R*	135,864	62.0
Stuart D. McLean, D	80,530	36.8
Joyce W. Stancliffe, AIP	2,651	1.2

Gubser plurality: 55,334

11 (San Mateo County, Redwood City, Pacifica)

Paul N. McCloskey Jr., R*	144,500	77.5
Robert E. Gomperts, D	39,188	21.0
Jack W. Wilson (write-in)	2,786	1.5

McCloskey plurality: 105,312

12 (South central coastal counties, Monterey)

Burt L. Talcott, R*	95,549	63.6
O'Brien Riordan, D	50,942	33.9
Herbert H. Foster Jr., P&F	3,682	2.5

Talcott plurality: 44,607

13 (Santa Barbara, Ventura counties)

Charles M. Teague, R*	127,507	58.5
Gray K. Hart, D	87,980	40.4
Maude I. Jordet, AIP	2,339	1.1

Teague plurality: 39,527

14 (Contra Costa County, Richmond)

Jerome R. Waldie, D*	148,655	74.5
Byron D. Athan, R	50,750	25.5

Waldie plurality: 97,905

15 (Central Valley counties, Stockton)

John J. McFall, D*	98,442	63.1
Sam Van Dyken, R	55,546	35.6
Francis E. (Gill) Gillings, AIP	1,994	1.3

McFall plurality: 42,896

16 (Central Valley counties, Fresno)

B. F. Sisk, D*	95,118	66.4
Phillip V. Sanchez, R	43,843	30.6
James W. Scott, AIP	4,237	3.0

Sisk plurality: 51,275

17 (Southern Los Angeles, Torrance)

Glenn M. Anderson, D*	83,739	62.2
Michael C. Donaldson, R	47,774	35.5
Robert W. Copeland, AIP	1,724	1.3
Thomas E. Mathews, P&F	1,292	1.0

Anderson plurality: 35,965

18 (South Central Valley counties, Bakersfield)

Robert B. (Bob) Mathias, R*	86,071	63.2
Milton Spartacus Miller, D	48,415	35.5
Nora E. Hensley, AIP	1,709	1.3

Mathias plurality: 37,656

19 (Southeastern Los Angeles County)

Chet Holifield, D*	98,578	70.4
Bill Jones, R	41,462	29.6

Holifield plurality: 57,116

20 (North central Los Angeles, Pasadena)

H. Allen Smith, R*	116,437	69.1
Michael M. Stolzberg, D	50,033	29.7
Earl C. Harper, AIP	2,100	1.2

Smith plurality: 66,404

21 (Central Los Angeles)

Augustus F. Hawkins, D*	75,127	94.5
Southey M. Johnson, R	4,349	5.5

Hawkins plurality: 70,778

22 (Northwestern Los Angeles)

James C. Corman, D*	95,256	59.4
Tom Hayden, R	63,297	39.5
Callis R. Johnson, AIP	1,880	1.2

Corman plurality: 31,959

23 (Central Los Angeles)

Del Clawson, R*	77,346	63.3
G. L. (Jerry) Chapman, D	44,767	36.7

Clawson plurality: 32,579

24 (Northeastern Los Angeles County)

John H. Rousselot, R*	124,071	65.1
Myrlie B. Evers, D	61,777	32.4
Brian Scanlon, AIP	3,018	1.6
Harold (Hess) Kaplan, P&F	1,858	1.0

Rousselot plurality: 62,294

25 (Eastern Los Angeles County)

Charles E. Wiggins, R*	116,169	63.3
Leslie W. (Les) Cravens, D	64,386	35.1
Kevin Scanlon, AIP	2,994	1.6

Wiggins plurality: 51,783

26 (Western Los Angeles, Beverly Hills)

Thomas M. Rees, D*	130,499	71.3
Nathaniel Jay Friedman, R	47,260	25.8
Lewis B. McCammon, P&F	3,677	2.0
Howard E. Hallinan, AIP	1,639	0.9

Rees plurality: 83,239

27 (North central Los Angeles, western Kern counties)

Barry M. Goldwater Jr., R*	139,326	66.7
N. (Toni) Kimmel, D	63,652	30.5
Edward Richer, P&F	3,306	1.6
John H. Hind, AIP	2,642	1.3

Goldwater plurality: 75,674

28 (Western Los Angeles, Santa Monica)

Alphonzo Bell, R*	154,691	69.3
Don McLaughlin, D	57,882	25.9
Derck A. Gordon, AIP	5,759	2.6
Jane E. Gordon, P&F	4,971	2.2

Bell plurality: 96,809

29 (Central Los Angeles)

George E. Danielson, D	71,308	62.6
Tom McMann, R	42,620	37.4

Danielson plurality: 29,048

30 (Central Los Angeles)

Edward R. Roybal, D*	63,903	68.3
Samuel M. Cavnar, R	28,038	29.9
Boris Belousov, AIP	1,681	1.8

Roybal plurality: 35,865

31 (West central Los Angeles)

Charles H. Wilson, D*	102,071	73.2
Fred L. Casmir, R	37,416	26.8

Wilson plurality: 64,655

32 (Southern Los Angeles, Long Beach)

Craig Hosmer, R*	119,340	71.5
Walter L. Mallonee, D	44,278	26.5
John S. Donohue, P&F	3,227	1.9

Hosmer plurality: 75,062

33 (San Bernadino County)

Jerry L. Pettis, R*	116,093	72.2
Chester M. Wright, D	44,764	27.8

Pettis plurality: 71,329

34 (Northern Orange County, Anaheim)

Richard T. Hanna, D*	101,664	54.5
William J. (Bill) Teague, R	82,167	44.0
Lee R. Rayburn, AIP	2,843	1.5

Hanna plurality: 19,497

35 (Northern San Diego, southern Orange counties)

John G. Schmitz, R*	192,765	67.0
Thomas B. Lenhart, D	87,019	30.3
Francis R. Halpern, P&F	7,742	2.7

Schmitz plurality: 105,746

36 (Central San Diego, La Mesa)

Bob Wilson, R*	132,446	71.5
Daniel K. Hostetter, D	44,841	24.2
Walter H. Koppleman, P&F	5,139	2.8
Orville J. David, AIP	2,723	1.5

Wilson plurality: 87,605

37 (Southwestern San Diego County)

Lionel Van Deerlin, D*	93,952	72.1
James B. Kuhn, R	31,968	24.5
Faye B. Brice, AIP	2,962	2.3
Fritjof Thygeson, P&F	1,386	1.1

Van Deerlin plurality: 61,984

38 (Southern counties, Riverside)

Victor V. Veysey, R	87,476	49.8
David A. Tunno, D	85,684	48.8
William E. Pasley, AIP	2,481	1.4

Veysey plurality: 1,792

COLORADO

AIP – American Independent Party
Ind – independent
LRU – La Raza Unida
SW – Socialist Workers Party

Governor

John A. Love, R*	350,973	52.5
Mark Hogan, D	302,406	45.3
Albert Gurule, LRU	12,179	1.8
Walter R. Plankinton, AIP	2,049	0.3
James Lauderdale, SW	1,143	0.1

Love plurality: 48,567

U.S. Representative (by district)

1 (Denver)

James D. McKevitt, R	84,643	51.5
Craig S. Barnes, D	74,444	45.3
Salvadore Carpio Jr., LRU	5,257	3.2

McKevitt plurality: 10,199

2 (Denver suburbs)

Donald G. Brotzman, R*	125,274	63.4
Richard G. Gebhardt, D	72,339	36.6

Brotzman plurality: 52,935

3 (Southeastern counties, Colorado Springs)

Frank E. Evans, D*	87,000	63.6
John C. (Jack) Mitchell Jr., R	45,610	33.4
Martin P. Serna, LRU	1,828	1.3
Walter N. Cranson, Ind	1,598	1.2
Henry John Olshaw, Ind	652	0.5

Evans plurality: 41,390

4 (Western and northern counties, Greeley)

Wayne N. Aspinall, D*	76,244	55.1
Bill Gossard, R	62,169	44.9

Aspinall plurality: 14,085

CONNECTICUT

AIP – American Independent Party
APP – A Public Party
CPP – Common People's Party
DI – Dodd Independent Party

Governor

Thomas J. Meskill, R	582,160	53.8
Emilio Q. Daddario, D	500,561	46.2
Scattered	76	0.0

Meskill plurality: 81,599

Senator

Lowell P. Weicker Jr., R	454,721	41.7
Joseph D. Duffey, D	368,111	33.8
Thomas J. Dodd, DI*	266,497	24.5
Scattered	24	0.0

Weicker plurality: 86,610

U.S. Representative (by district)

1 (Hartford)

William R. Cotter, D	88,374	48.7
Antonina P. Uccello, R	87,209	48.1
Edward T. Coll, APP	5,774	3.2
Scattered	10	0.0

Cotter plurality: 1,165

2 (Eastern counties)

Robert H. Steele, R	92,846	53.5
John F. Pickett, D	81,492	46.7
Scattered	4	0.0

Steele plurality: 11,354

2 (To fill vacancy)

Robert H. Steele, R	92,816	53.3
John F. Pickett, D	81,333	46.7
Scattered	1	0.0

Steele plurality: 11,483

3 (New Haven)

Robert N. Giaimo, D*	89,042	54.6
Robert J. Dunn, R	69,084	42.3
Richard P. Antonetti, DI	5,062	3.1
Scattered	14	0.0

Giaimo plurality: 19,958

4 (Part of Fairfield County, Bridgeport)

Steward B. McKinney, R	104,494	56.6
T. F. Gilroy Daly, D	78,699	42.6
Eileen M. Emard, AIP	1,428	0.8

McKinney plurality: 25,795

5 (Southwestern counties, Waterbury)

John S. Monagan, D*	96,947	54.7
James T. Patterson, R	78,414	44.3
Alphonse Avitabile, CPP	1,727	1.0
Scattered	4	0.0

Monagan plurality: 18,533

6 (Northwestern counties, New Britain)

Ella T. Grasso, D	96,969	51.1
Richard C. Kilbourn, R	92,906	48.9
Scattered	5	0.0

Grasso plurality: 4,063

DELAWARE

AIP — American Independent Party

Senator

William V. Roth Jr., R	94,979	58.8
Jacob Zimmerman, D	64,740	40.1
Donald G. Gies, AIP	1,720	1.1

Roth plurality: 30,239

U.S. Representative (at large)

Pierre S. du Pont IV, R	86,125	53.7
John D. Daniello, D	71,429	44.6
Walter J. Hoey, AIP	2,759	1.7

du Pont plurality: 14,696

FLORIDA

Ind — independent
X — Votes not tabulated: no contest.

Governor

Reubin Askew, D	948,305	56.0
Claude R. Kirk Jr., R*	746,243	44.0
Louis R. Beller, Ind	265	0.0

Askew plurality: 202,062

Senator

Lawton Chiles, D	902,438	53.9
William C. Cramer, R	772,817	46.1
Jim Fair, Ind	123	0.0

Chiles plurality: 129,621

U.S. Representative (by district)

1 (Northwestern counties, Pensacola)

Robert L. F. Sikes, D*	88,744	80.2
H. D. (Sam) Shuemake, R	21,951	19.8

Sikes plurality: 66,793

2 (North central counties, Tallahassee)

Don Fuqua, D*	X	100.0

3 (Jacksonville)

Charles E. Bennett, D*	X	100.0

4 (North central counties, Daytona Beach)

Bill Chappell Jr., D*	75,673	57.8
Leonard V. Wood, R	55,311	42.2

Chappell plurality: 20,362

5 (East central counties, Orlando)

Louis Frey Jr., R*	110,841	75.8
Roy Girod, D	35,398	24.2

Frey plurality: 75,443

6 (Tampa and suburbs)

Sam Gibbons, D*	78,832	72.3
Robert A. Carter, R	30,252	27.7

Gibbons plurality: 48,580

7 (South central counties, Lakeland, Sarasota)

James A. Haley, D*	78,535	53.4
Joe Z. Lovingood, R	68,646	46.6

Haley plurality: 9,889

8 (St. Petersburg and suburbs)

C. W. Young, R	120,466	67.2
Ted A. Bailey, D	58,094	32.8

Young plurality: 61,562

9 (South central counties, West Palm Beach)

Paul G. Rogers, D*	120,565	70.6
Emil F. Danciu, R	50,146	29.4

Rogers plurality: 70,419

10 (Northern Dade County, Fort Lauderdale)

J. Herbert Burke, R*	81,170	54.1
James J. Ward Jr., D	68,847	45.9

Burke plurality: 12,323

11 (Central Dade County, northern Miami)

Claude Pepper, D*	X	100.0

12 (Southern counties, part of Miami)

Dante B. Fascell, D*	75,895	71.1
Robert A. Zinzell, R	29,935	28.9

Fascell plurality: 45,960

GEORGIA

Governor

Jimmy Carter, D	620,419	59.3
Hal Suit, R	424,983	40.6
Write-in votes	1,261	0.1

Carter plurality: 195,436

U.S. Representative (by district)

1 (Southeastern counties, Savannah)

G. Elliott Hagan, D*	70,856	100.0
Write-in votes	32	0.0

2 (Southwestern counties, Albany)

Dawson Mathis, D	59,994	91.8
Thomas (Tom) Ragsdale, R	5,376	8.2
Write-in votes	2	0.0

Mathis plurality: 54,618

3 (West central counties, Columbus)

Jack Brinkley, D*	54,588	100.0

4 (Atlanta suburbs)

Benjamin B. Blackburn, R*	85,848	65.2
Franklin Shumake, D	45,908	34.8
Write-in votes	7	0.0

Blackburn plurality: 39,940

5 (Atlanta)

Fletcher Thompson, R*	78,540	57.3
Andrew Young, D	58,394	42.6
Write-in votes	26	0.0

Thompson plurality: 20,146

6 (West central counties)

John J. Flynt Jr., D*	92,500	100.0
Write-in votes	8	0.0

7 (Northwestern counties, Rome, Marietta)

John W. Davis, D*	80,149	72.5
Dick Fullerton, R	30,392	27.5
Write-in votes	12	0.0

Davis plurality: 49,757

8 (Southeastern counties, Brunswick)

W. S. Stuckey, D*	52,446	100.0
Write-in votes	1	0.0

9 (Northeastern counties, Gainesville)

Phil M. Landrum, D*	64,603	71.7
Bob Cooper, R	25,476	28.3
Write-in votes	3	0.0

Landrum plurality: 39,127

10 (North central counties, Augusta)

Robert G. Stephens Jr., D*	74,075	100.0
Write-in votes	5	0.0

HAWAII

Governor

John A. Burns, D*	137,812	57.6
Samuel P. King, R	101,249	42.4

Burns plurality: 36,563

Senator

Hiram L. Fong, R*	124,163	51.6
Cecil Heftel, D	116,597	48.4

Fong plurality: 7,566

U.S. Representative (by district)

1 (Honolulu)

Spark M. Matsunaga, D*	85,411	72.9
Richard K. Cockey, R	31,764	27.1

Matsunaga plurality: 53,647

2 (Remainder of state)

Patsy T. Mink, D*	91,038	100.0

IDAHO

AIP — American Independent Party

Governor

Cecil D. Andrus, D	128,004	52.2
Don W. Samuelson, R*	117,108	47.8

Andrus plurality: 10,896

U.S. Representative (by district)

1 (Western counties, Boise)

James A. McClure, R*	77,515	58.2
William J. (Bill) Brauner, D	55,743	41.8

McClure plurality: 21,772

2 (Eastern counties, Pocatello)

Orval Hansen, R*	66,428	65.7
Marden E. Wells, D	31,872	31.5
Joel A. Anderson, AIP	2,625	2.6
Marianne Condon (write-in)	134	0.1

Hansen plurality: 34,556

ILLINOIS

SL — Socialist Labor Party
SW — Socialist Workers Party
† — Rep. Charlotte T. Reid resigned October 7, 1971, to become a commissioner on the Federal Communications Commission.

Senator

Adlai E. Stevenson III, D	2,065,054	57.4
Ralph T. Smith, R*	1,519,718	42.2
Lynn Henderson, SW	8,859	0.2
Louis Fisher, SL	5,564	0.2
Write-in votes	77	0.0

Stevenson plurality: 545,336

U.S. Representative (by district)

1 (South side Chicago)

Ralph H. Metcalfe, D	93,272	91.0
Janet Roberts Jennings, R	9,267	9.0

Metcalfe plurality: 84,005

2 (South side Chicago)

Abner J. Mikva, D*	88,252	74.7
Harold E. Marks, R	29,853	25.3

Mikva plurality: 58,399

3 (Southwestern Chicago)

Morgan F. Murphy, D	97,693	68.9
Robert P. Rowan, R	44,013	31.1
Write-in votes	7	0.0

Murphy plurality: 53,680

4 (Chicago suburbs)

Edward J. Derwinski, R*	117,590	68.0
Melvin W. Morgan, D	55,328	32.0
Write-in votes	10	0.0

Derwinski plurality: 62,262

5 (Central Chicago)

John C. Kluczynski, D*	97,278	68.8
Edmund W. Ochenkowski, R	44,049	31.2

Kluczynski plurality: 53,229

6 (West side Chicago)

George W. Collins, D	68,182	56.2
Alex J. Zabrosky, R	53,240	43.8
Write-in votes	2	0.0

Collins plurality: 14,942

6 (To fill vacancy)

George W. Collins, D	68,949	55.7
Alex J. Zabrosky, R	54,746	44.3

Collins plurality: 14,203

7 (Downtown Chicago)

Frank Annunzio, D*	70,112	87.3
Thomas J. Lento, R	10,235	12.7

Annunzio plurality: 59,877

8 (Central and west side Chicago)

Dan Rostenkowski, D*	98,453	73.9
Henry S. Kaplinski, R	34,841	26.1

Rostenkowski plurality: 63,612

9 (Northeast Chicago)

Sidney R. Yates, D*	111,955	75.8
Edward Wolbank, R	35,795	24.2

Yates plurality: 76,160

10 (Chicago suburbs)

Harold R. Collier, R*	107,416	62.2
R. G. Patrick Logan, D	65,170	37.8
Write-in votes	6	0.0

Collier plurality: 42,246

11 (Northern Chicago)

Roman C. Pucinski, D*	137,090	71.9
James R. Mason, R	53,461	28.1
Write-in votes	1	0.0

Pucinski plurality: 83,629

12 (Northeastern counties, Waukegan)

Robert McClory, R*	84,356	62.1
James J. Cone, D	51,499	37.9
Write-in votes	1	0.0

McClory plurality: 32,857

13 (Chicago suburbs, Evanston)

Philip M. Crane, R*	124,649	58.0
Edward A. Warman, D	90,364	42.0
Write-in votes	24	0.0

Crane plurality: 34,285

14 (Chicago suburbs, Elmhurst)

John N. Erlenborn, R*	122,115	65.5
William J. Adelman, D	64,231	34.5

Erlenborn plurality: 57,884

15 (North central counties, Aurora)

Charlotte T. Reid, R* †	95,222	68.9
James E. Todd, D	43,014	31.1

Reid plurality: 52,208

16 (Northwestern counties, Rockford)

John B. Anderson, R*	83,296	66.8
John E. Devine Jr., D	41,459	33.2

Anderson plurality: 41,837

17 (East central counties, Bloomington)

Leslie C. Arends, R*	92,917	62.3
Lester A. Hawthorne, D	56,340	37.7

Arends plurality: 36,577

18 (North central counties, Peoria)

Robert H. Michel, R*	84,864	66.1
Rosa Lee Fox, D	43,601	33.9
Write-in votes	2	0.0

Michel plurality: 41,263

19 (West central counties, Rock Island)

Tom Railsback, R*	92,247	68.2
James L. Shaw, D	43,094	31.8

Railsback plurality: 49,153

20 (West central counties, Springfield)

Paul Findley, R*	103,485	67.5
Billie M. Cox, D	49,727	32.5

Findley plurality: 53,758

21 (Southern counties, Cairo, Carbondale)

Kenneth J. Gray, D*	110,374	62.5
Fred Evans, R	66,273	37.5

Gray plurality: 44,101

22 (Central counties, Decatur)

William L. Springer, R*	83,131	59.0
Robert C. Miller, D	57,781	41.0

Springer plurality: 25,350

23 (South central counties, Alton)

George E. Shipley, D*	91,158	54.0
Phyllis Schlafly, R	77,762	46.0

Shipley plurality: 13,396

24 (Southwestern counties, East St. Louis)

Melvin Price, D*	88,637	74.2
Scott R. Randolph, R	30,784	25.8

Price plurality: 57,853

INDIANA
Senator

Vance Hartke, D*	870,990	50.1
Richard L. Roudebush, R	866,707	49.9

Hartke plurality: 4,283

U.S. Representative (by district)

1 (Gary, Hammond, East Chicago)

Ray J. Madden, D*	73,145	65.6
Eugene M. Kirtland, R	38,294	34.4

Madden plurality: 34,851

2 (Northwestern counties, Lafayette)

Earl F. Landgrebe, R*	79,163	50.4
Philip A. Sprague, D	77,959	49.6

Landgrebe plurality: 1,204

3 (Northern counties, South Bend)

John Brademas, D*	87,064	57.5
Donald M. Newman, R	64,249	42.5

Brademas plurality: 22,815

4 (Northeastern counties, Fort Wayne)

J. Edward Roush, D	86,582	51.9
E. Ross Adair, R*	80,326	48.1

Roush plurality: 6,256

5 (Central counties, Kokomo, Marion)

Elwood H. Hillis, R	86,199	56.0
Kathleen Z. Williams, D	67,740	44.0

Hillis plurality: 18,459

6 (Indianapolis suburbs)

William G. Bray, R*	115,113	60.7
Terrence D. Straub, D	74,599	39.3

Bray plurality: 40,514

7 (West central counties, Terre Haute)

John T. Myers, R*	97,152	57.1
William D. Roach, D	73,042	42.9

Myers plurality: 24,110

8 (Southwestern counties, Evansville)

Roger H. Zion, R*	93,088	52.6
J. David Huber, D	83,911	47.4

Zion plurality: 9,177

9 (Southeastern counties, Jeffersonville)

Lee H. Hamilton, D*	104,599	62.5
Richard B. Wathen, R	62,772	37.5

Hamilton plurality: 41,827

10 (East central counties, Anderson)

David W. Dennis, R*	81,439	50.8
Philip R. Sharp, D	78,871	49.2

Dennis plurality: 2,568

11 (Indianapolis)

Andrew Jacobs Jr., D*	71,329	58.3
Danny L. Burton, R	50,990	41.7

Jacobs plurality: 20,339

IOWA

AIP — American Independent Party
INP — Iowa New Party

Governor

Robert D. Ray, R*	403,394	51.0
Robert D. Fulton, D	368,911	46.6
Robert Dilley, AIP	18,933	2.4
Scattering	3	0.0

Ray plurality: 34,483

U.S. Representative (by district)

1 (Southeastern counties, Davenport)

Fred Schwengel, R*	60,270	49.8
Edward Mezvinsky, D	59,505	49.2
Lee E. Foster, AIP	1,168	1.0

Schwengel plurality: 765

2 (Northeastern counties, Cedar Rapids)

John C. Culver, D*	84,049	60.5
Cole McMartin, R	54,932	39.5

Culver plurality: 29,117

3 (North central counties, Waterloo)

H. R. Gross, R*	66,087	59.0
Lyle D. Taylor, D	45,958	41.0

Gross plurality: 20,129

4 (South central counties, Ottumwa)

John Kyl, R*	59,396	54.6
Roger Blobaum, D	49,369	45.4

Kyl plurality: 10,027

5 (Central counties, Des Moines)

Neal Smith, D*	73,820	64.9
Don Mahon, R	37,374	32.9
John H. Grant, AIP	1,297	1.1
Roy E. Berger, INP	1,262	1.1

Smith plurality: 36,446

6 (Northwestern counties, Sioux City)

Wiley Mayne, R*	57,285	57.0
Fred H. Moore, D	43,257	43.0
Scattering	1	0.0

Mayne plurality: 14,028

7 (Southwestern counties, Council Bluffs)

William J. Scherle, R*	53,084	62.7
Lou Galetich, D	31,552	37.3
Scattering	25	0.0

Scherle plurality: 21,532

KANSAS

C—Conservative Party
P—Prohibition Party

Governor

Robert B. Docking, D*	404,611	54.3
Kent Frizzell, R	333,227	44.7
P. Everett Sperry, C	4,312	0.6
Marshall Uncapher, P	3,040	0.4
Scattering	6	0.0

Docking plurality: 71,384

U.S. Representative (by district)

1 (Western counties, Salina)

Keith G. Sebelius, R*	83,923	56.8
Billy D. Jellison, D	63,791	43.2
Scattering	2	0.0

Sebelius plurality: 20,132

2 (Northeastern counties, Topeka)

William R. Roy, D	80,161	52.3
Chester L. Mize, R*	68,843	45.0
Fred Kilian, C	4,145	2.7

Roy plurality: 11,318

3 (Eastern counties, Kansas City)

Larry Winn Jr., R*	74,603	53.0
James H. DeCoursey Jr., D	64,344	45.7
Warren E. Redding, C	1,820	1.3

Winn plurality: 10,259

4 (Central counties, Wichita)

Garner E. Shriver, R*	85,058	63.2
James C. (Jim) Juhnke, D	47,004	34.9
George W. Snell, C	2,452	1.8

Shriver plurality: 38,054

5 (Southeastern counties, Pittsburg)

Joe Skubitz, R*	94,837	66.1
T. D. (Ted) Saar Jr., D	48,688	33.9

Skubitz plurality: 46,149

KENTUCKY

AIP—American Independent Party
†—Rep. John C. Watts died September 24, 1971.

U.S. Representative (by district)

1 (Southwestern counties, Paducah)

Frank A. Stubblefield, D*	27,829	100.0

2 (West central counties, Owensboro)

William H. Natcher, D*	21,024	100.0

3 (Louisville)

Romano L. Mazzoli, D	50,102	48.5
William O. Cowger, R*	49,891	48.3
Ronald W. Watson, AIP	3,265	3.2

Mazzoli plurality: 211

4 (Ohio River counties, Louisville suburbs)

M. G. Snyder, R*	83,027	66.6
Charles W. Webster, D	41,659	33.4

Snyder plurality: 41,378

5 (Southeastern counties, Middlesborough)

Tim Lee Carter, R*	49,266	80.4
Lyle Leonard Willis, D	11,977	19.6

Carter plurality: 37,289

6 (North central counties, Lexington)

John C. Watts, D* †	44,322	64.9
Gerald G. Gregory, R	23,971	35.1

Watts plurality: 20,351

7 (Eastern counties, Ashland)

Carl D. Perkins, D*	50,672	75.3
Herbert E. Myers, R	16,648	24.7

Perkins plurality: 34,024

LOUISIANA

Ind—independent

U.S. Representative (by district)

1 (Southeastern counties, part of New Orleans)

F. Edward Hebert, D*	66,284	87.3
Luke J. Fontana, Ind	9,602	12.7

Hebert plurality: 56,682

2 (Jefferson County, part of New Orleans)

Hale Boggs, D*	51,812	69.3
Robert E. Lee, R	19,703	26.3
Benjamin E. Smith, Ind	3,279	4.4

Boggs plurality: 32,109

3 (South central counties, Lafayette)

Patrick T. Caffery, D*	48,677	100.0

4 (Northwestern counties, Shreveport)

Joe D. Waggonner Jr., D*	44,848	100.0

5 (Northeastern counties, Monroe)

Otto E. Passman, D*	31,087	100.0

6 (East central counties, Baton Rouge)

John R. Rarick, D*	36,632	100.0

7 (Southwestern counties, Lake Charles)

Edwin W. Edwards, D*	24,517	100.0

8 (Central counties, Alexandria)

Speedy O. Long, D*	26,607	100.0

MAINE
Governor

Kenneth M. Curtis, D*	163,138	50.1
James S. Erwin, R	162,248	49.9

Curtis plurality: 890

Senator

Edmund S. Muskie, D*	199,954	61.7
Neil S. Bishop, R	123,906	38.3

Muskie plurality: 76,048

U.S. Representative (by district)

1 (Southern counties, Portland, Augusta)

Peter N. Kyros, D*	99,483	59.2
Ronald T. Speers, R	68,671	40.8

Kyros plurality: 30,812

2 (Northern counties, Bangor, Lewiston)

William D. Hathaway, D*	96,235	64.2
Maynard G. Conners, R	53,642	35.8

Hathaway plurality: 42,593

MARYLAND

AIP — American Independent Party
† — Rep. Rogers C. B. Morton resigned January 29, 1971, to become Interior Secretary. William O. Mills, winner of a special election to fill the vacancy, was sworn in May 27, 1971.

Governor

Marvin Mandel, D*	639,579	65.7
C. Stanley Blair, R	314,336	32.3
Robert Woods Merkle Sr., AIP	19,184	2.0

Mandel plurality: 325,243

Senator

J. Glenn Beall Jr., R	484,960	50.7
Joseph D. Tydings, D*	460,422	48.1
Harvey Wilder, AIP	10,988	1.1

Beall plurality: 24,538

U.S. Representative (by district)

1 (Eastern Chesapeake Bay counties)

Rogers C. B. Morton, R* †	79,594	75.6
David S. Aland, D	24,923	23.7
Henry Joseph Laque Jr., AIP	822	0.8

Morton plurality: 54,671

2 (Baltimore suburbs)

Clarence D. Long, D*	87,224	68.5
Ross Z. Pierpont, R	40,177	31.5

Long plurality: 47,047

3 (Part of Baltimore and suburbs)

Edward A. Garmatz, D*	52,374	100.0

4 (Part of Baltimore and suburbs)

Paul S. Sarbanes, D	54,936	70.0
David Fentress, R	23,491	30.0

Sarbanes plurality: 31,445

5 (Prince George's, Charles counties)

Lawrence J. Hogan, R*	84,314	61.4
Royal Hart, D	52,979	38.6

Hogan plurality: 31,335

6 (Western counties, Hagerstown)

Goodloe E. Byron, D	59,267	50.8
George R. Hughes Jr., R	55,511	47.6
Audrey B. Carroll, AIP	1,873	1.6

Byron plurality: 3,756

7 (Part of Baltimore and suburbs)

Parren J. Mitchell, D	60,390	58.7
Peter Parker, R	42,566	41.3

Mitchell plurality: 17,824

8 (Montgomery County, Rockville)

Gilbert Gude, R*	104,647	63.4
Thomas Hale Boggs Jr., D	60,453	36.6

Gude plurality: 44,194

MASSACHUSETTS

Ind — independent
P — Prohibition Party
SL — Socialist Labor Party

Governor

Francis W. Sargent, R*	1,058,623	51.8
Kevin H. White, D	799,269	39.1
Henning A. Blomen, SL	6,747	0.3
John Charles Hedges, P	3,189	0.2
All others	78	0.0
Blanks	175,381	8.6

Sargent plurality: 259,354

Senator

Edward M. Kennedy, D*	1,202,856	58.9
Josiah A. Spaulding, R	715,978	35.0
Lawrence Gilfedder, SL	10,378	0.5
Mark R. Shaw, P	5,944	0.3
All others	451	0.0
Blanks	107,680	5.3

Kennedy plurality: 486,878

U.S. Representatives (by district)

1 (Western counties, Pittsfield, Holyoke)

Silvio O. Conte, R*	117,045	71.9
All others	34	0.0
Blanks	45,687	28.1

2 (Central counties, Springfield)

Edward P. Boland, D*	111,430	74.1
All others	18	0.0
Blanks	38,874	25.9

3 (Central counties, Newton, Waltham)

Robert F. Drinan, D	63,942	35.4
John McGlennon, R	60,575	33.6
Philip J. Philbin, Ind*	45,278	25.1
All others	5	0.0
Blanks	10,642	5.9

Drinan plurality: 3,367

4 (Central counties, Worcester)

Harold D. Donohue, D*	95,016	53.0
Howard A. Miller Jr., R	79,870	44.5
All others	4	0.0
Blanks	4,422	2.5

Donohue plurality: 15,146

5 (Northeastern counties, Lawrence, Lowell)

F. Bradford Morse, R*	116,666	60.5
Richard Williams, D	67,646	35.1
All others	2	0.0
Blanks	8,486	4.4

Morse plurality: 49,020

6 (Northeastern counties)

Michael J. Harrington, D*	114,276	59.4
Howard Phillips, R	70,955	36.8
Blanks	7,253	3.8

Harrington plurality: 43,321

7 (Northeastern counties, Boston suburbs)

Torbert H. Macdonald, D*	107,770	61.4
Gordon F. Hughes, R	52,290	29.8
All others	13	0.0
Blanks	15,419	8.8

Macdonald plurality: 55,480

8 (Boston, Cambridge)

Thomas P. O'Neill Jr., D*	89,875	67.2
All others	4	0.0
Blanks	43,783	32.8

9 (Boston)

Louise Day Hicks, D	50,269	50.1
Daniel J. Houton, Ind	17,395	17.3
Laurence Curtis, R	17,324	17.3
Blanks	15,358	15.3

Hicks plurality: 32,874

10 (Southeastern counties, Fall River)

Margaret M. Heckler, R*	102,895	55.7
Bertram A. Yaffe, D	77,497	42.0
All others	6	0.0
Blanks	4,218	2.3

Heckler plurality: 25,398

11 (Boston, Brockton, Quincy)

James A. Burke, D*	143,026	76.4
All others	23	0.0
Blanks	44,220	23.6

12 (Cape Cod, Bedford)

Hastings Keith, R*	100,432	49.3
Gerry E. Studds, D	98,910	48.5
All others	7	0.0
Blanks	4,426	2.2

Keith plurality: 1,522

MICHIGAN

AIP — American Independent Party
SL — Socialist Labor Party
SW — Socialist Workers Party

Governor

William G. Milliken, R*	1,338,711	50.4
Sander Levin, D	1,294,600	48.7
James L. McCormick, AIP	17,988	0.7
George Bouse, SW	2,546	0.1
James C. Horvath, SL	2,144	0.1
Scattering	104	0.0

Milliken plurality: 44,111

Senator

Philip A. Hart, D*	1,744,672	66.8
Leonore Romney, R	858,438	32.9
Paul Lodico, SW	3,861	0.1
James Sim, SL	3,254	0.1
Scattering	538	0.0

Hart plurality: 886,234

U.S. Representative (by district)

1 (North central Detroit, Highland Park)

John Conyers Jr., D*	93,075	88.2
Howard L. Johnson, R	11,876	11.2
Jacqueline Diana Rice, SW	617	0.6
Scattering	3	0.0

Conyers plurality: 81,199

2 (Southeastern counties, Ann Arbor)

Marvin L. Esch, R*	88,071	62.5
R. Michael Stillwagon, D	52,782	37.5

Esch plurality: 35,289

3 (South central counties, Kalamazoo, Battle Creek)

Garry Brown, R*	80,447	56.3
Richard A. Enslen, D	62,530	43.7
Scattering	3	0.0

Brown plurality: 17,917

4 (Southwestern counties, Benton Harbor)

Edward Hutchinson, R*	74,471	61.9
David R. McCormack, D	45,838	38.1

Hutchinson plurality: 28,633

5 (Kent, Ionia counties, Grand Rapids)

Gerald R. Ford, R*	88,208	61.4
Jean McKee, D	55,337	38.5
Frank Girard, SL	120	0.1
Kalter M. Kus, SW	87	0.0

Ford plurality: 32,871

6 (Central counties, Lansing)

Charles E. Chamberlain, R*	84,276	60.3
John A. Cihon, D	55,591	39.7
Scattering	1	0.0

Chamberlain plurality: 28,685

7 (Lapeer County, Flint)

Donald W. Riegle Jr., R*	97,683	69.2
Richard J. Ruhala, D	41,235	29.2
Eugene L. Mattison, AIP	2,194	1.6

Riegle plurality: 56,448

8 (Eastern counties, Saginaw)

James Harvey, R*	85,634	65.9
Richard E. Davies, D	44,400	34.1

Harvey plurality: 41,234

9 (Western counties, Muskegon)

Guy Vander Jagt, R*	94,027	64.4
Charles Arthur Rogers, D	51,223	35.1
Patrick V. Dillinger, AIP	811	0.6
Scattering	2	0.0

Vander Jagt plurality: 42,804

10 (North central counties, Bay City)

Elford A. Cederberg, R*	82,528	59.1
Gerald J. Parent, D	57,031	40.9
Scattering	10	0.0

Cederberg plurality: 25,497

11 (Upper Peninsula)

Philip E. Ruppe, R*	85,323	61.6
Nino Green, D	53,146	38.4
Scattering	1	0.0

Ruppe plurality: 32,177

12 (Macomb County, Detroit suburbs)

James G. O'Hara, D*	129,287	76.1
Patrick Driscoll, R	38,946	22.9
Milton E. Deschaine, AIP	1,562	0.9
Scattering	1	0.0

O'Hara plurality: 90,341

13 (Central Detroit)

Charles C. Diggs Jr., D*	56,872	86.1
Fred W. Engel, R	9,141	13.8
Scattering	3	0.0

Diggs plurality: 47,731

14 (Northeastern Detroit and suburbs)

Lucien N. Nedzi, D*	91,111	70.0
John L. Owen, R	38,956	29.9
Scattering	7	0.0

Nedzi plurality: 52,155

15 (Southwestern Detroit suburbs)

William D. Ford, D*	101,018	79.9
Ernest C. Fackler, R	25,340	20.1

Ford plurality: 75,678

16 (Detroit and suburbs, Dearborn)

John D. Dingell, D*	90,540	79.1
William E. Rostron, R	23,867	20.9
Scattering	3	0.0

Dingell plurality: 66,673

17 (Northwestern Detroit)

Martha W. Griffiths, D*	108,176	79.7
Thomas E. Klunzinger, R	27,608	20.3
Scattering	12	0.0

Griffiths plurality: 80,568

18 (Detroit suburbs, Royal Oak)

William S. Broomfield, R*	113,309	64.6
August Scholle, D	62,081	35.4
Barbara Halpert (write-in)	42	0.0
Scattering	6	0.0

Broomfield plurality: 51,228

19 (Detroit suburbs, Pontiac)

Jack H. McDonald, R*	91,763	58.8
Fred L. Harris, D	63,175	40.5
Hector M. McGregor, AIP	990	0.6
Scattering	1	0.0

McDonald plurality: 28,588

MINNESOTA

IG — Industrial Government Party
Ind — independent
SW — Socialist Workers Party
D — In Minnesota, D is Democratic-Farmer-Labor Party.

Governor

Wendell R. Anderson, D	737,921	54.0
Douglas M. Head, R	621,780	45.5
Karl Heck, IG	4,781	0.4
Jack Kirkham (write-in)	961	0.1

Anderson plurality: 116,141

Senator

Hubert H. Humphrey, D	788,256	57.8
Clark MacGregor, R	568,025	41.6
Nancy Strebe, SW	6,122	0.4
William Braatz, IG	2,484	0.2

Humphrey plurality: 220,231

U.S. Representative (by district)

1 (Southeastern counties, Rochester)

Albert H. Quie, R*	121,802	69.3
B. A. Lundeen, D	53,995	30.7

Quie plurality: 67,807

2 (Southwestern counties, Mankato)

Ancher Nelsen, R*	94,080	63.3
Clifford R. Adams, D	54,498	36.7

Nelsen plurality: 39,582

3 (Minneapolis suburbs)

William Frenzel, R	110,921	50.6
George Rice, D	108,141	49.4

Frenzel plurality: 2,780

4 (St. Paul and suburbs)

Joseph E. Karth, D*	131,263	74.2
Frank L. Loss, R	45,680	25.8

Karth plurality: 85,583

5 (Minneapolis)

Donald M. Fraser, D*	83,207	57.1
Dick Enroth, R	61,682	42.3
Derrel Myers, SW	783	0.5

Fraser plurality: 21,525

6 (West central counties, St. Cloud)

John M. Zwach, R*	88,753	51.8
Terry Montgomery, D	81,004	47.3
Richard Martin, Ind	1,625	0.9

Zwach plurality: 7,749

7 (Northwestern counties, Moorhead)

Bob Bergland, D	79,378	54.1
Odin Langen, R*	67,296	45.9

Bergland plurality: 12,082

8 (Northeastern counties, Duluth)

John A. Blatnik, D*	118,149	75.5
Paul Reed, R	38,369	24.5

Blatnik plurality: 79,780

MISSISSIPPI

Ind – independent

Senator

John Stennis, D*	286,622	88.4
William R. Thompson, Ind	37,593	11.6

Stennis plurality: 249,029

U.S. Representative (by district)

1 (North central counties, Greenville)

Thomas G. Abernethy, D*	42,367	100.0

2 (Northern counties, Tupelo)

Jamie L. Whitten, D*	51,689	86.5
Eugene Carter, Ind	8,092	13.5

Whitten plurality: 43,597

3 (Southwestern counties, Jackson)

Charles H. Griffin, D*	50,527	63.7
Ray Lee, R	28,847	36.3

Griffin plurality: 21,680

4 (Central counties, Meridian)

G. V. Montgomery, D*	66,064	100.0

5 (Southeastern counties, Biloxi)

William M. Colmer, D*	58,546	90.4
Earnest J. Creel, Ind	6,225	9.6

Colmer plurality: 52,321

MISSOURI

AIP – American Independent Party
Ind – independent
NP – nonpartisan

Senator

Stuart Symington, D*	654,831	51.0
John C. Danforth, R	617,903	48.1
Gene Chapman, AIP	10,065	0.8
E. J. DiGirolamo, NP	513	0.0

Symington plurality: 36,928

U.S. Representative (by district)

1 (Northern St. Louis and suburbs)

William Clay, D*	58,082	90.5
Gerald G. (Jerry) Fischer, AIP	6,078	9.5

Clay plurality: 52,004

2 (St. Louis suburbs)

James W. Symington, D*	93,294	57.6
Philip R. Hoffman, R	66,503	41.1
Sterling E. Lacy, AIP	2,206	1.4

Symington plurality: 26,791

3 (Southern St. Louis and suburbs)

Leonor K. Sullivan, D*	73,021	74.8
Dale F. Troske, R	24,651	25.2

Sullivan plurality: 48,370

4 (West central counties, part of Kansas City)

William J. Randall, D*	80,153	60.1
Leslie O. Olson, R	53,204	39.9

Randall plurality: 26,949

5 (Kansas City)

Richard Bolling, D*	51,668	61.3
Randall (Randy) Vanet, R	31,806	37.8
Jim E. Kernodle, AIP	778	0.9

Bolling plurality: 19,862

6 (Northwestern counties, St. Joseph)

W. R. Hull Jr., D*	74,496	53.6
Hugh A. Sprague, R	63,789	45.9
O. B. Chaney, AIP	686	0.5

Hull plurality: 10,707

7 (Southwestern counties, Springfield)

Durward G. Hall, R*	92,965	100.0

8 (East central counties, Columbia, Jefferson City)

Richard H. Ichord, D*	97,560	64.3
John L. Caskanett, R	53,181	35.1
Charles H. Byford, Ind	879	0.6

Ichord plurality: 44,379

9 (Northeastern counties, Hannibal)

William L. Hungate, D*	100,988	63.0
Anthony C. Schroeder, R	58,103	36.2
Orville C. Hale, AIP	1,197	0.7

Hungate plurality: 42,885

10 (Southeastern counties, Cape Girardeau)

Bill D. Burlison, D*	62,764	56.0
Gary Rust, R	49,355	44.0

Burlison plurality: 13,409

MONTANA
Senator

Mike Mansfield, D*	150,060	60.5
Harold E. (Bud) Wallace, R	97,809	39.5

Mansfield plurality: 52,251

U.S. Representative (by district)

1 (Western counties, Butte, Helena)

Richard G. Shoup, R	64,388	50.5
Arnold Olsen, D*	63,175	49.5

Shoup plurality: 1,213

2 (Eastern counties, Billings, Great Falls)

John Melcher, D*	78,082	64.1
Jack Rehberg, R	43,752	35.9

Melcher plurality: 34,330

NEBRASKA

AIP — American Independent Party
Ind — independent

Governor

J. J. Exon, D	248,552	53.8
Norbert T. Tiemann, R*	201,994	43.8
Albert C. Walsh, AIP	10,913	2.4
Scattering	160	0.0

Exon plurality: 46,558

Senator

Roman L. Hruska, R*	240,894	52.5
Frank B. Morrison, D	217,681	47.4
Scattering	391	0.1

Hruska plurality: 23,213

U.S. Representative (by district)

1 (Eastern counties, Lincoln)

Charles J. Thone, R	79,131	50.6
Clair A. Callan, Ind	40,919	26.2
George (Bill) Burrows, D	36,240	23.2
Scattering	15	0.0

Thone plurality: 38,212

2 (Eastern counties, Omaha)

John Y. McCollister, R	69,671	51.9
John Hlavacek, D	64,520	48.0
Scattering	96	0.1

McCollister plurality: 5,151

3 (Western counties, Grand Island)

Dave Martin, R*	93,705	59.5
Donald Searcy, D	63,698	40.5
Scattering	4	0.0

Martin plurality: 30,007

NEVADA

AIP — American Independent Party
Ind — independent

Governor

Mike O'Callaghan, D	70,697	48.1
Ed Fike, R	64,400	43.8
Charles E. Springer, Ind	6,479	4.4
Daniel M. Hansen, AIP	5,415	3.7

O'Callaghan plurality: 6,297

Senator

Howard W. Cannon, D*	85,187	57.6
William J. Raggio, R	60,838	41.2
Harold G. De Sellem, AIP	1,743	1.2

Cannon plurality: 24,349

U.S. Representative (at large)

Walter S. Baring, D*	113,496	82.5
J. Robert Charles, R	24,147	17.5

Baring plurality: 89,349

NEW HAMPSHIRE

AIP — American Independent Party

Governor

Walter R. Peterson, R*	102,298	46.0
Roger J. Crowley Jr., D	98,098	44.1
Meldrim Thomson Jr., AIP	22,033	9.9

Peterson plurality: 4,200

U.S. Representative (by district)

1 (Southeastern counties, Manchester)

Louis C. Wyman, R*	72,170	67.4
Chester E. Merrow, D	34,882	32.6

Wyman plurality: 37,288

2 (Remainder of state)

James C. Cleveland, R*	74,219	69.7
Eugene S. Daniell Jr., D	32,274	30.3

Cleveland plurality: 41,945

NEW JERSEY

AF — American First Party
DDD — Destroy Drug Devils Party
FTP — For The People Party
Ind — independent
NC — National Conservative Party
SL — Socialist Labor Party
UTR — Urban Tax Reform Party

Senator

Harrison A. Williams Jr., D*	1,157,074	54.0
Nelson G. Gross, R	903,026	42.2
Joseph F. Job, Ind	58,992	2.8
William J. O'Grady, NC	12,938	0.6
Joseph S. Mans, DDD	6,066	0.3
Julius Levin, SL	4,009	0.2

Williams plurality: 254,048

U.S. Representative (by district)

1 (Camden, Gloucester counties; Camden)

John E. Hunt, R*	83,726	61.2
Salvatore T. Mansi, D	52,567	38.4
Dominic W. Doganiero, SL	460	0.3

Hunt plurality: 31,159

2 (Southern counties, Atlantic City)

Charles W. Sandman Jr., R*	69,392	51.7
William J. Hughes, D	64,882	48.3

Sandman plurality: 4,510

3 (Monmouth County, Long Beach)

James J. Howard, D*	87,973	55.2
William F. Dowd, R	68,675	43.1
Clyde W. Hill, NC	2,831	1.8

Howard plurality: 19,298

4 (Northwestern counties, Trenton)

Frank Thompson Jr., D*	91,670	58.4
Edward A. Costigan, R	65,030	41.4
Joseph J. Frank, SL	393	0.3

Thompson plurality: 26,640

5 (North central counties, Morristown)

Peter H. B. Frelinghuysen, R*	111,553	66.4
Ronald C. Eisele, D	53,436	31.8
Robert G. Wright, NC	2,953	1.8

Frelinghuysen plurality: 58,117

6 (South central counties, Burlington)

Edwin B. Forsythe, R	88,051	53.6
Charles B. Yates, D	72,347	44.1
John V. Mahalchik, AF	2,936	1.8
Bernardo S. Doganiero, SL	806	0.5

Forsythe plurality: 15,704

6 (To fill vacancy)

Edwin B. Forsythe, R	89,565	54.8
Charles B. Yates, D	73,821	45.2

Forsythe plurality: 15,744

7 (Western Bergen County, Hackensack)

William B. Widnall, R*	90,140	58.6
Arthur J. Lesemann, D	63,928	41.4

Widnall plurality: 26,482

8 (Passaic County)

Robert A. Roe, D*	75,056	61.0
Alfred E. Fontanella, R	48,011	39.0

Roe plurality: 27,045

9 (Eastern Bergen County, Englewood)

Henry Helstoski, D*	91,589	56.6
Henry L. Hoebel, R	68,974	42.6
Hannibal Cundari, NC	1,241	0.8

Helstoski plurality: 22,615

10 (Newark and suburbs)

Peter W. Rodino Jr., D*	71,003	70.0
Griffith H. Jones, R	30,460	30.0

Rodino plurality: 40,543

11 (Newark and suburbs)

Joseph G. Minish, D*	68,075	68.5
James W. Shue, R	31,369	31.5

Minish plurality: 36,706

12 (Southwestern Newark suburbs, Plainfield)

Florence P. Dwyer, R*	109,537	66.2
Daniel F. Lundy, D	55,930	33.8

Dwyer plurality: 53,607

13 (Part of Hudson County, Elizabeth)

Cornelius E. Gallagher, D*	77,789	71.7
Raul E. L. Comesanas, R	27,929	25.5
Everett C. Miller, UTR	3,675	3.4

Gallagher plurality: 49,860

14 (Parts of Hudson County, Jersey City)

Dominick V. Daniels, D*	77,771	69.7
Carlo N. De Gennaro, R	31,161	27.9
Martha R. Whaley, NC	1,775	1.6
Vincent J. Dellay, FTP	823	0.7

Daniels plurality: 46,610

15 (Middlesex County, Perth Amboy)

Edward J. Patten, D*	94,772	61.1
Peter P. Garibaldi, R	60,450	38.9

Patten plurality: 34,322

NEW MEXICO

INMP – Independent New Mexican Party
PCP – People's Constitutional Party

Governor

Bruce King, D	148,835	51.3
Peter V. Domenici, R	134,640	46.4
John A. Salazar, INMP	4,652	1.6
Wilfredo Sedillo, PCP	2,237	0.7

King plurality: 14,195

Senator

Joseph M. Montoya, D*	151,486	52.3
Anderson Carter, R	135,004	46.6
William L. Higgs, PCP	3,382	1.1

Montoya plurality: 16,482

U.S. Representative (by district)

1 (Northern, eastern counties, Albuquerque)

Manuel Lujan Jr., R*	91,187	57.6
Fabian Chavez Jr., D	64,598	40.8
Anita Montano, PCP	1,763	1.1
Norbert J. McGovern, INMP	811	0.5

Lujan plurality: 26,589

2 (Southern, western counties, Roswell)

Harold L. Runnels, D	64,518	50.8
Ed Foreman, R*	61,074	48.1
Juan A. Roybal, PCP	1,388	1.1

Runnels plurality: 3,444

NEW YORK

Com – Communist Party
Con – Conservative Party
CSI – Civil Service Independent Party
Envir – Environment Party
IA – Independent Alliance
Lib – Liberal Party
RTL – Right to Life Party
SL – Socialist Labor Party
SM – Silent Majority Party
SW – Socialist Workers Party

Governor

Nelson A. Rockefeller, R*, CSI	3,151,432	51.2
Arthur J. Goldberg, D, Lib	2,421,426	39.4
Paul L. Adams, Con	422,514	6.9
Rasheed Storey, Com	7,760	0.1
Clifton DeBerry, SW	5,766	0.1
Stephen Emery, SL	3,963	0.1
Blank, void and scattering	137,616	2.2

Rockefeller plurality: 730,006

Senator

James L. Buckley, Con, IA	2,288,190	37.2
Richard L. Ottinger, D	2,171,232	35.3
Charles E. Goodell, R*, Lib	1,434,472	23.3
Arnold Johnson, Com	4,097	0.1
Kipp Dawson, SW	3,549	0.1
John Emanuel, SL	3,204	0.1
Blank, void and scattering	245,733	4.0

Buckley plurality: 116,958

U.S. Representative (by district)

1 (Long Island, part of Suffolk County)

Otis G. Pike, D*, Lib	108,746	52.2
Malcolm E. Smith Jr., R, Con	99,503	47.8

Pike plurality: 9,243

2 (Long Island, part of Suffolk, Nassau Counties)

James R. Grover Jr., R*, Con	107,433	66.1
Harvey W. Sherman, D, Lib	54,996	33.9

Grover plurality: 52,437

3 (Long Island, parts of Queens, Nassau Counties)

Lester L. Wolff, D*, Lib	94,414	54.4
Raymond J. Rice, R, Envir	66,196	38.1
Lola Camardi, Con	12,925	7.4

Wolff plurality: 28,218

4 (Long Island, part of Nassau County)

John W. Wydler, R*	91,787	57.0
Karen S. Burstein, D, Lib	56,411	35.1
Donald A. Derham, Con	12,701	7.9

Wydler plurality: 35,376

5 (Long Island, part of Nassau County)

Norman F. Lent, R, Con	93,824	51.0
Allard K. Lowenstein, D-Lib*	84,738	46.1
Vincent J. Carey, RTL	5,342	2.9

Lent plurality: 9,086

6 (Eastern Queens)

Seymour Halpern, R*, Lib	89,250	77.3
John J. Flynn, Con	26,244	22.7

Halpern plurality: 63,006

7 (Southern Queens)

Joseph P. Addabbo, D*, R, Lib	112,983	90.8
Christopher T. Acer, Con	11,515	9.2

Addabbo plurality: 101,468

8 (Northern Queens)

Benjamin S. Rosenthal, D*, Lib	93,666	62.8
Cosmo J. Di Tucci, R, Con	55,406	37.2

Rosenthal plurality: 38,260

9 (Western Queens)

James J. Delaney, D*, R, Con	102,205	91.9
Rose L. Rubin, Lib	9,025	8.1

Delaney plurality: 93,180

10 (Central Brooklyn)

Emanuel Celler, D*, Lib	78,324	73.0
Frank J. Occhiogrosso, R, Con	29,012	27.0

Celler plurality: 49,312

11 (Eastern Brooklyn)

Frank J. Brasco, D*	60,919	78.6
William Sampol, Con	9,462	12.2
Paul Meyrowitz, Lib	7,156	9.1

Brasco plurality: 51,457

12 (North central Brooklyn)

Shirley Chisholm, D*, Lib	31,500	81.8
John Coleman, R	5,816	15.1
Martin S. Shepherd Jr., Con	1,204	3.1

Chisholm plurality: 25,684

13 (South central Brooklyn)

Bertram L. Podell, D*	102,247	77.0
George W. McKenzie, R	20,550	15.5
Herbert Dicker, Lib	9,925	7.5

Podell plurality: 81,697

14 (Northwestern Brooklyn)

John J. Rooney, D*	31,586	55.2
John F. Jacobs, R, Con	15,222	26.6
Peter E. Eikenberry, Lib	10,452	18.3

Rooney plurality: 16,364

15 (West central Brooklyn)

Hugh L. Carey, D*	50,767	64.7
Frank C. Spinner, R	17,931	22.9
Stephen P. Marion, Con	5,307	6.8
Carl Saks, Lib	4,506	5.7

Carey plurality: 32,836

16 (Staten Island, southwestern Brooklyn)

John M. Murphy, D*, CSI	71,553	51.6
David D. Smith, R, Con	62,597	45.2
George D. McClain, Lib	4,415	3.2

Murphy plurality: 8,956

17 (East Side Manhattan)

Edward I. Koch, D-Lib*	98,300	62.0
Peter J. Sprague, R	50,647	31.9
Richard J. Callahan, Con	9,586	6.0

Koch plurality: 47,653

18 (Harlem)

Charles B. Rangel, R, D	52,651	86.8
Charles Taylor, Lib	6,385	10.5
Bohdan J. Wasiutynski, Con	1,033	1.7
Jose Stevens, Com	374	0.6
Paul B. Boutelle, SW	242	0.4

Rangel plurality: 46,266

19 (West and Lower East Side, Manhattan)

Bella S. Abzug, D	46,947	52.3
Barry Farber, R, Lib	38,460	42.8
Salvatore Lodico, Con	4,426	4.9

Abzug plurality: 8,487

20 (Upper West Side, Manhattan)

William F. Ryan, D-Lib*	73,779	78.8
William Goldstein, R	13,527	14.4
Francis C. Saunders, Con	6,315	6.7

Ryan plurality: 60,252

21 (Parts of Queens, Bronx, Manhattan)

Herman Badillo, D, Lib	38,866	83.7
George B. Smaragdas, Con	7,561	16.3

Badillo plurality: 31,305

22 (East central Bronx)

James H. Scheuer, D*, Lib	50,372	71.6
Robert M. Schneck, R, Con	19,994	28.4

Scheuer plurality: 30,378

23 (Western Bronx)

Jonathan B. Bingham, D-Lib*	78,723	76.2
George E. Sweeney, R	16,172	15.6
Norma M. Kardian, Con	8,456	8.2

Bingham plurality: 62,551

24 (Northern Bronx, Yonkers)

Mario Biaggi, D*, Con	106,942	69.9
Joseph F. Periconi, R, SM	38,173	24.9
John P. Hagan, Lib	7,970	5.2

Biaggi plurality: 68,769

25 (Parts of Westchester, Rockland counties)

Peter A. Peyser, R	76,611	42.5
William Dretzin, D	66,688	37.0
Anthony J. DeVito, Con	31,250	17.3
William S. Greenawalt, Lib	5,697	3.2

Peyser plurality: 9,923

26 (Part of Westchester County)

Ogden R. Reid, R*, Lib	109,783	66.4
Michael A. Coffey, Con	29,702	18.0
G. Russell James, D	25,909	15.7

Reid plurality: 80,081

27 (Southeastern counties, Newburgh, Poughkeepsie)

John G. Dow, D, Lib	89,787	52.2
Martin B. McKneally, R*, Con	82,191	47.8

Dow plurality: 7,596

28 (Southeastern counties, Kingston)

Hamilton Fish Jr., R*	119,954	70.8
John J. Greaney, D	41,908	24.7
Harry S. Hoffman Jr., Con	7,606	4.5

Fish plurality: 78,046

29 (Albany, Schnectady, Amsterdam)

Samuel S. Stratton, D*	128,017	66.2
Daniel E. Button, R*, Lib	65,339	33.8

Stratton plurality: 62,678

30 (Northeastern counties, Troy)

Carleton J. King, R*, Con	95,470	57.1
Edward W. Pattison, D, Lib	71,832	42.9

King plurality: 23,638

31 (Northern counties, Watertown)

Robert C. McEwen, R*, Con	90,585	72.4
Erwin L. Bornstein, D	34,568	27.6

McEwen plurality: 56,017

32 (Central counties, Utica, Rome)

Alexander Pirnie, R*, Lib	90,884	65.8
Joseph Simmons, D	47,306	34.2

Pirnie plurality: 43,578

33 (South central counties, Ithaca, Elmira)

Howard W. Robison, R*	90,196	66.5
David Bernstein, D, Lib	45,373	33.5

Robison plurality: 44,823

34 (Central counties, western Syracuse)

John H. Terry, R, Con	88,786	59.5
Neal P. McCurn, D	60,452	40.5

Terry plurality: 28,334

35 (Central counties, eastern Syracuse)

James M. Hanley, D*	82,425	51.9
John F. O'Connor, R, Con	76,381	48.1

Hanley plurality: 6,044

36 (Western counties, eastern Rochester)

Frank Horton, R*	123,209	70.5
Jordan E. Pappas, D	38,898	22.3
David F. Hampson, Con	10,442	6.0
Morley Schloss, Lib	2,165	1.2

Horton plurality: 84,311

37 (Western counties, western Rochester)

Barber B. Conable Jr., R*	107,677	65.9
Richard N. Anderson, D, Lib	48,061	29.4
Keith R. Wallis, Con	7,729	4.7

Conable plurality: 59,616

38 (Southwestern counties, Jamestown)

James F. Hastings, R*, Con	94,906	71.4
James G. Cretekos, D	37,961	28.6

Hastings plurality: 56,945

39 (Buffalo suburbs)

Jack F. Kemp, R, Con	96,989	51.6
Thomas P. Flaherty, D, Lib	90,949	48.4

Kemp plurality: 6,040

40 (Buffalo suburbs, Niagara Falls)

Henry P. Smith III, R*, Con	87,183	63.4
Edward Cuddy, D, Lib	50,418	36.6

Smith plurality: 36,765

41 (Buffalo)

Thaddeus J. Dulski, D-Lib*	79,151	79.7
William M. Johns, R, Con	20,108	20.3

Dulski plurality: 59,043

NORTH CAROLINA

AIP — American Independent Party

U.S. Representative (by district)

1 (Northeastern counties, Greenville)

Walter B. Jones, D*	41,674	70.2
R. Frank Everett, R	16,271	27.3
Gene Leggett, AIP	1,452	2.4

Jones plurality: 25,457

2 (Northeastern central counties, Rocky Mount)

L. H. Fountain, D*	38,891	100.0

3 (Southeastern central counties, Goldsboro)

David N. Henderson, D*	41,065	60.1
Herbert H. Howell, R	27,224	39.9

Henderson plurality: 13,841

4 (Central counties, Raleigh, Durham)

Nick Galifianakis, D*	49,866	52.4
R. (Jack) Hawke, R	45,386	47.6

Galifianakis plurality: 4,480

5 (Northwestern counties, Winston-Salem)

Wilmer Mizell, R*	68,937	58.1
James G. (Jim) White, D	49,663	41.9

Mizell plurality: 19,274

6 (North central counties, Greensboro)

Richardson Preyer, D*	47,693	66.0
Clifton B. (Pete) Barham Jr., R	20,739	28.7
Lynwood (Lyn) Bullock, AIP	3,849	5.3

Preyer plurality: 26,954

7 (Southeastern counties, Fayetteville)

Alton Lennon, D*	37,377	72.0
Frederick R. Weber, R	14,529	28.0

Lennon plurality: 22,848

8 (South central counties, Salisbury)

Earl B. Ruth, R*	51,873	56.1
H. Clifton Blue, D	40,563	43.9

Ruth plurality: 11,310

9 (South central counties, Charlotte)

Charles Raper Jonas, R*	57,525	66.6
Cy N. Bahakel, D	28,801	33.4

Jonas plurality: 28,724

10 (West central counties, Gastonia)

James T. Broyhill, R*	63,936	57.1
Basil L. Whitener, D	48,113	42.9

Broyhill plurality: 15,823

11 (Western counties, Asheville)

Roy A. Taylor, D*	90,199	67.0
Luke Atkinson, R	44,376	33.0

Taylor plurality: 45,823

NORTH DAKOTA

Ind — independent

Senator

Quentin N. Burdick, D*	134,519	61.3
Thomas S. Kleppe, R	82,996	37.8
Russell Kleppe, Ind	2,045	0.9

Burdick plurality: 51,523

U.S. Representative (by district)

1 (Eastern counties, Fargo, Grand Forks)

Mark N. Andrews, R*	72,168	65.7
James E. Brooks, D	37,688	34.3

Andrews plurality: 34,480

2 (Western counties, Bismarck)

Arthur A. Link, D	50,416	50.3
Robert P. McCarney, R	49,888	49.7

Link plurality: 528

OHIO

AIP — American Independent Party
SL — Socialist Labor Party

Governor

John J. Gilligan, D	1,725,560	54.2
Roger Cloud, R	1,382,749	43.4
Edwin G. Lawton, AIP	61,300	1.9
Joseph Pirincin, SL	14,087	0.4
John A. Crites (write-in)	321	0.0
Marcia Sweetenham (write-in)	106	0.0
Donald R. Lesiak (write-in)	100	0.0

Gilligan plurality: 342,811

Senator

Robert Taft Jr., R	1,565,682	49.7
Howard M. Metzenbaum, D	1,495,262	47.4
Richard B. Kay, AIP	61,261	1.9
John O'Neill, SL	29,069	0.9

Taft plurality: 70,420

U.S. Representative (by district)

1 (Eastern Cincinnati and suburbs)

William J. Keating, R	89,169	69.1
Bailey W. Turner, D	39,820	30.9

Keating plurality: 49,349

2 (Western Cincinnati and suburbs)

Donald D. Clancy, R*	77,071	55.9
Gerald N. Springer, D	60,860	44.1

Clancy plurality: 16,211

3 (Dayton and suburbs)

Charles W. Whalen Jr., R*	86,973	74.2
Dempsey A. Kerr, D	26,735	22.8
Russell G. Butcke, AIP	3,545	3.0

Whalen plurality: 60,238

4 (West central counties, Lima)

William M. McCulloch, R*	82,521	64.4
Donald B. Laws, D	45,619	35.6

McCulloch plurality: 36,902

5 (Northwestern counties)

Delbert L. Latta, R*	92,577	71.1
Carl G. Sherer, D	37,545	28.9

Latta plurality: 55,032

6 (South central counties, Portsmouth)

William H. Harsha, R*	82,772	67.8
Raymond H. Stevens, D	39,265	32.2

Harsha plurality: 43,507

7 (Central counties, Springfield)

Clarence J. Brown, R*	84,448	69.4
Joseph D. Lewis, D	37,294	30.6

Brown plurality: 47,154

8 (North central counties, Mansfield)

Jackson E. Betts, R*	90,916	100.0

9 (Toledo and suburbs)

Thomas L. Ashley, D*	82,777	70.9
Allen E. Shapiro, R	33,947	29.1

Ashley plurality: 48,830

10 (Southeastern counties, Lancaster)

Clarence E. Miller, R*	80,838	66.5
Doug Arnett, D	40,669	33.5

Miller plurality: 40,169

11 (Northeastern counties)

J. William Stanton, R*	91,437	68.2
Ralph Rudd, D	42,542	31.8

Stanton plurality: 48,895

12 (Central counties, part of Columbus)

Samuel L. Devine, R*	82,486	57.7
James W. Goodrich, D	60,538	42.3

Devine plurality: 21,948

13 (North central counties, Lorain)

Charles A. Mosher, R*	85,858	61.7
Joseph J. Bartolomeo, D	53,271	38.3

Mosher plurality: 32,587

14 (Akron and suburbs)

John F. Seiberling Jr., D	71,282	56.4
William H. Ayres, R*	55,038	43.6

Seiberling plurality: 16,244

15 (Central counties, part of Columbus)

Chalmers P. Wylie, R*	81,536	70.6
Manley L. McGee, D	34,018	29.4

Wylie plurality: 47,518

16 (Eastern counties, Canton)

Frank T. Bow, R*	81,208	56.2
Virgil L. Musser, D	63,187	43.8

Bow plurality: 18,021

17 (East central counties, Newark)

John M. Ashbrook, R*	79,472	62.2
James C. Hood, D	44,066	34.5
Clifford J. Simpson, AIP	4,253	3.3

Ashbrook plurality: 35,406

18 (Eastern counties, Steubenville)

Wayne L. Hays, D*	82,071	68.3
Robert L. Stewart, R	38,104	31.7

Hays plurality: 43,967

19 (Eastern counties, Warren, Youngstown)

Charles J. Carney, D	73,222	58.4
Margaret Dennison, R	52,057	41.6

Carney plurality: 21,165

19 (To fill vacancy)

Charles J. Carney, D	70,161	58.4
Margaret Dennison, R	50,005	41.6

Carney plurality: 20,156

20 (Eastern and central Cleveland)

James V. Stanton, D	70,140	81.3
J. William Petro, R	16,118	18.7

Stanton plurality: 54,022

21 (Western and southern Cleveland)

Louis Stokes, D*	74,340	77.6
Bill Mack, R	21,440	22.4

Stokes plurality: 52,900

22 (Northwestern Cleveland and suburbs)

Charles A. Vanik, D*	114,790	71.5
Adrian Fink, R	45,657	28.4
Sydney Stapleton (write-in)	49	0.0

Vanik plurality: 69,133

23 (Southern Cleveland suburbs)

William E. Minshall, R*	111,218	60.0
Ronald M. Mottl, D	73,765	39.8
Robert Wischmeyer (write-in)	500	0.3
E. L. Viets (write-in)	9	0.0

Minshall plurality: 37,453

24 (Southwestern counties, Hamilton, Middletown)

Walter E. Powell, R	63,344	51.5
James D. Ruppert, D	55,455	45.1
Joseph F. Payton, AIP	4,179	3.4

Powell plurality: 7,889

OKLAHOMA

AIP — American Independent Party
Ind — independent
— In Oklahoma, unopposed candidates receive total number of votes cast in the district.

Governor

David Hall, D	338,338	48.4
Dewey F. Bartlett, R*	336,157	48.1
Reuel Little, AIP	24,295	3.5

Hall plurality: 2,181

U.S. Representative (by district)

1 (Tulsa and suburbs)

Page Belcher, R*	67,386	55.7
James R. Jones, D	53,598	44.3

Belcher plurality: 13,788

2 (Northeastern counties, Muskogee)

Ed Edmondson, D*	87,131	70.8
Gene Humphries, R	35,989	29.2

Edmondson plurality: 51,142

3 (Southeastern counties, Ardmore)

Carl Albert, D* #	112,458	100.0

4 (Southwestern counties, Lawton, Norman)

Tom Steed, D*	67,743	63.7
Jay G. Wilkinson, R	37,081	34.9
Mary H. Rawls, AIP	1,000	0.9
Kenneth A. Kottka, Ind	534	0.5

Steed plurality: 30,662

5 (Oklahoma City and suburbs)

John Jarman, D*	62,034	73.1
Terry L. Campbell, R	22,801	26.9

Jarman plurality: 39,233

6 (Northwestern counties, Enid)

John N. Happy Camp, R*	81,959	64.2
R. O. (Joe) Cassity Jr., D	45,742	35.8

Camp plurality: 36,217

OREGON

Governor

Tom McCall, R*	369,964	55.5
Robert W. Straub, D	293,892	44.1
Doug Yeager (write-in)	1,545	0.2
Write-in votes	993	0.1

McCall plurality: 76,072

U.S. Representative (by district)

1 (Northwestern counties, part of Portland)

Wendell Wyatt, R*	147,239	71.8
Vern Cook, D	57,837	28.2
Write-in votes	18	0.0

Wyatt plurality: 89,402

2 (Eastern counties, Salem)

Al Ullman, D*	100,943	71.2
Everett Thoren, R	40,620	28.7
Write-in votes	153	0.1

Ullman plurality: 60,323

3 (Portland and suburbs)

Edith Green, D*	118,919	73.7
Robert E. Dugdale, R	42,391	26.3
Write-in votes	84	0.1

Green plurality: 76,528

4 (Southwestern counties, Eugene)

John Dellenback, R*	84,474	58.3
James H. Weaver, D	60,299	41.6
Write-in votes	13	0.0

Dellenback plurality: 24,175

PENNSYLVANIA

AIP—American Independent Party
Const—Constitutional Party
Consum—Consumer Party
SL—Socialist Labor Party
SW—Socialist Workers Party
†—Rep. Robert J. Corbett died April 25, 1971.
‡—Rep. James G. Fulton died October 6, 1971.

Governor

Milton J. Shapp, D	2,043,029	55.2
Raymond J. Broderick, R	1,542,854	41.7
Andrew J. Watson, Const	83,406	2.3
Francis T. McGeever, AIP	21,647	0.6
George S. Taylor, SL	3,588	0.1
Clarissa Cain, Consum	2,988	0.1
Pearl Chertov, SW	2,400	0.1
Others	153	0.0

Shapp plurality: 500,175

Senator

Hugh Scott, R*	1,874,106	51.4
William G. Sesler, D	1,653,774	45.4
Frank W. Gaydosh, Const	85,813	2.4
W. Henry MacFarland, AIP	18,275	0.5
Herman A. Johansen, SL	4,375	0.1
Robin Maisel, SW	3,970	0.1
William R. Mimms, Consum	3,932	0.1
Others	60	0.0

Scott plurality: 220,332

U.S. Representative (by district)

1 (Southwestern Philadelphia)

William A. Barrett, D*	79,425	69.2
Joseph S. Ziccardi, R	34,649	30.2
Paul K. Botts, AIP	677	0.6

Barrett plurality: 44,776

2 (Northwestern Philadelphia)

Robert N. C. Nix, D*	70,530	68.2
Edward L. Taylor, R	32,858	31.8

Nix plurality: 37,672

3 (Southeastern Philadelphia)

James A. Byrne, D*	54,755	56.4
Gustine J. Pelagatti, R	42,393	43.6

Byrne plurality: 12,362

4 (Northern Philadelphia)

Joshua Eilberg, D*	113,920	59.4
Charles F. Dougherty, R	77,817	40.6

Eilberg plurality: 36,103

5 (East central Philadelphia)

William J. Green, D*	80,142	66.9
James H. Ring, R	38,955	32.5
John Donahue, AIP	724	0.6

Green plurality: 41,187

6 (East central counties, Reading)

Gus Yatron, D*	96,453	65.0
Michael Kitsock, R	48,397	32.6
George T. Atkins, Const	3,469	2.3

Yatron plurality: 48,056

7 (Part of Delaware County)

Lawrence G. Williams, R*	91,042	59.2
Joseph R. Breslin, D	62,722	40.8

Williams plurality: 28,320

8 (Bucks County, Bristol)

Edward G. Biester Jr., R*	73,041	56.3
Arthur Leo Hennessey Jr., D	51,464	39.7
Charles B. Moore, Const	5,118	3.9

Biester plurality: 21,577

9 (Chester County, part of Delaware County)

John H. Ware III, R	76,535	59.2
Louis F. Waldmann, D	52,852	40.8

Ware plurality: 23,683

9 (To fill vacancy)

John H. Ware III, R	44,077	57.0
Louis F. Waldmann, D	31,353	40.5
Benjamin H. Winkelman, Const	1,916	2.5

Ware plurality: 12,724

10 (Northeastern counties, Scranton)

Joseph M. McDade, R*	102,716	65.4
Edward J. Smith, D	51,506	32.8
Stephen P. Depue, Const	2,731	1.7

McDade plurality: 51,210

11 (East central counties, Wilkes-Barre)

Daniel J. Flood, D*, R	146,789	96.6
Alvin J. Balschi, Const	5,123	3.4

Flood plurality: 141,666

12 (South central counties, Altoona)

J. Irving Whalley, R*	93,385	64.0
Victor J. Karycki Jr., D	48,738	33.4
Kenneth W. Ferry, AIP	1,923	1.3
Lloyd G. Cope, Const	1,848	1.3

Whalley plurality: 44,647

13 (Montgomery County)

R. Lawrence Coughlin, R*	101,953	58.3
Frank R. Romano, D	68,743	39.3
John S. Matthews, Const	3,356	1.9
Anthony S. De Meno, AIP	718	0.4

Coughlin plurality: 33,210

14 (Central Pittsburgh)

William S. Moorhead, D*	72,509	76.5
Barry Levine, R	21,572	22.8
Reuben Francis Chaitin, AIP	687	0.7

Moorhead plurality: 50,937

15 (East central counties, Bethlehem)

Fred B. Rooney, D*	93,169	66.9
Charles H. Roberts, R	44,103	31.6
Chester R. Litz, Const	2,093	1.5

Rooney plurality: 49,066

16 (Southeastern central counties, Lancaster)

Edwin D. Eshleman, R*	74,006	66.5
John E. Pflum, D	33,986	30.5
Walter B. Willard III, Const	3,319	3.0

Eshleman plurality: 40,020

17 (East central counties, Harrisburg)

Herman T. Schneebeli, R*	88,173	57.9
William P. Zurick, D	60,714	39.9
Robert C. Weber, Const	3,342	2.2

Schneebeli plurality: 27,459

18 (Northern Pittsburgh and suburbs)

Robert J. Corbett, R* †	87,246	60.2
Ronald E. Leslie, D	54,639	37.7
John E. Backman, Const	3,043	2.1

Corbett plurality: 32,607

19 (South central counties, York)

George A. Goodling, R*	71,497	53.9
Arthur L. Berger, D	58,399	44.0
Joseph Paul, Const	2,704	2.0

Goodling plurality: 13,098

20 (Southeastern Pittsburgh and suburbs)

Joseph M. Gaydos, D*	84,911	77.0
Joseph Honeygosky, R	22,553	20.4
Alan Staub, Const	2,840	2.6

Gaydos plurality: 62,358

21 (Westmoreland County)

John H. Dent, D*	76,915	68.5
Glenn G. Anderson, R	33,396	29.7
Lloyd G. Cope, Const	1,979	1.8

Dent plurality: 43,519

22 (West central counties, Johnstown)

John P. Saylor, R*	81,675	57.7
Joseph F. O'Kicki, D	58,720	41.5
Ellsworth L. Hahn, AIP	1,213	0.9

Saylor plurality: 22,955

23 (North central counties, State College)

Albert W. Johnson, R*	70,074	57.9
Cecil R. Harrington, D	50,908	42.1

Johnson plurality: 19,166

24 (Northwestern counties, Erie)

Joseph P. Vigorito, D*	94,029	66.8
Wayne R. Merrick, R	44,395	31.5
Robert Shilling, AIP, Const	2,424	1.7

Vigorito plurality: 49,634

25 (West central counties, New Castle)

Frank M. Clark, D*	92,638	69.7
John Loth, R	37,355	28.1
Albert H. Thornton, Const	2,959	2.2

Clark plurality: 55,283

26 (Southwestern counties, Washington)

Thomas E. Morgan, D*	80,734	68.4
Domenick A. Cupelli, R	35,083	29.7
Bernard M. Dae Check, Const	2,176	1.8

Morgan plurality: 45,651

27 (Southern Pittsburgh and suburbs)

James G. Fulton, R* ‡	86,932	60.5
Douglas Walgren, D	55,050	38.3
Harvey F. Johnston, AIP	1,618	1.1

Fulton plurality: 31,882

RHODE ISLAND

Ind — independent
P&F — Peace and Freedom Party
SW — Socialist Workers Party

Governor

Frank Licht, D*	173,420	50.1
Herbert F. DeSimone, R	171,549	49.5
John E. Powers Jr., SW	1,372	0.4

Licht plurality: 1,871

Senator

John O. Pastore, D*	230,469	67.5
John J. McLaughlin, R	107,351	31.5
David N. Fenton, P&F	2,406	0.7
Daniel B. Fein, SW	996	0.3

Pastore plurality: 123,118

U.S. Representative (by district)

1 (Eastern Rhode Island, part of Providence)

Fernand J. St. Germain, D*	86,283	60.9
Walter J. Miska, R	52,962	37.4
Stephen Bruce Murray, P&F	2,327	1.6

St. Germain plurality: 33,321

2 (Western Rhode Island, part of Providence)

Robert O. Tiernan, D*	121,704	66.1
William A. Dimitri Jr., R	61,819	33.6
Louis Dona G. O'Hara, Ind	518	0.3

Tiernan plurality: 59,885

SOUTH CAROLINA

SCI — South Carolina Independent Party
UCP — United Citizens Party (write-in)
†— Rep. L. Mendel Rivers died December 28, 1970. Mendel Davis, winner of a special election to fill the vacancy, was sworn in April 27, 1971.

Governor

John C. West, D	250,551	51.7
Albert W. Watson, R	221,233	45.6
A. W. (Red) Bethea, SCI	9,758	2.0
Thomas D. Broadwater, UCP	3,315	0.7

West plurality: 29,318

U.S. Representative (by district)

1 (Southeastern counties, Charleston)

L. Mendel Rivers, D* †	63,891	100.0

2 (South central counties, Columbia)

Floyd Spence, R	48,093	53.1
Heyward McDonald, D	42,005	46.4
Donald R. Cole, SCI	486	0.5

Spence plurality: 6,088

3 (Western counties, Anderson)

W. J. Bryan Dorn, D*	60,708	75.2
H. Grady Ballard, R	19,981	24.8

Dorn plurality: 40,727

4 (North central counties, Greenville)

James R. Mann, D*	52,175	100.0

5 (North central counties, Rock Hill)

Tom S. Gettys, D*	43,742	66.0
B. Leonard Phillips, R	21,911	33.0
James Burton Sumner, SCI	688	1.0

Gettys plurality: 21,831

6 (Northeastern counties, Florence)

John L. McMillan, D*	46,966	64.1
Edward B. Baskin, R	25,546	34.9
Charles H. Smith, SCI	773	1.0

McMillan plurality: 21,420

SOUTH DAKOTA

Governor

Richard F. Kneip, D	131,616	54.8
Frank L. Farrar, R*	108,347	45.2

Kneip plurality: 23,269

U.S. Representative (by district)

1 (Eastern counties, Sioux Falls)

Frank E. Denholm, D	71,636	56.0
Dexter H. Gunderson, R	56,330	44.0

Denholm plurality: 15,306

2 (Western counties, Pierre, Rapid City)

James Abourezk, D	55,925	52.3
Fred D. Brady, R	51,092	47.7

Abourezk plurality: 4,833

TENNESSEE

AIP — American Independent Party
Ind — independent

Governor

Winfield Dunn, R	575,777	52.0
John J. Hooker Jr., D	509,521	46.0
Douglas L. Heinsohn, AIP	22,945	2.1
Write-ins	4	0.0

Dunn plurality: 66,256

Senator

W. E. Brock, R	562,645	51.3
Albert Gore, D*	519,858	47.4
Cecil R. Pitard, AIP	8,691	0.8
Dan R. East, Ind	5,845	0.5
Write-ins	2	0.0

Brock plurality: 42,787

U.S. Representative (by district)

1 (Northeastern counties, Johnson City)

James H. Quillen, R*	78,896	67.9
David Bruce Shine, D	37,348	32.1

Quillen plurality: 41,548

2 (East central counties, Knoxville)

John J. Duncan, R*	85,849	73.3
Roger Cowan, D	30,146	25.7
William E. Butcher, Ind	1,116	1.0

Duncan plurality: 55,703

3 (Southeastern counties, Chattanooga)

LaMar Baker, R	61,527	51.3
Richard H. Winningham, D	54,662	45.6
Robert Shockey, Ind	2,124	1.8
Frank Massey, Ind	1,375	1.1
Write-ins	314	0.3

Baker plurality: 6,865

4 (East central counties, Oak Ridge)

Joe L. Evins, D*	86,437	82.6
Mrs. J. Durelle Boles, R	18,180	17.4
Write-ins	3	0.0

Evins plurality: 68,257

5 (Nashville)

Richard Fulton, D*	89,900	70.6
George Kelly, R	37,522	29.4

Fulton plurality: 52,378

6 (West central counties, Clarksville)

William R. Anderson, D*	87,517	81.7
Elmer Davies Jr., R	19,622	18.3

Anderson plurality: 67,895

7 (Southwestern counties, Jackson, part of Memphis)

Ray Blanton, D*	83,904	74.2
W. G. Doss, R	29,139	25.8

Blanton plurality: 54,765

8 (Northwestern counties, part of Memphis)

Ed Jones, D*	66,590	100.0
Write-ins	2	0.0

9 (Part of Memphis)

Dan Kuykendall, R*	72,498	62.2
Michael M. Osborn, D	43,279	37.1
Malley Byrd, Ind	744	0.6
Write-ins	4	0.0

Kuykendall plurality: 29,219

TEXAS

Governor

Preston Smith, D*	1,197,726	53.6
Paul W. Eggers, R	1,037,723	46.4

Smith plurality: 160,003

Senator

Lloyd M. Bentsen Jr., D	1,226,568	53.4
George Bush, R	1,071,234	46.6

Bentsen plurality: 155,334

U.S. Representative (by district)

1 (Northeastern counties, Texarkana)

Wright Patman, D*	67,883	78.5
James Hogan, R	18,614	21.5

Patman plurality: 49,269

2 (Northeastern counties, Orange)

John Dowdy, D*	52,634	100.0

3 (Western Dallas County)

James M. Collins, R*	63,690	60.6
John Mead, D	41,425	39.4

Collins plurality: 22,265

4 (Northeastern counties, Tyler)

Ray Roberts, D*	70,103	100.0

5 (Eastern Dallas County)

Earle Cabell, D*	57,058	59.7
Frank Crowley, R	38,481	40.3

Cabell plurality: 18,577

6 (East central counties)

Olin E. Teague, D*	74,038	100.0

7 (Northwest Houston and suburbs)

W. A. Archer, R	93,457	64.8
James Greenwood III, D	50,750	35.2

Archer plurality: 42,707

8 (Northeast Houston and suburbs)

Bob Eckhardt, D*	26,294	100.0

9 (Eastern counties, Galveston)

Jack Brooks, D*	57,180	64.5
Henry Pressler, R	31,483	35.5

Brooks plurality: 25,697

10 (Central counties, Austin)

J. J. Pickle, D*	78,872	100.0

11 (Central counties, Waco)

W. R. Poage, D*	59,641	100.0

12 (Fort Worth and suburbs)

Jim Wright, D*	62,057	100.0

13 (North central counties, Wichita Falls)

Graham Purcell, D*	80,070	64.9
Joe Staley, R	43,319	35.1

Purcell plurality: 36,651

14 (South central counties, Corpus Christi)

John Young, D*	62,560	100.0

15 (Southern counties, Brownsville)

Eligio de la Garza, D*	54,498	76.2
Ben A. Martinez, R	17,049	23.8

de la Garza plurality: 37,449

16 (Western counties, El Paso)

Richard C. White, D*	54,617	82.7
J. R. Provencio, R	11,420	17.3

White plurality: 43,197

17 (Central Counties, Abilene)

Omar Burleson, D*	70,040	100.0

18 (North panhandle, Amarillo)

Robert Price, R*	52,845	100.0

19 (West central counties, Lubbock)

George H. Mahon, D*	59,996	100.0

20 (Part of San Antonio)

Henry B. Gonzalez, D*	48,710	100.0

21 (South central counties, San Angelo, Odessa)

O. C. Fisher, D*	76,004	61.4
Richard Gill, R	47,868	38.6

Fisher plurality: 28,136

22 (South Houston and suburbs)

Bob Casey, D*	73,514	55.6
Arthur W. Busch, R	58,598	44.4

Casey plurality: 14,916

23 (South central counties, Laredo)

Abraham Kazen Jr., D*	61,068	100.0

UTAH

AIP — American Independent Party

Senator

Frank E. Moss, D*	210,207	56.2
Laurence J. Burton, R	159,004	42.5
Clyde B. Freeman, AIP	5,092	1.4

Moss plurality: 51,203

U.S. Representative (by district)

1 (Eastern, northern counties, Ogden)

K. Gunn McKay, D	95,499	51.3
Richard Richards, R	89,269	47.9
Daniel L. Worthington, AIP	1,489	0.8

McKay plurality: 6,230

2 (Western counties, Salt Lake City)

Sherman P. Lloyd, R*	97,549	52.3
A. H. (Bob) Nance, D	87,000	46.6
Stephen D. Marsh, AIP	2,094	1.1

Lloyd plurality: 10,549

VERMONT

LU — Liberty Union Party
† — Sen. Winston L. Prouty died September 10, 1971. Rep. Robert T. Stafford, R, was named by Gov. Deane C. Davis, R, as Prouty's interim replacement pending a special primary and general election.

Governor

Deane C. Davis, R*	87,458	57.0
Leo O'Brien Jr., D	66,028	43.0
Scattering	42	0.0

Davis plurality: 21,430

Senator

Winston L. Prouty, R* †	91,189	58.9
Philip H. Hoff, D	62,271	40.2
William H. Meyer, LU	1,416	0.9
Scattering	14	0.0

Prouty plurality: 28,927

U.S. Representative (at large)

Robert T. Stafford, R* †	103,806	68.1
Bernard O'Shea, D	44,415	29.1
Dennis J. Morrisseau, LU	4,315	2.8
Scattering	21	0.0

Stafford plurality: 59,291

VIRGINIA

Ind — independent

Senator

Harry F. Byrd Jr., Ind*	506,237	53.5
George C. Rawlings Jr., D	294,582	31.2
Raymond L. Garland, R	144,765	15.3
Write-in votes	30	0.0

Byrd plurality: 211,655

U.S. Representative (by district)

1 (Eastern Shore counties, Newport News)

Thomas N. Downing, D*	71,441	99.9
Write-in votes	38	0.1

2 (Norfolk, Portsmouth)

G. William Whitehurst, R*	44,099	61.7
Joseph T. Fitzpatrick, D	27,362	38.3
Write-in votes	1	0.0

Whitehurst plurality: 16,737

3 (Richmond and suburbs)

David E. Satterfield III, D*	73,104	67.2
J. Harvie Wilkinson III, R	35,229	32.4
Mrs. Ulrich Troubetskoy (write-in)	371	0.3
Other write-in votes	4	0.0

Satterfield plurality: 37,875

4 (Southeastern counties, Suffolk)

Watkins M. Abbitt, D*	55,233	61.0
Ben Ragsdale, Ind	25,399	28.1
James M. Helm, R	9,876	10.9
Write-in votes	3	0.0

Abbitt plurality: 29,834

5 (Southern counties, Danville)

W. C. Daniel, D*	54,261	73.0
Allen T. St. Clair, R	20,029	27.0
Write-in votes	2	0.0

Daniel plurality: 34,232

6 (West central counties, Roanoke)

Richard H. Poff, R*	62,311	74.6
Roy R. White, D	21,219	25.4
Write-in votes	6	0.0

Poff plurality: 41,092

7 (Northwestern counties, Charlottesville)

J. Kenneth Robinson, R	52,619	61.7
Murat Williams, D	32,617	38.3
Write-in votes	8	0.0

Robinson plurality: 20,002

8 (Eastern counties, Washington, D.C. suburbs)

William Lloyd Scott, R*	68,167	63.8
Darrel H. Stearns, D	38,680	36.2
Write-in votes	8	0.0

Scott plurality: 29,487

9 (Southwestern counties, Bristol)

William C. Wampler, R*	53,950	60.9
Tate C. Buchanan, D	34,609	39.1
Write-in votes	2	0.0

Wampler plurality: 19,341

10 (Washington, D.C. suburbs)

Joel T. Broyhill, R*	67,468	54.5
Harold O. Miller, D	56,255	45.5

Broyhill plurality: 11,213

WASHINGTON

B—Buffalo Party
SW—Socialist Workers Party

Senator

Henry M. Jackson, D*	879,385	82.4
Charles W. Elicker, R	170,790	16.0
William (Bill) Massey, SW	9,255	0.9
Edison S. (Pinky) Fisk, B	7,377	0.7

Jackson plurality: 708,595

U.S. Representative (by district)

1 (Part of Seattle, Bainbridge Island)

Thomas M. Pelly, R*	107,072	64.4
David A. Hughes, D	53,156	32.0
Stephanie Coontz, SW	4,388	2.6
Stan Iverson, B	1,724	1.0

Pelly plurality: 53,916

2 (Northwestern counties, Everett)

Lloyd Meeds, D*	117,562	72.7
Edward A. McBride, R	44,049	27.3

Meeds plurality: 73,513

3 (Southwestern counties, Olympia)

Julia Butler Hansen, D*	81,892	59.1
R. C. (Skip) McConkey, R	56,566	40.9

Hansen plurality: 25,326

4 (Southeastern counties, Yakima)

Mike McCormack, D	70,119	52.6
Catherine May, R*	63,244	47.4

McCormack plurality: 6,875

5 (Northeastern counties, Spokane)

Thomas S. Foley, D*	88,189	67.0
George Gamble, R	43,376	33.0

Foley plurality: 44,813

6 (Peirce County, Tacoma)

Floyd V. Hicks, D*	98,282	69.4
John Jarstad, R	42,213	29.8
Richard Congress, SW	1,180	0.8

Hicks plurality: 56,069

7 (Part of Seattle)

Brock Adams, D*	99,308	66.6
Brian Lewis, R	47,426	31.8
Russell Block, SW	2,378	1.6

Adams plurality: 51,882

WEST VIRGINIA

Senator

Robert C. Byrd, D*	345,965	77.6
Elmer H. Dodson, R	99,663	22.4

Byrd plurality: 246,302

U.S. Representative (by district)

1 (Northern counties, Wheeling)

Robert H. Mollohan, D*	61,296	61.5
Ken Doll, R	38,327	38.5

Mollohan plurality: 22,969

2 (Eastern counties, Martinsburg)

Harley O. Staggers, D*	56,263	62.7
Richard Marshall Reddecliff, R	33,509	37.3

Staggers plurality: 22,754

3 (Central counties, Charleston)

John M. Slack, D*	57,630	65.4
Neal A. Kinsolving, R	30,525	34.6

Slack plurality: 27,105

4 (Western counties, Huntington)

Ken Hechler, D*	62,531	67.4
Ralph Shannon, R	30,255	32.6

Hechler plurality: 32,276

5 (Southern counties)

James Kee, D*	48,286	71.1
Mrs. Joe (Marian) McQuade, R	19,585	28.9

Kee plurality: 28,701

WISCONSIN

AIP — American Independent Party
IND — independent
PLS — Progressive Labor Socialist Party
SL — Socialist Labor Party
SW — Socialist Workers Party

Governor

Patrick J. Lucey, D	728,403	54.2
Jack B. Olson, R	602,617	44.9
Leo James McDonald, AIP	9,035	0.7
Georgia Cozzini, SL	1,287	0.1
Samuel K. Hunt, SW	888	0.1
Myrtle Kastner, PLS	628	0.0
Scattering	302	0.0

Lucey plurality: 125,786

Senator

William Proxmire, D*	948,445	70.8
John E. Erickson, R	381,297	28.5
Edmond E. Hou-Seye, AIP	6,137	0.5
Elizabeth Boardman, Ind	2,022	0.2
Martha Quinn, SW	580	0.0
Adolf Wiggert, SL	428	0.0
Scattering	58	0.0

Proxmire plurality: 567,148

U.S. Representative (by district)

1 (Southeastern counties, Kenosha, Racine)

Les Aspin, D	87,428	60.9
Henry C. Schadeberg, R*	56,067	39.1
Scattering	4	0.0

Aspin plurality: 31,361

2 (South central counties, Madison)

Robert W. Kastenmeier, D*	102,879	68.5
Norman Anderson, R	46,620	31.0
Lavern F. Krohn, AIP	718	0.5
Scattering	15	0.0

Kastenmeier plurality: 56,259

3 (Southwestern counties, LaCrosse)

Vernon W. Thomson, R*	64,891	55.5
Ray Short, D	52,085	44.5
Scattering	3	0.0

Thomson plurality: 12,806

4 (Southern Milwaukee and suburbs)

Clement J. Zablocki, D*	102,464	80.3
Philip D. Mrozinski, R	23,081	18.1
John A. Zierhut, AIP	1,985	1.6
Scattering	46	0.0

Zablocki plurality: 79,383

5 (Milwaukee)

Henry S. Reuss, D*	60,630	75.9
Robert J. Dwyer, R	18,360	23.0
Earl R. Denny, AIP	640	0.8
James E. Boulton, PLS	208	0.3

Reuss plurality: 42,270

6 (East central counties, Oshkosh, Sheboygan)

William A. Steiger, R*	98,587	67.7
Franklin R. Utech, D	44,794	30.8
Rani V. Davidson, AIP	2,150	1.5
Scattering	10	0.0

Steiger plurality: 53,793

7 (North central counties, Wausau)

David R. Obey, D*	88,746	67.6
Andre E. Le Tendre, R	41,330	31.5
Richard D. Wolfe, AIP	1,189	0.9
Scattering	11	0.0

Obey plurality: 47,416

8 (Northeastern counties, Green Bay)

John W. Byrnes, R*	76,893	55.5
Robert J. Cornell, D	60,345	43.6
Joseph W. Dery, AIP	1,283	0.9

Byrnes plurality: 16,548

9 (Milwaukee suburbs)

Glenn R. Davis, R*	84,732	52.0
Fred M. Tabak, D	78,123	48.0
Scattering	2	0.0

Davis plurality: 6,609

10 (Northwestern counties)

Alvin E. O'Konski, R*	66,104	50.9
Walter Thoreson, D	62,991	48.6
William Hable, AIP	694	0.5
Scattering	6	0.0

O'Konski plurality: 3,023

WYOMING

Governor

Stanley K. Hathaway, R*	74,249	62.8
John J. Rooney, D	44,008	37.2

Hathaway plurality: 30,241

Senator

Gale W. McGee, D*	67,207	55.8
John Wold, R	53,279	44.2

McGee plurality: 13,928

U.S. Representative (at large)

Teno Roncalio, D	58,456	50.3
Harry Roberts, R	57,848	49.7

Roncalio plurality: 608

INDEX

This index excludes persons cited in Appendix I and Appendix II.